A Paradise out of
a Common Field

Garden parties were among the high points of the summer's social round.

A PARADISE OUT OF A COMMON FIELD

The Pleasures and Plenty of the Victorian Garden

Joan Morgan and Alison Richards

1817

HARPER & ROW, PUBLISHERS, New York
Grand Rapids, Philadelphia, St. Louis, San Francisco,
London, Singapore, Sydney, Tokyo, Toronto

BLACK AND WHITE ILLUSTRATION ACKNOWLEDGMENTS

The authors and publishers would like to thank the following for supplying black and white illustrations: Cambridge University Library pp 29, 105, 174; Kent Archives Service p 183; Mappin & Webb Ltd pp 87, 113; Mary Evans Picture Library pp 2, 13, 82, 155, 187; Suffolk Record Office p 15; Suttons Seeds Ltd pp 10, 25, 51, 70, 81, 91, 128, 152, 178, 200, 219, 223; Wye College, University of London pp 26, 44, 67, 77, 79, 132, 135, 149, 164, 192, 221. The other black and white illustrations are from the authors' collections.
For details of the colour plates see page 7.

This book was originally published in Great Britain by Random Century Group. It is here reprinted by arrangement with Random Century Group.

FIRST U.S. EDITION
LIBRARY OF CONGRESS NUMBER 89-45695

ISBN: 0-06-016034-9

Designed by Behram Kapadia
Set in Goudy Old Style by SX Composing Ltd, Rayleigh, Essex
Printed and bound in Great Britain by Butler and Tanner, London and Frome

90 91 92 93 94 10 9 8 7 6 5 4 3 2 1

CONTENTS

Acknowledgements

This book has its origins in a series of three programmes made for BBC Radio 3 early in 1986. They were broadcast under the title *A Paradise out of a Common Field*, and our thanks go to George Fischer, then Head of Talks and Documentaries, Radio, and Ian McIntyre, former Controller of Radio 3, for supporting this initial project. We also acknowledge our debt to Geoff Deehan, former Chief Producer Science Programmes, BBC Radio, and members of the Radio Science Unit.

During the preparation and writing of this book we received help from many people, all of whom gave generously of their time and knowledge. We thank Brent Elliott of the Royal Horticultural Society's Lindley Library, and the outstanding authority in this field, for innumerable helpful and instructive conversations. For advice on fruit and a wide range of horticultural matters we are indebted to Harry Baker, Fruit Officer at the RHS Gardens, Wisley, Surrey; Hugh Ermen and David Pennell of the National Fruit Trials, Brogdale, Kent; and Peter Dodd of London University's Wye College, Kent. We also thank the Royal Horticultural Society and the National Fruit Trials for allowing us to use their Fruit Collections.

Tom Wright, Jeanne Ingram, Lyn Garraway, Roger Price and Ian Lean of Wye College; Patricia and Michael Twyman of Olantigh Nurseries, Wye, and Stephen Torrode of Dyffryn Gardens, Glamorgan, answered many questions and gave valuable advice. Alan Mitchell; and J. McIntyre and G. Phillips of the Bedgebury Pinetum, Kent, advised us concerning conifers. For insights into the Victorian diet and attitudes we are grateful to Doris Morgan and the late Illtyd Morgan.

For help with finding and interpreting archival material relating to Linton we thank Bernard Thomas and the Archive Department, County Record Office, Maidstone, Kent. Special thanks are also due to Mrs Bridget Petherick, née Cornwallis; Mr R. G. Daubeny, the last private owner of Linton, and Mr L. Quick, its last head gardener; and Jean Cobbald of the National Council for the Conservation of Plants and Gardens. Recent owners of Linton were kind enough to allow us to visit the grounds.

Jane Fowles and Kate Harris, archivists at Longleat, were most helpful, and we thank the Marquess of Bath for providing material. Mappin & Webb, London, and W. Petre of IDG kindly supplied us with archival material. We are also grateful to the East Sussex Record Office, Lewes, and R. A. Scott, for material relating to Oldlands; and to the present owners for allowing us to visit the grounds. For information relating to other estates we thank Alison McCann of the West Sussex Record Office, Chichester; B. M. Gall of the Haddington Library, East Lothian; the Bodleian Library, Oxford; T. B. Groom of the Staffordshire Record Office; Bath Record

Office; Mr Watkins of Merthyr Tydfil Library; John Hughes of Swansea Central Library; the Belvoir Estate, Leicestershire; R. Kirton-Darling of the Lambton Estate, Durham; and Peter Walne of the Hertford County Record Office.

E. M. Lucas and the staff of Wye College Library, and the ladies of Wye Public Library gave us invaluable assistance. We also thank the RHS Lindley Library, and the London Library for their unfailing help, and Jane and Alan Davidson.

Michael Clarke and Bob Richards gave us considerable technical assistance, and we are grateful to Pam Richards, Beryl Littlewood, Gill Turner, Jonathan and Judy Hill, Vanessa Brodie, and Elizabeth Walker who all contributed in various ways.

Finally our greatest debt is to our husbands and children.

Authors' Note

Many Victorian measures for controlling pests are dangerous and are not recommended for present-day use.

Throughout the book the terms England and Great Britain have been used interchangeably.

Colour Plates

1. Harewood House from *The Gardens of England* by E. Adveno Brooke (1856-57)

2. Araucaria Imbricata at Dropmore by William Richardson from *The Pinetum Britannicum* by Edward James Ravenscroft (published by Charles Lawson, 1863-1884) *Bodleian Library*

3. *Rhododendron 'Trebah Gem', Trebah*, Cornwall by Beatrice Parsons, the frontispiece to Rhododendrons and the Various Hybrids by J. G. Millais, 2nd series 1924 *Private Collection, photograph: Christopher Wood Gallery*

4. *Still Life of Melons, Grapes, Peaches, Plums and a Pineapple* by Eloise Harriet Stannard *Sotheby's*

5. *Still Life of Asparagus, Cauliflower and Strawberries* by Adrienne Mols *Fine Art Photographs*

6. *Mr Schneider's neat garden at Belsfield, Bowness-on-Windermere* by J McGahey *Mary Evans Picture Library*

7. Plate from *La Mode Illustrée*, 1870 *Mansell Collection*

8. *A Happy Interlude* by Gustave Leonard de Jonghe *Fine Art Photographs*

Foreword

t is an evening in early December, 1867. The house and dinner guests have assembled in the drawing room at Linton Park, home of the Cornwallis family, and a glittering Palladian mansion that sits on the greensand ridge, overlooking the Kentish Weald. In a few minutes they will proceed ceremonially into the dining room where wreaths of evergreens garland the table and candles illuminate tall glass stands of flowers. Set around the table are bowls of fresh fruit for the dessert – black and white grapes with their velvety bloom still upon them, pears that have reached the moment of melting perfection and a magnificent pair of ripe pineapples. Among the dishes to be served are pheasant from the estate, and an *entrée* garnished with mushrooms and French beans. Everything has been home-grown and the house guests are looking forward to visiting the kitchen garden as well as the rest of Linton's celebrated grounds. Target shooting at the butts has been organized for the following day and there will be every opportunity to enjoy the pleasure ground which is immaculate, and full of interest despite the bleakness of the season.

From the terrace below the drawing room, steps descend to the flower garden. In summer, this is a mass of brilliant colour, as are the rose garden, basket garden and borders. In December the great oval bed of the flower garden is filled with evergreens, and an elaborate design is traced out in grey cotton lavender, green box and golden yew. From the terrace broad, smooth walks lead out into the pleasure ground. An easterly stroll passes a conservatory set into the southern wall of the kitchen garden, and arrives at a summer house at the edge of the pinetum. Going west, the visitor encounters ornamental shrubberies, collections of rare young trees and a wild dell. In the distance lies the lake, and beyond, the rising landscape.

The fame of the gardens at Linton Park was largely the achievement of the head gardener, John Robson, who came to work for the Cornwallis family in the late 1840s, and remained until his retirement in 1876. He was one of the élite group of head gardeners who, in the middle of the nineteenth century, were transforming the beautiful but restrained landscape parks of Britain, and carving 'paradise out of a common field' for the new country houses that were being built at an unprecedented rate. They had crossed the line which previously separated the practical men from the more esteemed landscape gardeners, and were responsible for everything from designing elaborate formal parterres to planting collections of orchids and conifers.

They also ensured that the mansion was filled with flowers, that the chef was supplied with vegetables in and out of season, and that there was always a splendid range of fresh fruit. Even the buttonholes, posies and hair ornaments were their concern.

This glorious heyday lasted from about the 1840s to the turn of the century, by which time social, economic and scientific developments had begun to erode the head gardeners' position. During this period they enjoyed a status and prestige unparalleled before or since, and made a profound and lasting contribution to the development of horticulture and taste. It is an achievement which has been largely ignored.

This book is an attempt to re-examine the head gardeners' accomplishments and their role in supporting the social function of the country house. It is a tribute to a forgotten group of men who helped to educate both the eye and the palate of British Society.

A Paradise out of a Common Field

uring the second half of the eighteenth century the fashionable country house sat in splendid isolation amidst a piece of idealized English countryside. Preferably designed by the sought after 'Capability' Brown, the view from the drawing room window presented a composed landscape of rolling meadow, glittering water and native woodland. It was a flowing, tranquil, almost abstract version of Nature, from which all obvious signs of geological drama and human spoil had been erased. In this setting, the transforming genius of the landscape designer was all. Once the excavation, damming and tree planting was complete, the scene had simply to be left to mature. The practical gardener's role was reduced to scything the grass, maintaining the drives, and a little woodland management. He retreated to the kitchen garden, where he concentrated his talents on the fruit and vegetables. With none of the chores of formal gardening which had burdened his predecessors, he was free to develop further the technically challenging possibilities of growing tender and exotic fruit, and the art of forcing vegetables.

A century later, most of this had changed. Gardeners still presided over kitchen gardens in which everything from pineapples to tomatoes now flourished alongside more traditional fare, but the setting of the country house was transformed. Outside the drawing room was a formal flower garden or 'parterre'. This usually took the form of one or more terraces, featuring as many as fifty rectangular or curved beds, closely planted with brilliant exotics such as the geranium, or more correctly, pelargonium. Statues, fountains and evergreens punctuated the vivid geometry, which would be set off by a background of gravel or grass. In the pleasure ground beyond there were roses in profusion, rhododendrons, lilies and all manner of conifers. A rockery and a fernery might also add interest, as would the tropical collections in the conservatory and glass-houses.

The garden had become a showcase for plants rather than for landscape, and even if the original ground plans had been the work of an architect, it was the gardener who realized them in terms of colour, form and seasonal variety. It was he who nurtured the thousands of tender bedding plants upon which the parterres depended, and determined the colour contrasts and harmonies. It was he who sited avenues and walks, and composed views. He positioned the specimen plants and planned the rose garden. He gave shrubberies form and conservatories brilliance, planted banks with spring flowers, and hillsides with winter cover. From his headquarters in the kitchen garden his influence extended to the furthest reaches of the pleasure ground.

This transformation of the English park, and of the gardener's position, was partly a reflection of a more widespread about turn of Taste. Inside the mansion as well as out, the 1820s and 1830s saw a change from purity and simplicity to ornament and eclecticism, 'from the rule of authority to the fancies of the individual'.[1] It was equally a reflection of the increasing availability of new and exciting plants from abroad. The variety and splendour of this new material begged for access to the garden, both exerting pressure for change, and providing the perfect medium through which to explore the freedoms of the new fashion.

The technological innovations of the nineteenth century also played an important role in changing the park back into a garden. Railways could transport plants swiftly and efficiently from nurseries all over the country. The gardener was made independent of local building materials and could indulge in all manner of geological fantasy if he so wished. The invention of concrete and of Portland cement – which resembled natural stone – allowed everything from urns and rockeries to ponds and grottos to be constructed with ease, and mass produced ironwork enabled conservatories and arbours to be prefabricated. Above all, improvements in the manufacture of glass, and in construction and heating, made glasshouses more efficient. Large panes of clear glass replaced the small, green-tinged 'fish scales' of the eighteenth century, and hot water pipes fed by reliable boilers made fireplaces and flued walls redundant. With the removal of the punitive tax on glass in 1845, and access to cheap coal, the gardener could have as much heated protection as he wanted, and undreamed of independence from the weather. He could raise plants for the parterre on a vast scale, and recreate the climates his new exotics required.[2]

Driving it all was the booming economy, and the social and political changes which came in the wake of rapid industrial and commercial expansion. The old aristocracy were making new fortunes out of mineral rights and enjoying the fruits of their fathers' agricultural improvements. Middle-class merchants and industrialists of sufficient means were buying their way into the landed gentry as never before. Money was poured into country estates. There was an epidemic of country house building and refurbishment.[3] Parks were remodelled and new gardens laid out, and every detail acquired significance in the social account book. In a world in which wealth, taste and acceptability were measured out – at least in part – in flower gardens and orchid houses, asparagus and grapes, the gardener's role gained new prestige.

The fame of individual gardeners also spread beyond their immediate locality. Society was nothing if not peripatetic, and many gardens were open to the public. More important, gardening had become a national preoccupation at all levels from the ducal pleasure ground down to the vicarage's couple of acres, and the villa front garden. There was an inexhaustible appetite for information and advice, and the advent of cheap printing and a band of experts eager to exchange and share ideas, led to the burgeoning of a horticultural press. John Claudius Loudon founded the first of the many journals with his monthly Gardener's Magazine in 1826. It closed on his death in 1843, but by then the weekly Gardeners' Chronicle had begun to roll off the presses, and within a few years its chief rival, the Journal of Horticulture and Cottage

Gardening had appeared. For the first time, practical gardeners had a forum in which to report, debate and criticize.

The Victorian head gardener became nurseryman and market gardener, florist and landscape artist, botanist and engineer, craftsman and gardening correspondent. As his qualifications rose, so did his status, helped along by the example of Joseph Paxton's meteoric career. Born in 1803, Paxton was the son of a Bedfordshire farmer. By 1826 he was head gardener to the Duke of Devonshire at Chatsworth, Derbyshire, where he set about altering the glasshouses, designing new buildings, rearranging the waterworks and planting trees. He succeeded in flowering the giant water lily, *Victoria amazonica*, wrote a treatise on dahlia growing and edited various horticultural journals. He laid out municipal parks and cemeteries, and in 1850-1 erected the Great Exhibition building in Hyde Park, the Crystal Palace. He died Sir Joseph Paxton, M.P. and railway millionaire.[4] Few could emulate Paxton's career, but all could now aspire to a measure of prestige in their own right. The practical gardener could begin to think of himself as a professional man.

Parks into Gardens

Changes to the landscape park were in many senses inevitable. A new generation of landowners with wealth at their disposal and social statements to make did not wish to sit around while their fathers' handiwork matured. They wished to make their own mark upon the landscape.[5] Besides, the political and economic conditions which had favoured the development of the landscape park were changing. Such empty vastness had often been made possible by enclosure, which enabled the aristocracy to enlarge their holdings at the expense of smaller landowners, farmers and local villagers.[6] It expressed wealth and power through breadth of domain, rather than through the intricacy of a garden.[7] The apparent lack of any practical purpose to the park reinforced the status of its owner, and the isolation of the house emphasized his lofty disregard for the livelihood and concerns of the local community.[8]

Even before the eighteenth century was out, revolution abroad and the spectre of unrest at home had begun to make such lordly disdain uncomfortable.[9] Humphry Repton, the successor to 'Capability' Brown as the most fashionable purveyor of gardens to the aristocracy, wrote explicitly of his distaste for a style which set the house 'solitary and unconnected in a sea of grass'. He believed a park should encompass, not deny, its owner's responsibility towards the community. 'The dairy farm,' he wrote, 'is as much a part of the place as the deer park, and in many ways more picturesque.' By the same token, if labourers' cottages 'can be made a subordinate part of the general scenery, they will, far from disgracing it, add to the dignity that wealth can derive from the exercise of benevolence.'[10] If the signs and apparatus of the working landscape were to be allowed to re-enter the view from the drawing room, then a new line had to be drawn between the house and the world beyond. There became once more a need for a garden in the vicinity of the house; a space in which to reflect the civilization and refinement which was still the prerogative of the landlord, however benevolent his gaze over the estate.

Blenheim Palace, Oxfordshire, 1787. In his critics' opinion 'Capability' Brown's landscapes left the house 'grazing by itself in the middle of the park'.

'Capability' Brown's parks had other, more practical, drawbacks. Just as he had banished the mundane realities of farming from the landscape, domestic offices such as the stables and kitchen garden had also been removed to some suitably distant point. This was highly inconvenient. The endless expanses of grass were also a problem. They might need little maintenance apart from the presence of a few sheep, but did little to cheer or divert the eye for a large part of the year, or to provide the shelter or surface for a stroll. As early as 1780, Walpole observed that '. . . the banishment of all particular neatness about a house, which is frequently left grazing by itself in the middle of the park is a defect. Sheltered and even close walks in so very uncertain a climate as ours are comforts ill exchanged for the few picturesque days that we enjoy.'[11] It was a view shared by Repton and eagerly adopted by his clients. As the eighteenth century turned into the nineteenth, flower gardens and terraces began to reappear around the house.

If changes in the political situation undermined the park, so did upheavals on a more philosophical front. During the second half of the eighteenth century, improvements in transport encouraged journeys to the wilder and more remote parts of the British Isles. Here mountain torrents and windswept crags appealed to the same temperamental streak that eagerly responded to Gothic literature. The Augustan version of Nature began to look increasingly tame and insipid.[12] The impact of this, and just how far thinking had moved on, became apparent during a public quarrel between Repton and two Herefordshire squires and intellectuals, Richard Payne Knight and Uvedale Price. It was essentially a debate over the degree to which landscape painting ought to serve as a basis for landscape gardening,[13] in the course of which Price and Knight attacked Brown's 'thin, meagre genius of the bare and the bald'.[14] Tamed and miniaturized, the crags and waterfalls of the picturesque theorists did find their way into the wildernesses, rock works and waterworks of later gardens, but as important for the transition from landscape park to pleasure ground was the growing belief that whatever else they did or did not sanction, painterly values reinforced the need for a suitable foreground to the view from the house, and the propriety of formal and obviously artificial features in its immediate surroundings.

The notion of an objective standard of Taste determined by classical values was also beginning to look uncertain. The eighteenth-century park was an attempt to evoke in an English setting the gravitas and tranquillity of classical landscapes. Its inspiration was the continental scenery through which the cultured gentleman passed on his travels through Italy, and the rendition of that landscape in the paintings of the seventeenth-century artists Salvator Rosa, Caspar Dughet, Nicolas Poussin and Claude Lorrain.[15] As long as the authority of ancient Rome was the measure of Taste, the style enjoyed some security. When this began to weaken, the park became vulnerable.

Walpole had built his Gothic villa at Strawberry Hill by 1750, pointing out the absurdities of small windows and deep porticos in the English climate and demonstrating that there was a respectable alternative to classical models in architecture.[16] As travel and trade with exotic parts accelerated during the second half of the eighteenth century, exposure to strange and wonderful artifacts, and to the accounts of returning travellers, began to challenge not only the Roman ideal, but also the belief in any absolute authority, or purity of style. Under the weight of a vogue for Chinoiserie, enthusiasm for things Indian, and the revelations of classical Greece, the notion of an objective standard of Taste began to break down.[17] Its demise was reinforced by the expansion of Society to include members from outside the closed and traditional world of the aristocracy. It was no longer possible or practical to sustain a single, authoritarian approach.[18] Instead the elements of fashion were constantly sifted and regrouped as a consequence of intense social jockeying. The gates of the garden were opened, not just to artifice, but to any number of exotic and diverse elements.

THE SEARCH FOR A STYLE

It is not hard to understand why a return to formality seemed such an attractive option. The landscape park was a remarkable aberration from a long and distinguished tradition of formal gardening. The notion of the pleasure garden as an extension of the house, to which Nature could be admitted within well-defined geometric or architectural limits, lay behind the gardens of classical antiquity, and the great Renaissance gardens which set out to recreate them. It inspired the gardens of sixteenth- and seventeenth-century France and Holland, and of Jacobean and Stuart

Shrubland Park, Suffolk, circa 1850. *The view from the terrace has been transformed.*

England. Almost every trace of these English formal gardens had been destroyed by the end of the eighteenth century, but in Europe they remained largely untouched. Repton had been sent to Rotterdam in 1764 at the age of 12 to learn the textile trade, and recalled in his *Memoir* the box hedges filled with chippings of coloured glass, pleached trees, statuary and 'a parterre. . . . in which the design traced on the ground was like a pattern for working . . . embroidery.'[19] In 1819, John Claudius Loudon, poised to become one of the most important influences on nineteenth-century gardening, returned from a series of continental tours entranced by the great geometric gardens of France and Italy.[20]

Formality offered everything that the landscape park did not. In the park, Art masqueraded as Nature. In the formal garden, artifice was self-conscious and unashamed. No longer, as one commentator put it, need a stranger be 'at a loss to know whether he be walking in a meadow, or in a pleasure ground, made and kept at very considerable expense.'[21] With the parterre as its centrepiece, the formal garden could be elaborated on a grand scale, or adapted to the smallest villa front garden. Planting could change from season to season to reflect the demands of the social calendar, and from year to year to include new novelties and changes in fashion. The parterre could be as colourful and ornate as the Neo-Rococo interiors which were all the rage from the 1830s until almost the end of the century.[22] Even during the more miserable months of the year it could provide interest and delight, whether viewed from the drawing room or explored on feet protected from the damp by gravel. Above all, it offered the supreme opportunity to employ the new plants.

Exotics, which had little place in the English pastoral of the landscape park, were made entirely at home by surroundings which were not only artificial but cosmopolitan and allusive. Trees were fastigated to resemble Mediterranean cypresses[23] and the scrolls, blocks and arabesques of the parterre could be coloured each summer with the most accommodating of the new exotics, the brilliant bedding plants. There were scarlet pelargoniums and blue lobelias from South Africa, and purple verbenas and yellow calceolarias from South America. Most European flowers bloomed in early summer, and were past their best by the time aristocratic families returned to their country seats in August, but these splendid plants flowered without ceasing from August until October.

It was a winning combination. The marriage of formal gardening and exotic plants introduced an intensity of colour and pattern that had never been seen before, and provided a powerful visual language in which to express the mood of the time. It was a style at once old and completely new, domestic and controlled, yet expansionist and outward-looking. It could only be made possible by new technology, yet lent itself to the nostalgic and heraldic associations required by old and new aristocrats alike. Whether measured in terms of architectural and engineering triumphs, the tens of thousands of bedding plants needed to fill the parterre, or the immense labour required to maintain the high level of finish on which the whole effect depended, it was an unsurpassed opportunity for the display of wealth and taste.

By the middle of the nineteenth century, many gardens had been laid out after the style of Trentham Park, the Staffordshire residence of the Duke of Sutherland. Here, the Society architect Charles Barry remodelled the house in the classical fashion during the 1830s, and then drew on his studies of Italian Renaissance gardens to set it within a grand architectural garden of several acres. Between the house and the distant lake he constructed terraces and two extensive parterres. Stone steps and balustrades linked the gardens, which were traversed by broad walks, and embellished with fountains and statues. Planted with spectacular success by the Duke's head gardener, George Fleming, the example of Trentham played a major role in popularizing the bedding system.[24] Barry went on to modify other houses and gardens, notably Harewood House in Yorkshire, Cliveden in Buckinghamshire and Shrubland Park, Lord Middleton's Suffolk establishment. The style received the ultimate accolade when adopted by Prince Albert at Osborne House on the Isle of White, and saw its ultimate expression in Paxton's park for the Crystal Palace in south London. Here the terracing, walks and fountains were taken out to the boundaries.

Eighteenth-century values were not, however, entirely abandoned. The Augustan ideal of a composed landscape in which house, park and countryside formed a unified whole was still a governing aesthetic of the 1850s. Formal gardens gave the mansion an appropriate setting but they usually occupied only a few acres at most, creating the need to shape a pleasure ground beyond, which both shared in the artifice of the parterre yet merged gradually into the surrounding landscape. Part of the solution was to extend architectural features such as formal walks and statuary out beyond the limits of the flower garden, but once again, the newest and most exciting possibilities lay in the use of exotic plants.

Beyond the strictly formal garden the presence of unusual plants in the landscape was a clear sign of artifice, and Loudon had coined the term 'gardenesque' as early as the 1830s to describe the multiplicity of effects exotic planting could achieve. At Biddulph Grange in Staffordshire, the home of the horticulturalist, James Bateman, rich collections of exotic specimens were accommodated outside the geometric garden in a series of themed gardens, separated by walls, tree-lined banks, rocky outcrops and even tunnels. Substantially complete by the mid-1850s, this approach was widely adopted in principle if not in scale.[25]

Additional possibilities were suggested by the 'natural' school of gardening inspired by Robert Marnock, the curator of the Royal Botanic Society's garden in Regent's Park, London. Marnock objected to the submission of plants to rigidly formal ends and advocated that they should be used in ways which drew attention to their individual beauty, rather than treating them as furniture in an architectural setting. From the 1860s onwards, there was an increasing trend towards a more naturalistic disposition of plants within the landscape. Environments were contrived which imitated as closely as possible those of the native homeland, and Nature was permitted to enhance the effect. Exotics such as rhododendrons could be allowed to self-seed in the woodland glades and narcissi and snowdrops to multiply among the wild primroses. Such an approach was both harmonious and practical, and became another means of including new introductions, particularly in the outer reaches of the pleasure ground.

The distinctive style of Victorian gardens was, therefore, both formal and eclectic. They were to borrow promiscuously from the English past and an exotic present. They took what they wanted from Renaissance gardens, and from the landscape parks they condemned. The whole was unified by an equally characteristic neatness and 'high polish'. By keeping every corner of the grounds 'clean as a drawing room',[26] there could be no question anywhere that Nature had not yielded to the artist's shaping intelligence.

New Plants for New Gardens

Exotic plants had, of course, been entering Britain for centuries via Royal and monastic networks, but until the pleasure ground became an essential adjunct to the great house in the sixteenth century, these introductions consisted mainly of useful fruits and medicinal plants. Once the demand for ornamental plants was established, the number entering the country increased dramatically. They came in not only from Europe but also from the New World. The South American passion flower and the New England Virginia creeper reached England in the seventeenth century, and when William III, Prince of Orange, became ruler of Great Britain in 1688, plants began to arrive from South Africa through the Dutch connection. This brought *Agapanthus*, discovered by the Dutch settlers at the Cape, and later the parents of the scarlet bedding pelargonium.[27]

The new ornamentals were highly regarded and throughout the eighteenth century a growing market helped to encourage both the volume and pace of introduction. Plants began to flow in from the east coast of America as English plantsmen financed collecting expeditions undertaken by their counterparts on the other side of the Atlantic. When the London merchant, Peter Collinson, first went into collaboration with a fellow Quaker, John Bartram, of Pennsylvania, the American was collecting seeds only for his partner and two other subscribers. By 1740, the number of sponsors had risen sufficiently that Bartram's consignments to England had become 'a setled Trade and Business'. He is said to have introduced over 200 new plants, including several magnolias and the first of the American evergreen rhododendrons, the Rose Bay of the Carolinas.[28]

Collecting plants, and producing and collecting paintings of plants became fashionable Augustan occupations. The celebrated Swedish botanist, Carl Linnaeus, had helped to promote the view that, as the world itself was a mighty collection, 'a museum, furnished with the works of the Supreme Creator', it followed that 'among the luxuries, therefore, of the present age, the most pure and unmixed is that afforded by collections of natural productions.'[29] Amassing examples of the beautiful, the rare and the strange became a preoccupation of wealthy enthusiasts who revelled in collections of minerals, shells, birds and, above all, plants.

Linnaeus' simple system of classifying plants did much to make botanizing a popular and improving pastime. George III's mother, Princess Augusta of Saxe-Gotha, set up a private botanic garden at Kew in 1751 and, following the Royal example, titled ladies took up flower painting and began to assemble herbaria and collections of rare plants. According to Repton, the second Duchess of Portland's garden at Bulstrode, in Buckinghamshire, included ancient, American, flower, and botanic gardens, a shrubbery and a parterre. She also bought around 220 drawings by the German artist, Georg Dionysius Ehret, who had illustrated Linneaus' work. He painted some 300 exotic and 500 English plants for her, and taught her daughters and those of other aristocratic families how to sketch.[30] Botanists such as Linnaeus' pupil, Solander, and his English translator, Benjamin Stillingfleet, became social attractions, and were eagerly sought after at *conversazioni* in London and Bath.[31] As enthusiasm increased, so did the desire for collecting become more far-reaching. When the collector Joseph Banks returned from his voyage to the South Seas with Captain Cook in 1772, George III appointed him as his Adviser on the Plant Life of the Dependencies. Banks, later Sir Joseph, and President of the Royal Society, was a rich young landowner with a passion for botany, and he put all his energies behind the new project. That same year the first of the long line of Kew collectors was despatched to bring back new and unique treasures for His Majesty's garden. Trips such as these were to yield Cape heathers, the parents of garden gladioli, and the Canary Island broom.

In 1786, the East India Company set up a Botanic Garden in Calcutta, which collectors from Great Britain could draw on. This garden also provided a staging post for plants from China, which was virtually closed to foreigners. Under Banks' influence the East India captains brought in the first tree peonies, and Chinese chrysanthemums and roses followed. The Kew gardens had recorded 5,535 foreign species of

Journal *readers could share vicariously in the plant hunters' quests.*

plants in cultivation in 1789, but by 1813 the figure had doubled.[32]

By this time, expeditions had acquired another sponsor – the newly formed London Horticultural Society, later to become the Royal Horticultural Society. This was set up in 1804 by Banks and John Wedgwood, son of the famous potter, with the cooperation of William Forsyth, the Royal gardener at Kensington, and Thomas Andrew Knight, the pioneer fruit breeder. The Society acquired large gardens at Chiswick in 1821 and sent plant hunters out to all corners of the globe.

The scope for collectors was enormous. At the beginning of the nineteenth century there were still large areas of the world untapped. The East had hardly begun to reveal its horticultural riches, and western North America and almost the whole of the Southern hemisphere were still unexplored. As these new territories were opened up and searching became more systematic, the flow of plants into Britain increased still further. Exotics also started to become more widely available. Material began to find its way out of mainly private collections into commercial channels and hybridization began in earnest. New varieties were raised to create yet more diversity, and hardier forms suitable for the British climate. By the 1830s and 1840s the wealth of material available had ignited a national passion for roses, chrysanthemums, dahlias, rhododendrons and bedding plants, and signalled the inevitable demise of the landscape park.

It proved worthwhile for many nurseries to send out their own collectors, and the closed environment of the sealed glass Wardian case, which had come into widespread use by the 1840s, did much to ensure that their tropical prizes survived the long journey home. The renowned Veitch nursery, founded in Exeter, Devon, by John Veitch in 1832, maintained collectors abroad continuously from 1840 to 1905. In 1853 the family took over the old firm of Knight and Perry in the Kings Road, Chelsea, and this became the Royal Exotic Nursery, where fashionable Society and their gardeners could be sure to find all the latest decorative plants. Both the range of material and demand soared, and many firms could afford to concentrate on limited groups of plants. William Paul of Cheshunt specialized in roses, Benjamin Williams of Highgate Hill, London, in orchids and Charles Turner of Slough, Buckinghamshire, in carnations.

The nursery trade boomed. Exploration of the Pacific coastline of America had yielded seeds of the giant conifers which the Horticultural Society's collector, David Douglas, started to send back in 1826. So rich were his finds that he wrote to his sponsors, 'You will think I manufacture Pines at my pleasure.'[33] By the 1850s the whole range of West Coast trees had arrived and avenues of wellingtonia and collections of conifers were being planted at grand – and not so grand – estates up and down the country.

From South America, now released from Spanish and Portugese control, and eager for trade with Britain, had came more dahlias and fuchsias, Argentine pampas grass and the monkey puzzle tree. Orchids came in from Central America, and from Africa, India and the Far East, as Britain's Empire spread. With the ending of the Opium Wars came the acquisition of Hong Kong and the right of entry to several Chinese ports. This gave the Horticultural Society's collector, Robert Fortune, access to nurseries and numerous shrubs including forsythia, weigela, and large flowering clematis. When foreigners were finally admitted to Japan in 1860, John Gould Veitch and Fortune were able to visit Tokyo and send back the imperial Japanese chrysanthemums, the golden-rayed lily, *Lilium auratum*, and *Ampelopsis veitchii* which rapidly replaced the old Virgina creeper everywhere.[34]

From the 1830s onwards, England was in the grip of an escalating floral mania. There were flowers inside and out, real and artificial. They embellished wallpapers, carpets, windows, ceiling ornaments, fireplaces, picture frames, mirrors, cabinets, silverware and inkstands.[35] There were pots of Mexican poinsettia in the drawing room and elegant palms in the hall. Every suitable niche held vases filled with the new, perpetually flowering hybrid roses. The Amazon lily, *Eucharis amazonica*, decorated the dining table and was the chief white flower used in ladies' bouquets.

Just a step away were conservatories resplendent with successions of exotics from the glossy foliage and waxy perfection of camellias to the brilliant blooms of Eastern azaleas and Brazilian fuchsias.

Almost everyone, from the wealthy collectors of rare specimens to the amateur botanists of the drawing room, was held in the thrall of the orchid. Beautiful, strange, and costly to cultivate, the mastery of orchid culture had nevertheless enabled some species to become cut flowers and pot plants without peer. In 1838 Paxton's glasshouses at Chatsworth boasted 83 species. The first hybrid flowered at the Veitch nursery in 1856. By 1885 there were to be 2,000 species in cultivation, and on her Diamond Jubilee in 1897, Queen Victoria was presented with a basket 'of endless spikes of all that are best and rarest from her Majesty's Dominions, being used together with the almost priceless blossoms of the hybridist's art raised in this country since our Queen's accession.' It contained species from the West to the East Indies, from Burma and India, from Africa's Table Mountain, and from British Guiana, illustrating 'the vast floral wealth in orchids of the many lands over which our Queen reigns.'[36] Two hundred hybrids were on record, and England earned the title 'The Motherland of Orchids'.

Long considered an educational and ennobling occupation, the contemplation and cultivation of flowers was by the middle of the century perceived as the key to respectability and refinement. Since the arrival of sentimental flower books such as Charlotte de Latour's, *Le Langage des Fleurs*, published in 1833, flowers had also acquired deeper moral and romantic significance.[37] The intricacies of flower symbolism saw plants as a series of spiritual messages from the Creator and also as the basis of an explicit code through which to pursue the delicacies of friendship. Whether in the garden or the drawing room, the ducal mansion or the urban parlour, much of social, romantic, and even spiritual life was conducted through flowers.

The passion for exotics extended to fruit and vegetables too. Pineapples, grapes and some Mediterranean fruits had been served at a small number of select Georgian dining tables, but the social calendar, and the Victorians' desire to capture the world's treasures and have all Nature at their command, created a demand for luxury fruit all year round. In this company, humble vegetables such as parsnips and cabbage no longer sufficed for winter dining, and the gardener was expected to furnish not so much exotic, as out of season, delicacies. Under the influence of post-Revolution French cookery and the new genre of gastronomic literature, food connoisseurship was fast becoming one of the hallmarks of sophisticated Society, and French chefs and discerning palates increasingly demanded a wide range of choice varieties throughout the year. Once again, it was the nurserymen, the hybridists and, above all, the gardeners whose responsibility it was to provide them.

As industry and the newly affluent middle classes expanded, nurseries, market gardens, florists and firms of professional floral decorators grew up to meet their demands. Against this fast-moving commercial background the Social élite had continually to stay ahead of fashion. The country estate could always count on having the edge over commercial suppliers in quality and freshness, but the gardener had to ensure that it kept the lead in novelty too. Whether consolidating the position of an established family, or making a bid for the acceptance of a new, it was upon the gardener's productions that much of his employers' social credibility depended. It was to this fact, above all, that the gardener owed his prestige.

THE GOLDEN AGE OF THE COUNTRY HOUSE

Houses and gardens have always made social statements, but the Victorian country house developed a particular role in supporting and maintaining the functions of Society. At the end of the eighteenth century, the landed aristocracy consisted of few more than three hundred families, most of whom had titles, and derived their income from the land. They all had in common the ability to support at least one country estate, and a house in town during the London Season.[38] Agriculture was still the largest single occupation and the wealthiest individual landowners were still the richest men in Society.[39] They made up, or controlled the Cabinet, the House of Lords and a large fraction of the House of Commons. Appointments in the Church and Armed Forces were in their gift.[40] They made up the glittering circles of London Society and, in partnership with their lesser relatives, the landed gentry, ran the social, political and administrative life of the Shires.

By the middle of the nineteenth century this supremacy seemed to be under threat. The Industrial Revolution had brought about an unprecedented expansion of industrial and commercial wealth, and a sharp decline in the relative importance of agriculture and the relative wealth of the landed classes.[41] The middle classes in the new towns – or the rapidly growing old ones – were demanding and obtaining a share in running the country. New towns were being given representation in Parliament, more people had the vote and the civil service was enlarged and opened up to competitive examination.[42] Yet even as the preconditions of landed superiority were ceasing to exist,[43] the prestige of the landed classes was, if anything, increasing.[44]

The aim of most Victorian merchants and manufacturers who had amassed a sufficient fortune was to establish themselves as landed gentry.[45] It was virtually impossible to buy directly into the aristocracy as the price of land and the limited opportunities to purchase an estate of sufficient size put an effective limit on the holdings they might acquire. They could only hope that an estate of at least 500 acres and a house to go with it would be the first step on the way to social acceptance, good marriages for their children, and perhaps, in time, a title. This massive expansion of the gentry presented the small, tightly knit circles of Society with a dilemma. They either had to close ranks or take the new candidates into partnership. In the face of widespread unrest in Europe and the threat of the mob at home, the latter course was more prudent.[46] The small closed world of Society at the beginning of the nineteenth century expanded to become the Upper Ten Thousand by the end.[47]

Admission to Society was not, however, made easy. In the face of the huge challenge to their exclusivity and way of life, the upper classes reacted by erecting a series of filters to exclude undesirables, and to ensure that all new entrants conformed to a set of rules and regulations of which they remained in control.[48] Every detail of dress and manners, taste and possessions, acquired critical significance. Etiquette became increasingly intricate and dinner services more elaborate. Entertainment, which had been largely public and unregulated when Society was small, became private. Routs, balls and public assemblies were replaced by house parties, shooting parties, dinner parties and elaborate calling rituals. Owning a country house was not only a certificate of common values, and the chief means of putting one's economic, social and aesthetic credentials on display. It was also essential if one were to participate in the rituals of upper-class life and the social and political engineering that accompanied them.

Since the eighteenth century these rituals had been increasingly bound up with land ownership. The agricultural revolution and the financial benefits that accrued from improving one's estate meant that landowners had become much more enthusiastic and involved in their land. In the meantime, improving transport had reduced the sense of exile that country life had once implied, and romantic attitudes towards Nature imbued it with the power of spiritual refreshment, a necessary counterbalance to the demands of the metropolis.[49]

As the benefits and enjoyment of land ownership increased, country sports became a popular way of passing the time. Enclosure had led to good fox hunting, especially in the neatly hedged, gently rolling grasslands of the Midland counties, where the Quorn and Belvoir hunts flourished.[50] With the interest in hunting came the development of Flat racing. The Derby and the St Leger were first run during the 1770s, and by the beginning of the nineteenth century had become major events in the Social calendar. Game shooting had also become popular, and was to play an even larger part in upper-class life after the arrival of the modern shotgun which was first shown at the Great Exhibition of 1851. This turned pheasants rather than partridges into the prime game birds as their faster flight made for more exciting sport and they could be reared in large numbers. The Victorians also invented grouse shooting, a pursuit which depended entirely on the expansion of the railways opening up the remote moors of northern England and Scotland to visitors. This had the splendid advantage of extending the shooting season into August.

Social and sporting calendars became completely intertwined. For those who owned or rented a London house, the Season opened with the Royal Academy's Summer Exhibition in May and continued with a series of dinner parties and receptions organized around such events as Royal Ascot, the Henley Regatta, the Eton and Harrow cricket match at Lords, as well as the balls and parties which culminated in the presentation at Court of the year's crop of debutantes. Social, marital, political and sporting interests would all be assiduously pursued at one and the same time.

When Parliament went into summer recess and the stench of the Thames became unbearable, Society took off for the Shires.[51] Having dispersed around the country, its members then embarked on a series of house parties and dinner parties which revolved, ostensibly at least, around the pursuit of grouse, partridge, pheasant and fox. Collections of guests whose mutual interests might be furthered by the opportunity for talk and acquaintanceship in civilized and unhurried surroundings would be carefully assembled. As in London, there might be a cabinet minister or two, a diplomat home on leave, a painter and, almost certainly, a musician who played to the company in the evenings. There was usually a sprinkling of women famous for their beauty and wit who 'either gave the conversation a sparkling turn, or were wise

Guests at a country house assemble for breakfast and a day in the field.

enough not to interrupt good talk and who accordingly sat looking statuesque or flower-like.'[52] It was also an opportunity for London and County circles to mix, and local notables would often be invited to join the house guests for dinner.

As guests moved from estate to estate, and acted as hosts in their turn, there was inevitably intense competition to offer the finest sport, the most attractive gardens, the freshest produce and the most agreeable company. Whether its purpose was to bid for advancement or to flourish ancient grandeur, secure a match for a daughter, or seek a political favour, the house party was the principle *raison d'être* of the Victorian country house.[53] In fulfilling the obligations of their position, head gardeners were essentially meeting the demands of this kind of entertainment. There is virtually no aspect of their achievement which was not determined by the demands of the social and sporting calendars and the social function of the country house.

Geometry and Geraniums

he geometric flower garden, or parterre, was the heart of the Victorian plea-sure ground. It usually lay to the south of the house which was deemed architecturally desirable as it could be seen from the drawing room and the terrace. The drawing room was an emphatically feminine room, which was always given a sunny aspect and the best view.[1] As the ladies received carriage calls and took afternoon tea, they were able to enjoy the glowing colours of the parterre at its best. The southerly situation was also the best horticulturally, as it gave the tender bedding plants maximum sunshine.

At first colours were mixed together within beds, but by the 1830s gardeners were beginning to explore the greater variety of artistic effects which could be achieved by using blocks of separate colour. This sharpened the geometric effect and opened the way for bold, contrasting designs. These usually consisted of simple shapes, such as circles, ellipses, squares and rectangles, filled in with red, blue or yellow blooms, but the more intricate curves and scrolls of the seventeenth-century French *parterre de broderie* were also used. The composition was symmetrical in shape and colour, and set off by a surround of grass or gravel.

The head gardener at Dropmore, the Buckinghamshire home of Lord and Lady Grenville, was widely credited with originating this massing system. His employers were devoted horticultural patrons, and as far as Robson, head gardener at Linton, could recall, the beds at Dropmore were drawn to the attention of the gardening public in an early number of Loudon's *Gardener's Magazine*. The 'design of the geo-metrical garden at Dropmore, with the mode of planting . . . appeared in one of the numbers of that periodical some time I think, about 1829 . . . It is possible the plan might have been adopted at other places before it was at Dropmore; and I know Scar-let Geraniums were planted in single beds before 1829; but I am not aware of any place where a regular set of beds were planted with distinct colours in such a way as to form a harmonious design before that time.'[2]

As Robson also observed 'its adoption . . . very much changed the features of out-door ornamental gardening', as gardeners and employers eagerly took up the oppor-tunities offered by the new technique. One of the first to experiment was John Caie, head gardener to the Duke of Bedford at Bedford Lodge in Kensington, whose basic principles of design were increasingly adopted over the next 20 years. In his view, the eye was continually agitated by small juxapositions, and he advocated 'clean . . .

The flower garden at Fordell Castle, Fife. The powerful geometric design is outlined by rows of box clipped to within 3 inches of the ground.

intelligible' colours, definite contrasts, and simple rather than complex shapes. He proposed keeping the height of plants proportional to the size of the beds, and a system of balance rather than strict symmetry. This required beds of equal size to be planted with equal brilliance, while a small bright bed could be used to balance a large one of subdued colour. The whole effect was intended to be one of dignity and 'greatness of expression'.[3]

With these ground rules established, the popularizing of the system was continued by George Fleming at Trentham Park, and by the writings and practice of Donald

Beaton at Shrubland Park in Suffolk. Encouraged by their employers, the Duchess of Sutherland – the 'Queen of Gardening' – and the artistic Lady Middleton, they explored the possibilities of contrast and harmony with increasing subtlety, and devised ways of creating shaded effects in which one colour blended into another.[4]

The keys to the success of the massing system were the brilliant colours and long flowering season of the geranium, or pelargonium, and the other new bedding plants which had been reaching Britain from abroad. When the first pelargoniums arrived from the Dutch colony at the Cape, they were greenhouse plants and until 1826 there were, as far as Robson could recall, very few varieties and 'these were slow growers and of course their multiplication was correspondingly slow.' There was the 'old Horseshoe-leaved Geranium [the zonal pelargonium], the flower of which was a dull red rather than a bright scarlet, and the petals narrow and windmill-like. This old scarlet was very soon followed by one under the equivocal title of 'The White Scarlet', a horseshoe variety with blooms of a dull white colour. This certainly was not common before the year 1832; and coeval with it were a gold and silver edged variety which I remember to have seen in cottage windows.' Nevertheless, he perceived that there was 'an important future . . . now in store for the Scarlets; both red and white were to be had, and the purpose of garden decoration to which they were destined to be put was by degrees developed.'[5]

Robson's first intimation of this came in 1829 when he tried planting them outside. A large plant of the 'old Horseshoe variety' had grown so well against the back wall of a plant house that 'it was much cut-in, furnishing a full wheelbarrow-load of shoots and stalks.' At the time, the flower beds on the lawn were being planted with annuals such as 'French Marigolds, Asters, Ten-week Stocks' and 'it was thought that some of the shoots of the Geraniums . . . might be stuck into one of the least promising of these beds.' By September, there was a fine display of healthy, if somewhat tall and unwieldy, plants, in full flower. Much encouraged, Robson planted a circular bed with pelargoniums the following year, surrounding it 'by wire basket work about 15 inches high, so that the unruly growth of the Geranium was carefully kept in bounds, and a good show of flowers was the result.'

Robson's experience was not a singular one. All over the country gardeners were experimenting with the new exotics. Breeders were working hard to improve varieties and by 1836 Robson believed that 'the importance of scarlet Geraniums as ornaments to the flower garden was fully acknowledged.' The increasing number of colours was followed in about 1842 by the introduction of more compact growing varieties, such as the scarlet Tom Thumb. With this development the full possibilities of colouring designs with flowers could really be explored.[6]

The arrival of purple and crimson verbenas from South America in the 1840s also did much to establish the bedding system. They made dense, continuously flowering masses, and a range of hybrids was soon available. To complete their palette, gardeners also had the little pouched-shaped calceolarias from South America to provide shades of yellow and orange, and South African lobelias for an intense blue.

As massing developed, so gardeners and nurserymen strove to increase their colour range still further. By the 1860s, there were pelargoniums with flowers from 'pure white up through the various shades of pink, peach, rose, cherry, salmon, scarlet, to crimson of various shades, with foliage of all shades of green, to say nothing of the shimmering beauty of the creamy, silver, golden-edged and bronze varieties . . . and all culminate in the gorgeous tricolor-leaved varieties which almost combine, in one leaf the colours of the rainbow, and vie in beauty of marking with the tenants of our stoves.'[7] Calceolarias sported every shade from bronzy crimson and orange brown, to buff and bright yellow, while verbenas came in white, crimson, scarlet and purple. Numerous other plants suitable for the 'highly artistic parterres' had also been recognized, including silver and grey leaved foliage plants such as *Stachys lanata*, *Cineraria maritima* and *Cerastium tomentosum*.

Combined with formal elements such as box hedging, gravel paths, clipped trees, statuary and so on, this colouring allowed almost infinite scope for the layout and design of the flower garden. In the grandly Italianate Trentham Park, for example, one parterre took the form of a complex design, incorporating and repeating the family's initial 'S', while at Shrubland an elaborate fan of scrolls was painted in flowers, gravel and turf. Both these establishments also had borders along the paths leading out of the flower garden into the pleasure ground. These were originally planted in parallel ribbons of colour, but by the 1860s had also become extremely complex with coloured scrolls and panels forming the groundwork beneath taller specimen plants.

The more slender and intricate the design, however, the more difficult it was to plant. While the practical men advocated simpler shapes, the designer William Nesfield aroused considerable controversy by a different approach. During the 1850s he introduced coloured sands and gravels into parterres such as those at Holkham in Norfolk and Eaton Hall in Cheshire. His precedents were the *parterre de broderie* which was laid out in box and gravel alone, and the old Tudor knot gardens which employed coloured earths to carry the design through the winter. By this means, he was able to create more elaborate patterns than would have been possible with flowers on their own, and one of his trademarks became the execution of monograms and heraldic devices with which the landed aristocracy old and new liked to emblazon their possessions. At the extremes, reaction was divided into those who found the 'chastity' of his effects a welcome relief from the blazing colour of the bedding plants, and those who considered the use of such artificial materials in the flower garden an 'abomination'. Used separately, however, rather than in conjunction with flowers, ornamental gravels enjoyed a brief period of popularity as adjuncts to the evergreen planting of winter designs.[8]

PLANNING THE PARTERRE

As he set out to design a new parterre or to replant an existing one, the gardener's first consideration had to be the characteristics of the site itself. Its scale, contours, relationship to the house and to any other vantage points from which it might be surveyed, all had to be taken into account.

At Linton, for example, the sloping ground in front of the house had been terraced, and from a broad terrace in front of the mansion an Italianate staircase led down through a series of landings and steps to a lawn. It was here that Robson made the flower garden in 1858. The area of level ground was comparatively small, so instead of dividing it up into a parterre, Robson adopted the novel solution of a single large bed measuring 90 feet by 68 feet in which he 'embroidered' a design. It was oval in shape so that, allowing for the effects of perspective, it would appear to be a perfect circle when viewed from the terrace. In the planting, Robson aimed for a bold, precise effect, tracing out the design in white, variegated alyssum or the dark brown foliage of perilla, and filling it in with the clear, bright colours of selected varieties of pelargonium, verbena, calceolaria and lobelia.

His first design was built around the letter 'C' for the Cornwallis family, but he changed the picture every year, and in 1861 the white alyssum outlined a flower. This was coloured with rosy crimson pelargoniums and set in a groundwork of pale blue lobelias. There was an outer rim of scarlet pelargoniums studded with circles of orange yellow calceolarias and a wide turf border. Encircling the whole was a path of crushed cockle shells which gave added sparkle to the creation, and inspired one visitor to draw comparisons with illuminated manuscripts and the rich colours of a Rubens painting.[9]

Large Central Bed

A Ten wedge-shaped, and one circular compartment, Geranium Trentham Rose.

B Groundwork surrounding the above a light blue Lobelia, of strong growth.

C Twenty circles of Calceolaria aurea floribunda.

D Border of Geranium Tom Thumb surrounding the Calceolaria circles.

E Alyssum variegatum forming an outer edging, and all the inner lines of stringwork; also dividing the central compartments, making the scrolls on the Lobelia groundwork.

Side Beds, Both Alike

F Twelve circles of Calceolaria aurantia multiflora.

G Ten panels or compartments of Horseshoe-leaved Geraniums (scarlet-flowered).

H Stringwork dividing and surrounding the above of Perilla nankinensis.

I Band 2½ feet wide of Geranium Mangles' Variegated.

J Band 3 feet wide of Tropaeolum elegans.

K Outer edging, Alyssum variegatum.

The design for the great oval bed at Linton, Kent, in the summer of 1861.

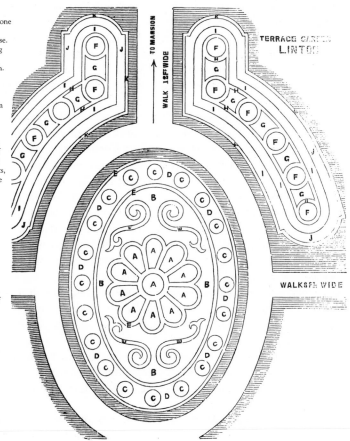

Robert Fish, a fellow head gardener, considered Robson's solution an admirable one which, in his report in the *Journal of Horticulture*, he recommended others might learn from. In 1859, the year he saw the bed, the design took the form of a bow, and 'the first peep I had of it by moonlight from the terrace was very striking – the favourable impression being more than confirmed the next day. It looked very well even when close to; but it looked better from the terrace; better still from the principal rooms above the colonnade; and best of all from the roof of the mansion. These facts will give an idea where such a plan could be most successfully followed. The spectator should be able to look down upon it and take it all in at once . . . The mode has given such satisfaction that it bids fair to be continued, especially as a new design can be adopted every season.'[10]

Fish faced a different set of problems at Putteridge Bury Park in Bedfordshire, where he had to contend with a flat, exposed site and a very limited range of glasshouses in which to raise the tens of thousands of bedding plants required. Nevertheless, despite the drawbacks, his peers considered he had 'created a Paradise out of a common field.'

The gardens lay around three sides of the mansion with the main flower garden on the southern side. This took the form of a sunken parterre of eighty beds set around a fountain. This afforded the plants extra shelter and was designed to be admired from the covered verandah above, which led from the mansion to the conservatory. There were also numerous other beds elsewhere, and hundreds of yards of borders, which included 'the striped ones Mr Fish is so famed for'.[11]

The feature which attracted most attention was an avenue made not of trees but of flower beds planted to resemble pyramids.[12] These were arranged in pairs across the lawn, leaving a grass walk, 24 feet wide, between them. Beds 10 feet in diameter alternated with ones half that size, and in the large beds, height was given by a tall conservatory plant, such as a fuchsia, the bright yellow *Cassia corymbosa*, or a form of the headily scented South American angels' trumpets, *Brugmansia knightii*. In the smaller beds the same effect was created by a showy, continuously flowering red China rose, Belle de Florence, or a large specimen pelargonium.

Around each central specimen were rings of bedding plants, and when Robson visited Putteridge Bury in 1860, he found 'the blending of the colours, as well as judicious dressing afterwards brought the beds to that state of artistic perfection not met with everywhere.' In one pair of beds, for example, the flowers were all in shades of rosy crimson with a centre of 'pink Nosegay Geranium; then a variegated Geranium edged with a dwarfer growing form.' In another pair, a red rose was 'festooned with Pearl Nasturtium', and in another pair the white angels' trumpets were ringed by red salvia, blue ageratum and a wide band of yellow calceolaria, with a rim of blue lobelia next to the grass.

The overall appearance of each bed was that of 'an agreeable pyramid or cone, or, what was more graceful still, a structure of flowers having a pent roof; for the centre was generally elevated so as to resemble that pointed appearance a circular tent has when the cords are slack.'[13]

The avenue stretched for some considerable distance and, according to a local newspaper correspondent, was 'especially patronised by the ladies.' This, he surmised, was because 'their full length dresses swept more agreeably over the turf than over the gravelled paths.'[14]

The extraordinary versatility of the bedding system, and the ingenuity of its practitioners, was perhaps even more evident in the gardens at Archerfield in East Lothian, which became a household name during the 1860s. Here the mansion was surrounded by parkland, and the ornamental flower gardens were a carriage drive away at the village and ruined castle of Dirleton. When David Thomson was engaged in 1858 by Lady Nisbet Hamilton as her new head gardener, she directed him to inaugurate the bedding system so that a mass of flowers could welcome her when she returned to Scotland in early August, and last until she left in November.

The site presented Thomson with a number of difficulties. It consisted of two separate areas, one of which was an open site beside the village green, while the other lay within the confines of the ruined castle. Enclosed by high walls and a beech hedge, this was irregular in shape, and would be seen both by visitors on the level ground and by those who chose to ascend the tower in the boundary wall or climb up to the castle itself which stood on a grassy knoll.

Thomson adopted quite different approaches in each of these areas, making two distinct and contrasting parterres. On the village site, he laid out a bold geometric design set off by grass. This was flanked by the large expanse of village green on one side, and an evergreen shrubbery on the western edge. In the planting, he concentrated mainly on strong, clear contrasts of red, yellow and blue, which beckoned the approaching visitor across the green and, on closer inspection, were admirably counterbalanced by the turf and shrubbery. A strategically positioned seat, sheltered by a tall yew hedge, offered a central vista framed by specimen conifers, and the southern aspect revealed the afternoon colours at their best.[15]

In the other parterre, Thomson made a virtue of the unsymmetrical shape and laid out an unconventional, almost paisley pattern, of sweeping curves and irregularly shaped beds. For the colouring, he used a richer palette than the heraldic primaries of the village display, employing more crimson and purple, lots of variegated-leaved pelargoniums, and grey and dark chocolate-coloured foliage. Carefully planned highlights of yellow were used to draw the eye over the design. The beds were bounded by low box hedging, and set off by broad gravel paths, which provided a more telling background than grass to the complex colour associations.

When Robson visited Archerfield in 1865 he reported that few 'could enter the door without being struck with the extraordinary blaze of colour spread out before them; even those who are well versed in the art of bedding for effect, and have followed it for years with success, have been compelled to confess they never saw the like before . . . I never saw so much bloom on any other class of plants, and the arrangement as to height and harmony of colour was faultless.'

CONTRASTS AND HARMONIES

The success of a parterre depended largely on its colouring, and this tricky subject occupied as many column inches in the journals as the cultivation of fruit for the dessert. It drew inspiration from the hybridists' ever expanding fund of tints and shades, and from the reverberations of colour theory which were echoing through the worlds of art and design.

Nineteenth century colour theory had its origins in the work of Johann Goethe, the German philosopher and poet.[16] He was interested in the phenomenon of after-images, the effect perceived when an experimenter transfers his gaze to a piece of white paper after staring at, say a red spot, and sees a green spot instead. The colour of this after-image always depends on the colour of the original spot, red invariably producing green; purple, yellow; and orange, blue. On this basis, Goethe concluded that these were natural, harmonious contrasts, which were 'immediately applicable to aesthetic purposes'. Furthermore, by editing and reordering the colours of Isaac Newton's spectrum after performing his own experiments, Goethe perceived a natural progression from darkness at the blue and violet end, through red and orange, to yellow, and light, at the other. This, in his view, implied that colours had intrinsically positive or negative properties. Blue was cold and associated with distance, yellow was warm and suggested proximity. As yellow intensified to red it became increasingly cheerful, while blue acquired grandeur and dignity as it approached the red part of the spectrum.

These thoughts soon gained acceptance in early nineteenth century art circles, and were rapidly embellished. In 1817 the colour maker George Field postulated that there could be no perfect harmony of colours in which either of the three primaries was wanting. In 1828, David Hay, who was to redecorate Royal Holyrood Palace in Edinburgh, published his *Laws of Harmonious Colouring Adapted to Houses*, in which he asserted that the direct union of opposites was harsh and unpleasant, and needed a 'harmonising colour to mark the full concorde.' Harmonizing colours were those which lay adjacent to each other if the spectrum was arranged in the form of a wheel, making orange the harmonizing hue to yellow, red to orange and so on. Principles such as these gave decorators of all kinds a vocabulary and explicit set of rules through which to explore colour combination.

They were given further guidance by the work of the French chemist, Michel-Eugène Chevreul, who was director of the Gobelin tapestry factory. His discovery of the importance of the background in perceiving colour reinforced the notion that the contrasting or complementary colours 'suited' each other. Red appeared brightest next to green and so on. It also showed how inserting a band of white between two colours which threatened to merge into each other, such as red and blue, could restore their distinctness.

By the middle of the century when Owen Jones, who decorated Crystal Palace, summarized these new rules as part of his *Grammar of Ornament* (1856), it was as if the visual volume of the Englishman's surroundings had been turned right up. On canvas, the sombre colours of academic landscapes had given way to brighter 'local' colour since artists in the second half of the eighteenth century had left their studios to paint in the open air. Turner's paintings had introduced new, heightened perceptions of light and colour, and the Pre-Raphaelites were even abandoning shade and shadow in their pursuit of pure, glowing tones. Since the founding of the Royal Academy in 1768, organizations of professional artists had also been holding annual exhibitions, which enabled a much wider public to see original paintings, rather than simply engravings.[17]

In the home, the new colour principles together with the discovery of new pigments such as rose madder, cobalt blue, cobalt green, and cadmium yellow, and the aniline dyes of the 1850s had brightened fabrics and paintwork. With the development of a satisfactory paste, wallpaper started to be used with increasing frequency. Small wonder that out in the garden there was also a demand for more brilliant colour, and earnest discussions on how best it might be employed.

Gardeners were kept abreast of the developments in colour theory by journals and lectures. In 1864, for example, Maidstone Gardeners' Mutual Improvement Society received the latest views from a professional artist.[18] They also kept detailed records of each year's colouring experiments, and were ready to modify theory in the light of any combinations which, if 'not strictly according to scientific dicta', had nevertheless turned out to be 'chaste and pleasing'. The journals were filled with reports and diagrams, discussions and advice. David Thomson, in particular, was said to have 'raised the whole subject to a higher status of art and enjoyment' and his book, the *Handy Book of the Flower Garden* which was published in 1868, remained in print until the end of the century.

Thomson's advice began with the recommendation to experiment first with a detailed plan on paper. 'Let the walks or ground work be coloured, if it be gravel, as nearly as possible as it exists in the garden when in a high state of keeping, and then colour the beds of a verdant green colour throughout. On this green, which is designed to represent the foliage of the plants, strew a few petals of the flowers, leaving green dots uncovered here and there. This will give an idea of what the plants look like when in bloom in the beds – much more correct and natural than can be given by water colouring.'

As an aid to design he suggested using the decorator's colour wheel to read off the correct contrasts and harmonies of each colour, although the application of these rules to plants was not always very straightforward, as he was the first to admit. Take 'purple King Verbena, which may be described as reddish blue . . . ; it is blue with a shade of red in it, the contrasting colour to which is green and orange. The blue being in the ascendant in the Verbena, the contrasting plant must have orange in the ascendant as the contrast to blue; but the red in the purple demands a greenish shade and consequently the contrasting plant must be greenish yellow, such as we have in Calceolaria amplexicaulis and C. canariensis, etc.' For the reddish black of the popular foliage plant, *Perilla nankinensis*, the contrast had to be greenish white, which variegated pelargonium leaves, and grasses could supply, and silvery grey foliage could always be relied upon to make a good contrast against 'all strong colours such as bronzy crimson, deep scarlets, blues and deep purples'.[19]

Just as important as contrast was harmony. 'There are a few things that afford more pleasure to the eye, however slightly trained in colour, than the contemplation of the soft gradations that may be worked out in a bed of flowers associated according to the principle of harmony' wrote Thomson. This required the blending of colours 'insensibly into each other' in the same way as adjacent shades merged on the colour wheel. On this basis one could take 'red or scarlet, dark pink, pale pink and white, and place them in that order named and a pleasing harmony from red down to white is the result. The transition is gentle and beautiful – something like a plaintive melody in music.'

The choice of colours and the way in which they were deployed depended upon the setting and the mood that the gardener wished to create. Thomson generally advised the use of the harmonizing principle for beds in 'a quiet sequestered spot, where the design has to be studied close to the eye.' In such a situation strong contrasts were to be avoided as there was more than just a 'stare in a harmonious group of flowers in a quiet nook – there is a calm benignant beauty which goes directly to the heart.'

On the other hand, 'where the garden extends over a wide expanse, and has to be studied from a distant point or where there are long stretches of borders, there must be a measure of boldness and distinctness.' A large parterre should employ contrast to make 'every line and figure . . . sparkle with expression, or it will not be easy to follow out and appreciate the length and breadth of the design as if it were a small picture under the eye.'

Heavy masses of colour could be avoided, and beds made to appear larger, by planting beds of more than 12 to 24 feet in diameter, with rings of two or more colours, with the strongest colour at the outer edge. In a group of beds this same principle helped emphasize the whole design for 'as anyone who has studied the matter knows, with soft tones towards the centre and bright ones towards the outside, the eye takes in and the mind can master the design much better than with the bold colours at the centre.'

It was principles such as these which Thomson put into practice so successfully at Archerfield, particularly in the irregular parterre which depended on colour to lead the visitor through the garden and unify the design.

As far as we can tell, the breadth and balance of the design were emphasized by using quieter colours in the key centre beds and darker ones towards the perimeter. Although not obviously geometric, the parterre was symmetrical about a line between the tower and the castle, and consisted of three sets of beds – those under the tower, a larger group below the castle, and a central display between them. These were linked by similar planting of the main beds lying along the central axis. This drew the eye down the parterre, and the effect was further enhanced by highlighting the centres of certain beds with 'advancing' yellow calceolarias, to form a triangle which had its apex in the central bed of the far group under the tower, widened through a pair of beds in the middle section and was completed by a final group below the castle.[20]

For the visitor on foot, complex sequences of contrasts and harmonies invited exploration. Entering the garden through a gate in the south west corner near the tower they found themselves gazing at a group of brilliantly coloured beds. There was a pair planted with scarlet pelargoniums, and edged with a gold-leaved variety, and another of purple verbenas set off by variegated cream foliage and cerise-flowered pelargoniums. The centre of the group was the striking mass of yellow calceolarias which formed the apex of the triangle. It consisted of 'nothing save the golden blooms . . . resembling a large honeycomb . . . relieved by the shrubby habit and purple foliage of Perilla with which they were edged.'

Drawn on by paired planting in the middle section of the garden, guests finally arrived at the beds immediately below the castle. The large key bed in this arrangement was planted in a combination of harmony and contrast that Thomson considered 'exceedingly lovely', giving 'both repose and beauty'. Its centre was filled with Flower of Spring pelargonium, which had cerise coloured flowers and leaves edged with cream. This was surrounded by a wide, contrasting band of blue lobelia studded with orange gazania, which harmonized with an outer ring of a golden-foliaged, red-flowering, pelargonium.

In order to achieve such clear, dazzling effects, gardeners had to be ruthlessly selective. At Linton Park, Robson's success with the oval bed depended upon his use of a very few varieties carefully chosen for their purity of colour. Verbenas with a white 'eye' were no good for his purposes, nor were pelargoniums with any suggestion of a horseshoe tint to the leaves, as this gave a 'dirty and unpleasing effect' when viewed from a distance. The habit of the plant was also important, and varieties which held their flowers 'well to the top' and displayed their foliage were best. All this had the effect of reducing the range of plants used and by the middle 1860s more and more gardeners found themselves relying mainly on pelargoniums which were 'now so varied in habit and colour that with geraniums alone a skilled artist can produce almost any effect that may be required.'[21]

Extending the Season

As the importance of the flower garden increased throughout the 1850s and early 1860s, so did the feeling that the beds could not lie empty for the eight months that the parterre was not in bloom. At many establishments the family was in residence, at least intermittently, for most of the year. Belvoir Castle, Leicestershire, was set in the midst of some of England's best hunting country, and the sporting Duke of Rutland and his family entertained visitors from the Autumn right through until April or May. With improvements in the speed and ease of transport, it was also delightfully possible to punctuate the frenzy of the London season with a refreshing country weekend, especially if the estate was as convenient as Cliveden Manor in Berkshire, where the Duke of Sutherland had his southern home. As the Duchess was a friend of Queen Victoria, and the Mistress of the Robes, her presence at Cliveden would be required whenever the Royal Family repaired to nearby Windsor, as at Christmas, Easter, and during Royal Ascot week. There were also many owners of smaller country properties who took no part in metropolitan life, and for them months of bare earth was a particularly depressing prospect.

The obvious solution to the need for spring colour lay in the use of bulbs, and as early as the 1840s gardeners were employing hyacinths and tulips to give colour in the parterre two or three months earlier than the summer bedders. Pansies, the early nineteenth century invention of Lord Gambier's head gardener, Mr T. Thomson, were another candidate. He raised numerous varieties which became commercially available when he set up in business as a nurseryman in the village of Cliveden. It was, however, John Fleming, the Duke of Sutherland's head gardener at Cliveden Manor, and William Ingram at Belvoir, who showed the fashionable world what spring gardening could achieve.

The house at Cliveden had been acquired by the Duke and Duchess of Sutherland in 1849 and rebuilt by Charles Barry. After the Duke's death in 1861 it seems to have become the Duchess's main residence and the setting for her son's social activities. He had a taste for radical causes and in early May 1864 entertained Garibaldi as a house guest. Whatever else this may have achieved, it gave the General a chance to see 'the most beautiful flower garden in England'. According to the *Journal of Horticulture* his sitting room overlooked the 'Duke's Garden', which was on the eastern side of the house. Here the flower border was gay with 'Aubretia, Arabis, Anemone, Pansies, Oxslips and Jonquils, with a broad belt of Italian Wallflower. This last named loaded the air with its perfume, which was diffused all through the apartments adjoining.'[22]

The main flower garden was enjoyed from the terrace in front of the mansion. Here there were 'large beds of blue Myosotis studded over with the white La Candeur Tulip, looking as if jewelled in honour of the visit . . . The centres of the beds were already gay with some of the early flowering scarlet Rhododendrons and yellow Azaleas.' A ribbon border ran along below the terrace and this was 'so full of bloom, and the colours so beautifully disposed as to extract from the usually undemonstrative hero the exclamation "Magnifique." The first row consisted of the pink Daisy, then white Daisy, Cliveden Blue Pansy, Cliveden Yellow and Cliveden Purple; mixed Virginia Stock, Gilia tricolor, Collinsia grandiflora, Dwarf Wallflower and Purple Honesty.'

At Belvoir, William Ingram introduced spring gardening on a grand scale, yet his creations were 'of a quiet beauty . . . gay enough to satisfy any lover of colour yet it was not gaudy.' The local nurseryman John Pearson, who often visited Belvoir, found them reminiscent of 'Indian Shawls, the quiet tertiary colours were so beautifully contrasted and blended. The whole left the impression on my mind that few refined ladies had the exquisite taste possessed by Mr Ingram.'[23]

The great baronial residence sat on a steep, thickly wooded hillside and commanded extensive views over the countryside. As one walked in the grounds, every turn of the path brought a change of scenery. The most notable feature was the Duchess's garden some half a mile away from the castle. This occupied a natural hollow and took the form of a glade surrounded by woodland. Extending to some five acres, it provided conditions eminently suitable for spring flowers, and enjoyed a climate far superior to that of any other Midlands garden. Trees and undergrowth sheltered it from the worst of the winds , frosts rolled down the hillside and, being high, the air was drier than it would otherwise have been. Alpines flourished on rocky outcrops, and the rising slopes were terraced and planted with formal beds and borders. Ingram specialized in aubretias and the primrose family, and polyanthus, oxslips and primroses produced a magnificent display of colour from cream and yellow to glowing crimson. There were wallflowers in profusion, including the dwarf Belvoir Castle yellow, and heathers, tulips and hyacinths completed the formal picture. As Pearson reported, 'You have variety and effect combined, yet without extravagance – lovely

Spring bedding in the Duchess's garden at Belvoir Castle, Leicestershire, 1873. The drawing is by Mrs Ingram, the head gardener's wife.

little plants rarely met with peeping here and there amongst their showy sisters. I shall never forget the effect produced by Hyacinths of different colours growing through a mass of Arabis caucasica.'

Paths wound out among trees where large expanses of violets grew, and clumps of the handsome *Veratrum nigrum* nestled in shady nooks. As visitors stood on a terrace walk, looking down on 'the carpet of lovely green backed by the feathery foliage of the birch' they found 'it was difficult to tear themselves away.'

Attempts were also being made by 1860 to extend the season in the other direction. Spring bedding still meant 'no flowers worthy of the name on the wintry side of March' and winter was not only the longest period owners spent in their country seats, it was often the most active socially. The aim of winter gardening was to provide interest right through from the end of the summer until the beginning of May when the bedding plants went in again, without requiring the interruption of a spring display.

To achieve this, gardeners turned to evergreens, using ivy and small specimens of trees and shrubs such as box, holly and yew, as temporary bedders. As early as 1848, George Fleming had filled the main parterre at Trentham with heathers and dwarf evergreens, and new introductions constantly suggested new possibilities. Young conifers were particularly valuable, and deodar cedars, western red cedars, and Lawson cypress were pressed into service. Patterns were formal with, for example, a conifer or standard silver holly at the centre, a surround of box and an edging of variegated ivy. For Christmas, the display would be enhanced by richly berried specimens

including skimmias and laurels put in at the last minute, while bulbs such as snowdrops and crocuses tucked into the margins provided colour from February.

One who felt as keenly as most the difficulty of keeping a prominent flower bed interesting from July to Easter was John Robson at Linton. At first, he followed Nesfield's example of embroidering a pattern using coloured earths and gravels. Crushed
waste kiln bricks made 'a bright and telling red', sifted cinder ashes provided black
and a local sand or crushed shells, white. These were laid down in an inch-thick layer
and the pattern outlined by broken stones of 'uniform size and hue'.[24]

By the late 1860s, he was combining this approach with the use of evergreens to
make the design. Only the hardiest shrubs could survive transplanting twice in a year
and the southwesterly gales which swept across the site. Box, laurel and yew were
suitable and a great favourite of his was the novel form of the American white cedar,
then called *Retinospora ericoides*, which had autumn foliage of a 'beautiful violet tint.'
He liked to combine these darker leaves with some light foliage, as the surface of the
ground was moist most of the time, and consequently a darker colour than in summer. For this he chose cotton lavender and a variegated form of arabis, whose 'soft
clear cream-coloured hue' was 'unequalled for general effect when seen at a distance
of a few yards.'[25] Two wild plants, the common sedge, or ribbon grass, and *Helleborus
foetidus* also looked very well, and were economical into the bargain. The hellebore,
which could also be used to fill the terrace vases, had 'Fern-like foliage spreading
evenly all around the stem' which contrasted 'by its dark green hue, very strongly
with the paler and more delicate tint of the inflorescence, which appears in defiance
of all weather during the dark days of winter.'

*Linton's oval bed in the winter of 1864. The design was executed in cinder ash, crushed bricks,
shells, and pebbles.*

In these combined patterns Robson used only cinders and white sand or shells to complement the living material. In 1868, for example, the groundwork was black and planted with circles of evergreen shrubs. These featured yew at the centre, which was surrounded by box and edged with cotton lavender. The design was completed by 'some bold lines of scroll work' in white, and the whole bed set off by a white border laid out in the style of the Greek key pattern. Robson's aim was to have it all perfect by the end of November, when it replaced a mass of pelargoniums destroyed by the frost with a 'pretty device' that was all the more admired if 'it had been accomplished during the few days absence of those for whose pleasure it had been made.'

Winter gardens of this kind were never, however, universally adopted. The trend towards more natural gardening effects began to take hold during the 1860s and the use of coloured earths smacked of heresy. They were decried as 'bricks and mortar' gardens, in which the transplanted shrubs served only to make the parterre resemble a nursery ground.

RELIEF AND REPOSE

The popularity of the brilliantly coloured, geometric parterre was at its height during the 1850s and early 1860s, but not everyone embraced its enamelled artifice with unqualified enthusiasm. Many found the strong reds, blues and yellows, which dominated the style, gaudy, and it was even argued that a liking for such colours was a 'remnant of primitive barbarism', unworthy of cultivated minds.[26] By the mid-1860s, upheavals in colour theory were also calling into question the use of high contrast, while the massing of plants on the basis of colour alone was under fire as both unnatural and monotonous. It offered 'nothing to study except what may be seen any day in a draper's shop window' said one head gardener, and subjected them to the annual tyranny of raising and planting thousands of tender plants. 'The sooner the masses of tender flowers, which vanish with the frost cease to be the alpha and omega of our flower gardens' declared Thomson in 1863, 'the better in many respects.'[27]

The vivid appeal of such parterres was too great for their detractors to win converts overnight, but the first heady thrill of colour for its own sake had inevitably begun to wear off. The pastel shades of spring gardening had also suggested a new set of colouring possibilities, and just as the previous decades had seen a complete reversal of taste from restraint to stridency, so the switchback of fashion lurched again. What had been seen as powerful, became overpowering and the cry began to go up for more 're-pose' in floral compositions.

Edward Luckhurst, head gardener at Oldlands in Sussex, and one of the rising talents of the 1870s, defined this quality as 'delicacy of colouring, tasteful combinations, quietness and softness of tone . . . an absence of glare, harsh contrast or any incongruous feature'.[28] The key to this was a much greater use of neutral shades. Nature, as one head gardener pointed out, provided its own relief. 'It is the blades of wheat that make red poppies so telling' and 'the green Barley that gives Charlock its peculiar richness in yellow.'[29] And it was to foliage that gardeners turned for the relief they required.

As parterres began to reflect the new thinking, gardeners were inspired, as always, by the new exotics. With the introduction from China of *Perilla nankinensis* had come dark foliage unlike anything ever seen before. Its inky maroon colour had been despised at first but by the mid-1860s was being widely used where strong contrasts were required. There was also the *Amaranthus melancholicus ruber* from Japan, a compact grower with large, shaded crimson leaves, and *Coleus verschaffeltii*. This was a form of the Javan *Coleus blumei* and was the most versatile of the crimson-leaved plants. Between them these provided a palette of subdued purple, pink and crimson tones which could be combined with silvery foliage plants, variegated-leaved pelargoniums and Golden Feather – a golden-foliaged pyrethrum – to give an effect at once rich and soft. There were no harsh contrasts, and glaring vulgarity was avoided without any danger of insipidity.

For the benefit of the *Journal*'s readers Luckhurst described a ribbon border which illustrated the new approach to colour. It consisted of four rows, the first of which was planted with 'Cerastium, pearly grey; the second of Lobelia Trentham Blue, deep blue; the third of Pelargonium Crystal Palace Gem, rich yellow [leaves]; the fourth of Coleus Verschaffeltii, deep rich crimson'. The pelargonium was not allowed to bloom and spoil the effect.[30] For a circular bed, he recommended the deep violet of the recently introduced 'glorious Clematis Jackmanii', which could be pegged down to fill the whole area and trimmed with a soft yellow edging of Golden Feather. In Luckhurst's opinion, the contrast of the clematis and the Golden Feather was rich rather than harsh, while harmonies of white, pink and soft grey were 'sprightly and pleasing'.

THE TRIUMPH OF FOLIAGE

Foliage started to play a more important role in bedding schemes, and interest in foliage plants grew. Ferns had already begun to enjoy wide popularity, and collectors took advantage of the expanding railway network to explore the more remote regions of the country in the search for novel forms. Ferneries became a feature of pleasure grounds, and Wardian cases filled with ferns became a fashionable addition to city drawing rooms.

The riches of the stove house also received attention. Here the most spectacular and luxuriant foliage plants were to be found: tree ferns and palms reaching up to the roof, and huge-leaved wigandias which added several feet of growth in a season. Some of these hothouse specimens were capable of surviving an English summer outside, at least in the south of the country, and their showy foliage proved irresistible to gardeners seeking to relieve the flat monotony as well as the garishness of summer bedding. Lawns and parterres began to sprout stately specimens of sub-tropical foliage.

The fashion was led by Jean-Pierre Barillet-Deschamp's experiments in Paris parks, and owed much to the development of South American cannas.[31] These had been grown as stove house plants since the beginning of the century, but in 1846 a retired French Consul at Valparaiso, Chile, began hybridizing them to create bolder

*Tall, bold-leaved cannas could relieve the
vivid evenness of summer bedding.*

leaved forms. By 1856 he was crossing these hybrids with scarlet-flowered species to
produce plants with brilliant blooms as well as handsome foliage. He distributed his
stocks to French nurserymen, and cannas rapidly became a key element in the Paris
bedding displays. Both the plants and the enthusiasm reached Britain and, as Fish reported in 1866, cannas were now available in 'innumerable forms bearing bright
flowers peeping through the foliage, some of which grew to five feet or more in
height.'[32]

Cannas were not the only suitable plants for use in the parterre. There were a number of other possibilities, and when tastefully combined they made a splendid display.
Fish suggested using the castor oil plant, *Ricinus communis*, with its purple parasol-
shaped leaves, at the centre, surrounded by cannas and gladioli, and a dark outer edging. Hardy Japanese hostas with gold-margined leaves also made an appropriate trim.
In particular, the glaucous-leaved *Hosta sieboldiana* made a 'lovely harmony of form
with a mass of lance shaped Cannas', and contrasted well with the bronzy *Ricinus*.

Plants which could be propagated easily were naturally the most popular. *Ricinus*
could be raised from seed, and roots of cannas 'overwintered as easily as potatoes.'
The large-leaved *Fatsia japonica* was almost hardy, and along with yuccas and dracaenas could form good centres. Others like wigandias from Caracas, which were prominent enough to form specimens on a lawn, made rapid growth and could be propagated from root cuttings, so avoiding the problem of finding overwintering space.
Where there was plenty of glass, bananas and palms could be wheeled out from the

conservatory when the season allowed.

The English leader in sub-tropical gardening, as it came to be called, was John Gibson, who as a young gardener at Chatsworth had been sent out to India in search of plants for the Duke of Devonshire's collection. He became Superintendent of Battersea Park and, by 1864, had established a sub-tropical garden as its major attraction. This included a 'cool and tropical forest scene' reminiscent of his plant hunting days and the lawns were set with formal beds of cannas and other foliage plants, and there were also imposing single specimens. In one 'picturesque nook' the terminal plant was 'a grand example of the Abyssinian banana, Musa ensete'. It had leaves 11 feet 6 inches long, which were 'enhanced in beauty by their deep red midrib', and was fast outgrowing its winter quarters. Fern Hollow, one of the most admired sections of Battersea Park, was filled with tree ferns and palm trees. Monstera deliciosa, the cheese plant, was trained around tree trunks and stumps supported the stag's head fern.[33]

Sub-tropical bedding was, however, only successful in warm sheltered gardens, which ruled out many Scottish establishments. Plants could be kept under glass until the last moment, but this needed plenty of glasshouse space, and an exposed site soon rendered tall specimens 'most hideous when torn and tattered by the wind.' At Putteridge Bury, Fish attempted to overcome the problems of an open site by making a small, sheltered sub-tropical garden around a fountain, but this had to be abandoned as his limited glasshouse space became occupied with the more pressing demands of fruit for the dining table.[34] It was a style which persisted in some gardens but, in many more, the most adaptable specimens were incorporated into the next horticultural fashion, carpet bedding.

By the mid-1860s a range of dwarf foliage plants had become available, including species of the dark-leaved Iresine, and pink and purple Alternanthera, from South America. These acted as edgings or ground cover, and could be carefully clipped to produce a surface as uniform and even as a carpet.

At the same time, exploration of the Alps and other mountain ranges, had focused attention on the neat, close growing masses of alpine plants such as mossy saxifrages, sedums, sempervivums and the rosettes of Mexican echeverias. It was soon realized that combining the new dwarf foliage plants with alpines and succulents opened up new possibilities for embroidering with plants.

Once again, the innovator was John Fleming at Cliveden. In 1868, he used plants such as these to make a bed featuring the monogram of Harriet, Duchess of Sutherland, who died that year. The HS pattern was composed of 'Arabis, Echeveria and Sempervivum species' against a background of different coloured sedums. A leader in the Gardeners' Chronicle suggested the name 'carpet bedding' for this new effect, and recommended it for the coming season.[35]

This approach changed the scale of geometric design in the parterre. It allowed the creation of detailed and intricate patterns without recourse to Nesfield's artifice of coloured sands and gravel, and provided an appropriate range of colours through which to achieve the harmonious effects now admired. The palette could easily be extended by the use of additional foliage plants. Perilla and coleus could be pinched to keep them small, and a dwarf form of the Mexican marigold, Tagetes signata pumila, with its flowers picked off, gave a soft green. Brighter colours could be introduced where needed by the use of lobelia and Golden Feather. By 1875 Luckhurst was reflecting that 'we now have a greater variety of designs containing such charming combinations of colour as not long ago would have been considered impossible . . . quaint succulent plants and pretty alpine gems of minute growth but exquisite form imparting a new interest to the beds, a rich yet quiet and refined tone that was altogether wanting in the glaring masses of scarlet Geranium and yellow Calceolaria, which found such favour a few years ago.'[36]

The practical advantages were also considerable. Once planted, the effect was more or less immediate, with little further growth required to bring the picture alive. The flat, scissored surface kept the design crisp, with none of the parterre's problems of varying plant heights. As carpet beds depended on foliage they were also much more durable than those composed only of flowering plants. At Hampton Court, where they went so far as to cover the beds with canvas at night, they could be made to last well into November if the frosts stayed away.[37] Carpet beds were also not so badly affected by rain and wind. A heavy shower could leave the usual summer bedding scheme looking sad and bedraggled but the appearance of carpet beds was positively enhanced by glistening water droplets. 'This lovely enamelling of foliage never fails us' observed Luckhurst 'but literally grows in beauty both under clouds and sunshine till the falling temperature of autumn prompts us to substitute the hardier winter plants.'

Not suprisingly the style was taken up with enthusiasm. Almost every villa and country house seemed to be experimenting. One scheme which was particularly admired was at Cleveland House, the suburban villa of Mr and Mrs Ralli in south London, and executed by their gardener Mr Legg. According to a correspondent for the *Journal*, the beds in front of the house were perfect in planting and finish, and a masterpiece of decorative art. 'Rich tones are imparted by Golden Feather and Alternantheras; a cool lively character is given by the free use of Mesembryanthemum cordifolium variegatum; while quietness and repose are afforded by a dense neutral carpet of Sedum glaucum, brightened gently yet effectively by glowing tufts of the lovely alpine plant Nertera depressa. The association of these two lowly gems is the "chefd'oeuvre" of Mr Legg's taste, the dense and brilliantly berried Nertera nestling in the silvery-grey carpet of the miniature Sedum is a happy idea admirably carried out. If the birds do not carry off the berries, the beauty of this combination will be sustained throughout September, while each will bear the closest examination; but to comprehend their beauty to the fullest extent, they must be looked down upon from the upper windows of the mansion. For that privilege I am indebted to the special kindness of Mrs Ralli, and I have been thinking of it and dreaming about it ever since.'[38]

This was carpet bedding *par excellence* employing no flowers at all. To show off the design to its best advantage the beds were raised, 'ramped up by turf to about a foot above the lawn level, and the surface of each has a very gentle rise towards the centre.' The immaculate finish and geometric precision demanded not only 'ungrudgingly devoted time, skill and labour', but also an intimate knowledge of the plants' habits. The plants had not only been pinched to form the carpet, but some were sunken and others planted on a mound, so that neither alpines nor foliage were

The centrepiece of Mr and Mrs Ralli's celebrated display of carpet bedding at Cleveland House, south London.

more than two inches high.

The central bed was almost fountain-like, resembling a broad-rimmed saucer out of which rose a central dome crowned by an elegant specimen of *Dracaena indivisa*. In between each of the surrounding beds, giving 'an agreeable relief to the bright colouring of the carpet-work' were further sub-tropical plants, and beyond 'a circle of choice Conifers planted at wide intervals.'

Others took the technique in different directions. At Belvoir Castle, for example, Ingram incorporated the style in his spring planting schemes. In one of the terrace beds in the Duchess's garden he set a simple design of circles against a background of golden thyme. The circles were of grey cotton lavender filled with aubretia and a centre of a white dwarf heather. The design was banded on one side by a line of yellow violas and sedums, and on the other side by oxslips and saxifrages.[39]

In the gardens of Crystal Palace, the superintendent George Thomson planted a series of beds in 1875 which were deemed to surpass anything so far. The design took the form of six butterflies, the markings and colouring of which were realistic down to the portrayal of particular species. The idea was widely copied, particularly in parks, with beds emblazoned with town names, civic slogans, portraits, and animal and human figures.

It was not, however, a development which found favour in all quarters. In Luckhurst's view butterflies and the like were a retrograde step, being 'mere pictorial delineation'; toys rather than the balanced harmonious compositions of mosaic work which could be worthy of 'high rank among art works'.[40] Nevertheless, once the pictorial possibilities of the style had been revealed, they could not be resisted. While municipal parks sported symbols of civic pride, country establishments saw a resurgence of interest in the display of monograms and heraldic emblems. Ancient families and those aspiring to the club seized the opportunity to add a statement of lineage to the already eloquent message of the parterre, and by the 1880s 'names, mottoes, coats of arms and other frivolities [were] becoming common.'[41]

Carpet bedding was a style which was set to continue into the Edwardian era and beyond, particularly in public parks. Even so, it did not provide the complete answer to the problems of bedding. Alternantheras, which were the key to the brightness of the designs, needed strong sunlight and were not much more successful than subtropical bedding in cold northern climates. *Coleus verschaffeltii* was not much better, and succulents could not survive prolonged damp weather. In David Thomson's opinion, the whole style also tended towards bleakness. It might be appropriate for a few beds, but was 'too bald and formal in its outline and general effect to be recommended for extensive planting.' A more enduring development, at least in a domestic context, was the revived interest in the herbaceous border.

THE HERBACEOUS BORDER REDEEMED

In parallel with the interest in foliage plants came a quite different response to the criticisms of the gaudy geometric parterre. This was a revival of interest in hardy perennial plants. In all the exotic excitement these had been relegated to the decorative sidelines, or even to the kitchen garden, where they provided cut flowers for the house. As dazzling geometry began to pall, however, the more modest virtues of herbaceous plants came once again to be appreciated.

This was a process which was underway long before William Robinson embarked upon his self-important rhetoric of rediscovery. He was Robert Marnock's assistant at Regent's Park, and an ardent disciple of the 'natural' school of gardening. His *Hardy Flowers* was published in 1871, and from the pages of *The Garden* which he helped found the same year, he inveighed against the pernicious bedding practices which treated plants as mere paints, and consigned 'our precious collections of hardy flowers' to the rubbish heap. By 1913, he was claiming to have revived interest in herbaceous plants almost single-handed.[42] In reality, the pressures which restored hardy plants to ornamental status were gradual and various.

The parterre suited the aristocratic social calendar, but for the growing numbers of middle class owners it was not ideal. They wanted more lasting effects without the fuss and expense of successive spring and summer bedding. The gardening clergy were particularly opposed to the prevailing fashion. In 1863 the Reverend gentleman, who called himself the Wiltshire Rector, confessed that he had been caught up in 'the Geranium fever of a very scarlet type' for the past ten years. With eighteen beds to fill in his lawn, his house 'for seven months of the year had been geranium rid-

Dahlias flowered well into the autumn.

den – laundry full, study windows full, dressing room ditto, and if I go down into my
cellar I knock my head against Tom Thumbs hung up from the ceiling.'[43] Herbaceous
plants offered relief from the tyranny of bedding, and a level of interest that small gardens, with no room for the roseries, dells and other features of a large pleasure
ground, lacked in the parterre alone.

The trend was encouraged by spring gardening, which of necessity made use of
winter hardy plants, and also by an increasing interest in garden history. Age and tradition became a commodity to be valued as much in garden plants as in architectural
style and family connections.

On a more practical front, croquet and tennis which had been growing in popularity during the 1860s, began to compete with the parterre for lawn space. Disease
was also beginning to take hold of verbenas and calceolarias, while the capricious
British climate had never been on the side of tender plants, particularly in northern
England and Scotland.

These hard-driven gardeners had been using less tender material in the parterre for
years. At Archerfield, in East Lothian, Thomson had employed a variegated form of
the old fashioned Jacob's ladder which 'had all the grace of the fern tribe' as an edging
in the 1860s.[44] He also found catmint an admirable bedder. 'Its colour is beautiful
and chaste in lines and masses, being a warm mauve lavender,' he wrote, and with
'half the kind treatment given to Purple King Verbena, it will flower longer and even
excel it in show.'

Mixed borders composed of the finest hardy flowers such as phlox and delphiniums, mixed with temporary occupants such as dahlias, gladioli and bedding
plants, were also nothing new. Those at Bothwell Castle, also in Scotland, and at

Loxford Hall in Essex, were considered particularly fine, and 'a garden without a border for mixed flowers is seldom to be met with' asserted Donald Beaton at the end of the 1850s.

As the criticisms of the artifice and monotony of the parterre grew, the diversity of form, colour and association offered by herbaceous plants became increasingly attractive to gardeners at all social levels. By the 1870s there were nurseries all over the country offering large and inspiring collections of hardy plants. In Scotland, the way was led by nurseryman, William Sutherland, whom Thomson credited with showing Scottish gardeners how to display these eminently desirable additions to their flower gardens. He had been a gardener at Kew, going on to set up his own business in Liverpool and, finally, near Edinburgh. His *Handbook of Hardy and Herbaceous Plants* appeared in 1871. At Longleat, the Marquess of Bath's new head gardener, William Taylor, was able to draw on the resources of Wheeler's in Warminster, while gardeners in the Midlands had Smith's of Worcester. In York, the Blackhouse nursery, which was famous for its alpine plants also had an immense list of hardy plants, and in London gardeners turned to Ware's, at Tottenham and Osborn's of Fulham. If any doubt as to the merits of hardy plants remained, the escalating price of coal, the bad summers of 1875, 1876 and the 'almost polar severity' of 1879 when the bedders hardly bloomed at all, more than confirmed their advantages.

At some establishments, such as Blickling Hall in Norfolk, hardy plants were introduced into bedding schemes,[45] but everyone agreed that the best place to appreciate the attributes of hardy plants was in a long deep border. Here 'their beauty of form, variety of character and fragrance' could be enjoyed at their best. The main walk in the kitchen garden remained a suitable spot, but if the decorative possibilities were to be fully exploited, then the introduction of the herbaceous border into the flower garden had to be considered. In Sutherland's opinion, siting it near the edge of the ornamental garden offered the best of all worlds. 'The brilliant colours of the parterre would be intensified as well as harmonised by the comparatively neutral effect of the motley coloured border.' It would also help achieve the transition of the formal garden into the pleasure ground and 'present a chaste finishing touch to the scene.'[46]

This was the position of the perennial border at Longleat, which William Taylor began to plant in 1874. The formal flower garden lay to the north of the 'princely mansion', and looked out over lawns and a distant lake. To one side stood the old Orangery, and on the other, backed by rhododendrons, was the permanent herbaceous border. This had a row of 'pillars and arches covered with climbers, not too closely kept' in front of it, which helped to join the more informal planting to the strictly geometric garden and to break the straight outline of the border.[47]

The arrangement was a great success. Although the formal garden was usually the first to receive the guests' applause, this was short-lived, Taylor observed, compared to the more subtle pleasures afforded by his herbaceous plants: 'the longer people examine collections of hardy plants lovingly cared for, the better they like them.'[48] The display was not, however, a simple return to the past. Gardeners judged that 'the old speckled borders with Geums and hardy Asters, Veronicas, and Potentillas, lashed tightly in bundles to stakes like faggots' would now be quite unacceptable to eyes accustomed to the glorious masses of the parterre, and the border contained not only old-fashioned plants, but also many new hybrids and introductions.[49]

Stately blue delphiniums now came in several different shades, while there were pyrethrums offering a range of tints from white through to pink and crimson. The border phloxes, first developed by nurseryman Wheeler, were particularly useful, as they made great masses of rich colour. The new Asian lilies made exquisite points of interest, as did the lovely *Anemone japonica* sent back from China by Fortune, which bloomed from August to November. In addition, a little winter protection enabled the brightly coloured flowers of Mexican penstemons, and tall scarlet perennial lobelias to be added to the list.

The ideal when planting a herbaceous or perennial border was to achieve an appropriate massiveness of effect without sacrificing diversity, which was one of the great attractions of hardy plants, and missing in the parterre. Plants were always arranged in order of height, sloping down from back to front, and within this basic framework some gardeners adhered to the strictures of bedding and planted in lines. The general trend, however, was away from geometry, with arrangements designed to be free from stiffness and formality, but still orderly and graceful.

One way of achieving this was to repeat bold groups of telling plants, such as delphiniums at equal intervals to 'carry the eye from point to point along the entire length of the border.' Skilfully executed, this could create an overall impression of 'regularity and continuity' while not detracting 'from the variety in form and foliage that may be introduced in the intervening spaces.'[50]

In 1876, Luckhurst began making a long perennial border, some 20 feet deep, at Oldlands. He favoured 'bold groups of a dozen or more plants of the same kind down its length, a row or two of hollyhocks at the back, edgings and margins *ad libitum* in front.'[51] The groups, which 'form the most important feature' could be of 'many varieties of one species or even comprising many species of one genus, the intersecting spaces being filled with mixed specimens . . . Such an arrangement would always be as interesting as it would be ornamental.'

For bold groups he used phlox, penstemons and sweet williams. The phlox quickly grew into 'large clumps 2-3 feet high with colours ranging from pure white to deep purple', while penstemons came in many different shades of crimson, pink and white. Sweet williams made 'most brilliant groups' of similar colours. In addition he made use of peonies, and shrubby plants such as lavender, rosemary, hardy fuchsias and 'the old monthly China rose, bright with gay flowers to November'.

For prominent positions he also selected from a range of plants that included delphiniums, tall growing campanulas and red hot pokers. Carnations, chrysanthemums, irises and lilies were also valuable subjects for the perennial border. Margins could consist of catmint and there was nothing better for an edging than 'a broad line of the old white pink'. For a particularly striking effect the plants surrounding the key groups or even the groups themselves might consist of one colour only but this, he felt, was to rob the border of much of its interest.

Some gardeners, such as the nurseryman William Sutherland, preferred less organization. He advocated an informal background of shrubs and climbers such as roses and clematis, against which all linear arrangement should be avoided. He considered the 'monotonous and frequent repetitions of the same effect in colour, habit

*Clumps of penstemons provided highlights
in shades from crimson through to white.*

or foliage were undesirable', and put great emphasis on 'harmony of colour and harmony of form and agreeable contrasts of both'.

To achieve this, careful account had to be taken not only of the colour relationships between flowers in bloom at the same time, but also of their shape, height
and foliage. Some plants such as *Aconitum autumnale* and *Veronica virginica* were tall
and slender, and looked well planted close together, while the wide-spreading *Anemone japonica* and hostas soon grew into large clumps that were of interest from all
angles. Others, such as lilies, although growing tall, needed to be close to the eye to
be appreciated.

The selection of plants was governed by the pattern of the family's comings and
goings, as the period of maximum interest had to coincide with that of the country
entertainments. In Taylor's case, it was stipulated that nothing should flower much
before August when the Marquess returned from London, but that the display should
then last as long as possible. This could be managed in part by combining plants with
overlapping flowering seasons, but it was also necessary to supplement the colouring
with temporary annuals, dahlias and bulbs. A reserve stock of large plants such as
chrysanthemums, kept in pots and ready to replace spent ones and fill any weak
points in the colour, was also essential.

Taylor's border consisted of a great diversity of plants running into several hundred
different species and varieties. These he grouped informally, while confessing that it
'needed a practised hand to arrange a perennial border straight off, so that the ground
may be fairly covered without the plants being too much in lines or in other ways too

stiff-looking.'[52]

In August the Marquess was greeted by the Japanese *Lilium auratum*, the showy blooms of yellow and white evening primroses, old red bergamot, and blue and purple michaelmas daisies. Spiderworts, *Tradescantia virginica*, were in flower and would last several weeks as would the blue sea hollies, the eryngiums, which by September 'were all exceedingly beautiful, especially E. amethystinum.' September also witnessed the full splendour of the giant sea lavender, *Stactice latifolia*, 'with beautiful large leaves and lavender coloured flowers', while 'the Double White Meadow Saffron, the best of the Colchicums, was still as spotless as a Tuberose and almost equal to it for a bridal bouquet' in early October. The Kaffir lily, *Schizostylis coccinea*, like a miniature gladiolus, continued to throw up 'its scarlet spikes until the first frosts', and the giant red hot poker could last until Christmas. Hostas made a fine display of foliage throughout the season, while stocks, sweet peas, heliotrope, chrysanthemums and so on were all used to fill in blanks and provide scent and additional colour.[53]

Over the next decade, the possibilities of the herbaceous border were taken still further. In 1882 Miss Jekyll, a lady of independent means, artistic training, and one of the new generation of amateur gardeners, planted her great border at Munstead Wood. In this she used hardy plants massed together in broad drifts. These blurred into each other in a quite new way to create 'a soft and insensible transition from one mass of colour to another'. The colours were so arranged as to draw the eye through an unbroken sequence along the length of the border, starting with white and grey at the outer edges and moving in stages through to warm bright colours at the centre. This gave the border a 'brilliancy . . . beyond anything we had hitherto seen in the way of hardy flowers.'[54]

By the mid-1880s, therefore, the ornamental flower garden could be formal, informal or a mixture of both. Old-fashioned plants co-existed with new exotics. Designs could be representational or abstract, their colouring bold or harmonious, and surfaces uniform as a carpet, or as uneven as the border at Munstead Wood, Surrey. The vocabulary of the flower garden was essentially complete and remains the Victorian head gardeners' great and enduring contribution to modern gardening.

3

The Mansion in Bloom

perfect, fairy-land, marble, gilding, mirrors, pictures and flowers; couches ranged round beds of geraniums and roses, every rare and sweet oddity lying about in saucers, bouquets without end, tiers of red and white camellias in gorgeous pyramids. The dresses too were beautiful and so fantastic they would have passed for fancy dress a few years ago . . . head-dresses with long creepers of flowers interwoven with diamonds.'
Lady Eastlake recalling an evening party at Devonshire House, London, May 1850.[1]

With flowers at every turn outside, it was inevitable that they should enter the house itself. The garden had been steadily creeping closer since the end of the eighteenth century. The main rooms, once above the rustic, had begun to descend to ground level, and acquire low-silled or French windows opening straight on to the garden or terrace.[2] Orangeries and other ornamental buildings designed to protect tender plants such as citrus trees and oleanders had become increasingly popular additions to the house itself.[3] By the middle of the nineteenth century the new glass-roofed conservatories had brought ravishing displays of tropical and sub-tropical plants to the very threshold of the drawing room, and plants of all descriptions were spilling into both public and private rooms.

Just as the parterre reflected the arrival of the new exotics, so the mansion welcomed the perfect indoor specimens which emerged from the plant hunters' trips. Palms, dracaenas and other ornamental-leaved plants enlivened corridors and hallways. Madagascan stephanotis scented the ladies' boudoirs. Orchids decorated the drawing room and the dining table, and there were tea roses by the score for bouquets and buttonholes. Plants and flowers came to be considered not just luxuries for grand occasions but a year round necessity in 'homes of refinement and taste'. Everyone, it seemed, agreed with Longleat's head gardener, Taylor, that, 'No proprietor, once having his mansion furnished with flowering plants throughout the autumn and winter is ever willing afterwards to be without them. He finds his paintings, his china, and his furniture, be they ever so valuable, do not light up the faces and bring forth the hearty admiration of the majority of his visitors as do the flowers.'[4] By 1875, one hard pressed gardener observed in the *Journal* that the demand for flowers in the house had doubled in the previous ten years and quadrupled over the last thirty.[5]

Pots of orchids became important items of floral decoration. The Journal *considered this rosy Lycaste 'one of the prettiest'.*

In the country, responsibility for everything from the conservatory to the cut flowers and dinner table decoration fell to the head gardener. In town, families without a country establishment to send up supplies had to rely on the commercial men, who were also called upon to help out when even the plant houses and reserve grounds of the estate could not meet the demands made upon them. During the 1850s and 1860s the landed classes had a clear lead in floral showmanship. Their extensive glasshouses could supply a wide variety of high quality blooms all year round. But, as the hothouse industry took off, it increasingly became the head gardener's task to ensure that they did not lose this superiority.

The new florists' shops and professional floral decorators could provide basketfulls of cut flowers, festoons of ivy, ballroom posies, and lofty rented palms to order. One Mayfair gentleman paid out more than £3,000 for floral decorations in one month alone and, according to John Wills of the leading London decorators Wills and Segar, a bill for £1,500 for a single event was not unusual in Belgrave Square. In 1874, he supplied two tons of ivy and 2,000 blooms of Maréchal Niel roses for the Mansion House Ball in honour of the Duke and Duchess of York.[6]

By the end of the century, flower culture had become the jewel in the crown of commercial market gardening. The new Covent Garden Floral Market had been opened in 1870 and by the 1890s specialist growers such as Thomas Rochford in north London were producing palms and dracaenas by the million. Chrysanthemums followed the tomatoes in glasshouses, while orchards were under-cropped with moss roses, narcissi and violets.[7] Even so, with skilful management, private forcing houses could still give a longer season and wider range than the commercial man could profitably contemplate. Flowers could be sent up to the town house several times a week during the Season, and improved railway timetables ensured that they arrived in a better condition than almost anything the florist could provide. Throughout the period, therefore, floral decoration remained as telling an indication of wealth and good taste as the paintings in the gallery and furniture in the drawing room.

GARDENS IN THE HOUSE

Potted plants were the mainstay of floral decoration in the house, although cut flowers were used to make up the dinner table displays and as features in the drawing room. The selection of indoor plants was a complex business which involved careful consideration of colour and form for each new situation, and the additional difficulty of striking a balance between aesthetic requirements and common sense. 'They must be plants which look well,' observed Taylor, 'or the architectural and other ornaments will throw them quite in the shade. They must be different to those in the flower beds or they will appear vulgar.' On the other hand, 'it would not do to use rare and costly plants', as dark and draughty corridors and the fumes from coal fires, oil lamps and gas lights, spelt disaster for all but the most robust specimens.[8] Wardian cases could be used to protect plants from 'dust, soot, and noxious gases with which town atmospheres are generally loaded', and in suburban homes these diminutive conservatories housed ferns, flowering plants and even orchids. But for the upper classes something showier was called for, and they relied on careful selection and frequent renewal to achieve the necessary potted splendour.

Foliage plants were widely used as they could withstand unfavourable conditions. Many palms were admirably resilient and according to John Wills, who hired them out by the hundred, the dwarf coconut palm, *Cocos weddeliana*, 'will last in a drawing room six months or more if kept watered and clean.' He also found asparagus ferns could be relied upon, and supplied crotons, dracaenas and the faithful aspidistra to town houses throughout the Season.[9] Taylor, who sent up pot plants from Longleat for the Marquess of Bath's London entertainments, favoured the castor oil plant, *Ricinus*, which could 'rival the palms for grand effect', together with the glaucous-leaved honeybush, *Melianthus major*, and the fresh green, fern-like foliaged mimosa, *Acacia lophantha*. These were all easily raised from seed, so that 'if the house maid should drown them or the footman allowed them to be dried up, the pecuniary loss would not be very great.'[10]

From an aesthetic point of view Taylor preferred to avoid the fashionable variegated and coloured-leaved plants. There was generally not enough light in halls and corridors 'to bring out the colours, and often the prettiest colouring is on leaves which are otherwise heavy in appearance as, for example, in the fine leafed Begonias.' In his view, it was 'safer, therefore, when experimenting, to trust rather to beauty of form rather than to beauty of colour.' Architectural constraints demanded similar rectitude. 'There are niches and corners in mansions where symmetry rather than colour is wanted; where a noble Palm or graceful Fern judiciously placed seems to harmonise so thoroughly with the architecture and other permanent ornaments that to remove the plant seems to leave an almost irremediable blank.'[11]

That was not to say colour and perfume were not important. Come the dark, chilly days of autumn, Taylor said, 'give me bright flowers as they contribute an enlivening effect to which foliage, however fine can have no real claim.'[12] And when the house parties were in full swing a good display of blooms lent not only a suitably festive air to the proceedings, but also reassured guests that their host had spared nothing to ensure their comfort and delight.

Meeting these demands required 'considerable forethought and management' and Taylor planned some six months to a year ahead what his 'principal flowering plants in each month from August until the following May' would be. This often required throwing 'old loves and special hobbies clean overboard as if they were your greatest enemies' and 'taking up your employer's hobbies and making them your own with all your heart.'[13] Satisfying the ladies was a particular consideration and the ideal solution was 'to produce as many as possible of those flowers for which ladies have a special liking and remain good a long time.'

The backbone of Taylor's summer and early autumn displays was the old chimney bellflower, *Campanula pyramidalis*. This came in blue or white and, he found, 'lasts good in the house for two months; it might not look so well in a small house, but in our stately apartments it is very imposing.' The plants were 5 to 7 feet tall and grew 7 plants to an 8-inch pot. For best effect, they were grouped together ten or a dozen pots at a time and, as Taylor remarked of the two oval china containers at either end of the Great Hall, when filled with a dozen pots each, there was 'nothing that we can ever put in them has a nobler appearance.'[14] He also had pots of lilies, scarlet vallotas and the silvery rose *Amaryllis belladonna* gracing the corridors and reception rooms throughout the autumn, together with 'Balsams and the Celosia or Feathered Cockscombs, 18 inches high, with plumes as graceful as Humea elegans.'

The greatest display was mounted in December when there was hardly a pause between the pheasant shoots and parties. Poinsettias and chrysanthemums, 'in two or three bright colours', and mignonette, were the principal plants, and there were also huge numbers of tuberoses to waft heady perfume along the corridors. In the drawing room, the feminine furnishings and decoration were complemented by delicate cyclamen, cinerarias, and hyacinths mingled with maidenhair fern. South American gesneras with their scarlet and orange foxglove-like flowers, also featured prominently and looked particularly well under artificial light. Taylor had a whole house devoted to these in the kitchen garden, and their elegantly marked leaves were brought to the quality of a rich silk plush in the stove house before being brought inside. He also grew hundreds of a blush white begonia, 'Begonia Knowsleyana', which he had treasured from his time as a gardener at the Earl of Derby's country seat of Knowsley. Chinese primulas, *Primula sinensis*, were another important winter plant particularly suited to the boudoir, and come the New Year Taylor would bring in pots of bright azaleas and branches of an ornamental peach, which in the warmth of the forcing house had produced 'glorious wreathes of little snowballs.'

Taylor's choice also included pots of orchids, which were becoming an increasingly important item of floral decoration. One of the most useful was *Dendro-*

The mansion welcomed exotic foliage plants such as this screw pine with bright green leaves banded in white.

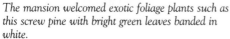

'How degraded would this Caladium appear if in a common flowerpot!'

bium nobile from the Far East. One of the oldest in cultivation, it was the cheapest to buy and easy to grow. Its flowers were large, pink and white, and had velvety crimson splashes at the throat. It flowered naturally in the spring, but by forwarding some plants a little each year, and bringing them into a stove house in the autumn it could be induced to flower at Christmas. Others, started in the New Year, would carry blooms until May. According to enthusiasts, it smelt of grass in the morning, honey at noon, and a faint primrose in the evening.

Orchids were even more prized at Drumlanrig. They were the particular forte of David Thomson, who had moved on from Archerfield to become the Duke of Buccleuch's head gardener in 1868. At Drumlanrig there were several orchid houses in the kitchen garden range. Thomson liked to supply the mansion with pots of *Cymbidium sinense*, which had scent 'as good as mignonette' and the white 'Bridal Orchid', *Coelogyne cristata*, could also be brought inside with impunity and was particularly requested for the drawing room and the ladies' private apartments. Most useful of all were the cypripediums, the Indian lady's slipper orchids. No one, said Thomson, 'who has a demand for decorative plants and cut flowers all autumn and through the winter should neglect [them].' The 'good old Cypripedium insigne, which flowers so freely and lasts so long' produced greenish yellow flowers streaked with brown, but in Thomson's collection there were many other species and 'always an interesting supply of Cypripedium blooms'.[15] The gardener could also call upon the quaint Columbian masdevallias with flowers ranging in colour from violet and magenta to white, and the beautiful lycastes, which were used as temple offerings in their native Guatemala. In Britain these flowered freely in the winter, and a number would last several months in the house.

With so much thought and care being given to the indoor plants themselves, it is not surprising that considerable effort was also put into the containers which showed them off. A fine-leafed caladium, for example, simply 'cried out for porcelain', and the Doulton, Wedgwood and Minton factories all turned out an immense array of jardinières and stands. The Chinese pots and silver and bronze containers already in the mansion were also pressed into service, especially as they often looked well in particular situations. This, however, frequently presented the gardener with the problem of fitting the plants in. As William Bardney, head gardener to the Liverpool banker, Heywood, reflected ruefully, 'some of the most peculiar shaped things have to be filled with a number of plants for which they are not adapted; plants have to be turned out of their pots and in some instances have half the roots pulled off to fit them in so as to produce the desired effect.'

In this respect, bulbs made admirable pot plants as did plants such as gardenias and ixoras which bloomed when small. Coleus was also invaluable and, what was more, confinement to a small pot induced its finest colours, ranging through 'every shade and hue of carmine and gold.' Handsome, even in tiny pots, it could be turned out and 'united with small ferns where plants have to be massed together in baskets or large vases.'[16] Orchids, too were wonderfully accommodating. Thomson had the lady's slipper orchid in all sizes of pot 'bearing 3-4 dozen blooms to 5 or 6, and no plant stands the atmosphere of the sitting room better.' Plants of *Dendrobium nobile* were equally useful and flowered when young and small, although, if necessary, a couple of flowering spikes cut from a large plant could be placed in moist sand in a small pot, and would last very well in the drawing room.

As a way of meeting the demand for containers which complemented their occupants without endangering their well being, Taylor devised a style of rustic basket which could be made up by his gardeners in a range of shapes and sizes, and used with perfect propriety everywhere in the mansion. For small ones, vine prunings as thick as a pencil were used, while for the large containers supple maple branches were ideal. The simplicity of the baskets, and the bright green moss which was used to cover the the soil, were the perfect foil for most plants, making them appear as 'gems amongst the magnificent decorations and works of art by which they were surrounded.' When they were used in the drawing room and the state apartments during the Prince of Wales' visit to Longleat in December 1881 everyone declared them 'perfectly lovely'.[17]

FLOWERS FOR THE HOUSE

As the century wore on cut flower arrangements became increasingly fashionable. This was almost certainly due, at least in part, to the expansion of commercial floristry which made loose flowers widely available. Previously, flowers were sold only in 'bouquets', and gardeners had also sent flowers from the herbaceous border and stove house up to mansion in this way. In addition, from the 1860s onwards, the introduction of elaborate floral displays to the dinner table escalated the demand for cut flowers elsewhere in the house.

The task of choosing and arranging these blooms was the lady's prerogative going back, perhaps, to the time when choosing and arranging a few flowers for the private apartments was a pleasing diversion rather than a fashionable necessity. In Charlotte M. Yonge's *The Daisy Chain* (1865) the daughter of the house 'cut sprays of beautiful geraniums, delicious heliotrope, fragrant calycanthus, deep blue tree-violet and exquisite hot house ferns', and at Drumlanrig there was a five-acre flower garden stocked with carnations, phlox and herbaceous plants for the ladies to enjoy. It was undoubtedly a custom which continued at establishments where the ladies were so inclined, but displays for the main reception rooms, and other public areas usually became the gardener's responsibility.

Once again, the choice of receptacle exerted considerable influence over the nature of the displays. Halls and landings often had large oriental vases which stood up to three feet high, and these had to be filled with flowers of a tall and stately aspect, such as delphiniums, gladioli and red hot pokers. In the drawing room and the private parlour of the lady of the house, shallow bowls and glass vases were favoured. Robson used glass baskets in the 1860s, and slender trumpet vases, of iridescent and crackled glass, were considered 'so beautiful that they are usually found in sitting rooms.' The use of coloured glass vases imposed obvious restrictions on the flowers they could contain but refined taste tended to consider these gaudy, and most gardeners had to contend only with plain English glass which 'when filled with clear water imparts an air of brightness that mingles most pleasantly with the varied charms of flowers.'[18]

Gardeners agreed that some flowers, such as chrysanthemums, tended to look best by themselves but whenever flowers were combined 'the harmonising and contrasting of colours was always a question of some importance, and in this the varied tastes of employers have in a great degree to be studied.'[19] Arum lilies, for example, set off by their own foliage and 'a few Pelargonium trusses or red Bouvardias added to impart colour' were considered very effective.

As a general rule, flowers were arranged thinly rather than crammed together. 'Every flower ought to stand entirely clear of its neighbour' stated Robert Brotherston, of Tyninghame, East Lothian, and author of a definitive work on cut flowers. 'I effect this by employing foliage freely, filling large glasses with foliage, and then inserting the flowers.' To this end he used the flowering shoots of ivy, ferns and yew. Alternatively, berried shrubs could form the background and he advocated graceful arrangements composed of a few cut flowers and, for example, 'Arbutus or berried Pernettya and maybe a single plume of Pampas grass in the centre'.

Small containers and low bowls demanded blooms that could bear close scrutiny, and examination from above. Passion flowers, whose strange form had long been endowed with the symbolism of the Crucifixion, were particular favourites for shallow displays, as were lilies which could float amidst a circlet of delicate greenery. The tropical allamanda was also greatly admired, and usually arranged 'with a few fronds of Maidenhair fern, or intermixed with a few sprays of any other flower that will contrast well, and rise lightly out from the ground of yellow.' For Bardney, at Norris Green, demand for allamandas was so great that the whole of a 40-foot long stove house was given over to two large pots of it, so that by retarding one and forwarding another, he could pick from the streams of golden blooms 'fully eight months out of twelve'.[20] For the boudoir, bunches of violets and lily of the valley had a delicate

*Roses, lilies, and ferns arranged for
an entrance hall or saloon.*

modesty, while glass baskets filled with white *Hoya carnosa*, from the East Indies, a frond or two of fern, and garlanded with a spray of the strongly scented stephanotis from the stove house were suitably chaste for 'the ornamentation of writing tables or other pieces of furniture in ladies' sitting rooms'.[21]

Roses, either alone or in combination with other flowers, such as the ubiquitous pelargonium, were also perfect for vases and bowls. Many new kinds had emerged from the marriage of Chinese and European roses and there was hardly a month when the gardener could not cut a bunch. They could be forced, and Taylor was 'expected to have roses by the score fit to cut at a moment's notice any time between the middle of March and the end of the year.'[22] Hybrid perpetuals such as the crimson Jules Margotin and Général Jacqueminot obliged with blooms in profusion up to May and so did Boule de Neige and La France, which was believed by many to be 'the most deliciously scented Rose known'. The more tender tea roses were usually grown under glass and were truly perpetual from May onwards, but pots of these could also be forced to provide ample quantities of refined, delicately coloured blooms a couple of months earlier. Yet more bunches of roses could come from the climbing tea rose Gloire de Dijon and the beloved Maréchal Niel. If trained against the back wall of a plant house, these would both furnish golden blooms month after month.

In June, the rose garden itself came into flower. Its hybrid perpetuals and Bourbons would be packed off to the London house until the Season ended, and they obligingly flowered again in August when the family had returned to the country. The favoured blush white Souvenir de la Malmaison continued to give sweet roses for another month, and for length of season there was nothing to touch the hybrid Chinas which went on flowering until the first frosts. Family and guests would then continue to enjoy the perfume of roses throughout the winter months from the great bowls of potpourri for which the gardener had gathered the rose petals, lavender and sweet herbs which the housekeeper dried and assembled.

Orchids rivalled, if not surpassed, roses as cut flowers 'for bouquets, glasses and personal adornment', and where 'really refined flowers are in request' gardeners were advised that 'it pays to grow a good many kinds.' Indeed the blooms lasted such a long time that 'lily of the valley or roses were fugitive in comparison.' The sprays of cymbidiums, bearing half a dozen flowers along their length, would last for weeks in water, and the lady's slipper orchids up to a month. At Drumlanrig, Thomson also grew large numbers of showy Indian calanthes in the warmest house. When a visitor called in 1875 he reported that 'armfuls of them were used as cut flowers when the family were staying at the Castle, and when they went to Bowhill a large boxful was sent once a week to them, and many decayed without ever being cut.'[23] In a cooler section he grew many species of Columbian odontoglossums, from which, in November 1883, he was cutting spikes with twenty or more flowers. 'To support these when placed in glasses, very slender green stakes are used, to which the spikes are attached, for the weight of the bloom is such that light glasses would be upset unless the spikes were kept almost erect.'[24]

DECORATIONS FOR THE TABLE

It was reputedly the Prince Regent who called 'the gardener to the aid of the cook and brightened the dining table with the choicest flowers of the conservatory',[25] but with the general enthusiasm for all manner of floral decoration, little encouragement was needed. The only thing which held the gardener back was the lack of space. Georgian and early Victorian dining tables were set out with all the dishes of a 'service' at once, and as this comprised a number of what would now be separate courses, there was little room left for much in the way of decoration beyond the candelabra and some ornamental plate.

In the late 1850s, however, things started to change. The old dining *à la Française* began to give way to *à la Russe*, which resembled today's restaurant service. Under the new regime successive courses were brought up from the kitchen, and each guest was served from the sideboard by a footman. This improved the quality of the food which could now be eaten hot rather than lukewarm or cold, and the conspicuous display of liveried servants added enormously to the host's prestige.[26] The new style of dining also left plenty of room down the centre of the table for floral masterpieces. The prospect of 'an exquisite mass of flowers and plants in pots' was generally agreed to be superior for health, temper and conversation than 'a table loaded with roasts, calf's head, [and] sirloin of beef', and dining table decoration became a new floral art form.

The favoured centrepieces were the tall glass flower stands invented by Thomas March, a senior member of Queen Victoria's household. These consisted of two shallow bowls – a large lower, and smaller upper one – supported on a slender glass stem, and solved the immediate problem of creating an elaborate arrangement which did not obstruct the guests' view across the table. They would be complemented by low vases or pots of flowers, and a tracery of foliage and blooms laid directly on to the cloth integrated place settings and floral displays into an overall picture. In winter, March stands were sometimes replaced by potted plants in silver or china containers. Palms, such as *Cocos weddeliana*, were not only wonderfully elegant and durable but, with their arching foliage above a slender trunk, also permitted guests to see their companions opposite.

Head gardeners soon rose to the challenge of dinner table display, and rapidly became arbiters of the new fashion. Robson was noted for his sound views and excellent taste in these matters, and John Perkins, head gardener to Lord Henniker in Suffolk, and William Low of the Duke of Grafton's Euston Hall gardens, also in Suffolk, both wrote books describing and illustrating their designs.

The guiding principles had been laid down first by March in his little book *Fruit and Flower Decoration* published in 1862, but were continuously modified and elaborated as innovations were made, new plants arrived, and fashions changed. The starting point for any design was always, however, the size of the table, and any particular 'fixtures' in the way of ornament. Dining tables were rectangular and never less than 5 feet 6 inches wide, and there would always be dishes of fruit, and candelabra or, perhaps, a many-branched silver epergne to accommodate. Epergnes supported both candle holders and flower vases, and looked well with the gold and silver plate the host might also wish to display.

The next considerations were then the number of guests, the nature of the occasion, and the time of day. Light and dainty flowers such as forget-me-nots and rosebuds were appropriate for lunchtime, for example, but scarlet pelargoniums and showy fuchsias would be required at dinner. And, as always, there were nice judgements concerning colour, form and perfume to be made.

Under artificial light, yellow flowers generally did not look well, and blue tended to appear dull and black. Deep pinks and carmines, on the other hand, looked splendid, as did a clear white 'when surrounded by a healthy mass of green.'[27] Robson also suggested that flowers with a circular outline looked best at night. Strongly scented flowers, such as tuberoses, were clearly inappropriate, as was heavy foliage. The fronds of ferns and fragile grasses were ideal, but much depended upon the circumstances. At Archerfield, for example, Thomson used the silver-leafed *Centaurea ragusina* – which was considered an ineffective foliage against a white table cloth – to great effect by employing the contrast of gold vases. When a guest at Oldlands requested violets for a birthday dinner, Luckhurst overcame the colour problem by

A *March stand for the dining table*.

using everything in the way of white china and white roses to set them off.

For dressing the March stands, the largest or the darkest of the chosen flowers would be used in the lower dish and roses, scarlet vallota and red pelargoniums were all widely used. Yellow allamandas, which appeared creamy white by candlelight, were also popular and Robson favoured the pearly white, star-shaped flowers of *Eucharis amazonica*. Maidenhair fern or ornamental grasses were used to soften the outline, and 'throw a thin veil over the beauty below.'[28] For the upper dish, flowers of a lighter, more feathery nature were required, and sprays of bouvardias, jasmines and pendulous fuchsias were ideal. A length of small-leafed creeper, such as a selaginella, twisted around the stem, completed the effect.

By the 1870s, the possibilities for an alternative centrepiece of potted foliage included screw pines, such as *Pandanus veitchii* which, with its leaves attractively edged in white, soon became one of the most acclaimed dining table plants. These were brought back from Polynesia by Veitch in 1869, during a trawl of the South Sea Islands which also yielded *Aralia veitchii*, a foliage plant whose slender, finely divided leaves were glossy green above, while presenting a rich red underside to the diners sitting below. The many new forms of dracaenas, their slender leaves streaked in crimson and purple, also made eminently suitable table specimens.

The enthusiasm of London decorators knew few bounds. They constructed arches of ivy and flowers which curved over the table like a conservatory roof, and erected jungle-like canopies of palms. Special table tops and table cloths had to be made, so that the large pots needed to support these tropical forests could be hidden away beneath.

Robson tended to draw the line at such extravagant ploys, but even he indulged in some novelties. For one summer event he organized a pair of tabletop fountains, with the water pumped up from the kitchens below. The pipework came up through the dining room floor and carpet, and into a specially constructed table leaf and 'there was more trouble than might be expected in arranging everything properly.' Nevertheless with 'its border affording good space for a floral display, while the internal fittings as well as the mechanical parts could be varied' the fountain lent itself to a variety of treatments, and could be decked out in completely fresh garb each evening.[29] Robson also made use of mirror glass, which was another fashionable feature. Large sheets measuring some 2 feet wide and 5 feet long would be laid along the centre of the table, and given a border of selaginella or wreathed evergreens. The usual centrepieces would be placed upon them, often with the addition of small glass baskets of flowers, no bigger than a deep tea saucer, and the myriad reflections would glint and glitter in the glass.[30]

These, however, were exceptional devices and Robson's more usual displays were low arrangements in accordance with his firm view that 'a dinner party is met for social enjoyment and guests should not have to peep around floral devices almost as big as a band-box.' He advised the use of shallow, rectangular or semicircular tin troughs, a mere ¾ inch deep and 2 inches wide. These would be filled with flowers such as the Blush China rose with its delicate foliage and bright pink buds. Sprigs of berried shrubs such as cotoneaster and pyracantha could also be used, together with the delicately perfumed flowers and evergreen leaves of laurustinus. Ivy leaves might overhang the edges and trail upon the cloth. Robson kept one set of troughs permanently planted with just the moss-like *Selaginella denticulata*. Its foliage tumbled over the sides of the troughs and displayed 'their beautiful configuration to best possible advantage against the white background of the cloth'. These troughs could be laid on the table in a number of different patterns which could easily be changed if guests were staying for a week or more.[31]

Conventional vases and pot plants were, however, the more usual means of setting off the central displays. This presented the gardener with the challenge of achieving a sufficient mass of blooms or foliage in small containers, although for large buffet tables, tall specimens such as fruiting vines trained up a trellis, or miniature orange trees, were quite in order. Feathery maidenhair ferns, such as *Adiantum farleyense*, which had 'a rich appearance by artificial light' were very useful as they attained an effective size and made low filmy features. Caladiums with almost translucent leaves also obliged, and azaleas made lovely spreading heads and flowered well in small pots. The Christmas cactus, *Epiphyllum*, which had drooping 'arms' tipped with bright rose flowers, was also admirable and, if grafted on to a stock, became a showy 'fountain'.

The gardener might have to resort to various other measures to persuade plants into dining table mode. The 'lovely stove climber Thunbergia Harrisii' raised from cuttings earlier in the year, would make a pot plant 'quite certain to be admired on the dining table' by the autumn, and the tops of poinsettias rooted in August would produce compact masses of scarlet for the winter entertainments. Failing this, cut bracts could simply be laid upon the table in a dish with a little moist sand.

For the garlands and tracery laid directly on the cloth, sprays of apple blossom, the

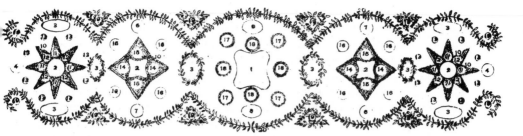

William Low's design for the Duke of Grafton's dinner table featured vases of flowers which were encircled by evergreens, and ferns and dahlia blooms were laid upon the cloth. Set around these were dishes of fruit and the table was garlanded with jasmine leaves.

fine twining stems of passion flower, circlets of coleus leaves and wreaths of evergreens could all be used. In one 'easily managed' pattern, Perkins made graceful scrolls out of the long fronds of the fern, *Asplenium marinum*, which were spiked along their length with the flowerheads of gladioli. For a breakfast table, he recommended gold variegated periwinkle and blue cineraria. Special occasions, such as a wedding breakfast, demanded particularly elaborate and often intricate effects. Perkins suggested embroidering the table with chains of myrtle studded with cyclamens. The bold curves of this design were composed of 'the broad-leaf Myrtle', while the linking bows were made of 'the small-leaf Myrtle'.[32]

When flowers were not too plentiful, Robson was particularly fond of using box, which was both economical and 'owing to the number of its bright shining leaves looks best at night.' The sprigs were tied to wire which, to render it inconspicuous, had been first weathered. These wreaths were laid on the table with great 'care being taken to turn upwards as many of the leaves as can be done.' The lengths could be arranged in patterns such as the curves of a Florentine Chain, or the Grecian Fret. The latter was a design Robson also used outside in the winter decoration of the great oval border, and although it required great precision of lengths and right angles, he found that 'when neatly done, the simplicity of the design has found a greater number of admirers than more elaborate devices.'[33]

The aim, especially from the 1870s onwards, was to unite all the diverse features of the table decoration into a perfect whole. Sometimes this was achieved by restricting the range of colour. In one of Low's arrangements, for example, the red-streaked leaves of the dracaenas in the centre of the table were echoed by star-like figures made of reddish purple passion flowers, and the bronze tints of the creeper *Ampelopsis veitchii* which garlanded the table. 'The perfectly decorated dinner table', he said, 'should be a finished picture without any visible sign or symbol of the artist's brush or paints, or undue predilection for the preponderance of any particular colour, or undue predominance of shadow or verdure.'[34]

The last twenty years of the century also saw a considerable change in the style of the main dining table displays. By the 1880s shaded candlesticks were becoming the preferred form of lighting and since these concentrated illumination down on to the table, tall centrepieces became less effective. Taste had also begun to shift towards

greater restraint in decoration, towards 'chaste simplicity rather than florid ornamentation.' As a result March stands began to fall out of favour, and ways had to be
found to make the most of lower, less dramatic, forms of display. One of Luckhurst's
solutions was to use a series of glass fish bowls with the largest in the centre of the
table, surrounded by smaller ones in various configurations. For one luncheon the
main bowl was delicately edged with fern fronds, on which rested clusters of yellow
Gloire de Dijon roses, and white spikes of Japanese privet. Its centre was filled with
larkspur, mainly in shades of blue but including some pink, and 'a dozen or two clusters of Quaking grass (Briza minima), springing irregularly out of the central flowers
imparted a pleasing air of sprightliness and finish to the whole.'[35]

For evenings, he liked to bring the chandelier suspended above the table into the
arrangement. In one design, the centrepiece was a gold cup, around which he
arranged a double chain of slender glasses connected by graceful loops of selaginella.
These were filled with the pink flowers and variegated leaves of a pelargonium, out of
which sprang maidenhair ferns and feathery grasses. Above them, suspended by thin
wires attached to the chandelier, were five glass bowls linked by pendant chains of
selaginella, 'just as from the glasses below, only it was much bolder in character.' The
four outer bowls held white fuchsias with bright pink corollas, while the central bowl
which was dropped slightly lower 'to give due importance to the central group was
filled with bolder, rosy pink fuchsias and Briza maxima . . . in the full beauty of its
glossy pink tinge just before ripening.'[36]

Graceful festoons of flowers and foliage intended to 'give the idea of a tent.'

Another approach was to draw attention to the display by using not only a single colour but also a single type of flower, which might feature as well in the pots and vases around the room, and in the bouquets and buttonholes. Orchids and roses lent themselves to this treatment, as did pelargoniums and carnations. Taylor grew the rosy crimson pelargonium, Guillon Mangilli, mainly as a cut flower, and on a sufficient scale to yield 300 trusses for one Longleat party held in March 1881. Perpetually flowering carnations, which had been introduced from France in the 1850s, were also a speciality of his. Taylor had a whole house of carnations and he relied on just three varieties, the flesh pink Miss Joliffe, cerise Belle Rose and white Purity, with some Souvenir de la Malmaison for its perfume. In December 1880, he was cutting 100 blooms a day and on March 31st the following year he recorded that 'I cut 860 blooms averaging 3 inches across of Belle Rose Carnation for decoration for a dinner party.'[37]

Such relatively simple arrangements were to grow in popularity and become the hallmark of the Edwardian dining table, but they were not to everyone's taste. At the Earl of Cork's house in Somerset, where William Iggulden was head gardener, they were considered unacceptably tame. The dining room at the Earl's residence, Marston House, was large and there were never less than twenty guests to be entertained, and frequently more. Brightness and richness were what was required, and Iggulden often used a profusion of red and gold plants such as dracaenas and chrysanthemums, concealing the pots in banks of moss studded with blooms. He liked to follow these 'heavy nights' by a 'silver night', at which the table was decorated with silver candlesticks, silver dessert dishes and silver flower receptacles filled with forced white lilac, set off by fern. Each candlestick base was surrounded by a ring of scarlet pelargoniums and golden chrysanthemums over a groundwork of moss and maidenhair fern laid directly on to the cloth. The dessert dishes were festooned with the red leaves of *Coleus verschaffeltii* and a single rhododendron bloom, and between them stood small glass globes containing a yellow allamanda and a frond of fern.[38]

BLOSSOMS FOR THE LADIES

As well as taking over the house and grounds, flowers proliferated about the person too. Ladies wore sprays in their hair, on their shoulders, and at the waist, and completed their outfits with bouquets. It has even been suggested that the origins of modern floristry lay with the ambitions of a lady's maid who, having lost her job, put her knowledge of dressing flowers for her mistress to good use. So successful was she at hawking her bouquets around fashionable London that she was able to set up in business on her own account.[39]

Certainly the bridal bouquet seems to have been a Victorian invention. The young Queen carried no flowers at her own wedding in 1840, but her eldest daughter, marrying some eighteen years later, was presented with a bouquet of orange blossom and myrtle by the Veitch nursery. In 1863, newspapers reported that the Prince of Wales' bride betrayed her nervousness by 'the tremulous motion of the large bouquet of orange flowers she carried.'[40]

Bouquets had also acquired a role to play before the wedding as flowers were drawn into the ritual of courtship. In the language of flowers, a posy consisting of mignonette, heliotrope and pinks declared: 'Your qualities surpass your charms. I love you with pure and devoted love', while an anemone reminded the flirtatious recipient that the sorrowing sender was 'Forsaken'.[41]

Not surprisingly, Victorian hand bouquets were characteristic celebrations of floral artifice. Closely packed and stiffly wired, they bore more than a passing resemblance to circular flower beds and evolved from the old florists' bouquets which were intended for placing straight in a vase. The design often consisted of a prominent central bloom surrounded by rings or segments of colour, and set off by a fringe of greenery and 'vandyked bouquet paper', or real Honiton lace. A typical example might contain a white camellia around which was banded a thick circle of blue violets, followed by an outer ring of scarlet pelargoniums, and a fringe of green leaves from a scented pelargonium.

This formality was dictated at least as much by practical as stylistic considerations. For any bouquet to withstand the crush and heat of a reception, or the exertions of the Gay Gordons and the Highland Fling, it had to be fairly solid and easily held. Only flower heads and a short piece of stem were used, the ends being wrapped in damp moss and wired on to slender fuchsia twigs. These made a narrow handle for the bouquet, which could be wrapped around with ribbon, or enclosed in a silver and jewelled holder.

Constructing these 'flowers on stilts' as their detractors dubbed them, was yet another of the head gardener's accomplishments. The best flowers to use were those of distinct form, delicate perfume and rich, pure colour. They also had to last well, making those with thick waxy petals, such as stephanotis, particularly popular. Since evening bouquets had to tone with gowns and jewellery, light colours were always in greatest demand, as orange was inadmissible and scarlet only used with caution. Eucharis was the chief white flower, and obligingly produced several flowers to a stem three times a year. Gardenias, camellias and hoya were ideal for centres and tuberoses met all the requirements, as did sprays of ixora, bouvardia, jasmine, lily of the valley and hyacinth pips. White and pink Chinese primulas were also used, especially the double forms which lasted longer. Pelargoniums and azaleas – again in the double forms – were employed too, but their centres had to be fixed with a drop of gum arabic as the petals had a tendency to fall. The sweetly perfumed *Narcissus poeticus* also made a 'posy not easily surpassed' and bouquets composed entirely of tea roses were considered 'very sweet'. The bright pink China rose, Cramoisi Supérieur, was often forced to provide hand flowers for Christmas events.

The ideal size for a bouquet was a somewhat vexed question. Fashion decreed that they be large, and florists' creations for the show bench were some 9 inches in diameter, and 'masterpieces of manufacture'. As to whether they were also objects of beauty was a matter of opinion. Such creations were felt by many to be an encumbrance rather than a decoration and Robson, who found judging this section even more controversial than adjudicating grapes, considered a diameter of 6 inches was quite large enough. The best model, he suggested, was the child's bunch of primroses bordered by violets, 'not only for its beautiful combination of colours but from

A lady's hand bouquet in a silver holder, circa 1870.

the fact that it seldom exceeds those modest dimensions to which all bouquets carried in the hand ought to accord.'[42]

Wedding bouquets could be larger and also more loosely constructed. Orange blossom was their main flower, but the small flowered gardenia which had a similar perfume could be used in its stead, or forced deutzia. Orchids were a desirable addition, especially the 'Bridal Orchid', *Coelogyne cristata*, with its snowy blooms tipped with yellow. Myrtle, the symbol of love, was always included. Princess Louise's bouquet in 1871 consisted chiefly of 'orchids and white roses, gardenias, orange blossom and myrtle'.[43]

The fashion for tight, formal bouquets did not, however, persist much beyond the 1880s. The general trend towards greater informality created a desire for less stylized displays while, at the same time orchids, which did not lend themselves to the mushroom-shaped posy, were becoming enormously popular.

Both these circumstances presented the gardener with considerable practical problems. Only strong twiggy sprays such as forced deutzia or rosebuds could survive standing proud of the body of the bouquet, and orchids, to be seen at their best needed to have the lip of the flower free to hang down. Whole orchid sprays could be wired into arching curves, and some florists went so far as to mount small blooms on a wire spring so that the slightest movement caused them to dance about like bees. Small wonder, then, that formal bouquets began to give way to looser more 'natural' sprays, a trend that was encouraged by the wide availability of long-stemmed carnations and hybrid tea roses. Sheaves of lilies were favoured by the debutantes of the 1890s and, for the last Royal wedding of the century, the future Queen Mary, carried 'an exquisite shower bouquet'.

Hair flowers also enjoyed enormous popularity while floral enthusiasm was at its height. These might take the form of individually fashioned ornaments to pin among piles of curls, or delicate coronets to complement a ball gown. The camellia was 'the belle of winter flowers . . . gracing our dinner parties, our balls and concert rooms; gleaming out in rosy crimson streaks from flaxen hair or showing off its depth of spotless whiteness among the dark braids of brown or black.'[44] It had been brought back from China in the eighteenth century but serious breeding had not commenced until the early 1800s when Loddiges' Nursery in Hackney, with its forests of camellias, became one of London's sights. At Longleat, the old Orangery was full of camellias, and at other sociable establishments such as Chatsworth and Syon House, there would be glasshouse upon glasshouse devoted to them. By keeping the houses at different temperatures and employing a range of varieties, blooms could be had from November right through until the spring. They were plucked without the woody stem, and wires gently threaded through the base. Two leaves similarly wired were attached at either side, and a piece of fern tucked in at the back. The wires were then drawn together to form a pin to hold the decoration in the hair.

Stephanotis, eucharis and gardenias were also used as were the pearly wax-like blooms of greenhouse rhododendrons. The bells of *Lapageria rosea* could form an eye-catching 'droop', and orchids were considered to look very fine nestling amongst the tresses. Once again, *Dendrobium nobile* was perfect, and of the useful odontoglossums there was 'no more beautiful wreath for the ladies' hair than Odontoglossum Alexandrae'. This had white petals two inches long, and touched with lemon and rose. With their 'whole outline being finely and beautifully fringed, [they] are in general appearance the most lovely and graceful objects conceivable', believed Thomson. 'The eye never tires of them.' He had some 250 pots of 'Odontoglots' at Drumlanrig, but 'any one with fifty plants of O. Alexandrae need not be many weeks of the year without a spike to admire, or a bloom for a lady's hair flower.'[45]

BUTTONHOLES FOR GENTLEMEN

Gentlemen, too, revelled in floral decoration. Buttonholes were reputed to have originated with another resourceful maiden – a French one this time – who stood on the steps of the Jockey Club in Paris and presented each member with a single flower as he passed. It became the fashion to have buttonholes for the gentlemen and tiny bouquets for the ladies waiting in glasses before each guest at the dining table. At some establishments buttonholes were placed under the napkin, while at others trays were sent in each evening and it was the eldest daughter's role to help each guest in his choice. Those in the habit of wearing buttonholes – and this included ladies in riding habit – would ask their tailors to make a little placket behind the *revers* to accommodate the slender glass tube of water which kept the blooms fresh. An alternative way of keeping the stems moist was to wrap them in a little damp moss bound with oiled silk.

As in the bouquet, the ideal buttonhole flower was one of distinct colour and exquisite form. Gardenias were cut by the thousand for buttonholes throughout the year, and perpetually flowering carnations were also eminently suitable. Orchids frequently adorned the lapel, with the pouch-like flowers and more sober colours of the lady's slipper orchids often the gentlemen's first choice. The all-round favourite was, however, the rosebud. The rosarian Shirley Hibberd was of the opinion that 'a half-blown moss rose was as perfect a buttonhole as the world affords', and the many varieties in cultivation certainly afforded colours 'both rich and delicate', which were admirably set off by the bright green and aromatic 'moss' which covered the sepals. Even so, it was probably tea roses, with their high pointed buds, scrolling petals and fragrance of the best orange Pekoe tea, which made the finest buttonholes. Grown under glass, they not only yielded perfect plump blooms and the most intense perfume, but could also be available from February onwards.

Such was the market's and the growers' enthusiasm that the question of which were the best varieties was the subject of never-ending debate. In the cream and yellow range, for example, many favoured the 'magnificent buds' of the old Devoniensis, which had outer petals touched with scarlet over cream. The apricot coloured buds of Gloire de Dijon also had their champions, as did the perfectly formed tall, white Niphetos, and creamy buff of Isabella Sprunt. Luckhurst's personal preference was for pinker blooms, in particular the flesh-coloured Goubalt, and Homère's 'pale salmon deepening outwards up the petals to deep pink, with edges beautifully recurved.' At Longleat, Taylor sent Devoniensis, pink Catherine Mermet and yellow and coppery Souvenir d'un Ami up to the mansion.[46]

The single bloom was very effective but nothing survived without elaboration during this period of grand floral display. The fashion for buttonholes grew into one for buttonhole bouquets. These consisted not just of a single bloom with its foliage but of a carefully wired mixed spray. By the 1880s, fashionable gentlemen would be sporting fetching combinations such as a yellow rose, blue forget-me-not and lily of the valley, or the stronger contrasts of a yellow rose, rich purple cineraria and white bouvardia. Such splendour was short-lived, however. With the increasing trend towards less, rather than more, ornamentation, the days when 'most people, from Mr Chamberlain with his daily orchid, to the artisan and his sweetheart going for an outing to Rosherville Gardens, the Isle of Man or Rothesay Bay, were bedecked with blossom and a bit of fern' had passed by the end of the century.[47]

Gardens Under Glass

he ultimate extravagance in domestic floral decoration was the conservatory. Here, family and guests could exult in a profusion of brilliant blossom and luxuriant foliage all year round.

From the 1850s onwards, private conservatories were a normal part of country house life, adorning an estimated quarter of the houses of the period.[1] The appeal of a greenhouse close to, or adjoining, the mansion had been recognized since the end of the seventeenth century. 'Can there be anything more agreeable in Winter', asked horticulturalist Richard Bradley in 1718, 'than to have a view from a Parlour or Study through Ranges of Orange Trees and Curious Plants of Foreign Countries, blossoming and bearing Fruit, when our Gardens without Doors are as it were, in a State of Death?'[2] Daniel Defoe records that Queen Anne 'oft was pleased to make the greenhouse, which is very beautiful, her summer supper house' and, according to his contemporary, the garden designer Stephen Switzer, William Blathwayt's greenhouse at Dyrham in Avon was 'whitewash'd and hung around with the most entertaining Maps, Sculptures, etc. And furnished with fine Chairs of Cane for the Summer.'[3]

Such buildings became steadily more popular. Not only did they have the seal of Royal approval, but with the fashion for landscape parks came a demand for ornamental buildings to help compose the scene, or provide an opportunity for contemplation. These lent themselves to a variety of functions and styles, including the very practical one of protecting delicate evergreen plants such as orange trees, myrtles and oleanders in winter, and providing an agreeable room in which 'either to drink tea, play cards or sit with a book, in a summer's evening.' Resembling classical temples, Palladian villas, or later, tiny Gothic or Chinese houses, these greenhouses were built of brick or stone with large side windows and a solid roof. Aethestics rather than horticulture determined their design and the serious glasshouses, known as stoves, in which the new exotic flowers and fruits could be grown, were consigned to the kitchen garden.[4] These were entirely functional in appearance, lean-to affairs, replete with stoves and pits of fermenting material to nurture the tender occupants. It was not until the nineteenth century that the two strands came together, and the full architectural, social and horticultural scope of the conservatory was realized.

Once the flower garden returned to the vicinity of the house, the lack of floral colour in winter was more keenly felt than ever before. As exotic introductions flooded into the country, the possibilities of year round displays under glass began to suggest themselves. The new plants, however, needed more light and heat than the old orangeries or greenhouses could provide. Since the more efficient stoves of the kitchen garden were neither beautiful nor convenient, the obvious solution was to build a new glasshouse close to, or adjoining the mansion. Inspired by the new technology at their disposal, the designers of these new conservatories seized the opportunity to erect structures of almost every architectural inclination, from Gothic and Indian, to Moorish and Italianate.[5]

Horticulturalists had realized that the most efficient shape for trapping the rays of the sun was a curved roof since it presented a face always at right angles to the sun's arc. Supporting such structures with wood was impractical as the thickness required to carry the weight cut out too much light but, in 1816, Loudon had solved the problem with a wrought iron glazing bar which could be curved without losing strength. With this, domes and all manner of curvilinear structures became a practical possibility.

Many gardeners, however, did not like iron, which tended to expand and contract, breaking the glass as it did so. An alternative way to maximise the amount of light entering the conservatory was to use 'ridge-and-furrow' glazing. The principle had originally been suggested by Loudon, and then developed by Paxton. It was essentially a system of pitching parallel rows of glass panes at angles to each other to form alternate ridges and furrows of glass. These captured both the morning and afternoon sun, were supported on wooden frames, and could be incorporated into large curved designs.[6] Nevertheless, iron still had a role to play.

Cast iron had been first used as a major construction material in 1779 when Telford built his Iron Bridge over the River Severn in Shropshire, and as manufacturing methods improved in the 1820s, demand and production soared. Cast iron had the advantages of being relatively inexpensive, decorative, and suitable for the prefabrication of parts. In the new conservatories, where efficient heating systems based on circulating hot water made the heat-retaining properties of stone and brick less important, it offered the chance to substitute uprights which were both sturdy and slender, and took at least some advantage of the economies of mass production.[7] With the availability of larger, and after 1845 cheaper, panes of glass, the growing enthusiasm for conservatory building was given every encouragement.

The 1840s saw the completion of Paxton's Great Conservatory at Chatsworth, and Decimus Burton's Palm House at Kew, and Winter Garden for the Royal Botanic Society in Regent's Park. Paxton's Conservatory at Chatsworth was both curvilinear in shape and employed the ridge and furrow system of glazing. It was 277 feet long, 123 feet wide and 67 feet high at the apex of the roof. Cast iron columns and a cast iron frame up to the top of the first curve supported the wooden ribs which held the billowing curves of the ridge and furrow glazing. It was by far the largest glass building in existence, and boasted the most and the first of almost every horticultural novelty. When the Queen and Prince Albert visited Chatsworth in 1843, they drove through the conservatory in a carriage and pair 'to see a building and collection of plants so grand and rare as to be deservedly ranked among the minor wonders of England.'[8]

Burton's Winter Garden was described in Knight's *Cyclopaedia of London* as 'a veritable fairy land transplanted into the heart of London. From the keen, frosty air outside, and the flowerless aspect of universal nature, one steps into an atmosphere balmy and delicious and not in the slightest degree oppressive. The most exquisite odours are wafted to and fro with every movement of the glass doors. Birds singing in the branches . . . make you again and again pause and ask, is this winter? Is this England?'[9]

With the erection of the Crystal Palace in 1851, the national conservatory craze took off. Six times longer than the Great Conservatory at Chatsworth, and four times the size of St Peter's in Rome, it combined breathtaking scale with simple construction and pleasing decoration. Of the six million visitors who saw it in the space of a few months, thousands returned home determined to build their own crystal palaces. Ranging in size from small rooms to veritable cathedrals, and from modest additions to the drawing room to huge covered winter gardens over 100 feet long, glass pavilions resplendent with domes, finials and delicate iron work began to embellish all manner of dwellings from country houses down to suburban villas.[10]

Setting up a conservatory in all its horticultural splendour was a serious and expensive undertaking. If space allowed, full grown specimens of tree-like proportions would be purchased, transported and installed in permanent beds. There would also be evergreen shrubs and smaller trees in beds or tubs. Climbers would be planted to clothe the rafters and cast valuable shade in the summertime.

When Robson stocked the new conservatory at Linton he travelled north to attend an auction at Combermere Abbey, Salop, on 13th April, 1865. Here he spent a total of £93.8s.9d on 4 orange trees, 2 citrons and 15 camellias.[11] The two largest orange trees, which cost £22.00 each, 'had been brought by Lord Com-

A prefabricated conservatory of the 1870s. Complete with dome and finials, it measured 45 feet by 28 feet and cost £700.

bermere from Paris in 1816, where they had belonged to Empress Josephine.' To look after these precious purchases a man was engaged and Robson left him a sovereign for his trouble. Robson's deputy at Linton, Mr Palmer, was then despatched to remove the large orange trees from the mansion and organize their transport back to Kent by rail at a total expense of £8.13s.7d.

Other purchases made that year included a tender New Zealand conifer, the Norfolk Island pine *Araucaria excelsa* which was considered 'one of the most elegant plants in existence.' It cost £26.5s.0d and had branches which resembled 'gigantic ostrich feathers and were a very delicate and pleasing shade of green.' Robson also acquired an ornamental-leaved South American *Rhopala* for ten guineas, and several large and small tree ferns, three *Alsophila* and three *Dicksonia squarrosa*. These, with their drooping leaves, were decidedly tropical in appearance but not overdemanding in their requirements.

Once the setting was established, the display would be completed by relays of pot plants brought in from the kitchen garden ranges when they reached their prime, and removed immediately they faded. This kept up the level of colour and interest all year round, and helped sustain an illusion of unfading brilliance. In small conservatories, where there was no room for permanent occupants, pot plants often composed the entire picture. They would be arranged on stepped staging along each side, and in tiers upon a central table.

At large, and even small establishments, the conservatory would be elaborately landscaped with pools, grottoes, fountains, and even a few song birds to warble among the trees. Mirrors, suitably positioned, would heighten the general effect, while hanging baskets suspended from the roof added to the air of luxuriance. For a society that placed the highest value on artifice in the garden, the conservatory represented a summit of achievement. It was 'entirely a work of art: the plants inclosed are in the most artificial situation in which they can be placed.'[12] It permitted mimosa from Australia and fuchsias from South America to grow alongside palm trees on the Kentish Weald, or even in the bleakest of Scottish gardens.

Grand establishments often had several conservatories, each serving a different function or creating a different environment. At Trentham Park there were no less than four conservatories, two adjacent to the house and two in the gardens. The entrance to the mansion lay on the west side of the house and, as Fish recounts after his visit in August 1863, instead of being 'ushered into a hall or lobby, you at once pass into a lofty conservatory chiefly ornamented with creepers and Ferns, and having broad stone pathways that to the north lead to the public rooms, and to the south to the more private apartments of the family. In connection with this is a sort of court with flower beds and beautiful stone plinth edgings.' This was a blaze of colour when he saw it, 'the Geraniums having a brighter hue than ever they have out of doors.'

From this inner court, Fish continues, 'you enter the private conservatory, which forms the west wing of the mansion on the south front. This, especially when the family is at home, is always kept a picture of floral loveliness.' Here the scene was enhanced by marble statuary, vases and a fountain in the centre. From the ornate roof were suspended decorative lanterns as well as baskets of ferns. Orange trees and 'the palm-like and elegant Seaforthia' were displayed in Versailles boxes mounted on

The conservatory at Bentley (Stanmore) Priory, the north London home of Sir John Kelk, railway contractor and engineer.

stone plinths, and every inch of soil was carpeted with the fresh green of a moss-like selaginella.[13]

Architects' conservatories attached to the house were not, however, as light or as well-ventilated as gardeners would like, although there were some notable exceptions. The conservatory at Harlaxton Manor, for example, opened off the drawing room and was divided into five compartments, each of which was maintained at a different temperature, 'so that some portions are devoted to tropical plants planted out and some are cool conservatories.'[14] Nevertheless, conservatories used mainly for social purposes did not generally house particularly rare or demanding specimens. This seems to have been the case at Trentham. The range of plants in the first two conservatories was relatively narrow, and suited to temperatures and humidities, which, if not imposed by the limitation of the building, were those most comfortable for its human occupants.

As one moved further away from the house, conservatories could, if desired, more closely match the gardener's requirements. There could be greater flexibility in the design, and guests could visit without having to linger too long in the heat.

At Trentham, the private conservatory opened onto the terrace, and a short walk led the visitor away from the mansion, across a footbridge over a stream, to a much more luxuriant indoor garden. This was built beside the main entrance gate to the walled kitchen garden, and was 'one of the most magnificent conservatories of the day. It is ridge- and- furrow-roofed, 14 feet in height, fully 70 feet in breadth, and 100 feet in length, as far as could be judged by pacing it.'[15] Walking through, Fish found the planning and arrangements in every way a success. 'The width of the pathways, and the neat stone edgings conjured up ideas of ease and gracefulness; whilst the somewhat stiff trimness of the massive specimens in the beds and tubs was relieved by the wild flaunting luxuriance of the dangling creepers and climbers.'

In here, conditions were much more favourable than in the conservatories adjoining the house. It was lighter, airier and less draughty, enabling all of the most fashionable plants of the day to thrive. Prominent among the climbers were many species of passion flower, trumpet vines – 'the Bignonia jasminoides, and the beautiful crimson B. cherere' – the convolvulus-like morning glories, with the brilliant blue 'Ipomoea Laerii in fine condition [and] the never-ceasing-flowering Habrothamnus elegans'. Trained up towards the rafters were also 'fine foliage Acacias . . . the light blue Plumbago capensis, and a huge mass of Cestrum aurantiacum, which produces long racemes of its golden flowers all the winter.'

It would be an endless task, wrote Fish, 'to enumerate all the fine plants in the beds of this house, mostly trained less or more in the pyramidal form, which gives more room for the streamers of climbers and the baskets of creepers suspended chiefly over the pathways.' Scented hedychiums, the Indian garland flower, were in bloom and the conservatory was 'always kept gay by fresh introductions during the season. At the end of August we were most struck with fine-flowered Fuchsias' and there were also large tubs of angels' trumpets. Many of the permanent shrubs were also showing every sign that they would be covered with flowers later in the year. Fish noted 'a fine plant of Luculia gratissima covered with buds', which would be decked with pink sweetly scented flowers by Christmas. The popular *Rhododendron Dalhousiae* from the Himalayas would bear its lemon-scented, lily-like blooms by the New Year and there were also many large camellias and azaleas in the 'highest state of luxuriance'.

When visitors were sated with this variety and brilliance, they could rest on a seat strategically placed at the corner of a pathway behind a large plant of New Zealand flax. From here 'you could see any one crossing the iron bridge over the river, and be yourself concealed by the thick foliage of the Flax.'

At large establishments which were botanically inclined, there might also be at least one more conservatory among the ranges in the kitchen garden department.

This would take the form of a stove house expressly designed for visitors. Here the intrepid might find themselves 'but a step from America into India through a glass door' or entering an atmosphere like 'Bombay in the rains'. At Dangstein, the Sussex home of Lady Dorothy Nevill, the kitchen gardens boasted a collection of plants 'which for rarity, number and diversity is scarcely equalled by any private collection in this country' and included a range of orchid houses, a palm house, and collections of foliage plants, filmy ferns and tropical fruit. [16]

At Trentham the fourth conservatory lay among the village of plant houses beyond the walled kitchen garden. It was a ' moist stove or tropical house aquarium' where guests would linger as long as they could bear, in order to gaze upon the exotic water lilies and luxuriant foliage plants. The heated water lily tank lay immediately inside the entrance and 'the back wall is formed into a rough rockery for Ferns, Mosses etc. The plants over the aquarium and elsewhere in pots were chiefly distinguished for the beauty of their foliage.' One of these was *Cyanophyllum magnificum*, which was said to be one of the most exquisite in cultivation. The upper surface of its leaves was velvety green and prominently marked by ivory white veins, while the under surface was scarlet. Fish also reports a bronzy leaved 'Alocasia metallica, very fine plants of varieties of Croton, Dracaenas, Marantas, Caladiums' and banana plants. Hanging down from the rafters were 'the rich leaved streamers of Cissus discolor', from Java, which ' mingled, shaded and contrasted with the foliage and flowers of Stephanotis floribunda', and ipomoeas, passion flowers and golden allamandas. Fish found it a scene which for 'natural magnificence (for the art to effect it was completely hidden) we have seen nothing to compare with it.'[17]

At Linton the conservatories were not on this exceptional scale. Nevertheless there were two for the family's enjoyment. A small semicircular conservatory opened off the ballroom and 'a spacious winter garden' lay a pleasant ten minute stroll from the mansion. The ballroom conservatory would have been furnished entirely with pot plants. In the winter garden Robson's new camellias and orange trees were planted around the sides, while the Norfolk Island pine made a stately feature in a central bed which was carpeted with a green selaginella. Some of the tree ferns, which had been planted in tubs, were large enough for visitors to walk beneath their branches, while overhead, the evergreen passion flowers and ipomoeas twining up from the borders made a tracery of flowers across the glass. Trained around a pillar there was a sweetly scented *Jasminum grandiflorum* that was almost always in flower.

The back of the house communicated with the kitchen garden via a corridor, and in this shady area Robson had constructed a fernery, spending a total of £124.15s.od on ferns. These were established in the ornamental rock work and around the edges of a pool equipped with a fountain and goldfish. 'Oh! The beautiful Ferns,' enthused a visitor the following March. 'From the palm-like tree ferns to the little wee ones at my feet, every graduation of size and form [was there]. What a charming place to sit and read in!'[18]

Considerable thought was given to the relationship of the conservatories to the house and other garden features. At Putteridge Bury, the conservatory overlooked the famous avenue of beds, while at Linton the winter garden, which 'resembled more a Grecian dwelling than a modern plant house' looked out over a Dutch garden.

This was always decorative, and even in winter Robson found the geometric pattern created by the box hedging and the bare earth 'presented an agreeable picture in harmony with the conservatory.'[19]

As far as the mansion was concerned, there were practical considerations as well as stylistic ones. The warm, moist air which plants required was widely regarded as injurious to health, which was why some conservatories were set a little away from the house or only entered from the garden. For other owners, this would have meant losing at least half the point of a conservatory, and they overcame the problem by link-

The date palm and veritable bamboo grove of the Great Conservatory at Syon House, London, gave visitors the frisson of foreign travel without its hardships.

ing it to the drawing room via a lobby or corridor. At Mentmore, the Rothschild mansion, and at some other establishments, the conservatory was also used as a kind of decontamination chamber between the smoking room and the rest of the house.[20]

All the problems and expense were, however, worthwhile. With their fragrant jasmines, forest trees and tropical flowers blazing through a green canopy, conservatories satisfied the Victorian desire for foreign travel without incurring any of its hazards. Orchids and more bizarre specimens such as the insect-eating pitcher plants from Borneo would be introduced to create features of special interest, and the armchair explorer could experience the wonder of the plant collector as he came upon great trees of rhododendrons in the remote Himalayas or hacked his way through the tangled luxuriance of tropical America. They were collections of 'natural productions' *par excellence*, and just as much fashionable showpieces as the dinner service and the ancestral plate. Gentlemen could enjoy their cigars as well as the camellias while walking the length of the conservatory, and ladies could take tea under the palm trees, or encourage their daughters to set up easels for a little flower painting. The concealing jungle also offered possibilities for assignations away from Mama's watchful eye, and made a refuge for the unsuccessful belle whose dance card remained less than fully marked.

CYCLES OF SPLENDOUR

Keeping up the displays in the mansion and kitchen garden pavilions was a formidable task. Once the parterre had faded, the conservatory was the main source of flowery entertainment and 'all floral strength had to be brought to bear in this important structure between November and April.' During the shooting season, chrysanthemums reigned supreme. They could be massed together near the entrance, or trained into pyramids or standards to line a path. At Margam Park in South Wales, Muir had chrysanthemums along the whole length of the old Orangery, which extended for some 300 feet.[21]

To provide more brilliant colour, there could be pots of the scarlet *Salvia splendens* of bush-like proportions and nothing was more effective for brightening up a conservatory than pelargoniums, which never appeared 'so beautiful and bright as when prepared for winter work.' Pots of heliotrope, massed together in ornamental troughs, would fill the air with 'a sort of reminiscence of the Rose and other sweet smelling flowers long since faded and gone' and features could be made of aloes, yuccas and dracaenas. These did service outside in the sub-tropical garden during the summer, and were equally prized in both situations. *Dracaena australis*, for example, could be 'a relief to the eye when the glaring sun is dazzling us or snow lies deep on the ground.'

Early in December the preparations for Christmas would begin. Roman hyacinths, brought on in a heated pit, would be moved in and if there was any suggestion that colour was lacking the gardener could call upon the scarlet bracts of a few dozen poinsettias. Cinerarias, which 'like a dry, cool atmosphere were ideal for the much frequented conservatory', and might be grouped in stands set off by a few ferns. The fes-

The Vanda House at Broomfield, the Essex home of Robert Warner, Esq., who retained his own orchid collector.

tive celebrations themselves would be brightened by the new varieties of Persian cyclamen, *Cyclamen persicum*, which had large blooms in shades from white to pink and purple and an exquisite fragrance. Chinese primula could 'figure to advantage' in mixed groups amongst the hyacinths and forced lily of the valley to further 'enliven the dreary months.' Mexican spurge, *Euphorbia fulgens*, 'the handsomest of winter flowering shrubs', displayed its long sprays of scarlet flowers, while up among the rafters was the rosy purple *Habrothamnus elegans*.

In the New Year, the camellias came into bloom to make groves of red, white and pink flowers. The orange trees would blossom and, with the encouragement of a little heat, the deep yellow flowers of the Canary Island broom would also fill the air with sweetness. From the forcing houses came Persian lilacs, which were 'easily excited into bloom' to replace chrysanthemums, and Japanese *Deutzia gracilis*, which made 'a foreground of snowy cylinders against the background of camellias and orange trees'. Pots of tulips and narcissi added interest, and no conservatory would be without the Queen of flowers, the rose. Hybrid perpetuals and the tea roses were the best for forcing in pots with 'blushing Goubalt' in Edward Luckhurst's opinion, the best for perfume. Little Fairy roses made pretty additions, as did pots of 'Indian azaleas', which guaranteed a show of colour. These did not come from India, but were derived from the *Rhododendron simsii* introduced from Chinese gardens. They could easily be induced to flower from Christmas to June, and by the 1870s were available in numerous varieties from white, through pink and crimson to orange and scarlet.

In a small conservatory, such as that at Linton, the spring display might be composed entirely of massed azaleas, with some trained as standards 'dotted here and there amongst dwarf plants to break the flatness and avoid an almost unbroken surface.' By the 1870s, these would be arranged to form banks of harmonizing rather than contrasting colour, and ferns and palms helped overcome 'any danger of being overdone with colour.'

This display lasted until after Easter when it was time for a complete change. Camellias in pots would be moved away to a shadier spot or sheltered yard, and fuchsias wheeled in to take their place. These had become 'one of the most decorative and useful plants' following the influx of new species from South America in the 1820s and 1830s. This led to the development of hundreds of large-flowering varieties in every permutation of pink, scarlet, white and violet. Easily propagated from cuttings, they could be produced in great numbers, and flowered continuously from spring to autumn as small bushes or tall, elegant pyramids. The distinctive flowers were popularly known as 'ear drops' after the way the blossoms swung from the sprays like long earrings, and they were a favourite subject for paintings.

By early July, gardeners said, 'the conservatory should be a perfect blaze of flowers with Balsams, Cockscombs, Hydrangeas, Gardenias, Fuchsias.' Pelargoniums and lantanas would also add to the effect and throughout the summer gloxinias would introduce further colour, the formal stiffness of their waxy blooms softened by the airy delicacy of ferns. Hanging baskets would now be planted up with bright Brazilian achimenes to make prominent globes of pink, mauve and purple. By the time the family returned to the country at the beginning of August, the passion flowers and ipomoeas would be in bloom and lilies, especially the Japanese *Lilium auratum*, would be loading the air with 'a perfume of orange blossom sufficient to fill a large room yet so delicate as to respect the weakest nerves.' Corners were brightened by the Guatemalan flamingo plant, *Anthurium scherzerianum*, which was the summer's counterpart of the poinsettia, and foliage plants such as caladiums and marantas, with 'their beauties developed in the strong moist heat of the stove house', would be tucked into shady nooks. The edges of paths would be given a metallic lustre by the olive green and silver leaves of *Begonia rex*.

Charming features were created by tropical stephanotis and allamanda trained over balloon-shaped frames and the great tubs of creamy angels' trumpets. Pillars were wreathed in blue plumbago and, as always, everything was set off by the sober tints of ferns, and mignonette trained into pyramids. Climbing along a rafter or trailing its dainty bells down from the corridor approach would be lapageria, its white and rosy forms twining together, 'as beautiful as stars in the milky way' and flowering right through the autumn.

5

Pleasures of the Table

The importance of private entertaining had consequences for the kitchen garden as well as for the flower garden and conservatories. Every month of the year brought a series of luncheons, dinners and supper parties, and the host's table was as much an advertisement of his wealth and taste as his house and garden. Menus had to be correctly constructed and perfectly executed, and the various courses chosen and garnished to reflect the finest ingredients the estate could offer. Not only would guests expect to be presented with the choicest fruits and vegetables of the season, they would anticipate those which were out of season as well. Even in winter, home-produced asparagus and mushrooms would be required, and many places liked to offer strawberries by Easter. Given the frequency of the entertainments, the horticultural inconvenience of the social calendar, and the large numbers of people to be catered for, the demands made on the gardener were awesome, but contributed enormously to his prestige.

According to E. S. Dallas, the Victorian journalist and observer of the gastronomic arts, the average eight-course dinner usually commenced with soup.[1] After this came fish, and the first service then progressed through a further dainty *entrée* of, for example, sweetbreads or lamb cutlets, to the *pièce de résistance*, the roast sirloin of beef or haunch of venison. The second service then opened with another lighter roast, usually of game or poultry, followed by an *entremets* of a dish of vegetables or salad. Each of the meat dishes had its fitting sauce or vegetable accompaniments such as peas with duck, celery sauce with pheasant, and turnip purée with the ragôut of mutton.

Next came the puddings. These might include a choice of pastries, a charlotte or fruit tart, moulded cream sweets and fruit jellies. Then followed the cheese and celery if it was being offered, a savoury perhaps, or a selection of fruit ices. The grand finale was a magnificent selection of luxurious fresh fruit, which would be followed by coffee.

Such dining came within the reach of affluent townspeople as the quality of produce reaching the markets improved, but it was the country house that was supremely placed to enjoy such fare at its best. Largely self-sufficient in raw materials, and unconstrained by commercial considerations, it had access to ingredients of the very first quality. The home farm could provide the most succulent young lamb, beef hung to perfection, and mild yet well cured bacon. In the poultry yard were fancy game

Dining à la Russe *encouraged the appreciation of fine food and splendid presentation.*

hens which were 'all breast.' From the dairy came firm, golden butter, thick Jersey cream and possibly their own cheese. Bread might be baked from home-milled flour made from home-grown wheat, and many establishments also brewed their own beer and cider. But it was in the kitchen gardens and orchards that, perhaps, their greatest advantage lay. Here all the fruit could be home-grown, ripened to perfection and brought to the table with painstaking care. Vegetables could be gathered while they were at their most tender and flavoursome and be with the cook within the hour.

The private kitchen garden could also afford to grow small quantities of a much wider range of varieties than most commercial market gardens. This not only ensured a fine selection, but the longest possible season. Almost every fruit and vegetable included varieties which cropped before and after the main season, and the most would be made of these by the skilled use of warm walls and sheltered borders. When these possibilities were exhausted, apples, pears and root crops could be drawn from the fruit and vegetable stores, and with the aid of a large and attentive staff and unlimited supplies of coal, crops such as French beans and strawberries could be forced under glass to provide a year-round continuity of fresh produce. Uncommercial treats such as new potatoes for Christmas could also be organized, and if the mistress of the house liked to have strawberries in February then have them she could.

This presented a very different culinary and horticultural picture from that of fifty years earlier, and the change, at least in part, can be attributed to the influence of events across the Channel. At the end of the eighteenth century, the hallmark of upperclass dining was 'good plain English country fare' with its emphasis on quantity and boiled or roast meats. There persisted considerable prejudice against those who 'admit nothing to their tables in its natural form or without some disguise.'[2] But, already, some of the grandest of the Whig grandees, including Lord Chesterfield and the Duchess of Devonshire, had begun to employ French chefs, so marking the beginning of a powerful association between French cuisine and social prestige. This was soon consolidated by the major overhaul of French cookery which took place at the beginning of the nineteenth century and led to the culinary takeover of the aristocratic tables of most of Europe.

An important stimulus for this was the multiplication of restaurants in France following the Revolution. This brought about increased competition and the growth of a discerning and vocal dining public. The centuries old traditions of *grande cuisine* were consequently opened up to scrutiny and to the possibility of improvement. In the kitchens and publications of Antonin Carême, all the elements of the new approach came together and out of his work and writings emerged the charter for the new French cookery, the *haute cuisine* of today.

Old procedures were rationalized and simplified, and extravagance curbed, a process which was also encouraged by the enforced austerity of the Napoleonic war years. Medieval trimmings, unnecessary complication and harsh flavours went by the board. In their place were appropriate garnishes and a central concern with fine ingredients and exquisitely balanced flavours. The taste of individual ingredients was to be enhanced, not obscured, and the value of the dish emphasized by the perfect artistry of its presentation. As Lady Morgan, a peripatetic Irish novelist, observed at a dinner Carême prepared for Baron de Rothschild in 1828, there were 'no highspiced sauces, no dark brown gravies, no flavour of cayenne and allspice, no tincture of catsup and walnut pickle . . . Distillations of the most delicate viands, extracted in silver dews with chemical precision . . . EVERY MEAT PRESENTED IN ITS NATURAL AROMA – EVERY VEGETABLE IN ITS OWN SHADE OF VERDURE.'[3]

The new approach soon crossed the Channel. Carême himself cooked briefly for the Prince Regent, while other culinary stars such as Louis XVI's former cook, Louis Eustace Ude, were tempted into the kitchens of the English aristocracy. Ude spent twenty years as chef to the Earl of Sefton, and then went on to make Crockford's Club in St James as well-known for its dining as its gambling tables. By the middle of the century the list of the most eminent cooks in England included only three English names,[4] and the two most famous figures in the English culinary world were Alexis Soyer and Charles Elmé Francatelli, both of whom had been pupils of Carême. After service in various esteemed households, including in Francatelli's case a brief spell as 'Maître d'Hôtel and Chief Cook' to Queen Victoria, they went on to preside over the kitchens of London clubs. This in turn helped to spread the French influence still further as the gentlemen who dined there returned home with new challenges for their English cooks.

One reason why the spirit of the new cuisine was readily embraced by the English aristocracy may have been that the new emphasis on clarity of flavour and fine raw materials accorded more closely with the ideals of the English dining tradition than did the barbarous Gallic hotch-potch of earlier satire. 'At Brambleton Hall' declares Matthew Bramble in Smollett's *Humphry Clinker*, 'my table is, on a great measure, furnished from my own ground; my five year old mutton, fed on the fragrant herbage of the mountains, that might vie with venison in juice and flavour . . . my game fresh from the moors; my trout and salmon struggling from the stream . . . My salads, roots and pot-herbs, my own garden yields in plenty and perfection.'[5]

Certainly this aspect of the new cuisine was being reinforced in a number of different quarters during the first half of the nineteenth century. In France, the growth of restaurants had also encouraged the development of gastronomy. This was the self-conscious cultivation of 'refined taste for the pleasures of the table' and, more particularly, its celebration in prose. The founding father of the genre was the lawyer, politician and writer, Brillat-Savarin, who dined regularly at Talleyrand's table, which was one of the best in Paris. The excellence of Carême's cooking reputedly reduced his gastronomic guest to silence,[6] but in his writing every aspect of the enjoyment of food was discussed at length, and the quality and character of raw materials emphasized as never before.

By 1814, gastronomic writing was flourishing in Britain, too,[7] and by 1835 an English gastronome, Thomas Walker, was urging that much more attention be given to obtaining the very best raw materials and to the pleasures of carefully cooked vegetables.[8] The Victorian digestion clearly found Brillat-Savarin's recommendation to dine upon 'dishes few in number but exquisitely choice' a sympathetic one. The habit of overeating had become widely regarded as a threat to health, and moderation rather than excess was becoming the mark of the serious diner – a change conceivably reflected in the shifting meaning of the term 'epicure', which lost its previous connotations of overindulgence and acquired quite the opposite sense of 'one who is choice and dainty in eating and drinking.'[9]

The high value placed by the discerning English diner on the range and quality of ingredients by mid-century was not only a cultural and philosophical development but also a practical one. Since the end of the eighteenth century, the freshness and quality of raw materials had improved markedly. In part, this was to do with better transport. The expanding road and railway networks enabled fruit and vegetables to reach city markets swiftly from almost any part of the country and even from abroad. By the same means, country house kitchen gardens could despatch hampers almost daily to keep the London house supplied with fine produce throughout the Season.

The range of fruit and vegetable varieties had improved too. This was a direct result of the increasing demands of an affluent urban population, together with formidable competition from abroad as import duties were lifted. Foreign growers enjoyed the advantage of a better climate which gave earlier and heavier crops than their British counterparts could achieve, and asparagus and peas, for example, arrived from Europe well ahead of the home-grown crops and commanded high prices as hostesses vied to launch the London Season in style. In order to oust the competition, and satisfy the demand of the markets, British horticulturalists such as the nurserymen Thomas Rivers and Thomas Laxton directed their considerable energies towards raising new varieties of fruits and vegetables. Yield, flavour and quality were all improved and the season extended in both directions.

These developments benefited not only the commercial growers but also the country house gardeners who were often the first to test the new material. They could afford to concentrate on quality rather than profit, and as they found strains which best suited their soil and kitchens, they were able to take advantage of the improved flavour and appearance of varieties which did not necessarily meet the commercial men's needs.

Luxury fruit and vegetables had also begun to feature more widely on English menus, cultivating British taste still further. The country estate had a long tradition of growing exotic fruits such as pineapples under glass, but the improvements in glass-house heating and design, and the removal of the glass tax had benefited the commercial men as well. The London markets were supplied with home-grown grapes; fine cucumbers and forced strawberries were available at a price. Peaches and pears came in from Europe and the Channel Islands, and exotics such as oranges and pine-apples were imported in increasing quantities. As in floral decoration, all with suffi-cient means could aspire to such splendours, but the country estate with its ranges of glass and ample resources continued to lead the way.

The celebration of fine ingredients, and of the French cooking which made such good use of them, was further encouraged by the introduction of dining *à la Russe* which allowed dishes to be served fresh from the kitchen, at the right temperature and in a carefully judged sequence. This did not become general practice until the end of the nineteenth century, but at fashionable country houses it was the rule – at least for large dinners – from the 1860s onwards. This was also the period during which the elaborate etiquette and paraphernalia of formal dining reached its height. The refined appreciation of food demanded equal refinement in presentation and consumption. Dinner services expanded to include bowls, plates and serving dishes for every conceivable menu, and specialized eating devices from fish knives and ice cream spoons, to grape scissors and asparagus tongs proliferated.[10] Not surprisingly, the new connoisseurship extended to the cellar too, and the correct wine in the cor-rect glass was the essential complement to each course.

VEGETABLES FOR THE TABLE

Provisioning the endless sequence of dinners, suppers, buffets and luncheons at a fashionable establishment required constant and reliable supplies of staples such as onions, potatoes, carrots, green vegetables and salads; as long as possible a season of choice vegetables such as asparagus and peas; and a wide range of new varieties in case family or guests wished to sample one of the latest prizewinners. An impressive selection of early and out-of-season vegetables was also important as these were ex-quisitely tender and carried particular prestige. It all imposed a great strain on Nature and, perhaps, an even greater one on the gardener.

Mushrooms, for example, were always required. Button mushrooms were an essen-tial garnish, while something nearer the size of 'Scotch bonnets' was needed for stuff-ing and grilling. They were a mainstay of ragôuts and sauces, and *duxelles* – a paste of equal quantities of chopped mushrooms, shallots and parsley – featured in some dish on almost every menu. 'In large establishments, during the winter months espe-cially,' wrote Taylor, 'the Mushroom is amongst choice vegetables what the Grape is amongst choice fruits – it is indispensable . . . If I were asked what it is which causes the greatest number of sleepless nights to the professional gardener I should say, Mushrooms . . . let the supply of either Mushrooms or Grapes fail, there is at once a blank which no substitute can fill, and the gardener's peace of mind is gone.'[11]

The excessive popularity of mushrooms could be laid at the French chef's door but the tastes of a traditional English gentleman were by now hardly easier to satisfy. There were few places where celery was not in great demand from at least September to April. This was mainly for eating with cheese, but also for use in salads and for heightening soups and sauces. It also appeared as a purée to accompany fowl or pheasant and, rolled in egg and breadcrumbs and deep-fried, made an interesting vegetable dish. At one establishment '10 heads a day were taken up to the kitchens for five months of the year',[12] while at Sandringham, the royal estate in Norfolk, it required an acre of ground to meet the demands of both the kitchen and the Prince of Wales' cheese course.[13]

The production of a successful celery crop was the source of much anxiety from the moment the seeds were sown in spring right through to the earthing up and blanching of the stems in autumn. Heavy rain, frost and attack by pests could all ruin the heads and out of every dozen lifted often only three were fit for table. 'Indeed', noted one correspondent in the *Journal*, they knew of 'more than one employer fond of having large and fine Celery who would be so dissatisfied in the event of its failure that the gardener was no longer secure in his situation.'[14]

The success rate could be improved by the astute choice of variety. The Dwarf White Incomparable, which came to be known as Sandringham White, had smaller heads than the 'Giants' which 'made people stare' but did not require immense banks of earth. As long as people kept saying they had 'never tasted such beautiful crisp celery', Fish found it an excellent choice, at least for the early part of the season.[15] Once the later maturing red varieties were ready no white could compare for a sweet nuttiness of flavour, although a mixture of both looked best in the celery glass.

Even when the crop had been safely delivered to the kitchen the worry was not over. As Fish observed, celery 'passes through so many hands, from the garden to employer . . . that it becomes reduced to a very little bit and is so pared and pared again that a lover of Celery scarcely knows what is before him.' He even knew of one case 'where there was no end of grumbling about the Celery for cheese, but the employer and his friends happened to pass the vegetable-washing shed one day, and were quite enraptured with the Celery, and as instructions were given that the Celery should go to the table exactly as it came from the gardener's hands he has never heard a word about it from that day to this.'[16]

THE VEGETABLE ÉLITE

The French made a feature of a separate vegetable dish as an *entremets* to follow the poultry or game of the second service, but with the exception of asparagus, seakale, globe artichokes and a few other choice vegetables, most English diners were loath to eat vegetables on their own.[17] This seems to have been a reflection of the fact that they were widely regarded as indigestible and a main cause of bad breath. Carrots, parsnips and cabbage were deemed a particular threat to the digestion, while the offensive odours produced by the consumption of onions and leeks were notorious. Fortunately, social acceptability and wholesomeness coincided in a few vegetables which were highly rated by gastronomes and hostesses alike.

Asparagus headed the list, followed by seakale and globe artichokes. During the summer, green peas dressed with mint and pats of fresh butter were highly prized, as were French beans and cauliflowers. Young carrots, which gave no digestive problems, were welcomed and according to Taylor salsify 'generally takes the place of a second course dish at the tables of the opulent, [although] ordinary people use it like a parsnip.' Cardoons were also 'an important crop where there is a French chef' while celeriac could be 'used as a second course vegetable and also as a salad, boiled and sliced liked beetroot.'[18]

Of **Asparagus**, Dallas wrote 'there is no cooked vegetable which raises expectation and lures the fancy so much.'[19] As a separate dish, it would be served with toast and English butter sauce, or in the French manner with oil and vinegar. Asparagus tips were also considered to make one of the most distinguished omelettes.[20] Its natural season ran from the beginning of May to early June, but it could be forced with great ease with a 'flavour nearly equal to that grown in the open air', and given sufficient re-

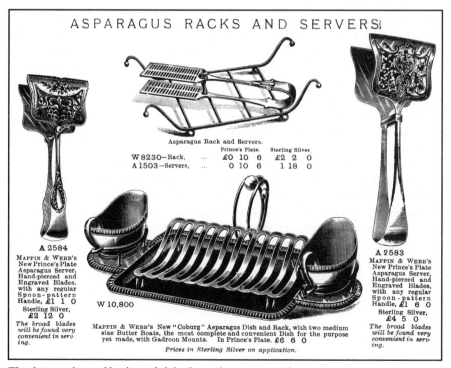

ASPARAGUS RACKS AND SERVERS:

Asparagus Rack and Servers.

		Prince's Plate.	Sterling Silver
W 8230—Rack,	...	£0 10 6	£2 2 0
A 1503—Servers,	...	0 10 6	1 18 0

A 2584

MAPPIN & WEBB'S New Prince's Plate Asparagus Server, Hand-pierced and Engraved Blades, with any regular Spoon-pattern Handle, £1 1 0 Sterling Silver, £2 12 0

The broad blades will be found very convenient in serving.

W 10,800

MAPPIN & WEBB'S New "Coburg" Asparagus Dish and Rack, with two medium size Butter Boats, the most complete and convenient Dish for the purpose yet made, with Gadroon Mounts. In Prince's Plate. £6 6 0

Prices in Sterling Silver on application.

A 2583

MAPPIN & WEBB'S New Prince's Plate Asparagus Server, Hand-pierced and Engraved Blades, with any regular Spoon-pattern Handle, £1 6 0 Sterling Silver, £4 5 0

The broad blades will be found very convenient in serving.

The choicest of vegetables demanded the finest silver serving implements.

sources could be available from Christmas to spring, if not quite from the 'last dish of peas until the new peas of early summer'.

As might be expected there was considerable debate in the journals as to the merits of the different varieties then becoming available and of the main growing methods. English taste had always been for slim, tender green stalks which 'can be snapped off like glass near the surface of the soil. The produce is then buttery, juicy and delicious . . . and of the greatest possible medicinal value.'[21] The French and Dutch favoured thicker stalks and grew them in such as way as to produce blanched stems with only a tiny rose or violet tip. Bundles of these were being imported in increasing quantities during the second half of the century, which caused great concern in the English markets, and even led to the offering of prizes as an inducement to adopt the continental system. Meanwhile, the country estate remained to be persuaded of the superiority of the foreign product. Luckhurst conceded that the imports took the palm for size, but the white parts were widely condemned as tough and inedible and more than one employer warned his gardener not to aim for size at the expense of the 'flavour and delicacy' which was the hallmark of home-grown asparagus.[22] 'Don't send any more of that big French Asparagus', wrote one employer after the hamper of vegetables arrived at the London house. The experiments in his kitchen garden had not been a success, 'as neither my family, nor friends like it so well as the other, and there appears to be so much waste about it.'[23]

Seakale, or *Choux de Mer*, which could be on the table in the New Year 'hinting at the approach of asparagus' was almost equally prized. The young, blanched shoots were the edible part, and these were forced under pots in a warm dark shed, or left in the ground and covered with a pot and a pile of fresh hot manure. With careful organization the tender stems could be available as early as the beginning of December and last until early June. It was particularly important for the chef and the gardener to understand each other as far as supply was concerned, as Fish knew of one place where instead of sending the 'whole head as cut to form part of the dish that is sent to table . . . the artiste of the kitchen was far too ethereal for such mundane treatments and cleared away all but the little knob in the centre.' Only acres of seakale could possibly cope with such profligacy.[24]

If the chef was French, he would want to offer **Globe Artichokes** as a separate dish from time to time. These, in Fish's experience, were 'nice things when people wish to linger at the dinner table', plainly served, boiled and dressed with butter sauce or oil and vinegar. Good form and colour were therefore as important as texture and flavour.

Artichokes were cut in summer from established plants, but their season could be lengthened by producing new plants raised from a piece of the old stool in May. These would come into bearing by the time the established crop was over, and carry on into the autumn when shooting parties made great demands on the kitchen.[25] The Purple or Violet Artichoke, with its scales tinged purplish red on the outside was the earliest variety, but the green Globe or Large Round-Headed Artichoke was the most esteemed in Britain, and considered to have the superior flavour.

The Great British Potato

Whereas the French ate bread throughout the meal, Dallas observed that the Englishman 'wants a potato with every dish that comes before him.' The great problem facing both gardeners and commercial growers was blight. English potatoes were generally agreed to have the best flavour, but the more prolific American varieties were introduced in an attempt to raise strains which would be resistant to the dreaded murain. Half a dozen varieties were generally considered to be quite sufficient to provide a good selection all year round, but a clutch of new varieties appeared every decade, and gardeners might have up to twenty on trial at any one time.

Such was the Englishman's devotion to the potato, however, that he was not always as discriminating as he might be. According to the well-known rosarian and potato fancier the Reverend Honywood D'Ombrain, a combination of good appearance and good flavour might be required in all other produce, but he knew of 'many persons who, provided a Potato is mealy (some, Goths indeed, like them waxy), care very little whether it is strongly or delicately favoured; and others think nothing of a Potato looking like a boy who has indulged in too much plum pudding – "all eye".' His own preference was to eat with butter 'a handsome, well flavoured and mealy potato, steamed in its jacket and gently laid in a white napkin when it comes to table.'[26]

This would have been the combination of qualities sought by the professional cook and the more gastronomically inclined of his diners. Floury potatoes were 'easily digested', and served equally well roasted with the beef, or reduced to a smooth purée for piping around an *entrée*. At Archerfield, David Thomson was particularly requested to grow a few of the very large American variety Ross's Early for baking whole. These came out of their skins 'sparkling like powdered sugar'.[27]

Selecting the right variety for each purpose was in D'Ombrain's opinion crucial if one was not to have to resort to paring, boiling with salt and the use of the drying cloth. He was inclined towards kidney rather than round potatoes and went along with the general view that the old variety Ashleaf was still the earliest, finest and the best for forcing. Planted over hot beds in frames it was ready for lifting in May. Compared with the watery, waxy lumps of some varieties, Ashleaf's mature, even-sized tubers were a mass of flour and had an excellent flavour. The best second early according to his trials of 1866 was Milky White, which he noted, was 'most beautifully white, very floury'. This he would follow with main crop Lapstone.

For a commercial field crop the most widely extolled varieties were Victoria Reds and Blues raised by Patterson's of Dundee. Although not quite as good as Lapstone, D'Ombrain conceded that they made 'excellent eating' and were 'very mealy and good flavoured'. By the mid-1870s growers were also pinning their hopes on Champion and Magnum Bonum. Victoria was said to be failing, and Taylor considered Champion to be 'white, floury and delicately flavoured' and reported that 'no other sort is desired in the Longleat dining room'.[28]

PERFECT ACCOMPANIMENTS

The pairing of meat, fish or game with the perfect vegetable accompaniment was a cornerstone of Victorian menu planning and considered essential to the appreciation and digestion of each. The serious dining table celebrated the finest ingredients at their seasonal best, and each of the top quality meats had its preferred partner. Gardeners had to ensure, therefore, that their vegetable supplies coincided with the hunting, fishing and livestock calendars. The first of the new peas, for example, had to be ready in time for the Easter lamb, while later varieties still had to be cropping for the autumn's roast quail and braised leg of mutton. Broad beans had to catch the last of the winter gammon, while mature beef called for savoy cabbage and baked onions.

Peas were 'the prince' of the new season's vegetables, and essential for duckling as well as for lamb. At Longleat in 1884, there were peas for the *Côtelettes d'Agneau aux Petit Pois* on April 26th[29] and the garden kept up a continuous supply until October. Another, northern, gardener described in the *Journal* how he had been able 'to supply an occasional dish of excellent Peas when the ground had been covered with 6 inches of snow, and once to a dinner party where the guests had sharpened their appetites by an afternoon's skating on the lake.' Alert to the possibilities of frost, he had pulled up the plants, and kept the pods fresh in soft sand for a fortnight. The guests' verdict was that 'the dish of Peas was decidedly late and undoubtedly good.'[30]

Once the season was properly established, no gap in the supply of peas to the kitchen would be tolerated. Continuity, at least from early June to October was ensured by successional sowings of early, second early, main and late crop varieties. By the 1870s there was a bewildering number of these, but the hybridists' interventions had been worth it. The 'ardent pea lover', Dr Maclean of Colchester, and the nurseryman Thomas Laxton of Stamford had succeeded in introducing the higher sugar content and superior flavour of marrow fat peas into the earlies, and also in raising larger peas. Another achievement was their development of lower growing varieties, as peas, 8 to 10 feet high, were 'awkward for a short man to gather'.

Previously, the earliest to crop had been of the hardier, smooth round type of seed that is used for drying today. Now gardeners keen to take advantage of the improved varieties could plant Maclean's Little Gem. Taylor was confident that he had never seen 'anything as good as Little Gem under a south wall. It comes into use as early as any of the round varieties, with its dwarf habit a great advantage.'[31] Others found that Laxton's Alpha and Harbinger would give peas by the end of May, while the prize for flavour was taken by Laxton's William I.

With so many good varieties to choose from, Taylor considered it now scarcely possible to go wrong with the successions. Much trickier, in his view, was the selection of the late crop. 'A good dish of peas at the end of October is reckoned to be amongst the best of dainties', he wrote in the *Journal*.[32] It was generally agreed that Ne Plus Ultra, which gave the largest peas of all, was probably one of the best varieties, although Laxton's Omega was nearly as good and only 3 feet high compared with its towering rival.

A vegetable order en route for the kitchen.

As gardeners experimented with the new varieties, they endured agonies of de-cision over the 'fine lively colour' and the 'very sweet and delicate texture' of the various types. Such concern may have been somewhat ahead of prevailing gastro-nomic preference. In Taylor's experience, cooks made size rather than colour or fla-vour their first consideration. 'I once knew a cook of great repute', he wrote, 'who would not have Veitch's Perfection Peas three parts grown (they were too large for him) if he could get some inferior round kind about the size of Canna seed.'[33]

Few, in his opinion, tasted peas in 'their true purity . . . If you would taste the full delicious flavour of Marrow Fat Peas, you must certainly not have them served with duck, which has highly-seasoned stuffing, nor with lamb and mint sauce – no, nor yet have the smallest particle of mint boiled with them, dear and time honoured as the custom is. If you grow the old fashioned bullet-shaped Peas under either old or new names, use mint with them by all means, for they have no particular good flavour of their own; but with the best Marrow Peas it is different.'

To appreciate these properly, Taylor recommended they should be nearly as pos-sible of one age, used straightaway and 'on no account must they remain in bulk long.' They needed no bicarbonate of soda to preserve their green colour, but should be boiled in a large volume of water with nothing but a pinch of salt. 'I am very sensi-tive to the least bit of soda,' he observed. 'It seems to have a depressing effect and I rarely venture to taste green vegetables out of my own house.'[34]

Peas could not be an all year round crop, as they did not respond reliably to grow-ing under glass, but dwarf **French Beans** were actually improved by forcing and, if necessary, could be grown indoors for nine months and outdoors for three. They were a popular garnish for meat dishes, particularly in the winter when green vegetables were scarce. English taste was for plainly boiled beans served with butter and a squeeze of lemon, and many considered the long, slender pods of Osborn's Early Forcing the best for all purposes, whether grown under glass or outside.

As far as other members of the bean family were concerned, the tall kidney beans or **Scarlet Runners** were largely precluded from the formal dining table by their appearance. 'No one tires of the flavour and peculiar roughness of the old Scarlet Runner,' observed one correspondent to the *Journal*, 'but it does not look quite so well cooked as the best dwarf varieties.' It did, however, have the advantage of being very productive and one sowing at Longleat 'kept up a continuous supply for servants and those who prefer it through the autumn from the beginning of July.'[35]

Cauliflower was another vegetable which Robson found 'usually a constant and acceptable accompaniment to the good things of the table.' Cauliflower *au gratin* could stand alone as a vegetable dish. Cauliflower, however, was not winter hardy and the succession from November to May was kept up by white broccoli, now known as winter cauliflower, which were more tolerant of the cold. For the earliest true cauliflower, which would be raised in a warm south border, Luckhurst recommended Early Snowball. This had small heads which, being well protected by leaves, kept their whiteness and were 'perfect models of what a first class cauliflower should be.' They could be sown again in August to 'give a capital supply for the October shooting parties.'[36] In between times, the 'crisp sweet' Autumn Giant from the Veitch nursery could be called upon. This was not usually left to grow to full size, but would be cut when the heads were 'little larger than a tea-cup'. It was generally considered that 'a dish of 3-4 of these is at all times more satisfactory on a gentleman's table than 1-2 heads so large that they must be smashed or mutilated to squeeze them beneath the dish cover.'[37]

As the frosts approached at the end of October, the last remaining cauliflowers would be pulled up, trimmed and hung in a cool shed. They would then 'keep in a fit condition for table' at a time when choice vegetables were scarce and the **Winter Broccoli** was not yet ready. Of the winter broccoli, Snow's Winter White was the hardiest variety and prominent amongst the vegetables brought to the table in the New Year celebrations, but new varieties were entering the catalogues every year. Luckhurst was particularly enthusiastic about Sutton's Leamington, which gave him some of the 'best heads I have ever sent to table . . . extremely compact, white and delicate, and so closely enveloped – that is to say protected by the leaves – that some care and pains are necessary in cutting them away in order to find the treasure which they guard so closely and well.'[38]

Another valuable addition to the table during the winter months were **Brussels Sprouts**. These could be gathered from August to February, and had become increasingly popular with both private and commercial growers. There was not, however, universal agreement over the improvements which had been made. The new large Brussels sprouts, for example, although 'fine for those for whom quantity is of the first consideration', were condemned by everyone provisioning the first class dining table as for 'appearance at the table as well as delicacy of flavour, smaller

Sprouts are preferred.' The perfect sprout, it was claimed in 1863 should be 'the size of a boy's play marble, at the same time very compact and firm'.[39]

Spinach, although quite high on the list of vegetables considered wholesome, seems only to have been grown in large establishments. Cooks generally preferred the more tender summer spinach, which many gardeners, like Taylor at Longleat, grew for all seasons.[40] It was used as a garnish for cutlets and ham, and puréed and dressed with butter and cream made an excellent dish by itself.

Cabbage had a certain popular following, being for most people 'second in importance to the potato'. But for those of more refined sensibilities it occupied a rather lowly position in the vegetable hierarchy on account of its coarseness and indigestibility. Nevertheless, it was an eminently serviceable crop, particularly when other green vegetables were difficult and expensive to come by. Young, close-hearted spring and early summer cabbages were the most sought after and, with careful cutting, could be made to produce a second crop of small, firm heads. Savoys would be used for the autumn's *Perdrix aux Choux* of braised partridge and cabbage. Red cabbage was grown for pickling, but there was little call for the cottager's standby, the tough hardy coleworts or **Kale**. Taylor, however, found 'Borecole . . . a very important vegetable of which I grow Dwarf Green Curled in large quantities. The tops of these succeed the Savoys for common use, and the side shoots keep up a good supply in early spring.' In his opinion Asparagus Kale, too 'supplies greens of excellent quality long after spring Cabbages come in.'[41]

SOUPS, SAUCES AND GARNISHES

As well as providing vegetables for serving separately and as accompaniments, the gardener also had to meet the demands of the soups, sauces and garnishes which completed every menu.

The presentation of a dish had been one of Carême's great enthusiasms. He finished his creations with silver skewers, or *attelets*, threaded with colourful vegetables, truffles and prawns, carefully chosen garnishes, and mounted the whole dish on a platform of sculpted paste. His followers emulated his flamboyant style. Soyer, for example, recommended sending in roast turkey with a pastry *croustade* resembling a ship's prow flying a mast of *attelets*.

Dining *à la Russe*, however, tended to discourage over elaborate constructions as the dish had to be served easily without growing cold in the meantime. Nevertheless, the ideal of a beautifully finished dish remained, and this usually depended on a series of well-chosen and skilfully executed vegetable garnishes. Colourful purées harmonized in *entrées* set off by a border of potato, while carrots and turnips were turned into fancy 'olives, small round balls, pillars, half moons, diamonds or fluted shapes'.[42] French beans were cut into diamonds, braised cabbage moulded into balls, and peas and asparagus tips presented in pastry tartlets or mounted on artichoke bottoms.

Vegetables were also the essential ingredients of the soups which were served at every main meal. Gastronomes were somewhat divided over the importance of the role played by this overture. Some saw soups as indispensable, whetting the appetite for all that was to come. Others considered them merely a preface that could easily be omitted. Most Englishmen, however, seemed to be of the same opinion as Carême, who invented several hundred *potages* and went to his death bed reiterating that he could not 'understand a dinner without it. I hold soup to be the well-beloved of the stomach.'

Soups in which vegetables starred were amongst the most highly prized. A *potage* of asparagus or celery was considered particularly fine, but as soups featured so frequently, almost every vegetable from Jerusalem artichokes to peas and even marrows made their appearance at some time or other as chefs strove for novelty. Many more recipes called upon vegetables as the supporting cast. Even a light clear consommé or a rich Turtle Soup required a basic stock flavoured with onions, carrots, turnips, leeks and herbs.

The same was true of sauces. One of the triumphs of Carême's rationalization of the old *grande cuisine* had been the development of a limited repertoire of basic sauces which lent themselves to many variations. A single Victorian dinner might include half a dozen different sauces, or even more, all of which might number vegetables among their basic ingredients.

In addition to the mushrooms which caused Taylor such sleepless nights, the first on the list of supporting ingredients which the gardener had to supply in quantity all year round were **Onions**. There was little doubt that a slight onion flavour enhanced the majority of savoury dishes and that, with proper preparation, the unsociable side-effects could be reduced. As well as flavouring stocks and soup, onions were the basis of many sauces such as the piquant *Sauce Robert* which accompanied the *entrées* of pork, and the *Sauce Soubise* which was *de rigeur* with mutton cutlets. Boiled, braised and stuffed dishes almost all demanded onions as did pickling. Large onions, boiled to attenuate their odour, and glazed or stuffed with a *duxelles*, were a popular garnish for beef and mutton. Button onions also provided many dishes with the final decorative touch.

Numerous varieties were in cultivation. There were tiny ones and large ones; round ones and pear-shaped ones; white, mildly flavoured sorts, and strong tasting varieties with dark red flesh. For pickling, very small varieties, such as early White Nocera, were grown. These were 'striped with fine green lines' and had a 'very agreeable appearance in pickle jars at table'. But for most other purposes, large mild Spanish onions were used. Of these, Nuneham Park was the most esteemed for its heavy crops, delicate flavour, generous size and good keeping qualities. Sown in the spring on its home territory of Nuneham Park kitchen garden, outside Oxford, it gave the head gardener Mr Stewart an August harvest weighing 19 cwt 5 stones 2 lbs in 1867.[43]

To take stores through to spring, sowing some of the stronger, reddish variety James's Keeping was also recommended. If the family had a taste for spicy colonial fare then the more intensely flavoured Deep Blood-red might be grown. This was highly decorative served raw with cold meats or in the form of a garnish of fried onion rings. It was also advisable to make a summer sowing of a variety such as the white-skinned Queen which Luckhurst found matured quickly to yield bulbs 7 inches in circumference by the following May. This avoided the embarrassing possibility of a gap

Francatelli's 'Braised Beef à la printanière' is
decorated with asparagus tips, French beans cut
into diamonds and turnip saucers filled with
peas.

The 'Dinde à la jardinière' (right) is garnished
with cauliflowers peas and carrots.

in late spring when, with the stores at an end, the cook would be crying out for large
bulbs, and there would be nothing to offer but little salad onions from the frames.[44]

Most kitchens also put **Shallots** high on the list of essential flavourings and required a few **Welsh Onions** as well. Shallots were milder tasting than onions, and
when used with steak and chops, their delicacy was infinitely preferable to 'the offensive odour of garlic.' With mushrooms, they were the main ingredient of the *Sauce
Duxelles* which graced numerous *entrées* from sweetbreads and ox-tongue to fillets of
fowl. As they were easily grown, hardy and stored well, they presented no problems
for the gardener. Welsh onions, too, were very tolerant. They could be relied upon to
withstand the hardest winter, and furnish marble-sized onions in the spring for garnishes and flavouring.

After onions, **Carrots** were the most useful vegetable. They were the main ingredient of *Potage Crécy* and helped to flavour almost every other soup in the repertoire.
The bright colour and solid flesh also lent itself particularly well to garnishes. Turned
or stamped into cones, stars, wheels, dice and other shapes, it could be glazed and
dusted with parsley and set around a joint. Small, young carrots also merited presentation as a dish on their own. For this elevated purpose, the stubby French Forcing
and Early Horn, would be brought on over hot beds in frames and could be on the
table by May. Further successions in the open ground would ensure tender baby carrots throughout the summer. For general use, a larger and longer variety such as
James's Intermediate would be grown outside and laid down to provide stocks for the
winter and spring.

Turnips were another ingredient expected to be available whenever the cook required. 'Great quantities were rarely wanted at one time', observed one gardener,
'but half a dozen to twenty roots are about the daily requirement for an ordinary
kitchen.'[45] As a vegetable it was not of the first rank but in some people's estimation
it rivalled peas when braised with duck.[46] The variety American Stone was particu-

larly good in Fish's experience, 'all white inside and so firm, juicy and sweet that every cook we know prefers it when it can be obtained to anything else . . . We have eaten a bit raw with our knife and thought it much sweeter than many a melon we have tasted when judging.'[47]

The turnip's main role, however, was as a flavouring and garnish. As well as being turned or cut into fancy shapes, they could be hollowed out to form little cups and filled with peas. They could also be carved into flowers. Cut to resemble camellias, for example, with the petals delicately tinted with cochineal, and the addition of a few glossy bay leaves to finish, they made a splendid decoration for cold turkey or tongue.

Another important garnish were **Cucumbers**. These were indispensable during the salmon and lobster season, which extended from March through to early summer, and again in autumn when they decorated the splendid buffet dishes served at the sporting balls and suppers. They could also be served as a hot dish on their own, stewed and coated with white sauce. This accorded with the strong feeling that raw vegetables were unwholesome although, as the century advanced, many Englishmen came to prefer their cucumbers crisp and freshly cut.

This was partly a reflection of the increasing ease and reliability with which good cucumbers could now be produced. They were a profitable market gardener's crop and numerous 'improved' varieties had come into the catalogues. In particular, the long, straight, smooth Telegraph was ideal for all purposes and a 'splendid winter cucumber'. Even more important, the new light, heated green houses were much better than the old dung beds in which the crop often succumbed to unaccountable death from the mysterious 'cucumber disease'. Taylor considered 'there was nothing more creditable to the gardener than a good house of cucumbers' and boasted in 1874 that, since coming to Longleat in 1869, 'with one exception of a month's duration caused by the failure of the heating apparatus, I have always been able to cut at least six Cucumbers a week.'[48]

The fruits would usually be cut young, when they were 12 to 15 inches long. Some varieties could reach 30 inches or more but, in Taylor's view, these were hardly worth bothering with. He advised gardeners to 'beware of large-growing kinds, none of them that I am acquainted with is fit to eat and few of them bear well.' The qualities he looked for were a flavour that is 'good and a large proportion of the fruit [that] is eatable.'[49] Also important was crisp flesh, which was solid to the centre, and a fine uniform appearance. Warts and ribs were not appreciated.

SUPERIOR SALADS

A carefully composed lettuce salad was one of the joys of the nineteenth-century French dining table but, for many traditional Englishmen, such an indigestible assemblage of raw 'green meat' was to be strenuously avoided. Given the way the dish was often interpreted in this country, they were probably wise. The Reverend Honywood D'Ombrain, who spent many weeks each year in France visiting nurseries and shows, despaired at the usual British 'mass of flabby green soddened by a solution of

Architectural splendour and horticultural extravagance made the flower garden an unequalled opportunity for the display of wealth and taste.

Exotic trees such as the strange, stiff monkey puzzle brought the excitement of foreign realms within a morning's stroll.

The pleasure ground became 'a veritable store house of rich and rare . . . rhododendrons mingling with other choice shrubs and a pleasing variety of conifers and deciduous trees'.

In its geographical variety and paradisian richness, the homegrown fruit produced for the dessert was a social and horticultural triumph.

Not only would the kitchen expect the choicest fruits and vegetables of the season, they would expect those which were out-of-season as well.

Gardens moved steadily closer to the house. Low-silled and French windows became fashionable and extensive conservatories de rigeur.

Ladies demanded flowers for their boudoirs, their hair, their dresses and their bouquets.

No proprietor once having his mansion furnished with flowers and plants is ever willing afterwards to be without them.'

vinegar and mustard and cream, in which it has lain for, perhaps, a couple of hours before dinner time.' It was, he declared, a travesty compared to the Continentals' 'crisp and dainty dish of well grown Lettuce or blanched Endive, simply dressed with oil, vinegar and salt.'[50] Nevertheless, at fashionable establishments, where the chef was French or the family gastronomically inclined, the composition, dressing and garnishing of a good salad was a year round preoccupation.

Part of the problem with the British salad bowl was that the lettuce leaves were washed, whereas French cooks merely wiped the leaves with a napkin. Where salads were prized, therefore, it became one of the gardener's priorities to provide 'good clean, crisp lettuces' with tight hearts of well-blanched leaves. As Fish pointed out, 'the proper arrangements of condiments, sweet herbs and having the bulk of the salad dry instead of wet will ever add to the attractiveness of this dish of raw vegetables.'[51]

Cabbage **Lettuce**, the French *laitue*, and Cos lettuce or *Romaine* would both be grown. The finest of the Cos was the large-hearted Paris White, which was 'very white crisp and excellent and blanches well.'[52] It was D'Ombrain's opinion that 'in the estimation of all real salad lovers, the Cos lettuce holds the foremost place; there is a crispness and flavour about them which we in vain look for amongst the Cabbage varieties.'

Cabbage varieties such as the solid Tom Thumb, which Taylor grew, were, however, hardier. They could be grown in frames during the winter, and Luckhurst, who knew only too well what was required when 'Monsieur Le Chef' demanded 'much laitue', planned for the 'early spring salads' by planting the variety Stanstead Park along the base of a warm peach wall. The outer leaves were worthless, but the heart was usable, and like other cabbage varieties, grew quickly.[53] Most gardeners also grew a few fancy-leaved varieties, such as the Oak-leaved, Asparagus, Crimson Cos and Small Dark Red lettuces.

The other salad staple was **Endive**. Lettuce was not a reliable winter crop, even under glass, and 'very often the produce does not pay one quarter for the labour bestowed upon it.' Endive, particularly the Improved Round-Leaved Batavian, was a surer bet and in 1878 Taylor declared that he had finally given up growing lettuces in autumn and winter. 'Once the warm weather is gone, the Lettuce grows slowly and blanches imperfectly, and this Endive is then decidedly the best. For it hearts well, blanches easily, is quite as sweet as Lettuce is at this time of year, and many people do not know it from a good Lettuce in the salad bowl.'[54]

Blanching ensured the leaves were not bitter. It could be achieved simply by putting pots over the plants, growing them in a mushroom shed or transferring them to a blackened frame. Some gardeners practised the so-called 'Spanish method'. This involved 'pressing the heart of the plant gently down, on which a fragment of tile is laid, over this a light covering of earth is sifted. The fringed edge of leaves are carefully freed from earth and exposed to light . . . to produce what gardeners particularly pride themselves in – *viz*, a plant of Endive white all over, excepting the edges of the outer leaves which show about two inches of green.'[55]

If the weather was really severe, and the endive failed, gardeners would then call on **Chicory**, which was even hardier. Roots would be lifted at intervals throughout the winter, potted 6 or 8 roots to a pot, and moved to a warm shed. Here, according to Margam Park's head gardener Muir, 'the crowns soon start into growth and throw up long cream coloured leaves, which are as tender and well flavoured as anyone could wish the best Lettuce to be. One or two dozen pots will give a daily supply for some months.'[56]

The finishing touch to a leafy salad was what in France was termed *la fourniture*. This was a sprinkling of chopped herbs which 'when cunningly selected and applied' gave ' a gaiety and sparkle to the composition of the salad'. The customary summer mixture was a *ravigote* of finely chopped tarragon, chervil, burnet and chives, with spring onions and shallot tops as substitutes earlier in the year. But people had different views about this, and where the diners were very particular, Fish found it best to let them compose their own salad. 'At one time', he wrote, 'neither the butler nor myself could do anything satisfactory with salads. What some considered essential, as young onions, sprigs of Tarragon, Burnet, etc., others thoroughly hated. The matter was set right in this way. The general make of the salad was approved as far as oil, vinegar, etc., were concerned; and to enable each resident and guest to suit his or her taste, there was a nice plate on the table supplied with young Onions, and small bundles of Tarragon, Burnet, Borage, Mint, Balm,Thyme etc, and every person could take and suit his own particular palate.' He had once 'served a gentleman who thought a salad in summer a failure without a few shoots of Borage mixed in with it' and in his experience some people liked 'the young shoots of Purslane in salads, but it is years since we have been asked for it.'[57]

In addition to the leaves and herbs which were the staples of the salad bowl, gardeners also had to make sure that a whole range of garnishes was available. Cress 'was expected to be at command winter and summer', and crisp radishes and cucumbers were always in demand. Endive would usually be garnished with a *chapon*, a piece of bread rubbed with garlic but, given that this was not always acceptable in English circles, Robson sought alternatives. He was particularly enthusiastic about a 'dish of finely blanched Endive set around with slices of Red Beet of the richest and best colour. This is of itself as ornamental as many vases of flowers are at the dull period of Christmas.'[58] Taylor, on the other hand, felt that the simple addition of 'sliced tomato and a very little good oil makes in my estimation a perfect salad.'

Tomatoes were long familiar to English herbalists and widely used in Mediterranean and Jewish cookery but it was not until the nineteenth century that they ceased to be regarded in Britain with anything other than suspicion. Once this was dispelled, however, attitudes changed rapidly. By 1880 William Iggulden, who wrote a book on tomatoes while head gardener to the Earl of Cork at Marston House, considered that nothing less than a complete revolution was taking place.[59] Whereas, once, they had been 'cultivated in gardens of the richer classes against a wall, and if the crop failed then Tomato sauce had to be dispensed with', now 'not only is it incumbent on those in charge of large gardens to maintain a supply of good fruit, but the owners of smaller gardens, amateurs, and even cottagers also are acquiring a taste for Tomatoes.'

Tomatoes came into the markets from the south of France, where they had become an important industry, and increasingly from local growers as British market gardeners responded to the challenge. A certain crop under glass, tomatoes were easily cultivated by any commercial grower who could manage grapes, and by the end of the century they had become big business in Britain too.

As always, the task for the country house gardener was to ensure the finest possible quality and to match his choice of varieties as closely as possible to the cook's requirements. Many sorts were in cultivation and could be used for sauces and soups but, for the salad, appearance was all important. Kitchens requested medium-sized fruits which had firm flesh and an even shape, and for this the old, ribbed Large Red had to give way to new improved varieties. Some of these came from America, where tomatoes had become an important field crop, and these Iggulden found 'were particularly good eaten as a salad in an uncooked state, and much as some epicures may like Tomato sauce, they will dispense with this rather than salad.'[60]

Tomatoes could be grown out of doors in the southern counties, and at the end of summer the last of the crop would be harvested green, ripened indoors and 'handed over to the cook for sauce.' The superior quality required for salads, however, came from glasshouses, which 'ensured that no one need be without tomatoes any day of the year.' At Longleat, tomatoes were a perpetual crop and, in Taylor's view, a good deal more straightforward than winter cucumbers. He found the new Orangefield Dwarf bore large fruit of excellent quality and was ideal for winter culture. In 1875, he sent up a dish of these to the Royal Horticultural Society's Fruit and Vegetable Committee meeting on 17th February, and they were 'much admired for their brilliant colour.'[61] An even more attractive, if less prolific, variety was the American Hathaway's Excelsior, which yielded fruit that was 'large, heavy and handsome, as round as a cricket ball, and an excellent sort for slicing up in tomato salads' – especially with the addition of chopped chives.[62] Ornamental Redcurrant and Cherry tomatoes that resembled their namesakes and produced racemes of tiny fruit for decorating fish dishes were also given a corner at most establishments.

THE KITCHEN HERBAL

Every kitchen garden had to have its quota of these essential garnishes and flavourings. Fish advised that gardeners should arrange to have 'a little piece of everything in the herb way', and make sure these were not too near the kitchen or 'the advantage is apt to be presumed upon by the culinary department.'[63] At Putteridge Bury he cultivated some thirty different herbs ranging from parsley, thyme and bay for the *bouquet garni*, through the more aromatic rosemary and coriander, of which 'very little will suffice', to the tall stems of angelica which the cook would candy.

The most important herb was undoubtedly **Parsley**. Gastronomes proclaimed it 'the crown of cookery . . . we wreathe our fish with sprigs of parsley; it would be impossible to eat cold meat without garlands of it round the dish; and the crowning grace of many a sauce and stew comes from a shower of minute parsley shed upon it at the last . . . Fried parsley is indispensable for fried fish, croquettes and rissoles.'[64] There was no meal which could exist without it. It garnished the kidneys at breakfast and the potato salad at lunch. Sprigs were set around the teatime sandwiches, and it adorned almost every course at dinner. It was also the main ingredient of *Maître* *d'Hôtel* butter, and Parsley Sauce, and the ubiquitous *duxelles* consumed it by the handful. 'The cook can be very fidgety without parsley,' observed one gardener. 'Pity the man who has not enough to send this in for use several times a day.'[65]

Cooks preferred the curly-leaved varieties they called 'double parsley' to the hardier and coarse-leaved kinds, and the gardener often met their demands with the 'beautifully curled' Myatt's Garnishing. Every gardener had a good-sized parsley plot, although not usually as large as at Thorseby Park, where the needs of the Earl's kitchen called for a bed of 'triple curled parsley 200 feet long and 10 feet wide'.[66] Supplies had to be kept up all year round, as to be 'without Parsley in winter' it was declared 'was like being without Mint in the Pea season.' In this instance, conflict between 'the ladle and the spade' could usually be avoided by planting a row of parsley in the orchard house, as Fish did at Putteridge Bury, or squeezing pots into the peach house.

Mint was also indispensable at any time of year, and a clump would be put into a frame in October so that there was mint for the new potatoes at Christmas. There had to be plenty of **Sage** for stuffing the pork and poultry, and since 'some like Red and some Green', it was Fish's opinion that 'it is always best to have both.' **Chives** were 'one of those useful little things that no garden should be without', **Chervil** and **Tarragon** were the essential ingredients of *ravigote* butter for steaks and fish, and for the delicate *Poulet Rôti à l'Estragon*. These would all be grown in pots in the vineries to keep supplies going throughout the winter.

Fennel and **Dill** were grown for the fish dishes, and there would be **Marjoram** and **Basil** in plenty. **Borage** and **Balm** would be on hand for the summer's Claret and champagne cup, and for making balm tea and balm wine. Another essential was **Horseradish**, without which many people considered roast beef to be 'as nearly as great a failure as without mustard' and, for an ordinary family's needs, a bed 15 feet by 8 feet was customary. At Bicton in Devon the kitchen garden even grew **Ginger** for the cook to crystallize. 'From 10 to 12 lb yearly was considered an ample supply to serve as a sweetmeat at the close of dinner.'[67]

THE GLORIOUS PUDDINGS

The chef's finale at dinner were the puddings. These brought the carefully ordered sequence of the menu to a close with the lightest and most perfumed dishes of his repertoire. Many of these would be made from or decorated with fruit. There would be meringues, pastries and creams; elaborately moulded iced sweets and jellies; charlottes and fritters, flans and Carême's exquisite invention, the soufflé. These consumed soft fruit, cherries, greengages and apples by the basket load, and there was also call for more exotic fruits such as pineapples, oranges and lemons. Everything, apart perhaps from the citrus fruits, would be home-grown. Imported pineapples might be used at some establishments, but at many places these would also be home-produced. At Petworth, Sussex, for example, Lord Leconfield's 'fruit was managed on a somewhat extensive scale.' Here 'as many as forty pines weighing 3½-4½ lb have been sent in at one time for preserving.'[68]

'Neapolitan Cake à la Chantilly'.   'Apples à la Portugaise'.

Gardeners tended to reserve their energies for producing the fresh fruit which would form the splendid dessert which followed the puddings, but they had to ensure that sufficient quantity and variety was available for the kitchens too. Some of the most tempting puddings, for example, would appear on the menu when the summer 'red fruits' were in season. These made possible such confections as Francatelli's pine-apple flavoured ice-cream mould filled with cherries, currants, strawberries and rasp-berries suspended in a cherry water ice, and garnished with more strawberries and en-titled 'Iced Pudding à la Chesterfield'. His strawberry jelly consisted of whole strawberries in a raspberry and redcurrant jelly , while in the fancier 'Macédoine of Whole Fruits in Jelly' a complete array of raspberries, cherries, peaches, strawberries and so on were suspended in the jelly.

Fruit tarts were an English passion. Lord Dudley, Foreign Secretary to George IV, and a well-known epicure, claimed he could never dine comfortably without apple tart on the menu, and that an apricot tart completed a dinner fit for an emperor.[69] Peaches, greengages and gooseberries also made fine tarts, and many gardeners, like Stewart at Nuneham Park, prided themselves on being able to supply the kitchen with freshly gathered gooseberries, currants and Morello cherries right through until Christmas.

This involved going to great lengths to preserve the fruit upon the trees with straw mats. Fish tended to the opinion that it was not worth the bother, observing that the fruit 'might as well have been bottled, preserved, or brandied at once when ripe, and thus saved all the attacks of birds and the trouble and expense of protecting them.'[70]

There was an extraordinary number of culinary and dessert gooseberries. Luck-hurst grew a hundred at Oldlands, while Petworth had over 150 varieties in the kitchen garden. They were used for pies as well as gooseberry fool, and made a good sharp sauce for mackerel and goose. Apricots were excellent in a charlotte as well as in a tart, and a *condé* of apricots with rice was always well-received.

Pears did not feature extensively in the cooked desserts but there were some vari-eties which, keeping sound until the following spring without any trouble at all, were used to make a refreshing compôte. Varieties such as the huge Catillac and Spring

Beurré were widely grown, and turned a pretty pink colour when poached and needed no help from an improving addition of redcurrant or plum jam.

The most useful culinary fruit for year-round use was undoubtedly the **Apple**. Purists enjoyed them plainly baked and served with thick cream, but apple purée was the basis of many elaborate moulded puddings such as apple charlotte and the meringue-topped 'Apples à la Portuguaise'. The apple's great virtue was its long season which ran from the end of July almost to the following June, and the range of texture and flavour which the different varieties offered.

Loudon had defined the criteria of a good culinary apple at the beginning of the nineteenth century. It should be distinguished, he asserted by 'the property of falling as it is technically termed, or forming in general a pulpy mass of equal consistency when baked or boiled, and by a large size.'[71] A collection of at least twenty varieties meeting these requirements was considered desirable to carry the crop through from the first codlins in July and August to the last of the Dumelow's Seedling in May.

All the early varieties, from Keswick Codlin to the esteemed Hawthornden, which was ready in September, made light juicy cookers. They were not too sharp and were equally good baked or turned into a purée for folding in with beaten egg whites for 'Apple Snow'. For the best apple tarts, however, it was best to wait until the end of September for Golden Noble. This cooked perfectly, and did not collapse into a thin purée like the early varieties. The sharp, strong Warner's King was the next off the tree, and Blenheim Orange would be requested if 'Apple Charlotte' was on the menu, as it formed a good stiff purée. Then came Dumelow's Seedling. This made a creamy baked apple, and kept its brisk acidity through until the spring rhubarb was ready, and even until the first gooseberries supplied the table with a welcome astringency.

Apples also appeared elsewhere on the menu. No self-respecting Englishman would allow goose or pork into his dining room without a good sharp apple sauce to offset the richness of the meat. According to an old proverb, 'A good goose will lay by Pancake Day', thereby ensuring that a brood of goslings would be ready for the first of the new season's codlins. The finest sauce apples cooked to a perfectly smooth purée and had a brisk flavour which needed no further embellishment. One of the best for this purpose was the Ecklinville Seedling, which was ready in time for the Michaelmas green geese. By the time the cold was in the ground and the first pigs were killed there were many more varieties to choose from. Herefordshire squires could relish their local Queen of the Sauce apple, and northern gardens were sure to have some trees of the very late keeping Yorkshire Goose Sauce.

Much of the fruit demanded by the kitchens was for turning into jams and jellies, or for preserving in spirits to add extra zest to the winter puddings. A fine apricot conserve made a 'perfect sweet omelette', the tea-time scones were served with strawberry jam and, at dinner, venison and hare would be accompanied by redcurrant jelly. Jams and preserves also served as the chef's 'paints' with which he decorated many of the more elaborate puddings such as 'Neapolitan Cake'. This was topped with cream and strawberries and decorated with a 'bright preserve such as greengage, apricot, redcurrant or apples and afterwards . . . ornamented with piping used for wedding cakes.'[72]

This did not mean that the gardener could send in any variety or condition of fruit. Less than perfect peaches and nectarines might jam successfully, but good preserving fruit needed plenty of acidity if it was to set well and not be cloyingly sweet. The best conserves also contained plenty of whole fruit so, as Fish observed, a preserving strawberry needed colour, flavour and substance. 'It must remain firm as all culinary varieties should during cooking.' Raspberries also needed to be specially selected for the kitchen. Luckhurst found that 'the order for the usual quantity of raspberries is always imperative with the housekeeper', and was best met by 'large fruit and plenty of it'. He recommended Prince of Wales which was 'very fine', though being 'not so sweet as some, it probably would not generally be liked for the dessert.'[73]

With the pastries, meringues and glittering jellies, the chef's contribution to the dinner was almost complete. The table would be cleared except for the magnificent display of fresh fruit which had awaited its moment throughout the meal. There would also be plates of tiny sponge cakes, almond biscuits or crystallized ginger, but the dessert to come was, above all, a celebration of the gardener's masterpieces.

6

The Dessert Triumphant

ictorian dinner menus were designed to please the palate and delight the eye, but the succulent roasts and exquisite vegetables were only the preamble to the grand finale of the dessert. This magnificent selection of fresh fruits was both the host's and the gardener's *pièce de résistance*. It was a dazzling demonstration of skill and resources, and offered guests the supreme opportunity to enjoy produce at its simplest and most perfect. From the estate's own hot-houses would come rich, juicy pineapples. There would be grapes from the vinery to equal the Mediterranean's finest, and bowls of home-grown peaches heavy with southern ripeness. Melons, apricots, figs and even tangerines might also be offered, as well as the choicest of more familiar fruits. Bone bladed knives would be supplied lest the fruit be tainted by metal, and the finest dessert wines would be served. In its visual majesty, imperial splendour and obvious debt to the quantities of glass, heat and labour expended upon it, the dessert was a social and horticultural triumph.

The practice of closing a meal with fresh fruit seems to have reached Britain from continental Europe during the seventeenth century or earlier, but the quality and diversity of fruit available for the Victorian dessert was very much a nineteenth-century achievement.[1] Before that, the choice of fresh fruit at most establishments was severely limited. During the summer, cherries, strawberries and well-ripened gooseberries and greengages could be offered, but for the rest of the year there were only apples and pears. Dried and candied fruits, almond biscuits and nuts and a range of confectionery were thus an important part of the pre-Victorian dessert and were only cast into the shade by the advent of superlative quality fruit.

New varieties of apples and pears had begun to proliferate during the seventeenth century, and Georgian gardeners, with their reduced role in the landscape park, experimented eagerly with the cultivation of tender fruits. Some, particularly in southern counties, had peaches and figs ripening successfully against warm, south-facing walls, and a few wealthy enthusiasts had specially constructed glasshouses devoted to pineapples and grapes.[2] But it took the improved glasshouse technology of the nineteenth century to enable a wide range of tender fruit to be grown reliably and well, and the new social and economic climate to give it such importance.

As in the flower and vegetable departments, the quality and variety of the fruit grown for dessert was influenced by commercial developments. The country house

A magnificent display of a homegrown pineapple and melon, and dishes of grapes, peaches and strawberries, arranged for a wedding party in June 1870.

had always given the lead in the cultivation of luxury fruit but, with the abolition of the glass tax in 1845, fruit growing under glass ceased to be the prerogative of the wealthy enthusiast. It came within reach not only of all country establishments of any size, but also of the burgeoning horticultural industry. Keenly aware of an affluent and expanding urban clientele anxious to emulate the tables of their landed neighbours, the commercial men were quick to extend the skills of the private gardener into the commercial world. The expertise of the English grape producers became renowned and Meredith's, of Garston outside Liverpool, sent boxes of grapes all over Europe. Market gardeners, particularly around London, also produced pineapples and forced early strawberries.

The fact that such high quality produce was commercially available acted as a spur to the country house to do even better. Taylor's brief when he commenced work for the Marquess of Bath was to 'improve the quality of the dessert' and the magnificence and variety which home-grown fruit could achieve became an important addition to the landowner's social armoury. The more exclusive and expensive it was to produce, the greater the kudos it conferred. Glasshouses were refurbished and extended, and the quantities of coal and labour which families were prepared to devote to the dessert seemed, for a time, to be limitless. Not surprisingly, the head gardener's expertise in cultivating fruit became a correspondingly important aspect of his increasing status.

The interests of commercial and private growers also coincided in the activities of the Horticultural Society. Besides its sponsorship of plant-hunting expeditions, the Society was concerned to improve the quality of fresh produce, both in kitchen gardens and the market place. From the very beginning its members had examined fruits and vegetables at their meetings, and collections of these, as well as of the latest conifers, shrubs and flowers, were planted in their gardens at Chiswick, London. Following the example of its president, the pioneer fruit breeder Thomas Andrew Knight, everyone from commercial growers and nurserymen to head gardeners and amateur enthusiasts was encouraged to seek out new varieties both here and abroad, and to themselves raise new strains. The range and quality of fruit in cultivation was thus considerably enhanced.

The task of cataloguing the Society's collection had also begun in the early 1800s, ensuring that the most meritworthy varieties soon emerged. Not only was the appearance, distinguishing features and performance of each carefully recorded but also the quality of its flavour. The choicest varieties for the dessert were clearly indicated.

As well as the Society, horticultural patrons and nurserymen also began to keep records and, eventually, to publish fruit books, some of which were beautifully illustrated with hand-coloured plates. The most useful, widely influential and lasting of these was Dr Robert Hogg's *Fruit Manual*. This first appeared in 1860 and covered the varieties then grown in Britain of every fruit from apples and apricots to pineapples, strawberries and walnuts. As the diversity and number of varieties expanded, and interest in every aspect of fruit increased, so each edition became larger and, by 1884, when the fifth and final edition was published, the *Fruit Manual* had become a weighty tome of nearly 800 pages.

Country house gardeners were ideally placed to benefit from as well as contribute to all these developments. They were probably the nurserymen's best customers and, at many estates, collections of fruit already existed and could be systematically explored and added to. They served as the trial grounds for the nurseymen's latest introductions which were duly reported and discussed in the literature. Head gardeners sat on the Horticultural Society's Fruit Committee which was set up in 1858 to assess new varieties, and they also took their place alongside nurserymen and professional fruitmen as judges at the increasing number of shows and exhibitions.

Their wide experience and continually expanding expertise ensured that the country house dessert excelled. They had the freedom to grow the choicest varieties regardless of economic considerations, and to select only the finest specimens which they would bring to the table with meticulous care. It was no coincidence that the emerging criteria of excellence at shows were essentially those demanded of the dessert at the mansion: perfection of form; richness of colour; and immaculate finish.

If the economic implications of the dessert display played an important role in focusing fashionable attention on fruit, so too did the growth of gastronomy and, during the second half of the century, the introduction of dining *à la Russe*. When dining under the old regime, the table would be cleared before the fruit and sweetmeats were brought in. 'At the dessert, the scene changed,' recounted one of the Duke of Argyll's visitors in 1784. 'The cloth, napkins, and everything disappeared.

The mahogany table shone in all the lustre that wood is capable of receiving from art; but it was soon covered with brilliant decanters, filled with the most exquisite wines; comfits, in fine porcelain, or crystal vases; and fruits of different kinds in beautiful baskets. Plates and glasses were distributed; and in every object elegance and conveniency seemed to rival each other.'[3]

Under the new regime, the ritual of removing the cloth was no longer necessary. The fruit, like the careful floral arrangements, and glittering array of crystal and plate, became part of the magnificent table display which greeted guests when they sat down to dinner and stayed in place throughout the meal. The Victorian dessert did not, therefore, only bring the meal to its triumphant conclusion, it signalled the splendour and generosity of the occasion from the outset.

The most kudos was, not suprisingly, attached to fruits cultivated under glass. Pineapples and grapes were held in greatest esteem and at the grandest places could be available all year round. More familiar fruits such as strawberries, peaches and nectarines were also highly prized and with the aid of glass their season could be extended in both directions. Melons were a celebrated summer fruit and, at some establishments, exotic novelties such as tangerines, passion fruit, mangoes and even mangosteens would occasionally make their appearance. Nevertheless, the traditional hardy fruits such as cherries, outdoor strawberries and greengages still found their place in the summer display, while throughout the winter the finest varieties of apples and pears were a welcome complement to the hothouse fruit.

By the 1870s, however, the emphasis had shifted a little. Pineapples ceased to enjoy quite such exalted status, while hardy fruit, particularly apples, began to receive more attention. The declining attraction of the pineapple was a direct result of the high quality imports, which by the 1870s, were starting to come in from the Azores. The enormous investment in time and money that growing tropical exotics required was only worth it for as long as the resulting quality and availability exceeded that of imported fruit. In the middle of the century an imported West Indian pineapple could only be compared to a homegrown specimen 'as a turnip is to a fine melon', but these latest imports were equal to the gardener's best. Pineapples lost their social cachet and, with it, their unchallenged supremacy at dessert.[4]

Apples became more important for both cultural and economic reasons. As gastronomic sensibilities developed, the infinite diversity of the apple came to be widely appreciated, and the efforts of pomologists, such as the redoubtable Dr Hogg, led to hundreds of local and traditional varieties being correctly identified and made more widely available. Apples and other homely fruits also began to seem increasingly attractive as the feeling grew in some quarters that it was imperative to recover the traditional skills and products that technology and mass production threatened to destroy.

This interest was strongly reinforced by economic circumstances. The expansion of the railway network had opened up industrial markets to the traditional fruit-growing areas of Kent and the west country, but the competition from imported continental and North American apples was formidable. In response, English growers during the second half of the century set about modernising their orchards and improving the quality of the crop. When British agriculture collapsed in the 1880s as a result of cheap grain flooding in from the prairies, the government campaigned for widespread investment in fruit growing as a supplement to farm incomes. By the end of the century, patriotism as well as economic necessity had transformed the growing popularity of the apple into nothing short of a crusade, and the area given over to fruit doubled during in the 1890s.[5]

THE DESSERT ON DISPLAY

The dessert was entirely the head gardener's responsibility. No details appeared on the menu as the chef played little or no part in the choice and presentation of the fruit. It was a matter to be decided between the gardener and his employers, and depended critically on the nature and social importance of the entertainments. A house party composed of the more fashionable and influential members of Society, for example, demanded the compliment of more luxurious desserts than a dinner party for the local gentry. A week of important luncheons and dinner parties culminating in a ball for over a hundred would take considerable planning to ensure that appropriate treats would be available for each occasion.

Once the choice of fruits had been settled, it was up to the gardener to select the finest examples for the table. Perfection of form and appearance were essential. The bloom of the grapes had to be unmarked, the velvety duvet on the peaches undisturbed, and the ripe fruit glowing with rich, well-developed colour. One London epicure even observed that main object of the dessert was 'its fragrance and its effect by way of ornament'.[6]

Even if this was sometimes the case in Town, where the fruit would have to travel up from the country estate or even be bought in, it does not appear to have been the position at the mansion. Here, gardeners were equally preoccupied with pleasing discerning palates. Guests expected to be offered only those varieties which displayed the finest attributes of each fruit. The muscat grapes had to show a high, aromatic quality, and the pears not only juicy melting flesh but also a range of subtly perfumed flavours. Indeed, the appreciation of flavour was 'something approaching to a science', in David Thomson's experience, and 'the man that can grow for exhibition and flavour' was the ideal gardener from many employers' point of view.[7]

The dessert display would be as carefully planned as the floral decorations. A dinner party for twenty guests would call for a prominent arrangement at either end of the table which might take the form of a selection of fruit assembled to show off its colour and splendour to greatest advantage. Pyramids of apples or pears, or a handsome pair of large, ripe pineapples both looked well. There would also be generous bunches of both black and white grapes in dishes at either side of the table, and smaller bowls of seasonal fruits between the place settings with, perhaps, some sweetmeats. For one such event William Low, who was head gardener to the Duke of Grafton, records that he prepared eight dishes of fruit which included 'Pine and Melon at the top and bottom, two dishes of Grapes, black and white, occupying the centre of the sides, these being flanked with Apples, Pears, Figs and Peaches.'[8]

At smaller gatherings, the entire display might be of individual dishes of a particularly special fruit such as Easter strawberries or the first perfectly ripe peaches. Only the prime fruits of the season would ever be served, and the selection would change during the week in case anyone should get bored. As one employer remarked to his gardener, 'Do you think I want to eat but one variety of grape?'

The dishes used to hold the fruit represented the mansion's finest lead crystal and most delicate porcelain. Many considered that fruit looked best on plain white china with a gold rim. Plain glass bowls were also favoured, as they enabled guests to glimpse the rich colours and glowing contrasts of their occupants.

The most fitting embellishment was usually judged to be a fruit's own foliage. A pineapple 'crowned by a towering rosette of its distinct foliage'[9] would be ringed with its own leaves at the base, and grapes were deemed particularly well set off by their autumn foliage. In late October, Taylor noted that leaves on the Black Hamburgh vine were turning 'a golden colour rivalling even our beautiful Tulip Trees', while 'the Muscats will have a mixture of russet and gold; Barbarossa, streaks and blotches of intense fiery scarlet, while Alicante is assuming a softer red in various shades, and is more beautiful than any of them.'[10] Some pear trees, too, developed a pronounced autumn colouring that might be usefully employed in the dessert.

There were occasions, however, when a different adornment was required. To some tastes, grapes showed 'best in frost', which might be provided by a few sprays of the ice plant, *Mesembryanthemum crystallinum*, whose leaves, covered with glittering hairs, had a suitably frosted appearance. If the pears and apples looked a little plain, then berries of pyracantha, cotoneaster, rose hips and tiny crab apples would wonderfully heighten the effect. Poinsettias were also a popular means of brightening up winter displays. 'Having ourselves last season upwards of two hundred plants,' wrote John Perkins, head gardener to Lord Henniker, 'we found that we were not encumbered with one too many. The richness which the scarlet bracts of this plant gives to almost any kind of fruit can scarcely be conceived, especially if arranged on white china with a few Fern fronds intermixed.'[11]

Due care was also taken to bring the fruit, with its embellishments, and the floral decorations into an integrated whole. The scarlet and gold of apples and pears, for example, harmonized well with a tracery of coleus leaves on the tablecloth, and for a grand Christmas display, the red berries of the bead plant, *Nertera depressa*, might be used to enliven the 'frost' of the grapes, and echo the holly and mistletoe berries which studded the evergreen embroidery. The ripening of the forced strawberries at Easter, and the first of the new season's grapes, would be a signal to bring in tea roses and give the whole table a lighter touch, while passion flowers and foliage, which were often used as table decorations, made the perfect foil to the summer melons. The miniature Queen Anne's pocket melon which was grown purely for decoration also enhanced both the dessert and floral displays of a summer table. It was 'like a small orange, beautifully striped with red and gold, and its aroma, too, is most delicious.'[12]

The King and Queen of Fruits

The King of fruits, 'the richest and most luscious of all' was undoubtedly the **Pineapple**. It was stately and exotic in appearance with a wonderful flavour, which was thought to combine 'the taste of peach, of the apple, of the quince and the muscatelle'.[13]

A native of South America, it was first known to have been brought to England in 1657. John Evelyn tasted one from the West Indies, at a banquet held by Charles II in honour of the French Ambassador in 1668, but did not think much of it 'the flavour being much impaired in coming so farr.' Twenty-five years later, what may have been the first successful homegrown specimen fruited in a stove house at George London's Brompton Park Nursery and was promptly presented to the Queen.

By the early eighteenth century England had succumbed to the pineapple fever which was to persist for the next 150 years. Pineapples became the most esteemed of gifts and sought-after adornments for the table. As they lasted for weeks, they were often passed on from party to party. Stone pineapples appeared on eighteenth-century gate-posts and roofs and, in 1761, the Earl of Dunmore even had a folly built in the shape of a pineapple. [14]

For a long time, the prime requirement for a fresh pineapple was, understandably, that it should be large. In 1821, one weighing 10 lbs 8 oz was considered so remarkable that it was presented to George IV for the dessert at the Royal table during the Coronation banquet. As the mystique surrounding cultivation gradually died away, quantity and quality became more important. For the Victorian gardener, the pinnacle of achievement was 'a constant supply of first rate pines', and half a dozen or more fruits weighing 2 lbs each were usually infinitely preferred to a monstrous 8 lbs specimen that hung on for days.[15]

As it took at least eighteen months from potting a young sucker to harvesting a ripe pineapple, the main requirements for a steady supply were large stocks of plants and unlimited amounts of coal to feed the boilers which heated the pineries. Success in the 'whole affair was one of pocket', declared Robson bluntly, 'coupled of course with some cultural details not difficult to understand.'[16] As possession of a coalfield offered a distinct advantage, it is not surprising that Lambton Castle outside Durham, and Raby Castle near Bishop Auckland were renowned for their pineapples, while one of the most productive pineries was at Cyfarthfa Castle, the Rhondda seat of the South Wales iron master R.T. Crawshay. Here during the 1870s, the gardener had thousands of plants and claimed to be able to cut a pineapple every day of the year and a hundred for Christmas.[17]

This was exceptional but when Robson – who confessed to a definite partiality to pineapples – looked back over his records, he found that during the six years ending in December 1875 there were only three months when no fruit could be cut. He managed about 150 a year altogether, with the greatest number, 171, being harvested in 1871. They averaged 2 lbs 10 oz each. This was not exhibition size but when 'in perfection, large enough'.[18] David Thomson, who was well-known as 'one of our best

Charlotte Rothschild was a splendid winter pine.

pineapple growers' also provided year round supplies of probably a dozen each month for the Nisbet Hamilton family from Archerfield and, at Drumlanrig, he recorded harvesting around 200 annually for the Duke of Buccleuch's table.[19]

The cultivation of two varieties was sufficient to maintain a year round supply and to meet the peak demands of the London Season and the autumn and Christmas entertainments in the country. It was usual, however, to grow several more to provide additional interest. The oldest and best known of the widely cultivated varieties was the Queen, which produced handsomely shaped fruit of a rich golden colour through the summer and autumn, when 'there was no pine to excel this for general excellence.' As a winter pine, however, it was 'generally wanting in juiciness and flavour', and from October to May, Thomson considered Smooth-Leaved Cayenne was the best choice.[20]

This was a more recent introduction, having found its way from Cayenne, the capital of French Guiana, to Paris by 1820, and thence to England.[21] It was a 'rich yellow' colour, rather barrel shaped, taller than the Queen and 'when well swelled, weighs a pound for every pip in depth.'[22] Thomson also advocated growing Black Jamaica which, in his opinion, was 'probably the highest flavoured winter pine in cultivation'. Although conceding that it was 'rather dull in colour', and that some people objected to 'its hardness of flesh and prefer the Smooth Cayenne on account of the melting juiciness of the latter', he was insistent that on the grounds of its excellent flavour alone 'it should be cultivated wherever winter pines are esteemed.'

Another splendid winter pine was Charlotte Rothschild. This had been found by one of Baron Alphonse Rothschild's sea captains and brought home to France in

1843.[23] It grew to a large size and had a good flavour compared with the old record breaker White Providence. This was now considered to be second-rate for flavour although, with its ability to reach 14 lbs, was still grown as 'a splendid centrepiece for dinner table decoration purposes'.[24]

From time to time a pineapple would seed and a new variety emerge. One of the most enduringly successful of these was probably the Lady Lambton Pineapple, raised by James Hunter. He was head gardener at Lambton, and a former pupil of Thomson. When grown by the master at Drumlanrig, it was found to be a large fruit of a 'high orange colour' and, as Thomson observed in the *Journal*, 'the very highest estimation of its flavour has been formed by all who have partaken of it, and I have been asked if it was Black Jamaica that was handed around. Personally I consider that Black Jamaica is the the only Pine to be compared to this much finer-looking fruit, the flavour of which is superb. The juice follows the knife in a stream and I know of no Pine more free from stringiness (if I may coin a word). It melts in the mouth like a marrow . . . It should be cut with a green tinge upon it, and this is the stage in which all Pines are best flavoured in autumn and winter.'[25]

If the pineapple was the King of fruits, then the **Grape** was the Queen. 'In no country in the world are Grapes grown with so much care, and brought to such perfection, as in Great Britain', claimed one leading authority.[26] When William Thomson, head gardener at Dalkeith, the Duke of Buccleuch's Edinburgh residence, was visiting the vine growing areas of the Continent in 1861 he was ' so struck by the inferior character of the Grapes in the hothouses I saw, that I wrote home for three bunches of Muscats to be sent to me in Paris, where I exhibited them at the first great exhibition of the Société Impériale et Centrale d'Horticulture on the 17th of September, and though the three bunches only weighed 10 lbs, they created as great a sensation as if the sea serpent, or some other semi-fabulous monster, had made his appearance.' They won the Emperor's Gold Medal and amazed the French that such grapes could be grown in Scotland.[27] By the mid-nineteenth century not only every country house, but also the more modest villa had to have its vinery, and there was no topic which received more attention in the gardening literature.

Over a hundred varieties of dessert grapes were in cultivation, but about a dozen would usually ensure a pleasing diversity of both black and white all year round. Both were preferably present in a dessert, and would be displayed in bunches from which the berries could be cut with silver grape scissors. Appearance, flavour and texture were all important, and the most highly valued were the soft juicy 'Sweetwaters', such as Black Hamburgh and Foster's Seedling, and the firmer fleshed and intensely aromatic 'Muscats'.[28]

Of them all, it was generally agreed that the most widely grown, accommodating and useful was Black Hamburgh. This, according to David Thomson, could be 'put on the table from April to February in such a condition that no other grape is preferred to it.' It could be forced for Easter; a vinery ripening slightly later would keep the family supplied while they were up in Town; and the main crop would reach its prime as the shooting season commenced. Part of the crop could even be preserved for a month or two by inserting the ends of the cut branches into bottles of water. This was a practice which started to become popular in the 1860s, although it was claimed by connoisseurs to dull the flavour.

The grapes would be grown, like everything else, as if for exhibition. To achieve this, the developing fruit was carefully thinned so that the remaining grapes reached a good size and formed compact bunches. These were not only easier to bring to the table with the bloom undisturbed, they also sat nice and plump upon the dish. Taylor maintained that berries 'none less than 3½ inches in circumference' were essential, and that the bunches should be a minimum of 2 lbs in weight. Appearance was not all, however, and could not compensate for a 'thin' flavour, or the 'mere sweetness' which, asserted the grape men dismissively, 'was often accepted by some palates for that vinous flavour which a properly trained palate requires in a Black Hamburgh grape.'[29] In Taylor's experience, the fruit was at its best when the berries were 'blue-black, after the manner of Sloes with a similar bloom to that handsome fruit . . . but no tinge of red on the skin'.

Among the white grapes, perfection of flavour and appearance was found in Muscat of Alexandria, which ripened slighter later and kept longer than the Hamburghs. This was the aristocrat of any collection but, like all muscats, was a demanding grape to grow. When well-ripened the pale amber berries acquired a cinnamon flush, and the flesh was firm, 'crackling' and 'exceeding sweet, rich and with a strong muscat flavour'.[30] To provide diversity, the esteemed black muscat, Madresfield Court, could also be offered, and in Scotland, the Duchess of Buccleuch, a white muscat with a 'sparkling champagne-like juice' was another, highly regarded alternative.

At the beginning of the season, to complement the first Black Hamburghs there

A silver grape stand
rom Mappin & Webb.

would generally be forced white grapes. These could include White Frontignan, which had a 'very sweet, rich and strong muscat flavour', and the easier to grow, 'sweet, refreshing' Foster's Seedling and Bucklands Sweetwater. In the most demanding circles, however, the showy good looks of the latter did not make up for its less than perfect quality. The Duke of Buccleuch would not have it on the table, and instructed David Thomson 'not to send it anywhere but to the cook.' For the dessert he preferred his own variety, the Duke of Buccleuch, which was another of William Thomson's new varieties raised in the Dalkeith gardens. This was forced in the early muscat vinery at Dalkeith for sending down to the London house, and also grown at Drumlanrig to provide a summer white grape. Here, a whole division of a vinery was devoted to its culture and 'peer and peasant alike' agreed no other early, white grape could compare for quality or had 'so imposing an appearance in the dessert.'[31]

To fill the gap between the end of the main crop varieties and the first of the forced grapes, there were a number of less refined, late varieties. These were handsome, but relatively harsh flavoured. They were only semi-sweet, seldom rich and had very tough skins. The most reliable of these was Alicante, which bore large bunches of finely bloomed black grapes that could rise to be 'brisk and pleasantly flavoured.' These would be ready by late autumn, but were probably not sent in to the table until Christmas or later, and would last fresh on the vine until early spring, although Taylor, who liked to clear all his vineries by February, preferred to conserve the last of the grapes by bottling. In 1880, he still had a dozen bunches of Alicante ready for use on 12th May.[32]

Other late varieties which could provide fresh grapes from the New Year onwards and give the necessary contrast on the dining table included the giant white Trebbiano. It was, however, a variety for show rather than good eating in the experts' opinion, and grape connoisseurs found the best flavour in Mrs Pince's Black Muscat. This had an intense muscat aroma but was difficult to 'finish' and kept poorly. The only sound late grape which was also well worth eating was Lady Downe's Seedling, which could be cut fresh from the vine until April. Taylor grew almost as many vines of this as Alicante. It produced large, purplish black berries which, by keeping their plumpness and bloom, more than made up for the looseness of the bunches. Given less than perfect treatment it, too, would lapse into harsh acidity but, skilfully cultivated, it could achieve a suggestion of the muscat flavour and was 'never destitute of that fine aroma.'[33]

More Fine Fruits

After pineapples and grapes, **Melons** were probably the most highly valued and ornamental of the dessert fruits. 'A noble Melon is a great addition to the dessert, especially where Pines are not grown,' declared Taylor and, in this case, it might form the centrepiece of the display. The melon's splendid appearance and distinctive flavour had made it a valued garden plant since the seventeenth century, when hot-bed technology first became understood and gardeners began using fermenting leaves and stable manure to grow musk melons and force vegetables. Melons hybridized freely and during the nineteenth century, there were numerous varieties in cultivation. These were divided into two broad categories by gardeners: those with white or green flesh, which were the finer flavoured; and the firmer, red-fleshed varieties.[34]

At Longleat, Taylor had five houses devoted to melons, 'this luscious fruit being in almost daily request here during the summer and autumn.'[35] His favoured variety was Meredith's Cashmere. This was yellow, with a smooth oval shape, and white flesh which was 'very juicy and of excellent flavour.' Other highly valued varieties were the golden Hero of Lockinge, with melting flesh, and Gilbert's Victory of Bath. This had been raised by the Marquess of Exeter's head gardener, and had 'juicy and richly flavoured' green flesh. The leader amongst the scarlets was the old Read's Scarlet but towards the end of the century this was ousted by the better flavoured Blenheim Orange from the Duke of Marlborough's gardens in Oxfordshire.

Melons helped to give the dessert display an air of exotic prodigality but, as with grapes, their presence was considered by many to be wasted if they were lacking in good flavour and texture. Taylor was well aware that there were those 'who do not know what a good Melon is, and can enjoy an inferior one with the same relish as children eat Crabs or sour Gooseberries', but he could not conceive 'of anything more disappointing to the connoisseur, who has been watching and longing for a slice all dinner time, than to find when the fruit is cut that it is not as good as it looked.' In his experience, good colour was a sure sign of fine flavour, while the development of a heady aroma combined with the fruit beginning to part from the footstalk was a reliable indication that it was ready to be cut and be taken off to 'finish' in the fruit room.[36]

The 'cool, refreshing, delicious' **Strawberry** was also 'ever welcome on the dessert and breakfast table' and regarded just as highly as its more exotic companions. Garden fruit would be available from June to late summer but forced strawberries , which could be on the table by Easter or even earlier, were especially valued. Good fruit was scarce after Christmas and the dessert, suffering from a surfeit of grapes, badly needed enlivening during these dull, cold months. Where strawberries were taken seriously, the task of growing them under glass could be formidable. During 1866 the glass-houses at Sandringham had kept the Prince of Wales 'continuously supplied since February 18th with 5,000 pots being forced' until the outside crop was ready in June.[37]

The modern strawberry, as opposed to the wild, woodland strawberries of Europe, was a comparatively recent development. For centuries, several of the wild species had been in cultivation and valued for their fine flavour. Their tiny berries were, however, time consuming to pick, and the large, new dessert strawberry was derived from two American species.[38] The first of these, the Virginian or Scarlet Strawberry, *Fragaria virginiana*, had reached England by the early seventeenth century. Its bright red, sharply flavoured berries were a great improvement in size over the indigenous species, but not in eating quality. On the other hand, the Chilean Strawberry, *Fragaria chiloensis*, which was being grown in France by the middle of the eighteenth century, had large berries that were sweet and soft. The first hybrid, raised by the young French botanist Duchesne, produced fruit of good size and flavour and was called the Pine Strawberry. Duchesne's work was cut short by the Revolution, but his studies and results were taken up and developed in England. There, strawberry breeding was pioneered by Thomas Andrew Knight but it was Michael Keen, a market gardener in Isleworth, London, who raised the first important modern strawberry, Keen's Seedling.

This caused a sensation in the 1820s, with its large, deep red, strongly flavoured fruit, which were borne high and clear of the ground and it continued to be grown for the rest of the century. In its wake, nurserymen, professional and amateur gardeners all started to breed new varieties with a vengeance and by the second half of the century there were dozens upon dozens in cultivation. The comparison of their relative merits assumed a Byzantine complexity. The Reverend W. F. Radclyffe, who was esteemed 'the best judge of strawberries in England' had trials of a hundred or more underway in his Dorset garden, and was driven to conclude that 'to select Strawberries to suit every man's taste and widely different circumstances' was about as difficult as trying to make 'a suit of clothes to fit the whole species of man.' One 'likes the Hautbois flavour, another likes a vinous, juicy strawberry; another prefers an acidulated flavour; another likes the Pine flavour; another does not care what the flavour is as long as he can get quantity, plenty of sugar, and Alderney cream.'[39] Nevertheless, all were to agree that Thomas Laxton's Royal Sovereign, introduced in 1892, was one of the finest flavoured varieties ever raised.

For very early forcing, the glossy, dark red Black Prince was one of the most popular varieties, although in Taylor's opinion anything before April was only ' a strawberry in appearance not in flavour.'[40] The ripening of the year's first, well-flavoured, forced strawberries made April the most important month for this crop, and the original Keen's Seedling was Taylor's first choice for this purpose. It was dark crimson and white fleshed with good sized fruits of which '5 berries would turn the scale at a quarter of a pound.' He also favoured Myatt's British Queen, which had 'a remarkably rich and exquisite flavour.' These were also good varieties for growing outdoors. In the garden they ripened in early June, and would be followed by the handsome Sir Joseph Paxton which, with its firmer flesh, was a good choice for supplying the town house, as it bore the travelling well. Then came the orange-red Dr Hogg, the largest of the late varieties, with pure white flesh and an intense flavour 'that remains long on the palate.'

Real devotees also sought out the Pine strawberries, which were descendants of the first hybrid and 'unquestionably allied' to the Chilean strawberry in Laxton's opinion. The flavour, ' rich and suggestive of the Pineapple' was probably at its most intense in the Scarlet Pine which, in the Reverend Radclyffe's opinion, was 'the highest flavoured and most pined sort that has been.' In the 1860s the Pine strawberry season commenced with the 'sprightly' Early Crimson Pine, followed by the 'exquisite' Enchantress, Scarlet Pine and Filbert Pine, and closed at the end of July with Frogmore Late Pine.[41]

The old, wild European species still retained a following, especially the Hautbois. It had a distinct, musky flavour, and was elected the best of all the varieties at Mr Knightley's famous strawberry picking party in Jane Austen's novel *Emma*.[42] Hautbois was the garden name for the musk strawberry, *Fragaria moschata*. It was a native of central Europe and was also known as the Bohemian Strawberry. Long cultivated

in England, it produced a larger, stronger plant than the native wild strawberry of the hedgerows, with larger berries. Several varieties had arisen and many Victorians considered it reached its finest expression in Rivers's Royal Hautbois. This, according to Dr Hogg, was 'the best variety of the Hautbois we have ever seen. It is the largest in size and the most abundant bearer, and the flavour is superior to any other of the Hautbois. The colour, like that of all other varieties, is partly purplish rose and partly pale yellowish; and the flavour as a friend remarked was "like Strawberries and cream".'[43]

Alpine strawberries were also a particular treat. These were a form of the common wild strawberry, *Fragaria vesca*, that had long ago been selected for its perpetual, or autumn, cropping habit. Grown in a south-facing border and given the benefit of a sunny autumn, the plants would furnish a plentiful supply of both red and white berries that were the 'most delicious strawberries grown', in Taylor's opinion.[44]

Whatever the variety, strawberries had to reach the table in perfect condition, and no fruit required more careful handling. The berries could not be pulled or crushed in any way for, as Robert Fish observed, if 'the surface was damaged in any degree a short period suffices to render them useless for table purposes.' He insisted 'on the fruit being picked with the footstalks to hold by, and sent to table in the basket in which they are gathered, or merely turned carefully into a suitable dish without any attempt at dressing them into cones or other shapes, which can only be done by handling every fruit separately. Artistic appearance in all such cases is gained at the expense of true delicacy and refinement.'[45] Having survived the journey to the table, they needed only the addition of sugar, Jersey cream and a glass of sauterne to provide the lightest and most exquisite conclusion to the meal.

Peaches and **Nectarines** were also valued as early fruits and for their continuing quality into the early autumn. Certain varieties responded well to forcing and, given the protection of glass, the main summer harvest as well as the earlier and later crops ripened with a good deal more certainty than on any south-facing wall. Grown in this way, a careful choice of at least a dozen varieties would produce fruit for seven months of the year and, even in Scotland, David Thomson could claim to have 'for years in succession gathered ripe peaches in the last week of April, and continued to do so till the last week of October.'[46]

The smooth-skinned nectarine was generally held to have the finer flavour of the two fruits, but the peach's buttery consistency was valued above the former's firmer and more fibrous flesh. The most favoured varieties were of the free-stone, rather than the cling-stone type, as the flesh fell away cleanly, allowing the diner to savour the fruit in neat, decorous slices. As with strawberries, perfection on the table depended upon the utmost care beforehand. At every stage, the fruit had to be handled with 'a great nicety of touch, the peach being very easily blemished when ripe.' It would not so much be picked as stroked off the branch, and then left in the fruit room to cool for six hours or so before being brought to the dining room.

The forced fruits would usually be ready in time for Easter, and set on the table with 'their crimson velvet glory enshrined in pale young vine leaves.' More would follow to keep the town house supplied for the duration of the Season and, by the time the family returned to the country in August, the main crop would be ready for the splendour of the summer and autumn entertainments. Peaches and nectarines would form part of the dessert at the August dinner parties in honour of the first grouse, grace the table when the partridge shooting began a month later, and still be on offer during the first weeks of October when the aristocracy took off in pursuit of pheasant.

At Longleat, Taylor grew Royal George, 'the sweetest of all peaches', and the dark red-cheeked Violette Hâtive nectarine, as his first crop. In his early house, neither of these ripened until mid-May but, as with strawberries, for the Longleat dining room 'flavour is of more importance here than earliness.'[47] Other favoured peach varieties included the 'peerless Bellegarde' which was 'deep red, striped with purple' with 'a rich and vinous flavour', and the 'first rate' Barrington, which could provide supplies for the London residence and, if further trees were grown in a cooler house, be ripe for the family's homecoming in August. Proprietors and gardeners also esteemed the 'sweet and very luscious' Noblesse. This was dappled with red and purple 'like a Pomeranian coach dog, very handsome and the richest of all peaches'. The season would be brought to a close by the late Walburton Admirable, which Thomson gathered 'till 24 October in a cool house'.[48]

Of the nectarines, the finest had long been held to be Elruge, an old variety known since the seventeenth century. This, however, was equalled if not surpassed by Stanwick, which had been raised in 1843 at one of the Duke of Northumberland's establishments and introduced commercially by Thomas Rivers. Stronger and more distinctive in flavour, it had flesh that was 'white, melting, rich, sugary and most delicious'. It lent itself to forcing, but also made a good summer variety.

Glass made for a certain crop but many southern gardeners, including Robson, Luckhurst, and Taylor, maintained that growing summer peaches and nectarines in the open air against a sunbaked wall, gave superior colour and quality. For this purpose, the new varieties being raised by Thomas Rivers for the commercial market were particularly useful. Rivers's aim was to persuade market gardeners to grow peaches, and although he did not entirely succeed in this – grapes being more profitable – the improved quality of his fruit, and the introduction of earlier and later ripening varieties, were just what these gardeners needed.

Luckhurst had all Rivers's new varieties on trial at Oldlands in Sussex and in 1875 recorded a succession of outdoor peaches which began with Early Beatrice in mid-July.[49] He sent up a dish of these daily until the second week of August when the 'rich and racy' Early Rivers took over, followed by the 'excellently flavoured Early York'. By this time, the first nectarine, Lord Napier, had started to colour. Rivers's new nectarines were large and well-flavoured, as well as better suited to the English climate. Lord Napier measured 'nearly 8 inches in circumference', and Victoria was 'pervaded with the flavour of a Stanwick with all the persistence of a subtle essence', but without the need for continual cossetting and a heated glasshouse to ripen it. His Pineapple nectarine, raised from the fine Pitmaston Orange, 'partook somewhat of the sprightliness of the pineapple', and was 'a very showy one for table'. The season was brought to a triumphant close by a peach, Rivers's Princess of Wales, which was large, 'primrose fleshed' and 'supreme at the end of September'.

Apricots were also traditional occupants of the walled fruit garden and few dessert fruits were as immediately evocative of their warm southern origins than the 'apricot shining in a sweet brightness of golden velvet.'[50] Prized as they were, however, good ripe apricots were not easily come by. Their season was very short, lasting only from late July to the end of August, and they did not respond to forcing. Despite Thomas Rivers's examples of trees under glass that were 'the picture of fertility', most gardeners still held that outside walls gave the best quality fruit, and the crop was consequently at the mercy of the British climate.

Linton's trees often obliged, however, and the Marquess of Exeter had '700 feet of south facing wall devoted to this esteemed fruit' at Burghley.[51] The old variety, Moor Park, was widely grown, and achieved 'great excellence' in some gardens. If protected from frost and well-ripened, the earlier Angoumois acquired a rusty brown flush, and the deep orange flesh 'charged with a fine aroma' that was much favoured. In the larger, late Peach apricot, Dr Hogg found not only a 'a very delicate, juicy and sugary' taste, but a 'rich and some what musky flavour'.

The elusive, perfect apricot might not often feature in the dessert, but **Figs** posed no such problem and could be made to produce two crops each year between spring and autumn. Many kitchen gardens had a fig tree in a warm corner, and there were often fig trees on the back wall of a vinery, but their splendid response to intensive methods led to whole houses being given over to them by the 1860s. They were widely held to be a particularly wholesome fruit, and the dessert provided the opportunity to celebrate figs in all their diversity.

They ranged through large and small fruited varieties, and those with dark or light coloured skins, and red and or opaline coloured flesh. Brown Turkey and Black Bourjassotte gave the greatest all-round satisfaction, with their deep red, stiff syrupy flesh, and both contrasted well in a dish with the pearly-fleshed White Marseilles, which was considered 'one of the most delicious in cultivation'.[52] There were also smaller

Figs would be forced for Easter.

varieties which many found irresistible. According to Dr Hogg, Oeil de Perdrix was 'dark chestnut or mahogany covered with a thin bloom', and flesh 'a sort of coppery colour, with a tinge of rose or salmon in it; juicy, tender and sweet'. Even more tempting was White Ischia, with skin so thin that 'the purple flesh shines through giving the fruit a brownish tinge' and, as grown at Petworth, 'even ladies can take [it] at a mouthful if they try – and they are fond of trying, so sugary sweet is this seductive Fig.'[53]

As with all other fruits, ripeness was all. A good fig, according to an old Spanish proverb quoted in the *Journal*, should have 'the eye of a widow and the cloak of a beggar'. In other words 'the tattered covering through which the flesh is seen is a good proof of excellence, and the weeping eye is desirable.'[54] At Putteridge Bury, whose owner Colonel Sowerby 'could manage a little basket of figs comfortably', Fish judged the moment was right for consumption when the fig 'was soft all over, cracked in three to six places and the rich juice oozing out of the cracks like so many honey drops.' Such perfection could only be experienced at the mansion. If figs had to travel to London then, as Fish observed, they had to be packed 'too unripe to let people know what a good Fig is.' In his view the only way 'if you wish to eat figs as luscious as they can be had in Italy' was to 'live near your Fig-tree.'[55]

EXOTIC NOVELTIES

As well as the accepted range of tropical and Mediterranean fruits that every self-respecting establishment had to produce, many kitchen gardens also managed to supply citrus fruits, bananas and passion fruit. A few others attempted rarities such as mangoes, guavas and mangosteens but these remained collectors' items and never became serious dessert fruits.

Lady Dorothy Nevill had such a collection in her tropical fruit-house at Dangstein in Sussex.[56] In it were 'planted Loquats, Mango, Guava, etc . . . and there were, besides the Nutmeg, and Pimento, Rose Apple (Eugenia Jambos) and various other rare and seldom-met-with fruits.' She was urgently trying to acquire a mangosteen as well, which was considered the most wonderful of them all. It was highly decorative, with camellia-like flowers, lychee-like flesh and a taste, it was claimed, worth a trip to Singapore. One enthusiast, who had succeeding in harvesting mangosteens, said it combined 'the flavour of the Pineapple, Grape, and Apricot, with one peculiarly its own'.[57]

The lesser novelties, on the other hand, were quite widely grown. **Bananas** and **Passion fruit**, were popular as conservatory plants but only fruited at those establishments where they were given the extra heat and space to do so. Of the bananas, *Musa cavendishii* or the Chinese banana, was the most compact growing species and the easiest to fruit. The first plant had arrived at Chatsworth in 1829, and Paxton's success in producing a crop in 1842 was soon being imitated at a number of establishments. In 1875, 'fine bunches ripened during the summer' in the tropical fruit house at Dalkeith, and 'are highly appreciated by the family.'[58] At the Earl of Durham's Lambton Castle, Robson reported 'bananas in plenty' ripening on the trees in 1873, and at Linton he himself had harvested a bunch of 136 fruits.[59] Bananas did not, however, earn themselves a lasting place in the dessert. Inelegant to eat and farinaceous in texture, they did not recommend themselves to the discerning diner.

Passion fruit was an altogether more interesting proposition. It appeared on the table at Drumlanrig in the early autumn, and its pleasing aroma and 'delicately flavoured jelly-like pulp' was also appreciated at Lambton Castle. Both establishments had a whole house devoted to passion fruit, and the plants, trained up and along the roof, bore a crop which hung down 'as thickly as in a well-managed Cucumber house, looking rich and good.'[60] Several species produced edible fruit. Of these, the giant granadilla, *Passiflora quadrangularis*, gave yellow fruit the size of a small melon, and this was considered to make a conserve 'of pleasing quality', while the more common and easier to fruit was the smaller, purple sweet-cup, *P. edulis*. According to the Royal gardener, Owen Thomas, the way to eat the sweet-cup was 'like a boiled egg – that is cut off the top and consume the contents with a spoon, adding a few drops of port wine instead of salt.'[61]

Citrus trees, like the first passion flower, had reached England by the seventeenth century, and were grown primarily for perfume and decoration, rather than for their fruit.[62] **Orange** trees adorned formal gardens during the summer months and, after these had disappeared, continued to be enjoyed throughout the year in specially constructed orangeries. Both the bitter Seville orange with its more strongly scented flowers, and the sweet orange were grown, but as no one wished to strip the trees of their golden baubles, assuming they had ripened at all, there was neither the quantity nor quality to make home-grown oranges available to the kitchens or dining room. Imported fruit began to arrive in England in the 1660s from the orange groves of Spain and Portugal, but remained an expensive luxury until the nineteenth century.

Then, as transport everywhere improved, oranges appeared in ever-increasing quantities, especially after the import duty was lifted in 1861, and British consumption soared to reach 700 million fruits annually by 1878.[63]

Few of these, however, found their way into the dining rooms of upper-class establishments. It was not just that imported oranges were vastly inferior, in Thomas Rivers's opinion, to what could be grown under glass using modern skills and technology, but that the fruit itself had considerable drawbacks. Attractive though oranges were, their strong flavour and acidity was ruinous to the appreciation of fine wine, and they were not at all easy to eat politely. Rivers himself was an enthusiast and had a collection of varieties and some 700 trees growing in pots at his nursery, but although many establishments would grow some citrus fruits for the winter dessert few, if any, went so far as devoting a whole house to them.

The most popular were the **Mandarin** and **Tangerine**, which had been introduced from China in the early nineteenth century. For the gardener they had the great advantage of making smaller trees which fruited after a relatively short time, in contrast to the true orange which could take up to 12 years. For the dessert, they not only looked charming, but peeled and divided easily. In Rivers's view the sweet tangerine took the palm in every respect. 'When freshly gathered no fruit could be more gratifying or delightful, as its aroma is so delicious, and its juice so abundant.' Homegrown, it also satisfied the essential country house criterion of surpassing anything commercially available by 'offering a pleasing contrast to those imported from Lisbon in November and December, the flesh of which is generally shrunk from the rind instead of being ready to burst, as in the case with those picked from the tree.'[64] All homegrown tangerines were thus placed on the table with some leaves and stalk 'so that they may be readily distinguished from foreign fruit', and most gardeners tried to have tangerines in the great Christmas display.

TRADITIONAL FAVOURITES

The magnificence of the dessert may have depended primarily on the splendours of the hothouse, but the traditional, hardy fruits remained indispensable. Cherries, plums and soft fruits would be called upon for the summer dessert, and apples and pears more than made up for their lack of exoticism in ease of cultivation and length of season. Between them, they could provide a succession of varieties throughout the entire period of the family's residence in the country, which began in August and lasted until late spring.

Pears were the most prized. 'Good melting pears were always in demand throughout the winter,' asserted Luckhurst and 'combined a range of subtle qualities which the educated palate so much delights in.' In the best varieties the melting, juicy flesh had a 'rich flavour and tempting aroma, full and pronounced in some, and ranging through many degrees of delicacy in others'.[65] The soft, yielding texture must also have been very appealing to those accustomed to grapes and forced strawberries, and mercifully easy on the digestion.

There were numerous varieties in cultivation, and most places maintained a substantial collection to ensure continuity, diversity and protection against a bad year. Nuneham Park, in Oxfordshire, had 120 varieties and Luckhurst, when making his new kitchen garden in Sussex during the 1870s, planted 70 varieties.[66] The first early summer varieties such as the prettily flushed Doyenné d'Été and Jargonelle were refreshingly sweet and ready for the family's arrival at the end of July, but distinguished flavour was the prerogative of the later maturing varieties, whose ranks were greatly expanded by the efforts of the nineteenth-century fruit men.[67] The *crème de la crème* of pears combined this distinctiveness of flavour with flesh that was 'fondant' or buttery, and bore not the slightest trace of grit in its make-up.

The season began in earnest in September with the new Williams's Bon Chrêtien, which had a powerful, musky aroma. Then came Fondante d'Automne, another new variety, which made 'one of our best October pears' in Luckhurst's experience. The new Beurré Superfin was as good or even better, as was the crimson-flushed Louise Bonne of Jersey. This had been raised in about 1788 at Avranches, on the coast of Normandy, and subsequently taken up by the Jersey fruit growers. It had a 'rich sugary and brisk vinous flavour'. Then came Thompson's, a variety that honoured the Royal Horticultural Society's first pomologist, Robert Thompson. Ready by November, it was covered in warm russet, highly perfumed, and so full of juice that it must have been an embarrassment at any decorous dining-table.

It was, however, in Doyenné du Comice that epicures found the perfect pear, and mere prose was scarcely able to convey its charms. First fruited in 1849, at Anger on the banks of the Loire, it was introduced to England in 1858 and swiftly found a place in most collections. Ready to eat by November, it possessed a yellowish-white buttery flesh that Hogg described as 'rich, sweet and delicately perfumed with a sort of cinnamon flavour'.

The season continued with the tender, scented Glou Morçeau which was ready by Christmas, and Winter Nélis, which, if given a warm wall, could earn the highest praise: 'yellowish flesh, sugary, vinous, a fine aroma'. The richly perfumed Joséphine de Malines was hardier and kept until March or longer, providing the dessert with high quality fruit through the bleakest months. It had red-tinged flesh with 'a high rose water aroma'. For spring there was Easter Beurré, the name reflecting its buttery flesh, which in a good year could be finely flavoured, with a touch of musk.

Pears were not, however, the easiest fruits to grow well. They needed warm walls and, in the north, even protection under glass, if late spring frost and sunless summers were not to spell disaster. They also had to be stored carefully, and telling when the right moment for eating had been reached was a difficult judgement. Pears are fickle fruits whose well-coloured cheeks may conceal 'sleepy' and decaying centres. In order to avoid the calamity of a diner's knife cutting into an unsound pear, gardeners had to rely on experience and meticulous records. Each year, the quirks, ripening and keeping qualities of each variety would be noted in the fruit book, to provide guidance for the next. Good colour was one of the surest signs, and a slight softening around the stalk usually meant the time had come to send them in for dinner. They would be put on the table with the chill of the fruit room still upon them, and by the time the dessert was served, would have reached just the right temperature for the melting flesh to release the distinctive aroma in all its fullness.

More reliable a proposition than the pear was the **Apple**. It brought brighter colours to the dessert and, in the estimation of epicures in the 1890s, could yield the greatest range of flavours of any fruit. At its best in the English climate, it had been the staple fruit of the dessert and of commercial growers for centuries, and the number of varieties available was correspondingly large. Dr Hogg documented in detail over 900 worthy of cultivation in Britain in his *Fruit Manual*, and more than 1,500 varieties went on display in 1883 at the historic Apple Congress, which drew exhibits from as far away as Sweden and Canada.[68]

The essential features of a good dessert apple, if not already well-known, had been laid down by Loudon in 1824. He wrote that varieties for the table 'are characterised by a firm juicy pulp, elevated, poignant flavor, regular form and beautiful coloring.'[69] Large size was not called for as it would have been unseemly to share a fruit over dinner. As apples gradually came to occupy the position of a premier dessert fruit at many establishments towards the end of the century, the merits of different varieties, regions and years would be discussed as seriously and enthusiastically as the the different châteaux and vintages of clarets. Were the Ribstons up to scratch? Strong and aromatic, but not too sweet? Had the Blenheims, sent down from Oxford for the occasion, the right crumbly texture and good nutty taste? And was this the true old Golden Pippin with that characteristic tang enthusiasts remembered from their youth?[70]

Many estates had collections of well over a 100 varieties,[71] and at such establishments a new selection could be offered for dessert every month from August until the end of April, or even May. The season began at the end of July with crisp, brisk Jenettings and drew to its close with another ancient variety, the Nonpareil, or one of its new seedlings. In between came many more of the recent additions to the fruit lists. There was Irish Peach which ripened in August and, eaten straight from the tree, possessed 'all the rich flavour of some of the winter varieties with the abundant and refreshing juice of the summer fruits'. It was an exception to the rule that there were no good apples until the autumn, and by the middle of the century had become indispensable to any collection. So, too, did Kerry Pippin, which ripened in September and combined a rich flavour with an attractive tortoiseshell-flushed cheek. Pine Golden Pippin and Cornish Gilliflower, were also valuable additions. Ready in October, Pine Golden Pippin hinted of pineapple, while the later maturing Cornish Gilliflower had, by December, developed a delicate flowery flavour that no one wanted to miss. After Christmas came a Gloucestershire variety, Ashmead's Kernel, to surpass its parent the Nonpareil, with a 'more sugary juice' but retaining all its strong, sweet-sharp flavour. This was also found in the new Sturmer Pippin which, provided it had received plenty of autumn sunshine, would be well-flavoured and ready to eat by February. It could last long after the old Nonpareil had finished, and even until May or June. At this late period, 'when the other favourite varieties are past', the Sturmer's crisp refreshing taste must have been a welcome contrast to the soft flesh of the forced grapes and strawberries.

The most important of the new varieties was Cox's Orange Pippin. This was descended from the Ribston Pippin and, like its distinguished parent, was at its best from late October to Christmas. It had the same intensity and complexity of flavour but was sweeter, with a softer flesh in which people were to discern hints of pears, spice and nuts. The more austere Ribston was still preferred by many connoisseurs as an accompaniment to claret, but by the 1860s, the Cox was being planted in gardens all over Britain. Its more delicate, richer flavour and regular shape fitted admirably with the dessert's requirements, and it was swiftly proclaimed one of the finest apples ever raised. By the 1870s, the equally famous Worcester Pearmain had also made its appearance. Sweet, with a strawberry-like flavour, and completely flushed in scarlet, it soon became highly prized in the dining room.

Many varieties were, like Worcesters, particularly valued for the bright colour they brought to the dessert. The sequence began in August with the crimson Devonshire Quarrenden, which also had 'cool refreshing vinous juice'. To harmonize with the autumn chrysanthemums and winter pelargoniums, there was bright red Fearn's Pippin and the prettily striped little Margil, which almost matched Ribston for flavour and was 'a better size for the dessert'. For Christmas, when the table was decked with evergreens and berries, the tiny red Api apple made a sweet and perfumed, as well as traditional, addition to the dessert, and from January to March, the displays of late grapes and pears were enlivened by the vermillion-cheeked Court Pendû Plat.

For large displays of fruit on particularly grand occasions, gardeners might also employ well-coloured culinary apples such as Lady Henniker. This was used by John Perkins on its home ground of Thornham Hall in Suffolk 'when large and handsome dishes of mixed fruit are required. Its appearance by lamplight is most telling.' For the buffet parties which continued throughout the fox-hunting season, the striking scarlet and gold colouring developed by the very late keeping Norfolk Beefing could also be employed to good effect.

None of the other hardy fruits could match apples and pears for variety and length of season. **Plums**, however, could be a welcome feature of the dessert from late July until the end of October. Good-flavoured plums were usually called gages, and were nearly all descended from the old greengage, which in France is known as Reine Claude.[72] Allowed to hang on the trees until perfectly ripe, gages could provide devotees with a succession of gilded and crimson mottled fruits, with juicy, rich and honied flesh, and a stone that fell away with obliging ease.

The indefatigable Rivers had raised an Early Transparent, or Early Apricot Gage. Then there was Oullins Golden Gage, the American variety Denniston's Superb, Golden Esperen and Bryanston Gage. The finest of all was Transparent Gage, with its almost translucent flesh, which ripened in early September, and the season closed with Reine Claude de Bavay in October. It did, however, require a good summer to produce really sweet fruit and avoid the digestive catastrophe of an unripe plum. In the north, gages were always grown against a warm wall, or even under glass.

Of the other hardy fruits, most of the **Cherries** and **Raspberries** were over before the family returned to the country, although there might still be late ripening varieties for a dish or two in August. Cherries could be forced, but peaches and grapes had first claim on the glasshouse space, and at most places they remained an outdoor crop. Perfectly ripe cherries, like raspberries, were poor travellers and families who spent the Season in London had, therefore, to be content with enjoying them in puddings, but for those who took little part in metropolitan life, they were one of the treats of early summer.

The best varieties of cherries would often be trained against a wall, which made it easier to net them against birds and helped ripen them to perfection. The Duke cherries were the epicure's first choice with their tender, rich flesh and thin, melting skins.[73] Their season began in June with the old May Duke, and a series of black and red Dukes followed throughout July. Victorian hybridists had applied their energies to cherries, too, and May Duke would be followed by a number of well-flavoured new varieties such as Early Rivers. This large black cherry was soft and sweet by the middle of June. Knight's 'rich and delicious' Waterloo, which ripened in early July was the best black cherry of all, in many people's estimation, while the melting, juicy Frogmore Bigarreau, which was raised by the Royal gardener Thomas Ingram in 1864, was soon esteemed as the best early white cherry.

Gooseberries, although regarded as a much humbler fruit, were also a welcome addition to the dessert at many establishments.[74] Displayed in glass bowls, the crimson, green, white and yellow fruits had a glowing translucence which made them look particularly inviting. The hundreds of different varieties owed their existence to the enthusiasm of Midlands factory workers who bred them as a hobby during the early part of the century. Although they tended to concentrate on size, their experiments also yielded some interesting experiences for the connoisseur. Early, sweet Green Gascoigne, for example, was particularly well thought of and so, too, was pure white Snowdrop. This, Hogg claimed to be 'one of the most beautiful gooseberries grown', and in the perfectly round, bright orange Catherina, he found a 'first-rate' flavour. Later in the season, Red Champagne, which was 'very rich, vinous and sweet' might complement the 'sugary', Pitmaston Greengage.

Similarly decorative was the 'beautiful table dish', which 'could be made up by red and white currants.' They looked like jewels glinting in the candle-light but, unlike the gooseberries, would not usually be eaten.

To complete the autumn dessert's magnificent display of fresh fruit, there might also be a selection of **Nuts**. These had been considered an appropriate way to conclude a meal since ancient times and had appeared on English dining tables for centuries.

Dessert gooseberries were valued for their glowing fruits and vinous flavour.

Robson had his own nuttery to provide for the dessert, and was something of an expert on the whole subject.[75] In his experience, the Lambert Filbert, or Kentish Cob, was the best, producing 'large full kernels'. This was a new variety introduced in about 1830 and its heavy crops and good keeping properties had soon ousted most of the older filberts. Red-skinned Filbert was, however, still 'by many esteemed the finest Nut grown, and for a month or more after gathering is unquestionably so.' It also brought a welcome contrast of colour to the selection, which might also include the new Cosford nut and the Frizzled Filbert. Cosfords had the novelty of a very thin shell that could easily be cracked between finger and thumb, and the Frizzled Filbert had an unmistakeable fringed husk. This, recorded Robson, had 'its admirers and the nut is also good.'

Hazel nuts were always presented with their decorative husks intact and their removal, followed by the skilful manipulation of the crackers, and the extraction of the nuts from their shells, was all part of the leisurely ritual of the nineteenth-century dessert. A few bletted medlars could also provide an interesting item to contemplate with the port, and round off this rich and varied ceremony of good food and good conversation.

7

Producing the Plenty

'Monsieur le Chef', observed Taylor, 'expects his demands for Concombre, Tomate etc. to be supplied as easily as his order to Messrs Barto Valle for macaroni,' and, as far as possible, this was the illusion that the head gardener sustained. Whatever the season, and come glut or shortage, five guests or fifty, he fulfilled whatever orders came down from the kitchen. His ability to do so depended on superlative husbandry, an ever widening range of fruit and vegetable varieties, and the ingenuity with which he fought the British climate. His battleground, and the horticultural stronghold from which he directed operations in every corner of the pleasure ground, was the walled kitchen garden.

This was often to be found behind the mansion, and to one side, carefully screened by trees and shrubs and convenient both for supplies of manure from the stables and delivery of produce to the mansion. Some, however, like those at Longleat and Burghley, had been banished from the vicinity of the house in the course of eighteenth-century landscaping, and were half a mile away, or even more.

The garden consisted of a main enclosure of several acres, surrounded by walls between 10 and 16 feet high.[1] These afforded shelter, and also created a series of useful microclimates. Sun-baked, south-facing walls, for example, provided the warmth necessary to ripen tender fruits, while the wide borders running below them could be used for hastening crops such as early strawberries, peas and potatoes. A shady northern aspect, on the other hand, would delay ripening for as long as possible. Judicious use of these differences enabled gardeners to extend a crop's season as far as possible in both directions, and maintain supplies to the kitchen without a break. Wall borders, particularly the west- and east-facing, were also used for cut flowers, and for the violets and lilies of the valley which would be dug up in the autumn and moved under glass for forcing in relays throughout the winter.

At Nuneham Park, in Oxfordshire, which was claimed to have one of the finest kitchen gardens in the country, a visitor in late September 1867 found strawberries planted in south- west- and north-facing borders in order to provide a succession of ripe fruit over an extended period of about three months instead of the usual six weeks.[2] French beans had cropped in a south-facing border during the summer, which now held a bed of 'young Intermediate Carrots' ready for the table. Further down this border were onions and more carrots, but this crop had 'grown too large' and 'would go to the lodge keepers and others in the park whom Mr Stewart [the head gardener] has to supply with vegetables.' In readiness for the autumn there was a large area of parsley. Mr Stewart, having once been 'caught napping in the matter of Parsley', and so chastened by 'the wiggings I had from the cook' had vowed he would 'never more remain minus that indispensable herb for a single hour.' A north-facing border held spring bedding plants – pansies and polyanthus – which were destined for the flower garden.

In southern England, peaches, figs and apricots would be trained against south-facing walls, while pears and gages would often be given a westerly aspect, which was the next best position. The east wall might be used for early plums or cherries, while the north wall, which was not generally used for dessert fruit, might bear a fan-trained specimen of the culinary Morello cherry and trained currant bushes.

Much of the main south-facing wall would, however, be taken up by a range of lean-to glasshouses. These took maximum advantage of the sun, and could be used to manipulate the climate still further. With the addition of more, or less, heating and ventilation, the gardener could reproduce in these almost any growing conditions, from those of a Mediterranean orchard to the tropics of Central America.

The borders and the glasshouses were separated from the main ground in the centre of the enclosure by a perimeter path wide enough to accommodate heavily laden barrows and carts, and to allow groups of visitors to stroll at their ease. Further paths divided the open ground into four or more sections – always called quarters – depending upon the area. Drumlanrig's eight acres, for example, were divided up into eight quarters. In some gardens there were also internal walls providing more space for tender fruit and successions of produce. Nuneham was divided across the centre by a single east-west wall, while the Marquess of Exeter's 14-acre kitchen garden at Burghley had no less than six internal walls.[3]

Asparagus would take up at least half an acre of this 'open' ground, and often more, while the celery patch, which could contain as many as 2,000 plants, would also occupy a large area. Peas, which were needed continuously from June to October, were similarly conspicuous. There would also be substantial plots of all the usual vegetables and salad leaves, while soft fruit might have as much as a whole quarter to itself. At Drumlanrig, an acre was given over just to strawberries,[4] while raspberries, currants and gooseberries occupied further space in a shadier quarter of the garden.

The walled garden was by no means the full extent of the kitchen garden complex. Considerable areas outside, but adjacent to the walls, would also be cultivated. These 'slips', as they were known, often accommodated the coarser or more space-consuming vegetables, such as main crop potatoes. At Nuneham, for example, the south slip contained 'a repertory of vegetable produce', including beetroot, seakale and parsnips, while in the 'broad eastern slip' there were turnips and large plots of Jerusalem and globe artichokes.

The slips could also be used for fruit, flowers and herbs – as at Linton – and even as nurseries for shrubs and trees being grown for the estate. The south slip at Trentham Park, for example, took the form of a reserve flower garden, which was used to provide stock plants for cuttings, replacement specimens for the parterre, and cut flowers for the house.[5] Nuneham also had an apple orchard and filbert plantation in the eastern slip, while an extra area beyond the southern slip was sheltered by a holly hedge, and acted as a nursery for conifers, forest trees and thorn for hedging. At many establishments, there were buildings to the west and north but, if not, a northern slip could be useful for soft fruit. At Longleat this area was netted over to make a 'gooseberry house', and more gooseberries, as well as currants and cherries were grown against the wall.[6]

Large numbers of pits, frames and further glasshouses would also be clustered outside the walls, while the back of the wall supporting the great glass range would be taken up with boiler rooms, offices and sheds. These would include fruit and flower rooms, a shed for trimming and washing the vegetables before they were sent up to the kitchen, and a room for packing the hampers which were sent up to the family's house in London at least once a week during the Season. There would also be fruit stores, stores for keeping root vegetables through the winter, and the warm dark cells where mushrooms were grown, and the seakale, chicory and rhubarb forced and blanched. Here, too, were the potting sheds, and bothy where the young gardeners lived. Close to the warmth of the boiler room, and convenient for the glasshouses which needed attention last thing at night, this usually consisted of sleeping quarters and a mess room. The head gardener's own house – a substantial residence befitting his status – would be built on to or close to the walled garden.

The slips and outer areas also harboured the more basic necessities of the kitchen garden – the dung and compost heaps, garden refuse which was waiting to be burnt, and, often, some means of drawing or collecting water. Nuneham was fortunate in having a horse-powered pump in the east slip which raised water from a pool in the park and distributed it to the grounds including a 'large deep round tank in one of the kitchen garden quarters'. Many places had, like Putteridge Bury, to make do with filling a water barrel at some distant point and then dragging it 100 yards or more to where it was needed, 'a severe undertaking, . . . making a man glad of other work when he had half a day of it.' Fish's dream was to have a 'cistern at a great height above the level of the garden, and a good supply of pipes, with taps and a hose to screw on, to enable a man to sprinkle water or deluge the ground without any more labour than holding and clenching the hose distributor.'[7]

There would also be the manure, and various piles and barrels of other nourishing concoctions. Supplies of manure would come from the stables, poultry houses and cow sheds, and there would be a manure tank close by to collect the drainings. This, diluted with water, provided liquid feed for all the glasshouse crops and pot plants. Should it run dry, the gardener might resort to a peck of sheep dung in 40 gallons of water for the forced fruit and vegetables, while others swore by guano water, made from imported Peruvian guano, the dried excreta of sea birds. A bag of soot in the bottom of a barrel was another standby. Soot, being rich in ammonia, when made into a liquid feed the colour of tea, was reputed to be suitable for everything from strawberries to mignonette.[8]

Stacks of turf, breaking down into fine loam for the potting shed, would occupy another corner, while several heaps of garden refuse would await their different fates.[9] One would be on its way to making a compost 'only inferior to the best half decomposed farmyard manure', while another, consisting of prunings and the roots of pernicious weeds such as convolvulus and thistle, would receive 'the firey treatment' to provide burnt earth and ashes for surface dressing. Nothing was wasted, and anything woody 'from old pea stakes to shoots as thick as your wrist' would end up on a third refuse heap to make charcoal for keeping the pots and flower vases sweet.

The extent of the whole kitchen garden complex depended upon the numbers being catered for. At Linton, the household – family and indoor servants – numbered between 25 and 30, while at Longleat it was nearer 60.[10] In addition, there were house guests and their servants to feed, often for a week or more at a time, and a succession of dinner and supper guests to provide for. One acre was reckoned to feed about 16 people, so Linton had two acres within its walls, Longleat had five, and both had almost as much again outside the walls. At large and sociable Belvoir, the enclosed area extended to 15 acres. The nature of the social calendar also meant that the demand for out of season luxuries was high, so the acreage under glass was an even keener reflection of an owner's social commitments. Taylor claimed half an acre of glasshouses,[11] while the Crawshay family at Cyfarthfa Castle in the less clement Rhondda Valley, probably had twice that amount. Colder Scottish gardens, such as those of Drumlanrig and Dalkeith, would have even more, as all but the hardiest fruit had to be grown under glass and forcing would go on for several weeks longer than in the south.

KINGDOMS OF GLASS

It was under glass that the Victorian head gardener made his ultimate conquest of Nature. Here he could grow almost anything, from any corner of the globe, and in defiance of its natural season. Cheap glass and large panes meant that glasshouses were lighter and more spacious than ever before, while modern heating arrangements rendered the British climate little more than an expensive inconvenience.

During the eighteenth century, the gardener had had to rely on the warming effects of a network of flues built into the solid walls of the glasshouse, which drew their heat from strategically positioned stoves and fireplaces. This was neither a reliable nor easily controlled form of heating, and often had to be supplemented with pans of glowing charcoal. Heating by steam circulating in pipes did not turn out to be a complete success either. It was not until the introduction of systems based on the circulation of hot water that gardeners had any real hope of achieving efficient, even and adjustable heating temperatures. Good coal-fired boilers were reaching the market by the 1830s and 1840s,[12] and from then onwards glasshouses could be warmed by runs of cast iron hot water pipes, with efficiency improving by the decade.

Around the mid-nineteenth century, for example, Drumlanrig was using 40 stoves to heat a series of ranges, and 'each house had a fire and chimney to itself. When these were all lighted, the place resembled a small village, the consumption of coal was enormous, and the smoke and dirt quite equal to it.' By the 1870s it took only four boilers to heat the same area, and these were housed in a 'subterranean chamber, the smoke being conducted to a shaft half a mile away among the tree clad hills.'[13]

Appliances such as these stayed in overnight and could supply heat rapidly if the

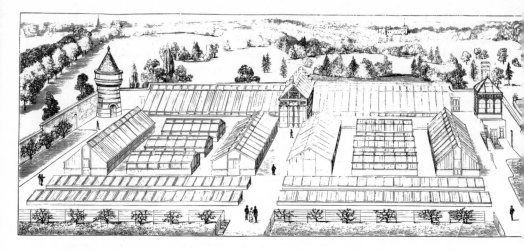

The village of glass constructed at Buchan Hill, Sussex, in 1885. The lean-to range consists of a central conservatory flanked by vineries and peach houses. There are span roofed houses for roses, stove plants, and late vines, and pits for pineapples, melons, cucumbers and forced vegetables.

weather should take a turn for the worse. A system of stopcocks and valves allowed the gardener to raise or lower the temperature relatively easily, and to keep the different compartments or 'houses' in a range, warmer or cooler as required. With troughs of water evaporating over the hot water pipes to provide the right humidity, and generous ventilation at the top and sides of the glasshouses, he had the main atmospheric variables at his command for the first time. He could do everything from just keeping the frost off the pear blossom to growing pineapples and tropical flowers.

Taylor's glass kingdom, 'in proportions that are expected in an establishment the size of Longleat', comprised not only the range which was some 400 feet long in the five-acre walled garden, but also, in an upper garden, three 'very commodious and useful' ranges each 100 feet by 18 feet, and a huge new vinery.[14] The first range, which also contained a vinery, as well as peach and fig houses, was an old structure, probably a lean-to, built against a south-facing wall. Such houses caught the full force of the midday sun and, being narrow, were the easiest to heat in winter, and often used for forcing. They were, however, poorly ventilated and not as light or as easy to manage as a half- or three quarter-span house, which was still a lean-to but had extra glass in the form of a pitched roof overhead. Taylor's three new ranges were constructed in this way, and included a cucumber house, a house containing strawberries and tea roses and several plant houses.

The gardener's ultimate glasshouse was a full-span structure, free standing and all glass. This was the lightest and most spacious of all but correspondingly the most expensive to heat. It was, however, ideal for crops that did not require forcing or tropical temperatures and Taylor's new vinery, which was pronounced the finest of its kind in the kingdom, apart from the Royal Horticultural Society's vinery at Chiswick, was a celebrated example.

All this glass gave the gardener enormous power, but the cost, in all senses, was high. The amounts of labour and coal required were prodigious. In 1864, for example, even Linton's relatively modest glasshouse ranges consumed 28 tons of coal costing 24 shillings a ton, while their total fuel bill was a fraction of Rangemore's, the Burton-on-Trent seat of the brewery magnate, Bass, where 40 glasshouses containing 3½ miles of hot water pipes fed by three boilers cost £700 a year to run.[15] In addition, tending the fires amounted to a full-time occupation for one of the garden lads, while all the watering, ventilation, insect chasing, pollination and general fussing over that the delicate occupants required could absorb limitless quantities of time and effort.

These glass palaces were not, however, the limit of the gardener's controlled environments. He also had row upon row of pits and frames. A pit, the larger of the two, functioned rather like a small sunken glasshouse. It had brick sides and was covered by a glass roof. Traditionally, the bottom heat for the beds inside was provided by fermenting manure and oak leaves, while the whole structure was also warmed by a jacket of fermenting manure. Once hot water heating became available, however, pipes took over wherever resources allowed. In a small pit, the gardener had to open the glass sashes in the 'roof' to tend the plants inside, but a large pit could be deep enough to have a central path flanked by beds on either side. They were much more economical to build and heat than glasshouses, but could take only low-growing plants such as pot vines, cucumbers, or forced vegetables. At Drumlanrig, the yard behind the walled garden contained pits for melons and cucumbers amongst other things, and at Blenheim Palace 'a number of useful pits, [were] used for growing Pines, Strawberries and for vegetable forcing.'[16]

Frames were smaller versions of pits and not necessarily heated. They could also be temporary affairs, made of wood, and easily moved on to freshly prepared hotbeds. In the spring they would be used for forcing vegetables, and then for hardening off the bedding plants before they were planted out in the parterre. During the summer they housed pots of bulbs such as amaryllis and tuberoses, and in winter sheltered lettuce and endive. In the autumn, pots of strawberry plants were brought into the shelter of frames until the time came to move them into the forcing house. Drumlanrig had a whole acre of frames, while at Linton, there was a double row of frames, 140 feet long, running from east to west across the walled garden.[17]

PINEAPPLES IN PROFUSION

Among the gardener's greatest triumphs over the British climate was the production of luxury fruit for the dessert, and at most establishments, supplying ripe pineapples throughout the year was the most exacting task of all. It took nearly two years to grow a pineappple plant from sucker to fruit and, as one batch of plants would provide fruit for cutting for about three months of the year, there had to be four separate batches in progress at any one time.[18] At Drumlanrig, where Thomson harvested 200 ripe pineapples a year, there was a long pit in the yard outside the walled garden for rooting and growing on the suckers, and two large stove pineries, each about 100 feet long to which the mature plants were moved to fruit.[19] At Cyfarthfa Castle, where a stock of some 1,500 pineapples was kept up during the 1870s, there were nine succession pits and four pine-stoves, each as large as a vinery.[20]

As pineapples required the tropical temperatures of Central America, the amount of coal needed to produce them was enormous. It was also recommended that pineapples were kept separate from all other plants to avoid picking up pests as eradication was difficult. As a result, pineries usually served a single purpose and stood in splendid isolation, although at some establishments they were also used for forcing French beans and, as at Bicton in the 1870s, for growing ginger. If the feared white scale or mealy bug did appear desperate remedies were called for. Plants had to be dipped in water at 130°F, or an equally hot solution containing soft soap, sulphur, camphor and turpentine, which just showed 'how very desirable it is to avoid getting a breed of them on pines.'

Throughout their production cycle the plants were entirely surrounded by a warm humid atmosphere. They were usually grown in pots, which were plunged up to their rims in moist fermenting tanner's bark. This would fill the propagation and succession pits and also the deep beds or pits in the centre of the lighter fruiting houses. It not only warmed the roots, but gave off ammonia which was said to deter pests, and bathed the foliage in liquid feed. This method was considered second to none for producing high quality, clean, juicy fruit. Such was the labour involved in freshening the tan in severe weather, however, and the degree of watchfulness required to control the heat, that many places turned over with relief to hot water pipes instead.

Each cycle began with taking suckers from mature plants after they had fruited. These would then be rooted in pots. As they grew, they were moved on into larger pots and, in a year or 18 months, would be mature plants, which could be induced to yield ripe fruit six months later.[21] To have ripe pineapples in June, for example, a batch of mature plants would be moved into the fruiting house in January and started into active growth. Another batch would be started a month later, so as to extend the period of ripening, in this case until October.

Temperatures would be raised to 85°F in the pit, and the fruiting house temperature kept at 70°F by day, and never lower than 60°F at night. The paths would be sprinkled with tepid water two or three times a day to increase the humidity, and the plants would be stimulated by the application of warm, weak, guano water, or a similar brew made of sheep or deer dung. Thomson also liked to add a little of this solution to the evaporating pans once or twice a week. 'I find it gives that fine dark green hue and thickness of texture so desirable to see in pines.'

By the end of February the first batch would be showing fruit. The temperature would be pushed up to a minimum of 75°F, and the generous watering continued. The fruits swelled rapidly, and as the weather improved in May, which was 'the very best month for swelling pines', began to colour. By June they were ready for cutting and despatching to the London house. If too many pineapples started to ripen at once, some could be held back in a cooler vinery. This slowed them down, but they remained 'excellent in flavour', and in this way the season could be extended still further. In the meantime another batch would have been started in June to provide pineapples up to Christmas, and another in September to give fruit to Easter. A new generation of suckers would also have been taken during August and September, to start a new cycle. Even Thomson, however, confessed that it was difficult to produce pineapples in the depths of winter and have good ripe fruit in March and April.

FRUIT FOR ALL SEASONS

After pineapples, which not everyone attempted, the gardener's greatest challenge to the weather was supplying grapes all year round, and bringing peaches, nectarines, figs and strawberries to the table as early in the year as possible. Glasshouses enabled him to persuade his tender charges that spring arrived in January or February, and come the New Year, forcing would begin with a vengeance.

In preparation for this *tour de force*, the fruit houses would all have been cleaned and disinfected while the trees were dormant.[22] Any house which required fumigation would either be subjected to the fumes of half a pound of tobacco burning slowly over a small pot of glowing charcoal in the centre of the house, or to the exhalations from a bushel of laurel leaves left to smoulder overnight. This was a considerably cheaper alternative and worked particularly well if all the chinks in the house were sealed by a blanket of snow. Walls and woodwork in all the houses would be given a coat of whitewash made up of hot lime and a little sulphur. At forcing temperatures,

The Pine-stove at Chatsworth in June 1887. Dozens of Queens are ready for cutting and sending up to the Duke's London residence.

this would emit small amounts of sulphurous fumes which helped keep the fungi and mites at bay. Some gardeners also painted their trees and vines with a paste made of 'two parts flowers of sulphur, two parts soot, one part soft soap and two parts clay, reduced with water to the consistency of a thick paint' to destroy any remaining pests.

Once the borders had been top dressed with well-rotted manure, all was in readiness. The first batch of strawberries would be moved in from the frames, and at the end of December or earlier the heating would be turned up, the paths kept sprayed and, encouraged by the warm moist atmosphere, new growth would begin. Now was the critical time for the gardener. The hours of daylight were few and sunshine was in short supply. Outside there could be frost and even snow on the ground. Stretching the technology at his disposal to the limit, he had to nurture the new growth into strong and precocious maturity.

Taylor kept a detailed dairy and during 1875 records that on 22nd January, after a little frost, 'We have actually had a whole day's sunshine, a blessing not to be lightly esteemed. I was a little timid in the morning, anxious to make the most of every ray of light, but half afraid that tender Vine leaves which had never seen real daylight before, would not bear such an abundance of it. Peaches, too, with flowers fully expanded under adverse circumstances, would they bear it? Cucumbers with strong vigorous shoots, but with scarcely so dark a green colour as they should have, and some of the little fruit damping at the end, barely keeping pace with the daily demand for salad, and affording none for culinary purposes, if they could be induced to stand three or four hours of this heavenly sunshine would never look back again. Strawberries with their crowns just opening, Roses with shoots an inch long and just coming into leaf, Asparagus is *Asperge blanche* when we would rather have it *Asperge verte*. Everything, excepting, perhaps, French Beans, shows a want of daylight.' [23]

His main concern was to keep control over the humidity and temperature in the houses to maintain a genial atmosphere. The sun would overheat the houses and harm the tender growth if he did not adjust the ventilation and turn down the heating, but this could only be done very gradually. Too sudden a drop in temperature would cause condensation, and rot the flowers and tiny fruit. 'Fortunately,' Taylor's entry continues, his round at sunrise revealed 'no house with a higher temperature than $57°$ . . . Drops of moisture hang like beads round the edges of the leaves, and when the sun shines through the roof it feels inside the houses as nearly like a fine morning in May as anything I can imagine.'

As soon as the temperature began to rise, it was time to start opening the ventilators as swiftly as possible. 'There is not time to stop long in a place; there is much running backward and forward, just putting the least bit of air on one house and then running on to the next. There is not even time to look at the thermometers, temperature now is immaterial. The all-absorbing question is, will the foliage, which is comparatively thin in texture and short of chlorophyll bear the sunlight?'

The fresh air, however, could be treacherous. 'Very little air must be admitted at once. It is still a frosty air. A leaf must not be seen to move, nor a breath of cold air felt. All the air must be admitted at the top, not the least bit anywhere else, or a draught will be the consequence.'

By 9.30 a.m. there was not a wisp of cloud in the sky, and the sunshine looked set to continue. Each house, with its different crop, required special treatment and all was now under control. Taylor's hour by hour account records with relief that 'The temperature has not yet risen more than 5° in any of the houses, but it is gradually rising in all; not a leaf is drooping, and there is now every prospect of the plants being able to stand the glorious sunlight. Fires of course were stopped long ago and the pipes are already cooling; it will soon be nothing but Nature's own genial atmosphere. A day like this will do more for the gardener than weeks of hard firing.' Indeed, he hoped to see benefits right away. In the cucumber house not a leaf was drooping and the growth 'after three hours' bright sunshine must be considerably consolidated, and I shall expect by to-morrow morning to have a visible difference in both leaves and fruit.'

But this was no time for complacency. By midday, he had to start anticipating the fall in temperature that the early afternoon would bring. Heat had now to be conserved, as a fierce blast from the boiler later on would not be tolerated. Consequently, he ordered the ventilation to be reduced, 'and all excepting the Peach house are entirely closed soon after one o'clock. Were the peaches a little forwarder, and fairly commenced swelling they would be closed up too; but probably all the flowers are not yet fertilised, and during the process of fertilisation a close atmosphere is not good for them.'

Apart from imposing on the gardener this nerve-wracking business of controlling temperature and humidity, forcing also involved him in the delicate matter of pollination and the more aggressive concerns of pest control. With no bees or insects about in the winter, pollination lay, as it were, in the gardener's hands. A gentle shaking of the trellis would usually suffice in the vineries but peaches might need additional help. Wielding a camel hair brush or a rabbit's tail, the gardener would painstakingly transfer a dusting of pollen from flower to flower. Strawberries, Taylor found, were best assisted by waving his hat over the blooms.

Pests, particularly the red spider mite, could still be troublesome, despite all the gardener's careful preparation. A daily syringing of the plants and paths with water helped keep it down, but Taylor was haunted by the fear of a careless lad, who after 'tying up a Cucumber plant where there was just a suspicion of spider had gone immediately into the early vinery to pull off a tendril or similar thoughtless act.'

If pests did take hold in a forcing house, the gardener was prevented from using anything harsh because of the tender foliage. Fish had a repertoire of gentle homemade remedies which, given repeatedly, he believed to be far superior to any patent insecticide.[24] He relied on soft water or clear lime water to keep strawberries and peaches clean, and also used soot water which contributed to the plant's vigour giving them a 'greater luxuriance and better green to the foliage'. With laurel tea, made from crushed laurel leaves, he 'slew myriads of greenfly', while prussic acid tea did for most insects. This was brewed by covering peach and nectarine bud thinnings with boiling water, and in Fish's experience 'most stone fruits like it over their foliage, and the houses after the syringing will smell like as sweet as a confectioner's shop.' Vineries, however, presented a particular problem as once the fruit had formed, syringing had to cease as the spray marred the bloom on the grapes. If the dreaded red spider mite did appear then the leaves had to be sponged by hand.

When the fruit began to set in the forcing houses, the gardener could breathe a sigh of relief. The major hurdle was past and careful husbandry should now see it safely to the table. Strawberries, for example, needed frequent watering, but not drowning. They stood on shelves lined with turf, which avoided any standing pools of water and also allowed the roots to go down into the soil. The plants would be fruited and harvested in successive batches, and at Petworth this amounted to 5,000 plants a year. Queen Victoria's household required nearly twice that number, while demand at the Duke of Rutland's spring hunting parties at Belvoir Castle was so great that his gardener, William Ingram, devised a special strawberry house in which the roof was stepped so that the banks of shelves were brought closer to the light. [25]

Meanwhile, new growth in the fruit houses would be tied back, and curbed, so that as much air and sunlight as possible could reach the developing fruits. In the peach and nectarine houses, the tiny fruitlets had to be thinned and given their final spacing of a fruit every 6 to 7 square inches as soon as the stones had formed and the crop was certain. At the same time the vineries would be busy with men on ladders thinning the grapes as they reached the size of peas. It took the utmost care and attention to avoid head, hands or even scissors touching the fruit, and so rendering whole bunches useless for the dessert.

Grapes, which at many places were a year-round crop and the most important dessert fruit after pineapples, occupied the largest area of all under glass. At Dalkeith, where Thomson senior, 'the great master of grape culture, achieved his greatest triumphs' some three ranges were devoted to, or contained, vines. These were managed so that supplies continued without a break. One very early house was 'started in October to be ripe by Easter, the supply of old and new Grapes always overlapping by a few weeks.' Four vineries produced grapes for May, June and July, and another whole range was given over to autumn grapes. A further house 100 feet long contained the late vines which kept grapes coming to the table until the following April. [26]

Longleat was also renowned for the quality of its grapes under Taylor, and here all but the early vines, which were in the kitchen garden, were housed in his celebrated new vinery. This had been built to Taylor's own specifications. Light and well ventilated, it measured 216 feet by 30 feet and was heated by two boilers – one in reserve in case of disaster – which fed ten rows of 4-inch pipes. As vigorously growing vines took between 60 and 100 gallons of water at a time, each of the three compartments was equipped with an 2,000 gallon underground tank, which held rainwater collected from the roof. Each had its own pump and could be topped up if necessary from a new reservoir in the upper garden. [27]

Here was everything required to create a corner of the Aegean in the middle of the English countryside. The first compartment contained five Black Hamburgh vines, while the third housed the late grapes, 'two Alicante, two Lady Downe's and one Mrs Pince'. The central section, which was the largest and warmest, was home to four vines of Muscat of Alexandria, which covered 3,000 feet of trellis suspended beneath the roof. Entering the house, a visitor recalled that 'you passed under an arch of Grapes, all so near the eye, and see the timber like stems in the corners, and the horizontal rods trailing along the front like huge cobras [and] the sight is a truly re-

Rows of hot water pipes help create the balmy climate of a Muscat house.

markable one.' When the Prince of Wales was entertained at Longleat in 1881, lunch on Saturday, 10th December was taken in the Muscat House, which 'although it had supplied dessert in no stinted quantities to over five hundred people at the ball the previous evening, looked still to have a full crop; and the late Grapes, which are all black hanging in the adjoining compartment amongst foliage of crimson and gold made such a picture as needed no further ornamentation.'[28]

At many establishments, the vineries also housed a fig tree or two trained against the back wall, but at other places there were whole houses devoted to figs. Putteridge

Bury had at least two houses set aside for them, and Dalkeith an 80-foot range. There might also be an additional fig tree in a corner of the kitchen garden itself. In 1866, the *Journal* reported that at Nuneham Park there was a wall of Brown Turkey 'laden with remarkably fine fruit . . . which Mr Stewart attributed to the copious waterings with soap-suds from the laundry.'[29]

A Vanguard of Vegetables

The provision of out-of-season vegetables to the mansion was almost as important as the supply of luxury fruit. In 1878 one head gardener noted that 'Asparagus , French Beans, Mushrooms, Seakale, Rhubarb, Tomatoes, Broccoli, Brussels Sprouts, Cabbage, Savoys, all kinds of roots, and plenty of Celery, Lettuce, Endive, Mustard and Cress, Radishes, Chicory and Cucumbers are the principal vegetables from the kitchen garden with which we are furnishing our employer's table during the Christmas week.'[30]

Asparagus could be forced *in situ*, or the roots could be dug up and brought inside.[31] The former method conserved the plants, and after a year's rest they could be forced again, but it required vast amounts of hot fermenting manure. This was used not only to cover the beds themselves, but also to fill the 3-foot deep alleys which ran between them. The same effect could be achieved more easily by running hot water pipes between the beds, as they did at Royal Frogmore, but this was not the cheapest expedient. At many establishments, including Longleat, the roots were simply transferred into large wooden boxes of soil, which were stacked on top of each other at the back of a forcing house. Another method was to pack asparagus roots into frames over a hotbed.

The roots had to be replenished every month by new stocks from the garden if the continuity of crisp green shoots from December to May was to be maintained. This, however, used up huge numbers of plants, as Rangemore's annual bills of £70 for asparagus roots testify.[32] Although they were easily raised from seed in the kitchen garden, it took four years before the plants were ready for forcing. Nevertheless, such a process of continual renewal was said to be able to 'keep the whole thing going like clockwork.'

Asparagus could be supplemented by the alternative winter delicacy – seakale. This was forced outdoors by placing a pot over each plant and covering it with fermenting manure. No one, however, much relished having to go out in the snow to replenish the manure, or dismantle the edifice every time seakale was required. As an alternative, roots could be dug up and the crowns brought into the mushroom shed, or specially prepared beds in a cellar. One head gardener in 1875 reported that he forced 100 plants every fortnight in this fashion, beginning on 9th November, and continuing until 13th March.[33]

The dark warmth of the mushroom shed could also be employed for forcing and blanching chicory and rhubarb, but its main function was, of course, to ensure a continuous supply of mushrooms. Many gardeners gathered field mushrooms during August and September, but relied on cultivated mushrooms for the rest of the year.

Mushroom beds consisted of mounds of horse manure seeded with spawn and could be made up outside in the yard. They had to be protected from the rain, however, and gave up in the severe weather. A mushroom shed was a much more satisfactory alternative. If it was well-insulated, and sited in the shade, it could be maintained at the ideal temperature of 55°F and produce mushrooms all year round.

In a shed, beds would be made up on slate shelves, with pockets of dry hay tucked in at the sides to trap the mushroom grower's perpetual enemy, woodlice. One bed might crop for as long as five weeks but, in order to be certain he never ran short, Taylor made up fresh beds every three weeks and aimed always to have two bearing at the same time. As he said, 'there is always an excuse for having too many, but no excuse for having none.'[34]

Longleat's chef also expected French beans to be available every week, which meant that boxes of beans had to be grown under glass from November until the following May. They responded well to forcing and one gardener reported that from pits of modest proportions he gathered between 1,000 and 1,500 beans per week in April 1878.[35] Such profusion went some way towards compensating for the hosts of red spider mite that always accompanied them. Taylor was always relieved when June came and he could turn out the last of the 'filthy' beans and strawberries.

Cucumbers were also grown all year round at Longleat but the poor light and dull days of winter produced a much smaller crop than the gardener could achieve in summer, and large stocks had to be maintained where demand was high. Grown in the most up-to-date manner, the cucumbers were planted on top of turf which had been laid on slabs, below which ran hot water pipes. The cucumber house also had tomato plants growing against the back wall. These were a year-round crop, and the plants would continue 'in bearing for two years, when they were thrown away and new ones raised from cuttings.'[36]

The gardener's 'small stuff', his lettuces, radishes, young carrots, and early potatoes, were usually forced in frames which at many places, including Putteridge Bury, drew all their heat from fermenting manure. To build the hotbeds, strawy litter would be collected from the stables and home farm, and tossed to take 'the fire out' and reduce the level of ammonia to a beneficial rather than harmful level. It would then be shovelled into a series of mounds, each of which would be packed down and surfaced with a layer of soil. To this a spadeful of soot and lime might be added as a precaution against worms and maggots attacking the carrots. After covering with frames, the beds were planted and by Easter young vegetables would be ready for harvesting.

Hotbeds were, however, the favourite haunts of mice and rats. Painting tar around the bottom of frames could discourage them, but Fish often found that the only way he could deter rats was to send out an unwary victim as a warning to others. 'Catch a fine fellow in a trap,' he instructed, 'singe his hair, paint him a little with tar and let him free again.'[37] The mice, who one year ate out 'the hearts of half a dozen Strawberry plants in pots, nibbled Asparagus, cut over Radishes, and cropped over a nice bed of young Carrots,' had to be dealt with by putting down traps, or even, if there were no prize poultry around, sprinkling bran sugared with arsenic in their runs. It was something of an irony, Fish reflected, that 'if the plants stand plunged in an open

'Nothing was more creditable to the gardener than a good house of cucumbers.'

bed mice will rarely touch them; but set them in a frame or cover them in a pit, and the mice will soon begin to taste them . . . strange that mice like men, should relish most that which is forbidden and most difficult to obtain.'

THE FRUIT GARDEN

Indispensable as all the glasshouses, pits and frames were for supplying luxuries and out-of-season produce, the bulk of the gardener's crops came from plants grown out in the open. Neither the kitchen nor the dessert could have survived without the acres of vegetables and fruit trees grown within and beyond the walled garden. Here the gardener's key to success was not his ability to override the British climate, but having the ingenuity and judgement to work with it.

At many places fruit was grown outdoors on the equivalent of what would now be considered a commercial scale. In the mild and sunny climate of Sussex, for example, Edward Luckhurst planted no less than 800 fruit trees in and around Oldlands' new kitchen garden, while the 14-acre kitchen garden complex at Petworth boasted 2½ miles of trained fruit trees.[38] These, more than anything else he had ever seen, conveyed to the Reverend Honywood D'Ombrain a 'wondrous notion of the princely manner in which our great magnates of the aristocracy live on their estates.'

The training of fruit trees was a traditional practice, which had been used in gardens since the seventeenth century. It not only produced decorative trees, but also improved the quality of the crop by exposing the branches and ripening fruit to more sunshine and air. Trained against walls, the trees also benefited from the extra warmth, and could be protected from spring frosts by matting hung from the permanent copings that projected from the top of the wall.

The way fruit trees were trained depended largely upon their natural habit. Peaches, nectarines, plums and cherries, which all bear fruit on the current season's growth, were most effectively trained as fans, with the branches tied on to the wall with 'shreds' – pieces of old cloth – nailed to the brickwork. Pears fruit on old wood and so could be more elaborately trained in the form of many armed, horizontal espaliers. Apples could also make espaliers, but were rarely honoured with wall space, although, like pears they were used to make the decorative espalier fences planted as screens in the kitchen garden. For these, only the best dessert varieties would be selected, and particularly those which needed plenty of sunshine to ripen and colour. The little Api apple and Calville Blanche d'Hiver, the French chefs' favourite cooker, were both popular choices.

By the 1870s a third system had become 'an ever growing source of interest'. This was the cordon, which took its name from the French word for a cord or chain, and required the tree to be pruned back and trained as a single diagonal stem bearing fruit all along its length. This method enabled a great many trees and varieties to be fitted into a relatively small space, and Luckhurst planted his new pear wall on this principle. He arranged the trees in order of ripening, with the earliest at one end and the seventieth, and latest, at the other.[39] At Barham Court, outside Maidstone, the gardener filled six walled gardens with row upon row of espaliers and cordons.[40] The fruit they produced was of prize-winning quality and amply demonstrated the benefits to be gained from careful training.

The culture of all fruit, and particularly of apples and pears, was also greatly influenced by the nurseryman Thomas Rivers, who vigorously promoted other intensive methods. He advocated his new dwarfing rootstocks for apples, and quince rootstocks for pears. Dwarfing rootstocks had long been used as a means of producing more manageable trees than the usual orchard standards, but Rivers's advocacy of his new stocks brought small trees to the forefront of horticultural fashion, and they were said to have revolutionized gardens by the 1870s.[41] Shaped into bushes and pyramids, such trees looked very fine lining a walk, were easier to care for and, like espaliers, could produce better quality fruit.

Pests and disease, however, remained perennial problems. Fruit trees and walls would be winter dressed with a mixture of soft soap and lime sulphur – flowers of sulphur dissolved in quicklime – which was thick enough to be applied with a brush and had a little soot added so that it was not too glaringly white. Surface soil would also be renewed to get rid of overwintering insects, and the trees closely inspected for any signs of infestation.

In spring, the fruit trees and bushes might be treated with evil pastes to keep the birds off the fruit buds. Two or three tom-tits could clear a gooseberry bush and leave a row of pears 'little else than bare poles' unless the crop had been syringed with a thick wash made of soot, lime, clay and cow dung. This, with the addition of a handful of salt, reported Fish, 'sticks on pretty well by the help of the clay and the cow dung; and should continued rains come before the buds are safe we must just repeat the operation and try thread, looking glass, pieces of tin suspended and all the rest of it . But so long as the buds are thus crusted they will hardly be touched by any bird that has any pretensions to epicureanism.'[42]

Birds, together with frost, damp and poor summers, ceased, however, to be a problem if another of Rivers's innovations, the orchard house, was employed. This was a light, airy glasshouse which will 'without the assistance of fire heat . . . give us the climate of the south-west of France, without the liability to injury from spring frosts . . . and approximate to one of its more temperate districts, *viz:* Angers.'[43] So protected, the fruit trees – and these could include plums, pears, cherries and even apples, as well as peaches and nectarines – were grown in pots and could be ripened and finished to perfection in this sheltered environment. Orchard houses were damned by many southern gardeners as amateur's toys, incapable of producing the quantities needed, and a watering nightmare. In the north, however, they could be invaluable.

Drumlanrig, in Dumfries, probably had the largest orchard house in the country and visitors testified that crops were achieved there which would not otherwise have have been possible in 'this dull and wet locality'.[44] It was, however, a considerable elaboration of Rivers's original plan. The far wall of the kitchen garden had originally been filled by peaches and nectarines, but even though these faced south, the crop had never been a success. Therefore, as the reporter for the *Journal* recounts, when the wall gave way, 'instead of rebuilding it as before, the whole was cleared away and in its place the finest glass house of its kind in the world was erected. It is a lofty, span roof house, 16 or 18 feet wide and 500 feet long.' It had 3,000 feet of piping, which could be called upon if required, and down the centre of the house ran a broad cast iron path whose 'side curbs act as metals for a railway wagon for conveying materials in and out of the house.' By the 1880s, the house was filled with pear, plum, peach, nectarine and fig trees trained up wires strung from the roof. This formed a veritable tunnel of fruit, and as the men carried out the long and arduous task of tying the fruit trees to the roof wires, they set up a step ladder on the wagon, and could easily move themselves along 'from tree to tree by touching or pulling a wire'.

The Vegetable Department

Just as a good position was important to the success of fruit in the kitchen garden, so success in the vegetable department also depended on making the best use of the different conditions within the enclosure. Here, however, the selection of varieties was more crucial and much depended on the careful preparation and execution of a cropping plan.

The first thing to be decided upon was the seed order. Each garden had its own characteristics, and it took experience and skill to select the varieties which gave the best quality as well as quantity in a particular place. It might also, in the case of peas for example, take as many as six different varieties to ensure a long season and continuous cropping. Taylor, like all head gardeners, kept records from year to year, and also noted in the margin of his current catalogue how much seed of each variety was purchased. This was usually sufficient to tell him the following year which orders should, or should not be repeated. 'There is no need to refer to other memoranda, a figure signifying so many quarts of Peas or so many ounces of Onion seed will bring the whole crop very vividly before one's eyes, when judgement is easily passed on them at this distant date.'[45]

Quantities, of course, varied widely according to the nature of the establishment. At the large and intensely sociable Longleat, Taylor had to supply a bushel of potatoes every day and considerable quantities of broccoli and cauliflower,[46] while Rangemore's gardener would expect to cut 12 dozen cauliflowers weekly during January.[47] Most private families, however, needed lots of different vegetables, said Robson, not wagonloads of one sort.

Tastes varied enormously, too, so it was important not only to anticipate the quantities correctly, but also the range. No one wanted to be caught out by the demands of a new guest or a change of management in the kitchen. It was also just as well to allow a margin for failure, both in quantity and variety. A break in the continuity or lack of a particular item was not something that cooks took lightly and it was 'not pleasant to be told by the cook at the end of the London season that they have been paying two shillings a bunch' for turnips.[48] Decisions also had to be made as to how much space, time, and money should be devoted to the nurserymen's novelties in the search for new and better varieties.

With the order settled, the next step was to draw up a cropping plan showing the proposed site of every spring sowing and its successor, so that 'nothing be left to memory or chance.' Rotation of crops so as not to 'tire the land' or build up pests had long been recognized as a sound approach, but now, with gardens so intensively cultivated, it was more a question of having two or three successive crops in mind when devising the planting arrangements than of sticking rigidly to theory.

Taylor's plan was to have all crops which remained in the ground for a similar length of time planted together. Thus broccoli 'which turns-in in December and January should not be mixed up with such sorts as are only fit for use in April and May; the former will be off in time for early Peas, to be again followed by an autumn crop of Cauliflowers, Broccoli or salading, while the latter may be succeeded by Celery or late Peas. Early Potatoes, such as Ashleaf or Myatt's Prolific, will be off in June and July in time for Carrots, Turnips, Borecole and a host of other crops including Winter Spinach; while late Potatoes will only be off in time for Cabbages.' More than half the garden was capable of being cropped twice a year in his view, and a large area of ground lying bare in late autumn and winter displayed, to his mind, a lack of proper forethought in the spring.[49]

Practical considerations also had to have a bearing, however. 'If one part of the garden is light, dry, and warm we should not by preference plant Celery in that particular spot, nor Potatoes where it is comparatively wet and heavy . Then again, Celery takes a large quantity of manure, necessitating much wheeling, therefore we try to make the distance as short as possible. Onions like a heavy soil, but they also like sufficient heat to ripen them not later than the end of August. Peas, Cauliflowers and Lettuce can scarcely have the ground too rich in manure; but Broccoli if grown too luxuriantly will not endure the frost.'

Every natural advantage was turned to good account, and full use was made of the borders in front of the trained fruit trees, especially those with a southerly and westerly aspect. These warmer and more forward borders, which could be up to 20 feet wide, provided the successions to follow the first vegetable crops from the hotbeds and frames, and in winter their extra warmth came in useful for late peas, lettuce and a bed of parsley.

At any time the cooler north borders could be employed for prolonging the season. In spring, for example, cauliflower plants were divided up into batches, some going into a warm sheltered border, others to a more exposed place in the open, and the remainder planted in a north border.[50] Likewise in the summer, shady borders were useful for turnips which soon went fibrous in the open garden.

Every bit of space had to be utilized. Lettuces and turnips were sown between the celery trenches and these would be finished before the time came to earth up the celery. Potatoes were earthed up 'before they had scarcely appeared above ground and the Sprouts were planted in the furrows.' Summer spinach, which needed moisture and shade if it was not to run to seed, was grown in between the widely spaced rows of peas.

Another example of double cropping Taylor sometimes favoured was to plant 'alternate rows of late Broccoli and Cauliflowers 2 feet apart. When the Cauliflowers come off, the Broccoli is left 4 feet from row to row, which admits plenty of air to harden it and plenty of room to walk between when it is wet in winter and spring . . . It is all very well to say, Keep off the ground when it is wet . . . but crops have to be gathered for monsieur the cook will not wait for fine weather or dry soil.' If the ground was wanted before 'the Broccoli turns-in, the crop can to taken up and laid elsewhere at almost any time.'

As ever, much of the execution of the plan was a contest with the weather. As the gardener was dependent upon having the right conditions before many jobs could be done, one of the first rules, according to William Iggulden, was to strike while the iron was hot, 'One man should not be set to do all the important work as that means many opportunities lost. Muster a sufficient number of hands where possible so as to get a job completed quickly.' It was also important to do as much as possible to ensure that the adverse effects of weather were reduced to a minimum. Despite the fabled wetness of the British climate, water was a precious commodity and not always in plentiful supply when needed. Considerable pains would be taken to make the best use of natural moisture. Deeply cultivated soils 'well hoed will stand a wonderful amount of drying up', wrote Fish, and as soon as the rows were showing men would be worrying the weeds with Dutch hoes and 'surface stirring' to cut down the moisture loss by capillarity. Mulching with spent hotbed litter and grass cuttings also helped. Raspberries were always mulched and celery, 'if mulched thickly with short grass as soon as planted . . . seldom requires more than one or two good waterings . . . The mildew which affects the Pea in dry summers is greatly checked, or altogether prevented, by good mulchings along the rows . . . Brussels Sprouts, Broccoli, Cauliflower etc, which often hang fire after planting in a dry June, make marvellous progress with their roots under a good layer of short grass .. The health of Gooseberry and Currant bushes is greatly promoted by mulching.'[51]

Whether it was a dry spring, a wet summer, or snow fell on Derby Day, being prepared was the best protection. Every gardener was his own weather man, watching the barometer, recording the rainfall, looking back over his records and seeing if he could forecast what change was in store. Gardeners also had their own in-built system of weather forecasting. They had finely tuned rheumatics, sensitive to the least draught or hint of damp. They also tended to be pessimists, always anticipating the worst. When a late spring frost threatened the fruit walls wreathed in blossom, they would have the men up and down the ladders fixing shelters as soon as blink. .

The gardener's other constant battle was against pests. As the crops moved forward so did the platoons of caterpillars, slugs, snails and other unwelcome visitors. Soot and lime were recommended as a precaution against the parsley grub and turnip beetle, and a sprinkling of this concoction deterred the insects from laying their eggs on the vegetable leaves. Quicklime was fatal to slugs and a dusting beside a row could protect new seedlings. A cover of burnt refuse also kept them off the peas and beans, and did for the mice too if barley awns were mixed in, which 'prick the sleek sides of the former and stick in the beard of the latter.'[52]

The garden boys also came into their own as pest destroyers. They were sent out, armed with branches, in pursuit of cabbage white butterflies, spurred on by 'the desire of boxing the greatest number'. When wet weather brought out the slugs and snails in vast numbers to hold 'high festival peregrinations on the hardest walks of the kitchen garden', picking them off the stems of lettuces and cabbages and the box edging was another task for the young lads.

Birds, too, had to be deterred. Both game birds and small birds were a problem. Planting tall growing peas put at least two-thirds of the crop out of reach of visiting pheasants, but Fish prophesied that if game preserves were maintained nearby, the whole kitchen garden would have to be netted. Already it was folly to expect to get a row of peas up without wire netting, and 'what small birds do for Peas, partridges and pheasants will soon do for Broccoli, Cauliflowers, etc.' And what the small birds did was dreadful indeed! Often in early summer, Fish could only get a 'nice dish of young Peas to please company by setting a boy with wooden clappers to keep the winged tribe at a distance . . . It is very trying to the patience when you expect to gather a superb dish of Peas or some first rate Strawberries, to find that the birds have shelled the first without your leave, and carried off or dug their bills into the best of the latter.'[53]

FROM GARDEN TO TABLE

The head gardener's responsibility for his fine – and often hard won – produce did not end with harvest. Through his assembly line of stores and preparation rooms, he had to ensure that it reached the kitchen and dining room of the mansion in perfect condition.

In the autumn, fruit and vegetables would be gathered and prepared for their winter quarters. Late-keeping apples and pears, picked and handled with the greatest care to avoid any bruising, were taken to the fruit store and inspected for blemishes.

Any imperfect fruit was rejected, as it would be sure to spoil the whole batch, and then the finest varieties might be individually wrapped in soft paper or cotton wadding and put into drawers, while the rest would be stacked on the wooden slatted shelves lining the walls. Cooking fruit would probably be consigned to bins on the floor.

Fruit collections as large as Lord Derby's at Knowsley, near Liverpool, produced sufficient crops to need a fruit store 80 feet by 100 feet long,[54] but all sorts of makeshift sheds could serve as fruit stores. The ideal, however, was a brick building which had been well insulated to keep out the frost and to maintain a reasonably constant, low temperature until late the following spring. It should also be dark with some means of ventilation and, said Robson, as 'sweet as a dairy'. As fruit was easily tainted, and would pick up the smell of onions, herbs or earthy dahlia roots, this meant resisting the temptation to use the store for anything else.

Throughout the winter the fruit would be regularly checked, any that was decaying removed, and more traps put down for the mice who inevitably sampled only the best and ripest apples and pears. In the centre of the room, a table with a lamp allowed the fruit to be examined for the evening's selection, and if employers enjoyed a walk around the fruit room, then a labelled display of the varieties which might be expected at the dessert would be laid out.

More sheds would be taken up with storing root crops. Onions, after a good baking by the sun, were plaited and hung in ropes from the roof. Carrots survived in the ground in a mild year, but most were dug up, and like the parsnips and beetroot, packed into boxes of sand. The main potato crop, which could run into tons, was usually stored in an outside thatched clamp. Potatoes would be lifted early to avoid the blight and with good fine weather they drew clean and free of earth.

Whether coming out of store, or straight from the plant, all fruit and vegetables had to be prepared and presented before they could be despatched to the mansion. Vegetables were trimmed and washed in a room devoted to the purpose, and any spiked with the fork or showing signs of being past their best were not sent up to the cook. Indifferent specimens, such as poorly coloured beetroot, would also be held back, 'or it may have the effect of influencing some of these hard-to-please individuals against one.' Together with the culinary fruit, everything would be packed into wicker baskets, with lettuce, radishes, herbs and so on attractively tucked in. It would then be loaded on to wheelbarrows, or into the pony and trap, and the garden boys would take it across to the house.

There was also another room that, during the London Season, would be devoted to the meticulous and complex operation of packing produce for the town house. Families departed for the metropolis after Easter – even earlier at some places – and remained there at least until July. It was during these months, however, that some of the estate's finest produce would be ready and, as no gentleman wished to miss the outdoor asparagus or first tender peas, it all had to be sent up to him. It was also up to the estate to supply as far as possible all the staples which would normally be expected for the time of year, together with fruit and flowers to satisfy the Season's heavy round of private entertaining. Everything could, of course, be purchased from the London markets but not only was the quality more variable, there was also the question of

Harvesting the pear wall. Cordons improved the quality of the crop and enabled many varieties to be fitted into a small space.

cost. With forced strawberries at 6 shillings a pound and grapes as much as at 25 shillings a bunch, 'employers were no more averse to paying green grocer's bills than during the London Season!'

If quality was not to suffer, the shortest possible time had to elapse between the fruit, vegetables and flowers leaving the kitchen garden and arriving at the London house. With the expansion of the railways, this could now be a matter of hours in some places. In Kent, for example, Linton was only five miles – a mere half an hour in the pony and trap – from Marden Station, and an hour from London on the Dover train. William Iggulden could leave the West country early in the morning and be up in town with his boxes of roses in plenty of time for an evening function. The extra expense of the passenger train was, however, only necessary for special occasions. Iggulden's usual practice was to 'start our hampers by goods train about 6 p.m. and the next day about 11 a.m. they are delivered to the town residence, having travelled 115 miles in the interval.'[55]

As a rule, hampers were sent up at least every week, and railway vans would take them from the London stations to the fashionable town houses of Mayfair and Belgravia. Here, the owners would often inspect the contents as they were unpacked by the butler. The wealthiest grandees could, of course, call upon the resources of more than one country establishment. Thomson, when at Archerfield, supplied the Nisbet Hamilton family's flowers and luxury fruit, while their English residence, Blox-holm Hall in Lincolnshire, sent down the more routine fruit and vegetables.[56] The Duke of Buccleuch could call upon the resources of the kitchen gardens at both Dal-keith and Drumlanrig and they, in turn, supplied his other residences. Luckhurst's employer benefited from his gardener's skills and the Sussex sunshine whether he was only 50 miles away in London, or at his northern Ireland residence of Lismore, in County Cavan. For Robson, the parliamentary and social commitments of Viscount Holmesdale and Lady Julia meant that he would often be packing for the town house outside the Season.

Vegetables such as asparagus and beans would survive the journey packed and separated by spinach leaves, but the dessert, and even the culinary, fruit required much more elaborate treatment if months of careful work were not to be ruined. Luckhurst confessed that he felt as much pleasure when informed 'of the satisfactory condition of such soft fruits as ripe Peaches and Nectarines after a journey of 800 miles as in winning a well-contested prize at a flower show.'[57]

Some fruits, such as pineapples, were relatively tough, although special care had to be taken of their crowns by wrapping them in cotton wool. A bruised specimen might be taken for imported fruit – a most shameful confusion for the dining room! Other fruits, such as grapes, would never arrive pristine, as preserving the bloom was almost impossible. Laying them in open boxes inside the hampers did not work, and each gardener tended to have his own patent solution. Luckhurst favoured wrapping the bunches in fine tissue paper and surrounding them with 'a slight padding of sweet bran as the fruit is placed side by side in a box', while Taylor enclosed the grapes in cones of stiff cardboard, and filled the gaps in between with chopped straw.[58]

Peaches and nectarines were best gathered slightly early if they were to be sent on the long journey down from Scotland, but Taylor packed each fruit perfectly ripe and ready for immediate use 'because we cannot expect those whose hands it afterwards passes through to have the requisite knowledge of judging when it is fit for use; this takes a considerable amount of experience, which even those who profess to have it are often short of.' The peaches, each wrapped in soft tissue paper and a layer of wad-ding were 'packed so closely that they cannot possibly move.'

Figs required even more care. They were individually wrapped in a soft vine leaf, which served to keep the fruit fresh, and contributed to the pleasing appearance when the boxes were opened in London, 'a definite advantage when the employer re-quests to see it before it is unpacked.' Strawberries were also separated from each other by a soft, dry leaf.

Inside the wicker hampers, tin boxes were often used and had different-sized com-partments for different fruits. These, however, could easily be dented and Taylor found that deal boxes made by the estate's carpenters to his exact instructions were more satisfactory. His boxes were numbered '1 to 66, and their sizes are known by their numbers; for instance 1-20 are flower boxes all of one length and breadth out-side, the lid of one fitting any of them. Another series is for Peaches, Nectarines, and Grapes, varying in depth but not in length and breadth. Strawberry boxes are another size, and these three measurements answer the purpose for almost every-thing. They are so distinct in size and appearance, and there being only three or four sizes of lids, there is no time lost in hunting them up and fitting them. I have tried boxes with hinges and fastenings; but as both hinges and fastenings soon come to grief, I have long since gone back to loose lids and 1½ inch brads, and I find they last as long as any and are most convenient.'

Taylor had a particularly well-organized packing shed, which he considered essential if boxes were not to be lost, lids found to be missing, or the continuity of supplies interrupted. As it left, every box and vegetable hamper would be marked down in the packing book under the headings 'Date', 'Destination', 'Description', 'Contents', 'Numbers', 'Remarks' and registered on the facing page when it returned. These 'forms and figures', he observed, 'have a wonderful power to bring the packages back and keep them in place. Of course they often come back broken but that I fear is out of my control. Stock is taken at intervals to see that nothing is short when likely to be required.' As, in June 1877, 'no fewer than 133 packages were dispatched and it is still increasing', the operation must have run smoothly. It did, after all, have to take its place alongside all the other tasks that not only the kitchen and flower gardens but also the rest of the pleasure ground required.

8

The Mansion in a Landscape

n many establishments, the head gardener's role extended far beyond the creation of a flower garden and the provisioning of the mansion. He also had to shape and plant the surrounding pleasure ground. This might consist of anything from 40 to 100 acres of parkland, which he had to transform into a setting appropriate to the house and the interests and position of its owner. During the nineteenth century this task enhanced his prestige even further for, despite his central role as a creator of the parterre and supplier of the table, there still lurked the shadow of the eighteenth-century distinction between the humble practical man and the landscape artist. As the Victorian head gardener became the shaper of the pleasure ground any confusion over status was resolved and he could take his place as a member of a respected 'practical' profession.

THE PLEASURE GROUND

The pleasure ground had a number of functions to perform. It was both a backdrop and a playground; a further opportunity for display and, equally important, a means of entertaining and amusing the guests, who for days or weeks on end made up the house parties around which country life revolved. As in the eighteenth century, the surrounding acres had to provide an aesthetically pleasing setting for the house when viewed from a distance, and a suitably impressive carriage approach which in scale, atmosphere and the tantalizing glimpses it offered of the surrounding estate, prepared visitors for arrival at the house itself. They also had to provide a series of pictorially composed views from the main rooms and carefully contrived vantage points within the grounds. But here the similarities with the landscape park ended. The previous century had advertized wealth and influence by extent, and 'restored' Nature by exclusion rather than inclusion. The nineteenth-century squire had to impress by diversity and artifice. Just as the heady possibilities of introductions from abroad had transformed the English flower garden, so they offered infinite scope for embellishing and 'improving' the English countryside. The magic of foreign realms was extended beyond the conservatories and hothouses into the parkland itself. Exotic trees and shrubs brought the Himalayas and the American Pacific Coast within a morning's stroll. Walks, rides, vistas and botanic collections abounded.

Providing this 'continuous and pleasing variety', and integrating it into a harmonious and congruous whole, was the gardener's awesome task. On the one hand, he still faced the perennial problems of accomplishing the transitions between the house, its immediate surroundings and the open countryside. On the other, he had the fresh challenge of siting and displaying the new exotics.

CREATING THE WHOLE

By the middle of the nineteenth century it was generally agreed that an architectural setting was appropriate to the mansion, and a geometric flower garden the most fitting extension of the house into the grounds. From the convenient, all-weather vantage point of his French windows on the terrace, a fashionable country house owner would look out over the brilliant intricacies of the parterre, his gaze moving from the elegant urns and balustrades in the foreground, across to the statues and fountains which focused the complex patterning of the beds. Strategically positioned vistas and avenues extended his view out into the pleasure ground, and to the hillsides and pastures beyond.

The gardener's skill lay in combining the architectural elements of the parterre, the controlled informality of the pleasure ground, and the wider expanses of the surrounding landscape. Unity could be sustained by the construction of formal avenues and walks to connect the house with various destinations in the grounds. Curving borders might be used to link the regular geometry of the parterre to the more clustered and serpentine arrangements beyond. Water, which was tightly controlled in fountains and basins near the house, could be gradually released into lakes and streams. Planting, too, could become less formal by degrees. Flowers might extend out of the parterre into herbaceous borders, specialist gardens and finally into the self-seeding blooms of copse and meadow. Trees and shrubs could appear in every possible guise. There were ornamental standards for the flower garden, and ranks of dignified conifers for the avenues. The pleasure ground could feature stately formations of specimen trees, ornamental clumps and semi-formal shrubberies. Out near the perimeter there was the apparent simplicity of dells and woodland.

Within this aesthetic framework, exotics could be employed in a number of ways. The first and most obvious was to confine them to enclosed themed gardens. The idea of separate gardens-within-a-garden, defined by species or country of origin, had appealed to Repton, who designed rose gardens and 'American' gardens. The geographic and botanical diversity of plants now available made the possibilities seem almost endless, and the brilliant example of Biddulph Grange in Staffordshire was enormously influential.

Here, by the mid-1850s, the collector and horticulturalist James Bateman had established an Italian garden, an Egyptian Court, a Chinese garden with bamboos, tree peonies, and newly arrived Japanese hostas and maples, a dahlia walk, rhododendron ground, a pinetum, an arboretum, a stumpery, an ornamental cherry orchard and a Wellingtonia Avenue.[1] Within a unifying framework of hedges, rock work and shrubberies, these separate gardens drew attention both to the individual

beauties of their occupants, and their collective characteristics. They prevented horticultural and botanic chaos, and the danger of visual offence. Specialized environments could be sustained, formal and informal woven together, and abrupt contrasts
avoided.

At some establishments, the status of the specialist garden could be elevated to
that of botanic collection. In this case the intention was not just to follow a particular
theme, but to display a botanic group in all its diversity. Coniferous trees were appropriate candidates for this approach, and although climatic conditions made a wholly
comprehensive collection impossible, there were many splendid pinetums, such as
that at Dropmore, dating back to the beginning of the century. By the 1860s there
were, in Robson's experience, more or less successful examples of the genre to be 'met
all over the country.'

The possibilities of form and colour offered by the new introductions were, however, too exciting to hide behind hedges or restrict to collections. Inspired by Loudon's concept of the 'gardenesque', and influenced by the 'natural' school of gardening initiated by Robert Marnock and, towards the end of the century promoted more
vigorously by his disciple, William Robinson, gardeners also introduced the new exotics into the semi-formal planting of the pleasure ground. New shapes, colours and
seasonal interest were introduced into traditional features such as shrubberies and
tree belts, while broad resemblances between native and foreign habitats were exploited to provide harmonious conjunctions of indigenous, or 'naturalized', plants,
and their more exotic relations. Forest rhododendrons sheltered quietly under
English trees, dwarf mountain evergreens clothed miniature hillsides, and reeds and
grasses of all denominations mingled at the lakeside.

The balance between formal and informal elements, and the manner and extent of
the exotic planting, varied according to personal taste, and as the century progressed
also reflected successive waves of plant introductions and the shifting emphasis in
aesthetic and horticultural philosophy. During the 1840s and 1850s the dominant
style was the Italianate formality of Trentham Park and Shrubland. At Trentham,
the parterres in front of the house extended down to a lake and were balanced by a
similarly large area which had been cleared on the opposite shore.[2] This featured an
ornamental shrubbery which consisted of rhododendrons, daphnes, heathers, yew
and arbutus planted in huge regular beds, as well as groups of hollies and conifers, all
surrounded by grass, and there was a rosery containing 'all the best roses'. By the
1870s, gardens of rather less formality and a much wider range of plants had also
become favoured models. At Lamorran, the home of the Honourable and Reverend
J.T. Boscawen, plants from Tasmania to Chile thrived in the mild climate of a
Cornish valley. On a visit in 1877, Luckhurst found 'a veritable store house of rich
and rare, so skilfully cultivated and arranged in such good taste as to be always fresh
and always attractive.'[3]

The gardens lay at the head of Lamorran creek, sheltered by natural woodland,
and took the form of a series of grass slopes stretching down to the water. These were
thickly planted with irregular clumps of rhododendrons and azaleas 'mingled with
other rare and choice shrubs, and a pleasing variety of conifers and deciduous trees.'
As Luckhurst accompanied his host along the paths which wound in and out of the

The gardener had to create a series of pictorial compositions.

shrubberies, he noted that every turn revealed an object of interest, such as the Himalayan 'Lilium giganteum with its spikes more than 10 feet high.' He also delighted in the *Lilium auratum*, which grew along the edges of the path and mingled with the rhododendrons, whose foliage made 'a charming foil to the delicate tints of the flowers'. It was all, he said, like 'a poet's dream – always beautiful, yet ever changing' and 'the very embodiment of repose'.

Throughout the whole period one common criterion of success prevailed. The gardener had everywhere to create a perfect picture. Whatever the stylistic emphasis, every juxaposition of plants, ornaments, buildings and natural or contrived scenery, had to qualify for the label 'picturesque' – it had to meet the accepted requirements of 'painterly' composition. As well as devising the intricate groundwork and perspectives of the parterre, and colouring it with due respect to the rules of harmony and contrast, the gardener had also, therefore, a much wider artistic function to fulfil. He had to structure the viewer's experience of a broader, more complex, and emphatically three-dimensional composition, whose elements changed with the seasons.

LINTON: THE SHAPING OF A GARDEN

At some establishments, and particularly where a house was being built, the new garden was laid out in its entirety over a relatively short period of time. At other places, gardens developed gradually over several decades, as money, changing circumstances and inclination dictated. This was the situation at Linton, where Robson became head gardener in about 1849.

The transformation of the garden from a typical eighteenth-century park with lawn right up to the mansion had begun as early as 1825, when Earl Cornwallis invited Loudon to recommend some improvements.[4] The small conservatory seems to have been added to the ballroom about this time, and a lake created to the south of the house to provide a distant prospect from the drawing room and the terrace.

Some twenty years later, alterations to the grounds began in earnest. In 1844, under the guidance of a noted Canterbury nurseryman, William Masters, a substantial number of exotic trees were selected and installed, and the steeply sloping site in front of the house was terraced.[5] Shortly after this, Robson came on the scene and took over the further development of the grounds.

For a man who wished to make a garden, the moment was right both historically and in terms of his employer's fortunes. In 1851, the old Earl died and responsibility for the future of the grounds fell to his daughter, the Lady Julia. It was she who, in 1858, directed Robson to design and plant his celebrated flower garden and, after her marriage to Viscount Holmesdale in 1862, initiated an ambitious programme of improvements to bring the appearance of both house and garden into line with her new social responsibilities. An avenue was planted, a croquet lawn laid out, and a splendid rose garden established. The dressed grounds were extended, the winter garden rebuilt, and hundreds of new and, frequently, rare shrubs and trees planted.[6] By the time Robson retired in 1876, Linton had become a fine example of everything that a fashionable family should aspire to.

The experience of arriving at the mansion was made suitably impressive by a long and somewhat indirect carriage approach, intended to err on the side of generosity in indicating to visitors the size of the estate. It was lined by a series of stately elm trees which met overhead, adding even further to the gravitas of the occasion. From the entrance lodge, it curved across open parkland, passed through a dense shrubbery, and opened out into a dignified entrance court.

The image of the house was also carefully prepared and presented from other vantage points within the pleasure ground. Robson was fortunate enough to inherit – and artist enough to preserve – the venerable beeches which, when viewed from the boating lake, lent 'dignity and grandeur' as well as 'an air of comfort to the mansion'. Guests pausing in the new summer house near the Pinetum to enjoy the young conifers, red oaks and tulip trees, would have their gaze drawn inexorably back towards the house by the stately gleam of a white façade beyond a sweeping emerald lawn.

Close to, however, the house revealed a more exotic aspect. In keeping with the fashionable desire to have the colour and gaiety of the garden coming as nearly indoors as possible, and to have new introductions mingling harmoniously in their English surroundings, the south side of the house sheltered brilliant and tender shrubs. Growing against the outside of the colonnade were not only 'Ivy, Roses and Scarlet Geraniums', but 'Ceanothus in great beauty', and fuchsias, myrtles, wisterias, the Chinese wintersweet, *Chimonanthus fragrans*, Australian parrot's bill, *Clianthus puniceus* with its bright red claw-like flowers, and magnolias which were rising up to the top of the columns.

Below the terrace wall, and observed by leaning over the parapet, was a long wide border containing a collection of yuccas, and several small Chusan palms. These, which had been introduced from China by Fortune, had proved to be the only palms sufficiently hardy for the British climate. Growing against the terrace wall itself were more choice shrubs and climbers such as jasmines and the lovely yellow Banksian rose *Rosa banksiae* Lutea. The shrubs to be admired included more Californian *Ceanothus*, the South American coral tree, *Erythrina crista-galli* and heather-like *Fabiana imbricata*; bright yellow *Coronilla glauca*, fragrant brooms, an acacia, and from New Zealand the showy, deep purple *Veronica speciosa*, now known as *Hebe speciosa*.[7]

In addition to Robson's great oval bed below the terrace, which linked house to garden when viewed from the pleasure ground, and offered a fine prospect from all the windows on the south side, there was also another flower garden on the eastern side which was reached by a walk from the terrace. This was the Basket garden. It consisted of eight large circular flower beds arranged around a central bed. Each one was surrounded by rustic timber work and truly resembled a basket of flowers, with an arch over the top covered with creepers. The garden was bounded by curved beds containing climbing roses which grew up tall pillars linked together by festoons of more roses trained along chains or ropes. The entrances to the garden were marked at either end by monkey puzzle trees.

The other 'gardens-within-gardens' were strategically sited around the pleasure ground. The rose garden was to the west of the house, convenient for ladies – but not so convenient that it would always be in view – and formal in design. Further out, the western flanks also contained a circle of lime trees, and a combined rockery and fernery enclosed by an atmospheric cluster of evergreen shrubs. Linton's celebrated Pinetum was to the east.

Visitors were guided to the various destinations by walks carefully designed to control what they saw along the way. Trees, banks, shrubberies and specimen plants were all used to screen or direct the gaze. The Broad Walk, for example, led eastwards from the terrace right out to the boundary of the pleasure ground. It passed shrubberies which masked the game larder and dairy, and a pair of deodar cedars which, set off to one side, beckoned visitors to the steps of the winter garden or conservatory. The main entrance to the kitchen garden presented another possible diversion, while straight ahead the famous cork oak, planted in 1778, and by the 1860s one of the sights of Kent if not of the whole of southern England, drew strollers onwards. Soon they came to a remarkable 15-foot high laurel bank which, closely cut into broad slopes and verticals, provided a fine shelter for a large old camellia tree, and persuaded the viewer to turn and behold the Pinetum laid out to the south.

This eastern section of the garden was also traversed by a formal walk which started at the conservatory, crossed over the Broad Walk and led down, via a series of landings, to a fountain enclosed by an ironwork dome festooned with roses. From here the descent continued to an opening in the dense belt of shrubbery that formed the boundary of the dressed grounds and obscured the more informal areas beyond. A summer house allowed visitors to rest and look back at the stepped landings rising above them, before proceeding through to the rest of the grounds that skirted the open parkland. Here, they might stop and admire the young, silvery-blue Mediterranean stone pines, which were just beginning to bear their weighty cones.

The western side of the grounds was also developed during the 1860s, and here Robson planted an avenue of wellingtonias which ran in a straight line from the house to the parish church. This had the church spire as its focal point and offered splendid views southwards over the croquet lawn and the open countryside. If visitors were not bound for Sunday service, however, they could take a small winding path which led off to the outer reaches of the western pleasure ground, and discover a Gothic summer house and a wild dell 'with roots Ferns, [and] Pampas Grass'.

GARDENS WITHIN GARDENS

Most self-respecting Victorian country houses would, like Linton, have a rose garden, a rockery or fernery, or both, and often an American garden – or rhododenron area – as well.

Ferneries reflected the lure of the wilder regions of the British Isles which, to many people, seemed only slightly less romantic than the forests of America or the foothills of the Himalayas. In addition, they had an aura of remoteness and contemplative mystery which was intimately connected with the ability of Nature to provide spiritual nourishment and renewal. It was a combination of all these qualities that the gardener and his employer hoped to suggest in an enclosed and peaceful fernery. 'To retire from the full glare of noon and the flower garden with all its brilliant colours and somewhat stiff and formal trimness, into cool retirement, perhaps on the north side of a wall or rock or under the shade of a spreading tree in which Ferns generally luxuriate,' made in David Thomson's opinion 'a most refreshing change to both body and mind . . . The beautiful forms and varied shades of green which the Fern tribe present are acknowledged as one of the most pleasant treats of the garden.'[8] To satisfy both plants and their visitors, he continues, 'these denizens of shade and rock . . . should occupy some quiet and shady and, if possible, romantic retreat.' This was easily produced with 'the aid of hillocks and banks of soil, and tree roots to form a rugged natural looking site for the Fern'.

Rockeries were generally intended to be a little more awe-inspiring, offering images of Nature in a more sublime mood. They also, like the conservatory, offered something of the traveller's thrills, without the hardship or terror. At first, the main interest of rockeries was their geological content and physical form, but the growing interest in alpine plants made the botanical dimension increasingly important. The most remarkable of all rock gardens was made at Friar Park, the Oxfordshire home of alpine enthusiast, Frank Crisp. Here, the main feature was an alpine landscape that boasted some 2,500 species of plants growing in broad masses amongst the rocks. Beneath was a network of caves and, towering over the garden, was a model of the Matterhorn, complete with cast iron goats to emphasize its Swiss inspiration.[9]

ROSES, ROSES EVERYWHERE

Ferneries and rockeries were both to some degree curiosities. The rose garden, in contrast, held a much deeper appeal. The old European roses – the tall albas, the damasks and gallicas which scented pot pourri, and the luxuriant centifolias, so often celebrated in Dutch and Flemish painting – had always been popular in England, but with the exception of the autumn damasks, bloomed while the aristocracy were away from their country seats. By the beginning of the 1790s, however, there had arrived from China a new kind of rose, which was to make this social disadvantage a thing of the past.

The first of the four most influential examples of China roses to reach English gardens were known as Slater's Crimson and Parson's Pink and these had the splendid virtue of flowering continuously from May until the first October frosts. They were rapidly crossed with the traditional roses, and hybrid Chinas were commercially available by the early 1800s. Not only did these new plants have the quality of repeat flowering but they also introduced brighter tones and a deep true red into the rose palette – most of the old roses were white or blush pink.

A few years later the Chinese tea roses arrived – Hume's Blush Tea in 1809 and Parks' Yellow Tea in 1824. These brought the distinct and exquisite tea rose scent, and with the Parks', a new colour – the yellow of its name. They were also, like the other Chinese roses, more refined than traditional roses, having more delicate foliage, fewer thorns, and loose, silky blooms, whose appearance in bud or partially open, was soon preferred to the full-blown effect of the old roses.

Breeding and crossing proceeded at a furious pace, particularly in France, where roses were a passion of the Empress Joséphine. By the 1840s several new and distinct rose groups had appeared. These included the Bourbons – the first to arise; the hybrid perpetuals – which were by far the most numerous; and the tea roses which were the most highly prized.

The Bourbon roses bloomed in June and again in August and September, and had flowers rather like those of the old roses, although more refined. The hybrid perpetuals were hardier and more vigorous, and their frequently large flowers came in every shade of bright red and pink. The favoured tea roses possessed high-centred, pointed blooms that were ideal for buttonholes and bouquets; were often truly perpetual; and had the most subtle range of colours. This ranged from ivory-white to salmon pink, and from buff apricot to primrose. They did, however, have to be grown under glass, and it was not until the 1860s that intensive cross-breeding produced the hybrid teas which were the forerunners of modern roses. These had all the merits of the tea roses combined with the hardiness of the hybrid perpetuals.[10]

By the middle of the century the 'Queen of Flowers' had become a national obsession at all social levels. The gardening clergy embraced the cultivation and assessment of roses with the same intensity they brought to the appreciation of strawberries, setting up rose shows in the case of the Reverend Reynolds Hole, who became the Dean of Rochester, and, in 1876, the National Rose Society, which was largely the achievement of the Reverend Honywood D'Ombrain. Nurserymen such as William Paul of Cheshunt, who was the leading man in the field, introduced dozens of covetable new roses every year, and rose shows became important Society events.

These versatile flowers were used in every conceivable way. They were grown in pots to decorate the conservatory and, at Archerfield and Longleat, there were hundreds growing in the kitchen garden to provide cut flowers for the house, and more under glass to provide buttonholes and blooms during the winter. In the flower garden, they could be used in a similar way to bedding plants and the old Blush China or Parson's Pink bore this treatment particularly well. The branches would be pegged down over a domed bed and nearly every eye would send up a bloom, creating a cushion of roses which would last until the first frosts. They could be used at the edge of the parterre and in herbaceous borders. They would also be trained up walls and pillars, and draped over balustrades, while seats could be 'embowered with wisteria, jasmine and roses.'

The ultimate celebration of the rose was in the rosery, or rose garden itself. Here, 'a luxurious profusion of flowers filled the eye with colour and the atmosphere with fragrance.' It would usually be set away from the house and out of view of the windows for 'roses when not in bloom were anything but pleasing.' The finest hybrid perpetuals and those others which could be relied upon to bloom for a second time in late summer would fill the beds. The red Général Jacqueminot, Jules Margotin, Beauty of Waltham and Duke of Edinburgh, would be sure to feature, as would the pink Duchess of Sutherland, Baroness de Rothschild and Paul Neyron. For everyone, the white rose of choice was Boule de Neige.[11]

The design of the rose garden often took the form of a parterre set off by grass or gravel and, according to Luckhurst, it was advisable to make the beds either long and narrow or circular 'so as to facilitate that close inspection of all flowers which is so desirable, and which ladies are debarred from when they are planted in deep masses.'[12] Blocks of a single, rather than mixed, colours were the rule, as in Lord Meyer de Rothschild's garden at Mentmore in Buckinghamshire, where there were over 200 varieties planted in the form of crimson, deep pink, pale rose and white beds arranged symmetrically so that 'due balance of the design is maintained.'[13] The beds themselves might be edged with box, or at some places 'densely grown very dwarf hedges of the lovely double white Scotch Rose, the Burnet Rose'.

The parterre of roses might be surrounded by a perimeter walk along which were spaced arches of climbing roses, such as the ever popular Gloire de Dijon, and the pale cream and lemon Céline Forestier, which also flowered continuously and had the delicate tea rose perfume. Paths leading to the rose garden might be lined by pillar roses, such as tall Bourbons, trained up poles. Sometimes the whole garden was surrounded by a rose hedge.

Linton's rose garden was, during the 1860s, considered to be a particularly fine example of the genre. It was oval and had at its centre four beds planted with hybrid perpetuals, each with a border of aubretia tumbling over a brick edging. Paths ran between the beds, and the group was surrounded by a decorative framework of turfed shapes in the form of scrolls. At either end of the garden were round beds, filled with Crimson and Blush China roses, and edged with the rose-coloured blossoms of thrift. Encircling the whole was a broad perimeter walk, surrounded by a curved border. Planted in the border, and following the line of the walk, was a series of pillar roses whose branches were also swagged along ropes to form festoons between the pillars. These were high enough to allow people to walk beneath, but not so high that the roses could not be gathered.[14]

Climbing roses trained up poles and chains drape in graceful swags beside a walk.

At Nuneham Park, the planting was similarly formal, but the garden was more elaborate. At the centre was a 'triangular trellised seat or bower with iron uprights supporting chains covered with climbing roses, surrounding which, and for the greater part of the plan, are flowing devices in beds of Roses, among which are stone pedestals bearing figures and statuettes also of stone.' The circular garden was bounded by ribbon borders containing sub-tropical plants such as scented angels' trumpets and cannas. Enclosing it were thorn trees, 'bearing their bunches of haws of different colours. Arbor Vitaes [and] Hollies slope upwards all around, so as to embrace at last the forest trees completely screening this pretty retired spot.' [15]

A less formal effect was achieved by Robert Fish's brother, David, for Lady Cullum at Hardwick House near Bury St Edmunds in Suffolk. During the 1870s, her gardens were said to be 'a standing monument to his talents', and roses, being her ladyship's favourite flower, were a prominent feature.[16] As well as having tea roses growing against walls and trained over arched walks in the flower garden, Fish had planted in the lawns a series of oval and circular beds containing 1,000 standard roses. These were predominantly hybrid perpetuals, but may also have included some other new roses which, though not producing blooms for exhibition, made 'beautiful weeping standards'.

These were the rambling or 'running' roses which could either clothe a bank or rose trellis or, suitably grafted, produce tall, fragrant showers of blooms. The sempervirens, or evergreen roses, were particularly favoured for this purpose, especially Félicité et Perpétué, which had shiny dark green leaves and constellations of little creamy blossoms. The hardy Ayrshire roses made even larger standards, of which Ayrshire Splendens would fill the air with the scent of myrrh. The beds beneath standard roses would often be filled with bedding plants 'in colours to harmonise with the roses', or by mignonette to create gardens of 'sweet odours' in the evening.

A RIOT OF RHODODENDRONS

As trade between the nurserymen of New England and Great Britain began to develop towards the end of the eighteenth century, the first 'American' gardens began to appear in English gardens.[17] These contained plants such as scented orange azaleas, the Virginian Swamp Honeysuckle, *Rhododendron viscosum*, and a number of evergreen shrubs, including the calico bush, *Kalmia latifolia*, the low growing checkerberry, *Gaultheria procumbens*, and the bog rosemary, *Andromeda polifolia*. There would also be rhododendrons and European heathers.

American gardens retained – and increased – their popularity for most of the nineteenth century but, although the name persisted, their contents were dramatically changed by the emergence of the new, brightly coloured rhododendron hybrids. The first rhododendrons to be cultivated in this country came from both North America and the Middle East, but the number of species was limited and their pink and lilac flowers were rather pallid. By the early 1800s hybridists had already succeeded in crossing the large flowering American species with the more colourful azalea to create azaleodendrons. These represented an improvement, but the real breakthrough came after the first Himalayan rhododendron, the blood-red *Rhododendron arboreum*, flowered in England during the 1820s. This slightly tender plant offered the enticing possibility that its marvellous colour could be introduced into gardens, and successful crosses were made. With Hooker's expedition to Sikkim between 1848 and 1850, which sent 25 new species back to Kew, the English love affair with the rhododendron was consummated. His discoveries included the spectacular red *Rhododendron thomsonii* and, best of all, the *Rhododendron griffithianum*, which had white flowers up to five inches across, and was very sweetly scented. This flowered outdoors for the first time at Lamorran in Cornwall. Hybrids for the conservatory and the pleasure ground proliferated, and nurserymen such as Waterer's of Bagshot were soon offering dozens of varieties.[18]

The only limit to the planting of rhododendrons was their dislike of a limey soil, and the new hybrids made splendid additions to – and were usually, by the 1860s, the main occupants of – so called American gardens. They were also planted extensively in shrubberies, although where the site was exposed, or bordered a carriage way, the older species still had their uses. Forms of the 'hardiest of all rhododendrons', the deep blush American *Rhododendron catawbiense*, could contribute 'fine foliage and good trusses of bloom of good form and substance' in shades of pale to rosy lilac and light to deep rose, while the lilac-coloured *Rhododendron ponticum* of the Middle East was splendidly robust.

In 1865 Robson ordered '100 rhododendron hybrids' and '50 of the newer kinds' that, in his words, 'were rendering many a poor plantation gay by their flowers.'[19] Luckhurst also extolled their virtues, considering them to surpass ' all other shrubs in the bright and varied loveliness of the flowers that were produced in such profusion.' His recommended list in 1873 included the rosy scarlet Titian, crimson Vandyke, and the dark purple Nigrescens.[20]

The main show of blooms came in May, which was, of course, a disadvantage to those owners whose estates were too far from London to allow the privilege of a country weekend. Nevertheless, there were a number of earlier varieties, which, if the frosts kept away, could enliven the Easter displays. Oldlands, in Sussex, was only 50 miles from London, with a good rail connection, and here Luckhurst planted thousands of rhododendrons in a range designed to give as long a season as possible. He massed them together in clumps of about 20 varieties in large circular beds surrounded by grass. Each presented a rich mixture of colour, but always included the pure white Purity, and other light coloured varieties which, in a large group, 'cannot fail to impart a relief and brightness which it is very desirable it should possess.' [21]

The blaze of colour was over by June, but as in the original American gardens, interest could be sustained by their traditional, if no longer strictly geographical, associates. Luckhurst adopted this principle in some of his planting at Oldlands, and observed with satisfaction that 'as the rhododendrons began to fade the clumps of Kalmia began to expand into beauty, the persistent flowers lingering on until the first opening of roses [in the rose garden] gave promise of a rich display' which would divert the visitor elsewhere.

Surrey was prime rhododendron country, both geologically and geographically, and at The Dell, Baron Schroeder's home in Egham, rhododendrons were the main occupants of a large walled garden situated close to the house. Here, a visitor in 1886 again found a mixture of plants designed to give as long and as rich a display as possible. There were 'choice Conifers, a magnificent collection of rhododendrons, flower beds and lawns'. The rhododendrons were massed together in beds of a great size, and it was clear that much thought had been given to the arrangement of varieties 'so that one colour does not "kill" another but rather heightens its beauty by suitable contrast.' Hardy azaleas in shades of bright yellow, orange and red filled the air with fragrance, and 'the Kalmia latifolia, similarly attracted atttention and very seldom is this seen in such luxuriance as at The Dell, producing its large clusters of pale pink wax-like flowers by the hundreds.'[22]

Conifers, with their North American associations, and potent appeal for the Victorians,[23] became an increasingly common feature of rhododendron gardens as the century progressed. Together with glossy evergreen shrubs, they provided foliage and contrasts of colour and form throughout the year. Lilies, also became a popular nineteenth-century addition to the original range of North American plants.

Relatively few kinds of lily had been cultivated in British gardens before the beginning of the century, but further exploration of North America and, particularly, the Far East brought in many new species.[24] They rapidly acquired popularity as pot plants for the house and conservatory, as well as entering the rhododendron garden, where, set off to perfection by their evergreen surroundings, they would 'lift their noble heads out of the rich green beds, and fill the air with fragrance' from July, when the rhododendrons were past, until the autumn.

Among the first of the new acquisitions were the bulbs of the Chinese tiger lily *Lilium tigrinum*, and the classic trumpet lily, *Lilium Brownii*, both sent home by collectors from Kew. These were followed some years later by the Japanese lilies which included the white lily, *Lilium longiflorum*, the florists' Easter lily; the showy white and pink *Lilium speciosum*; and, most sumptuous of all, the golden-rayed lily, *Lilium auratum*. This had large, open star-like flowers, which were ivory-white, spotted with pink and barred with gold. When the flowers from the first imported bulbs went on show in London in 1862 it was proclaimed 'the grandest lily that has ever been seen' and gentlemen removed their hats in deference to its exquisite beauty. The bulbs, however, were sold for as much as 15 guineas a time, and it was to be five years and many 'false' bulbs later before the cost came down to half a crown for a bulb guaran-

Lilies 'lift their noble heads out of the rich green beds' of rhododendron foliage in James M'Intosh's garden, Duneevan, at Walton-on-Thames.

teed to produce a specimen of the fabled *Lilium auratum*. This, observed the *Journal* triumphantly meant that 'now the million may be possessors of this lovely flower'.[25]

By the 1870s the rhododendron enthusiast, James M'Intosh had hundreds of *Lilium auratum* in his gardens at Duneevan, in Walton-on-Thames, Surrey. They were not only planted near the front of the rhododendron beds, but ran along the edge of a 100-yard walk which led down to a stream, and formed part of the display of rhododendrons on the opposite bank.[26]

THE PINETUM

As well as adding interest to rhododendron gardens, examples of the new conifers were often planted together as a feature in their own right to form a pinetum. A pinetum in its most comprehensive sense was 'a complete collection of all the Coniferous trees and shrubs known', but as many factors, including the British climate, made completeness impossible, the term was fairly elastic. It could refer to 20 or 200 trees and, while a serious collection presented the opportunity to study a wide range of conifers and might be planted in botanical family groups, the main or equal function of most pinetums was to be outdoor winter gardens, and they would be arranged accordingly. Such assemblies had the supreme Victorian virtue of being both decorative and didactic, providing 'an artistic effect which shall at once be a permanent source of attraction, of instruction and of ornamentation.'[27]

The fascination that conifers held for nineteenth-century gardeners and garden owners was many faceted. They offered great diversity of form, from slim and stately wellingtonias, and graceful deodars to the strange, stiff monkey puzzle trees. Their flowers were inconspicuous but their foliage and cones were both curious and ornamental. Above all, they were evergreen, most were hardy, and many grew rapidly. Britain has few widespread native evergreens, apart from the yew, holly and Scots pine, and the new conifers presented gardeners with the perfect means to relieve the bleak emptiness of the winter landscape within a relatively short space of time. As Luckhurst observed in 1873, once the autumn winds had swept off 'the pale yellow leaves . . . most trees that are indigenous and as many acclimatised exotics, appear cold and bare. On all sides the monotony of bare branches assails us' and everyone longs for the 'warmth and fullness of aspect that is gone. It is then that the value of evergreen forms is fully appreciated.'[28]

European larch and Norway spruce had been planted as forestry trees during the eighteenth century, and cedars of Lebanon were fashionable accessories in Augustan gardens. The Duke of Richmond, for example, had planted a thousand cedars at Goodwood, and they were the only non-native tree used by 'Capability Brown' in his landscape parks. It was not, however, until conifers started arriving from the Pacific Coast of North America that their immense diversity and decorative potential began to emerge.[29]

News that these exceptional trees existed had reached England at the very end of the eighteenth century from one Archibald Menzies. He was a scientist who had accompanied a naval squadron on their voyage to Alaska in 1792, and on his return had reported that he had found trees twice as high as anything he had ever seen. It was, however, the Horticultural Society's collector David Douglas who was responsible for the first introductions, when he began sending back seeds from Columbia in 1826; subsequently he moved down the coast to California.

Conifers offered great potential as new timber trees for the estate, and Douglas' Sitka spruce became the chief British forest tree, but gardeners and collectors also thrilled to the possibilities offered by these Pacific giants. Loudon was a strong advocate of the pleasure and satisfaction to be gained from collecting trees and the intrinsic botanic and aesthetic interest of conifers undoubtedly gained an extra frisson of excitement as tales of Douglas' exploits came to the attention of the gardening public. Part of his journal was published in 1836, and armchair travellers were brought to the edge of their comfortable seats by terrifying accounts of his encounters with Indians and grizzly bears, and sundry other difficulties such as having to eat his own horse or die of starvation. Douglas' tragic demise in a buffalo pit in 1832 had also done nothing to lessen the powerful appeal of his introductions.

By this time, too, other collectors had joined in the search, and the west coast of America was soon in the midst of a Green, as well as Gold Rush. By 1854 nearly all its conifers had reached Britain, while European and Asian species were also being systematically gathered. Veitch's visit to Japan in 1861 yielded yet more gems, and by the end of the century there were nearly 250 possibilities for a potential pinetum owner to choose from.

While most establishments of any pretensions had a pinetum of some kind by the 1860s, there were collections of particular renown at Chatsworth, Elvaston, Woburn, Bicton and, most acclaimed of all, at Dropmore in Buckinghamshire. Lord and Lady Grenville were both enthusiastic botanists, and as a member of the Horticultural Society, his Lordship had had immediate access to the seeds being sent home by David Douglas. He also had a skilled and sympathetic gardener in the person of Philip Frost, who joined him in 1822, becoming head gardener in 1833.

Under Frost's watchful eye several of these early introductions had grown into notable specimens by the 1880s. The 79-foot Monterey pine, for example, had been nurtured from a half-inch seedling that Frost had carried home from the Society's gardens between two thumbnail pots in his waistcoat pocket, while his Douglas fir, planted in 1827, reached an astonishing 120 feet. Dropmore's deodar cedar, which had been grown from the first seed brought back from India in 1831 by the Honourable Leslie Melville, was the tallest in Britain until struck by lightning in 1881, and its monkey puzzle tree was 'proclaimed the most magnificent in Europe.'[30] Having overseen one of the most magnificent collections of the century it was perhaps fitting that her Ladyship's last public appearance, two days before her death at the age of 92, was at the Botanic Society's Exhibition in London.[31]

Although conifers tended to thrive best in the milder, wetter areas of western Britain, Linton's deep greensand soil also produced some outstanding examples which the Veitch nursery turned to for information when compiling their *Manual of Coniferae* in 1881. The Pinetum and grounds contained over 70 species at the time of Robson's retirement, including what may have been Britain's third oldest monkey puzzle tree after those at Kew and Dropmore, and examples from all the conifer families. Robson kept an annual record of each tree's height and girth, and discussed the virtues and foibles of each at length in the literature.[32]

The pines, the most widely distributed and largest genus, were well represented by nine different species, all easily recognizable by their long needles, and pine candles of young growth. Of the western American pines, Robson considered Douglas' Ponderosa pine the finest and he had an equally tall, 55-foot Austrian pine whose 'deep green hue and upright timber-like bowl recommend it alike for use and ornament.' He was also attached to the beautifully coloured Himalayan Bhutan pine, which was not only 40 feet high but 'quite 55 feet in the spread of its branches . . . The rich silvery grey foliage is in a great measure pendulous; and differing as it does from most other Pinuses in its glaucous hue, this species is of great value in a collection.'

His vigorous Silver firs, which exuded scented gum, had fine, spire-like forms, and solid, shapely cones which were also an asset. Linton had specimens of the Grand, Magnificent, Beautiful and Noble firs as well as an example of the forester's ideal tree – the Douglas fir – which, unfortunately, failed to flourish in Kent's dry climate. Robson's Spanish fir, on the other hand, was considered 'to be the best of its kind in England . . . of a deep dark green hue, with a conical outline, almost as close and true as if it had been pruned into that shape.' He was also fond of his Himalayan fir, which although often nipped by frost had 'noble cones of a rich purple black so widely different from everything else [that they] give it claim to attention which no other species possesses.'

The collection also contained several members of the Cypress family and as everywhere else, nothing equalled the Californian Monterey cypress or *Cupressus macrocarpa* for rapidity of growth, or the ornamental value of its deep green foliage. Robson was, however, less enthusiastic about the generally popular Lawson cypress, which he believed had been overpraised. He preferred the Alaska or Nootka cypress, which he considered most handsome and 'of the darkest green hue'.

He was also justly proud of his western red cedar, or *Thuja plicata*, which although only 'planted in 1860' was by the 1870s '35 feet high, straight and tapering as a fishing rod . . . with a handsome foliage equalling many of the choicest ferns in the manner in which it gracefully droops over.' For sheer height, however, nothing could surpass the Californian coast redwood and the giant sequoia or wellingtonia. They had 'singular spongy bark . . . like coconut fibre united together and feeling soft to the touch' and, true to Robson's prophecy that the wellingtonias would one day be 'monarch of our forests', they were ultimately to become the biggest tree in every British county.

From the Orient he had examples of *Cryptomeria*, or Japanese cedar, which was also a Chinese timber tree and had been introduced via Shanghai by Fortune in 1844. This was generally prized as an ornamental tree on account of its young spring growth, which was a 'bright fulvous green'. Another even more decorative form of this species was later found by Veitch when Japan opened its doors to visitors in the 1860s. This had fluffier foliage that turned purplish red in winter. Robson's collection of Japanese conifers included the sacred timber trees, the Sawara and Hinoki cypress, and these were represented in a number of different forms which had more feathery, moss-like and richer coloured foliage.

A pinetum such as that at Linton was full of interest at any time of year but even the most modest examples always had something new to offer the visitor. In the spring, for example, there was the lacquer-bright new foliage to admire, and the bright pink flush of flowers on the Lawson cypress. During the summer, the air was filled with the sharp, resinous fragrance of firs, and strange and wonderful cones could be seen developing on many of the trees. The Atlas cedar's male cones, which were tipped with purple, were once described as standing upon 'the flat fields of foliage like mushrooms in the meadows of fairies', while the monkey puzzle tree produced cones resembling hedgehogs. In autumn, conifers were a continuing source of various and decorative foliage and, in winter, the powerful, angular forms stood out more strongly than ever in a landscape largely bereft of colour and interest. This was also the time to gather the cones for display in the glass-topped cases of the library.

The success of the pinetum as a winter garden – or as a source of delight at any season – depended not just on the choice of trees, but also on the pleasing disposition of the specimens. 'Avoid all approaches to overcrowding,' directed Luckhurst in 1873.[33] 'Let each plant have "ample space and verge enough" for its fullest development, and for effect,' which, in practice, meant allowing at least 30 feet between trees. Planting in straight lines was also to be abjured, as no matter how 'rich in botanic interest, [it] can never afford much satisfaction for its beauty.' A good scheme was to have the trees on 'a raised mound 2 or 3 feet above the general level; the smallest plants thus gain something in appearance . . . and this renders the trees quite safe from the hurtful effects of stagnant water.'

In his plan for a pinetum of two dozen conifers, Luckhurst planted the columnar incense cedars in a group of three, and the slower growing junipers near the walk. The deodar was also positioned so that passing visitors could admire its delicate habit at close quarters. The tall growing Douglas fir, wellingtonia, and a clump of Silver firs were placed in the background, 'not because any of them might not be brought to the very margin of the walk with the greatest propriety, but that an an open expanse of turf around the trees of such lofty growth, and huge proportions presents them to the eye in all the fullness of that dignity and majestic grandeur for which they are so justly esteemed.'

Combining Old and New

In the parterre, exotics were accommodated by geometry; in the special gardens and collections they were contained by theme or enclosure. In other areas of the pleasure ground, however, gardeners had to find various ways of employing exotics to good effect without offending the viewer by visual or botanic incongruity. The problem applied to all kinds of plants and situations, but the nature of their solutions can be seen most clearly in the use of conifers, structuring of shrubberies, and in the methods of 'semi-natural' planting.

The rich diversity of the pinetum offered too many decorative possibilities for the temptation to plant conifers elsewhere in the grounds to be resisted. When young, and still in the nursery ground, the more tolerant species could be transplanted into the parterre to make a low, interestingly textured, evergreen display for the winter. Larger specimens with their varied, graceful forms, and dark foliage with its 'marvellous beautiful, glaucous haze equivalent to the bloom on a carefully grown fruit', also invited themselves into the flower garden, as the perfect foil for the brilliant colours of summer bedding plants. They could punctuate the formal layout of the parterre, enclose it or, like the monkey puzzle trees at the entrance to the Basket garden at Linton, become semi-architectural features in their own right.

This last approach became one of the main ways in which more mature specimens were used out in the pleasure ground. They could make telling signposts, as did the cedars in front of Linton's conservatory, and when carefully chosen and positioned, made splendid features on lawns. In this guise they became a means by which gardeners could 'diffuse' the artifice of the house and flower garden outwards into the grounds. The slender spires of the wellingtonia, the stiff trim monkey puzzle, the graceful deodar and the spreading Bhutan pine, all looked particularly fine in such situations, and in Luckhurst's experience gained in beauty each year. Their lower branches swept down to the turf 'from whence they taper upwards with an elegance and diversity of contour that are always pleasing and never distasteful nor offensive.'[34]

Formal avenues, which had gone out of fashion during the vogue for landscape parks, were rediscovered by the Victorians as a way of organizing and unifying the pleasure ground, not to mention its visitors! Elm, chestnut, lime and beech were all favoured for long carriage approaches, and spaced to allow glimpses of the parkland beyond. For a more 'stately and picturesque effect', however, conifers could not be surpassed.

Wellingtonias, for example, would soar up into symmetrical cones to create 'vistas not easily forgotten', while Lawson cypress and the deodar cedar were also suitably dignified. At Bicton, in Devon, there was a striking avenue of monkey puzzle trees. These had been grown from seeds contained in the first large despatch sent back from Chile by Veitch's collector, William Lobb, in 1844. The avenue extended for a full 500 yards, and formed a 'magnificent vista of these strangely wonderful trees with their dark plexus of branches and rigid bristling foliage'.[35]

Planted close together conifers could also create permanent screens of greenery, which might be used to make a series of niches for statues – the whiteness of which would gleam out against the soft dark greenery – or to prepare visitors for their arrival at some slightly mysterious destination, such as a Grecian temple. Luckhurst was particularly of the opinon that 'like every feature of ornamental planting an avenue must have expression, or in other words there must be an apparent meaning for its presence.' Without this purpose 'it will fail to please not matter how fine it may appear.'[36]

SHRUBS FOR ALL SEASONS

Shrubs and small trees were used everywhere in the pleasure ground. They provided a glorious variety of blooms and foliage, colour and form, and successions of seasonal interest from spring blossoms, through summer flowers, to autumn berries and winter evergreens. They could stand alone as specimens, or be grouped together to form ornamental clumps. They could line walks and provide every kind of screen, from a small, strategically positioned shrubbery to an entire shelter belt. Similar plants could be massed together, or different species combined in careful compositions. They could be marshalled into straight lines or confined to geometric beds; they might enclose a parterre, arc into a bay, or meander along the sweeping curves of a shrubbery walk. They could be clipped and pruned into order, or allowed to spread in dense and wonderful profusion. In the opportunity they offered for the creation of a series of finely graded effects from the most formal through to the most 'natural', they were one of the principal means by which the transition from the parterre to parkland might be accomplished.

This versatility was almost entirely a reflection of the wide range and varied attributes of the new introductions. From North America, for example, Douglas had despatched seeds of the showy flowering currant and the valuable evergreen *Mahonia aquifolium*. From South America had come *Berberis darwinii*; from India the richly berried *Cotoneaster simonsii*; from China, garden hydrangeas, and from Japan colourful maples. Another of the Horticultural Society's heroic collectors, Robert Fortune, had sent forsythia and winter jasmine from China and also found weigela which, transposed from a mandarin's garden in Chusan, caused a sensation when it flowered in England. It produced a mass of pink blooms and 'had even attracted the notice of Her Majesty the Queen.'[37] Among his other prizes were red-berried skimmias and the handsome flowering privet, *Ligustrum japonicum*. In the courtyard of a temple near Yokahama, in Japan, he was also to find the double pink deutzia, *Deutzia crenata flore pleno*, which made a splendid addition to the already popular deutzia range. It was, therefore, the shrubbery – in its widest sense – which provided one of the main and most successful means of integrating exotics into the pleasure ground.

Near the house, for example, a backdrop of dark, glossy laurels, or sombre yew, made a splendid foil to the brilliant colours of the summer parterre, but the addition of spring flowering and autumn berried exotics helped sustain interest either side of the main display, and would complement whatever scheme the gardener employed to fill the beds for the remaining months of the year. At Easter, for example, Luckhurst had a display of pansies and tulips in the parterre, but also a surround of rhododendrons, 'the rich golden clusters of Berberis darwinii, and Mahonia aquifolium so glossy bright in growth foliage and flowers'.[38]

Further away, the choicest of the new shrubs and trees might be used singly as features in the deep recesses of shrubbery walks, or composed into ornamental clumps on the lawn. A tree peony, for example, made for a splendid encounter as visitors followed a curving path through a shrubbery on their way from the flower garden to another part of the pleasure ground. It would, said Luckhurst, 'burst into beauty in early summer, meeting the eye like a pleasant surprise.' The peony was the Chinese 'King of Flowers', celebrated in festivals, ceremonies and decorative designs for centuries. It carried all the allure of the Orient and, following Fortune's consignment of a large number of new varieties in 1844, gradually became available in a range of colours from white to rose, and in lilac, purple and carmine.[39]

Shrubbery bays might also provide a harmonious spot for a more elaborate feature such as a stumpery or collection of rocks. One or other of these, 'placed on the bold sweep of a shrubbery border so that the back or higher part of it became merged into the growth of the shrubs', could look splendid, in Luckhurst's opinion, planted with one of the new clematis varieties.[40] The first of the famous large, violet *Jackmanii* hybrids appeared in 1862, and clematis in colours from deep crimson and bright blue to mauve, lilac and pale-shaded whites were soon entering the nurserymen's lists. With their luxurious flowers trailing over the stumps or rocks, and twining in and out of the dark foliage of the shrubbery walk, they made a fine and picturesque display. Perfume could be provided by honeysuckles, and to clothe the stumpery in permanent greenery there was the dense, low growing Himalayan *Cotoneaster microphyllus*, with its bright red berries.

In the ornamental clumps that dressed the lawn or acted as screens, small trees were usually a key element. Holly and the evergreen strawberry tree, *Arbutus unedo*, were frequently used, together with conifers and a variegated maple to give a lighter note. Shrubs would be added according to the effect required, and just as the composition of the parterre and the herbaceous border received endless attention in the literature, so the makeup of shrub and tree groupings was a topic of earnest debate.

Luckhurst was particularly well qualified to give guidance in these matters as he had been responsible for planting thousands of shrubs and trees at Oldlands. On his arrival in 1870 the house was still being built, and beyond it lay nothing but ancient woodland. In the vicinity of the house he laid out 'all the usual ornamental and useful adjuncts of a gentleman's residence', including a formal parterre, a large herbaceous border, masses of hydrangeas, great beds of rhododendrons, many decorative tree clumps and a series of shrubbery walks. There were also lawns separated from the meadow by a ha-ha, a large kitchen garden and orchard, and in the outer reaches of the pleasure ground a series of 'wild woodland walks'. [41]

The composition of his groups of shrubs and trees depended upon the role they played. Where the shrubbery or ornamental clump was to be of interest in its own right, rather than simply providing a backcloth or the culminative impact of a massed display, its success, in Luckhurst's view, depended on whether 'the effect of one form with another is here fully realized, and the peculiarities of each plant are turned to the best account.' To achieve this, plants had to be carefully selected to provide contrasts of both colour and habit. Those 'of sombre hue and heavy mould', for example, 'forming admirable foils to others possessing the sprightly grace which slender growth, upspringing or pendulous and light coloured or variegated foliage impart.'[42]

Seasonal balance was also important and evergreens afforded 'the most pleasing variety when associated with deciduous forms; imparting an air of warmth and fullness in winter to what would otherwise appear naked and sterile in a very great degree during that cold period of the year.' It also provided the clump with a necessary animation. 'When the warm skies of spring and early summer clothe the bare death-like deciduous forms with fresh foliage, crowning many, too, with gay flowers, an air of freshness [and] life pervades the group, which thus changing in its aspect with the seasons, at no time appears heavy and monotonous, but contains within itself that charming variety so justly admired and sought after.'[43]

A detailed knowledge of the changing colours of shrubs as the seasons progressed was also essential if 'harmonious combinations, pleasing contrasts and picturesque effects' were to be achieved. Luckhurst's advice to his readers in November, for example, starts with the instruction to take 'Virginia Creeper in the full glory of its crimson autumnal colourings. Plant near it a Pampas Grass, and do not the silvery plumes seem brighter and the crimson foliage richer by force of contrast? . . . Bring near it the common holly, laden as it is now with the scarlet berries clustering so thickly among the glossy green leaves, and Arbutus unedo, which is also most attractive this autumn, with an abundant crop of its large crimson berries and numerous clusters of its waxen flowers. If possible, plant the Holly and Arbutus thinly upon a slope above, and sweeping around in a semicircle behind, the Pampas grass. Higher up, have the soft tapering forms of the conifer Thuja plicata, the Western Red Cedar, mingling with a white stemmed birch or two. On a lower slope, in front of the Pampas Grass, make a large bed of the Irish Heath, which is now one mass of purple flowers, and you have a picture most lovely – and not a mere fanciful conception, for I am painting from Nature, and really giving a description of a scene that has been growing in beauty for years.'[44]

As Luckhurst's account implies, sensitive arrangement and organization was just as important as the initial selection of plants. The group he described is likely to have been one behind the ornamental pool, which lay between the house and the start of the woodland walks. The creeper probably wound up over the rocks piled to one side of the pool, while cushions of evergreens, and glimpses of the crimson leaves of Japanese maples and azaleas of adjacent groupings, all contributed to the overall composition.

For an isolated ornamental clump that had to bear inspection from all sides, Luckhurst considered a circular arrangement 'the simplest and most elegant of forms.' He built his schemes around a minimum of 13 items, and always chose a prominent subject for the centre. The white magnolia, the Chinese Yulan lily, M. *denudata*, which had been described as 'a naked walnut tree with a lily on every branch' when it first flowered, was a good choice for a mixed assembly, while a young conifer would be used in an evergreen group. The common birch was always distinctive, whether in 'its pretty summer greenery' or 'picturesque winter guise of pendulous spray that in its red brown hue contrasts so charmingly with the silvery sheen of the glossy white bark' and made an elegant centrepiece for another mixed display.[45]

Around the central tree would be arranged a quartet of shrubs and in an outer circle, another eight. Each one was chosen and placed so that no colours clashed and that from all aspects the group showed colourful flowers, interesting foliage or engaging form. The shrubs could either be planted close together, so as to form a picturesque thicket and ornamental screen, but Luckhurst usually preferred to site them more spaciously. This allowed them to reach their full stature and beauty, while in the meantime, the empty areas could be filled by temporary low growing plants.

One such group, planted in the early 1870s and 'rich in shrubs for all seasons', had by 1884 become a large and 'very attractive' composition.[46] Describing it to his readers in the *Journal*, Luckhurst notes that 'In front came Japanese Maples, Kalmia glauca, Erica carnea, Potentilla fruticosa, Yucca gloriosa, and Fuchsia Riccartonii; in the centre Spiraea Douglasii, S. ariaefolia, Forsythia viridissima, a group of early flowering Rhododendrons . . . a Deutzia crenata flore-pleno; and behind a Siberian Crab, a mop-headed Acacia (Robinia), an Arbutus and a Holly.'

The first spring flowers to appear were on the forsythia, followed by the white crab apple blossom, which would be complemented by the rosy heathers in front. Then came the rhododendrons in a splendour of scarlet, pink and white, with the lilac kalmia and pink and white spiraeas opening soon after. In the summer, colour would be provided by the pink deutzia and yellow potentilla, with the deep red bells of the fuchsias and the creamy panicles of the yucca providing more striking notes.

Throughout the year contrasts of form were provided by the feathery robinia leaves and evergreens while the fern-like maple and bold, strap-leaved yucca, each set off the other's qualities. In terms of colour, the reddish leaves of the fuchsia and maple in the foreground were set off by glaucous yucca and kalmia, while attention was drawn to the fresh green of the robinia by the darker glossy leaves of the holly. A spiraea lent a silvery note, and interest continued into the autumn with the appearance of crab apples, berries and the yellow and scarlet autumn tints.

Oldlands was a small place by a Victorian head gardener's standards. It was not nearly as grand as Linton, and quite different in scale from a ducal establishment. Nevertheless, Luckhurst was able to explore a virtuoso range of planting effects. In sharp contrast to his highly contrived, semi-formal clumps near the house, he also employed native and exotic trees and shrubs in a more naturalistic manner in the outer reaches of the grounds.

To the east of the house lay a valley with a stream which near the edge of the estate fed three ponds that had once been part of the local iron workings. Luckhurst turned these into a lake and along the stream created a series of features whose effect became increasingly natural the nearer they came to the lake. His aim was to create a Highland glen in miniature and, with this image in mind, the whole valley seemed to call out for planting in 'bold irregular spreading masses. There should be no sharply defined lines of demarcation, no formal angularity of outline in such a scene, but a blending of growth and a certain air of irregularity of nature.'[47]

The framework of the planting was provided by holly 'so flourishing [in its aspect] on the steepest hillside and under the deep shade and drip of umbrageous trees, and so fine is the effect of high banks clothed with its deep rich glossy foliage.' For ground cover there were large masses of common heather and ferns, while lichens and mosses 'enamelled rocks' by the stream. Into this basic structure Luckhurst then introduced new and familiar trees and shrubs. The upper slopes of the valley were planted with clumps of Scots pine to compensate for the leafless winter forms of the old oak trees. These conifers provided the necessary 'relief, richness and warmth of colouring' as well as a 'crisp, bold contrast', which was also given by Norway spruce, the Silver fir and native yew.

On the valley floor, and close to the paths, he planted exotics such as the North American conifers. In the area closest to the house he made the largest and most formal of the glen's attractions. This was a large pond created by widening the stream, and spanned by a stone bridge complete with a stonework balustrade. From

Conifers frame a carefully contrived scene of exotic profusion at Lamorran, Cornwall.

this vantage point visitors could gaze down at the native yellow waterlilies, and then take a path leading to a rock face, which acted as a fernery. The setting was enhanced by handsome conifers, such as the deodar cedar, wellingtonia and Californian coast redwood, and plantings of rhododendrons and arbutus.

Further down the valley, Luckhurst dammed the stream to form another pond and a waterfall, and installed a rustic bridge. Weeping birch overhung the water's edge, and to this cool, shady spot visitors might be driven in a pony and trap. The approach and immediate vicinity of the pond were planted with less showy exotics, such as grasses, and a range of trees and shrubs to provide relief and variety. There were May trees, laburnum, guelder rose, various brooms, mock orange, mountain ash and lilacs.

The pathway through the glen took no formal line, but curved alongside the stream and offered 'at different points full views of its most interesting features'. It terminated at the large lake at the edge of the demesne. Luckhurst planted silver birches on the slope at the far side and planned a beech plantation, from which seats would offer the visitor looking westward, 'the pleasing vista of the waters of the lake with the soft turfy slopes broken by a few noble specimens of Oak, Elm or Lime.'

Enhancing Nature

Luckhurst's use of semi-natural woodland planting reflected a trend which had been gaining popularity since the 1830s when rhododendrons were found to be seeding themselves in gardens, most notably at Caen Wood in Hampstead, Bagshot Park in Surrey and Fonthill Abbey in Wiltshire. The charm of the natural effect was immediately recognized, encouraging leading gardeners to enhance and imitate it by broadcasting seed in appropriate settings. By the 1850s, for example, Frost, who had discovered self-sown seedlings of *Rhododendron ponticum* in the woodlands at the edge of the pleasure ground at Dropmore,[48] was busy creating his own deceptively artless and enchanting scenes.

The groundswell of criticism which had always accompanied the strict formality of the flower garden further encouraged experimentation with more natural effects elsewhere in the grounds, and the fashion for spring gardening inspired many gardeners to plant bulbs, which naturalized readily, in drifts at the foot of trees and on distant banks. By the 1860s Fleming had planted thousands of bulbs and primroses in this manner at Cliveden, and at Linton, Robson was edging paths and clothing naked places with snowdrops, letting 'the cheerful little winter aconite' seed itself in the turf around trees, on the edges of rockeries and margins of shrubberies.[49]

It was a manner of gardening that was quickly recognized as an ideal way of blending exotics into an English setting. The natural formations and interminglings of native and exotic species looked entirely at home and became more so with every passing year, as the foreigners gradually settled themselves into ancient nooks and crannies. In addition, it had the further advantage of being an economical style of gardening. Letting the new plants fend for themselves in grass or woodland was infinitely less trouble than the twice-yearly renewal of the flower garden, or the upkeep of formal roseries and shrubberies. Amidst the general passion for introductions, it also helped to refocus attention on the decorative value of the native plants with whom the exotics shared territory. Robson, for example, pointed out that the wild cherry 'when arranged in its white apparel in April and early May is a striking object, well worthy of a place at the back of the shrubbery, or front of a plantation or wood. Not less ornamental is the common Hawthorn. And many gentlemen's parks are beautified by old venerable Thorns scattered about in all directions, each one vying in symmetry with the best-managed exhibition plants.'[50]

The most vocal proponent of this semi-natural approach was William Robinson, although the principles had been established well before his book *The Wild Garden* was published in 1870. Reinforced by the outpourings of his new journal *The Garden*, which appeared the following year, his writings provided a source of ideas and suggestions for choosing exotics and ensuring they were happily naturalized. Many of these principles he considered to be exemplified in a piece of woodland at Longleat which lay between the mansion and the kitchen garden. It was here that William Taylor put into practice the ideas that he had explored in an article of his own in 1875 entitled 'Semi-Natural Flower Gardening.'

The wood was traversed by rides and it was along the edges of these and in open clearings that shrubs and flowers were planted, creating, according to Taylor's description, 'one of the most enjoyable spots on earth . . . half wood, half shrubbery, carpeted with low growing plants producing a succession of flowers through the four seasons, and with a well-drained walk, not too trimly kept, but such as can be used in all weathers, where there are gigantic timber trees to shelter from sun or rain, and rustic seats at intervals to rest while listening to the music of the birds and inhaling the odours of flowers.' Away from the constraints of the flower garden, he found daisies and primroses 'did not have such an uncomfortable look, as if conscious of being out of their proper place and cutting about as sorry figure as I should expect a journeyman chimney sweep to do in Her Majesty's Drawing Room.'[51]

Much of the natural woodland would not, of course, require the gardener's attention, being perfect unto itself with drifts of wood anemone, foxgloves, and bugloss needing only a little circumspect thinning as 'beauty is best appreciated when half veiled.' On the other hand, there were bare spots which skilful planting might improve. 'It is very little that is required', but one had to be in the right mood to select and place the embellishment. Wait, Taylor advised, until inspiration comes. 'Perhaps some fine morning, if we rise at the same time as the cuckoo does, and take a walk to the spot before we face the dozens of failures and vexations we are sure to meet in the garden, the happiest of thoughts will flash across our mind and the notebook is all that is required.'

As to the choice of material, there was no lack of handsome plants that would thrive as readily as the commonest weeds but the object was to achieve an effect that would convince everyone they were wild plants. 'The greatest art lies in concealing art' he wrote. 'If I am asked concerning a plant or a mass of plants, which has only been in position a year or two, "Did you plant that or was it always there?" I feel it is the greatest compliment I can receive on the score of good taste.'

To earn compliments such as this, the exotics had to merge with the indigenous background. Rhododendrons did not look out of place in a glade, while lily of the valley would spread as readily as wild garlic or dog mercury. Woodbine and traveller's joy festooned nut trees out of native habit but so, by design, could many of the cultivated honeysuckles and the new 'gorgeous clematis'. Dog roses twisting up stems of old trees found sympathetic companions in garden roses, such as the golden Gloire de Dijon, which would flower for longer.

As everywhere else in the pleasure ground at Longleat, Taylor strove to provide flowers and a succession of interest while the Marquess and his family were at home to enjoy their woodland drives. Rhododendrons, for example, which looked a little tame in early spring, were fringed with snowflakes and lit up by late summer with red hot pokers. The composition of pictures was also important, even at this distance from the mansion. A foreground might consist of 'Golden Thyme, Stachys, Musk, St John's Wort, London Pride, variegated Coltsfoot, etc. Specimens may include Spiraeas, Fuchsia Riccartonii, and others, Japanese Anemones, Martagon and other Lilies and Paeonies. Bulbs too will make a pleasing feature, and may include Snowdrops, Snowflakes, Daffodils, Narcissus and Jonquils.'

For most head gardeners in the 1870s and 1880s, woodland walks and the more obscure corners of the pleasure ground remained the only right and proper places for such 'wild gardening'. Changing taste, however, particularly in the gardens surrounding the newly built and self-consciously, 'old worlde' country houses, was calling for the introduction of similar principles in the vicinity of the house itself. It was not the signal to banish formality completely, but rather to replace French and Italian allusions with a late Victorian version of the 'old fashioned' gardens of 'Merrie England.' In such designs, flowers, although still contained in beds, were allowed to spill over the paths. Sundials and topiary, rills and dipping wells, replaced statues and fountains, while hedges, trellis work and pergolas provided enclosures, shady walks and retreats. It is a lasting tribute to the head gardeners' success in integrating exotics into the garden that, despite a similar call for 'old fashioned' plants to replace the brazen and intrusive foreigners, distinctions were already so blurred that even the most 'antique' of the new gardens were full of recent introductions.

9

The Perfect Whole

he success of the Victorian parterre, like that of all formal gardens, depended not just upon the original design but also on perfect execution and maintenance. Lines had to be kept crisp and precise, edges neat and the box hedging never less than trim. No glimpse of naked earth, wilting blooms or bedraggled foliage could be allowed to disrupt the immaculate geometry of the flower beds, nor moss, moles or daisies mar the velvet brilliance of the lawns.

Such a high level of finish held a deep appeal for the Victorians. It was deeply reassuring to contain the unruly energies of Nature and to transform them into Art and represented, like the production of pineapples at Christmas, another triumph over geography and climate. In addition, such polish could only be achieved by immense diligence and craftsmanship – the same qualities celebrated in the enamelled, miniature-like perfection of pre-Raphaelite paintings and, against a background of increasing mass production, strong statements of both moral,[1] and – in a garden setting – financial worth. As a result, the finish associated with the parterre was extended as far as possible out of the flower garden into both the mansion itself, and the outer reaches of the pleasure ground. It was the hallmark of the floral displays in the house and conservatories, of the presentation of fruit for the dessert, and even of the supplies sent to the kitchen, which were always delivered washed, trimmed and beautifully garnished. Outside, grass, shrubs, walks and drives all displayed the same meticulous attention to detail, helping to achieve the successful marriage of formal and informal features and to unite, through their uniform gloss, the diverse elements of the gardener's kingdom.

No detail was too minor to receive attention. The colour and style of fencing and ironwork was carefully selected to harmonize with its setting. Gravel had to be of exactly the right shade and size, and even the most appropriate kinds of stake and string were the subject of debate. Plants everywhere had to be at their best, wayward growth checked, and spent blooms and damaged foliage swiftly removed. Weeds were vigorously exorcised from every corner so that they should neither sully the picture, nor offer refuge to the platoons of pests whose attentions could wreak havoc among the flowers and foliage. Steps and stonework were kept scrubbed and well-pointed, while lawns were cut using a mower drawn by a pony wearing leather boots in order to leave no imprint behind. If a sudden gust of wind brought down a flurry of leaves a boy would be on hand to sweep them up, wielding his broom in one direction only so that no sign of the birch should remain. If carriage wheels disturbed the gravelled perfection of the courtyard he would be there, too, waiting with a rake to smooth out the offending marks.

Not only could no trace of neglect be allowed to disturb the view from the house or unsettle an afternoon stroll, but the sensibilities of the family and their guests also had to be protected from the sight of anything remotely disagreeable. The flower garden, for example, would be in full bloom when they returned from London in August, but walks and views were contrived so that other areas which were not at their best could be avoided. Even the gardeners themselves had to strive to stay invisible. One old-style practitioner recalled that, 'We must never be seen from the house; it was forbidden. And if you had a great barrow-load of weeds, you might have to push it as much as a mile to keep out of view.'[2]

It was also incumbent upon the kitchen garden, which might be visited by guests wishing to enjoy the hothouse collections, not to present too strong a reality. Obvious offenders such as manure heaps were kept well out of sight beyond the walls, and coarser vegetables such as potatoes and parsnips were grown outside in the slips. In the enclosure itself, the less seemly aspects of production were screened by ranks of sweetly scented flowers, and the fruit and plant houses were kept as immaculate as the conservatories in case their contents should invite a visitor's gaze. Such overwhelming discretion was not only an expression of exquisite sensibility but, in a gratifying paradox, served to draw attention to the very labours it denied.

With his ability to furnish the table and fill the house and conservatories with flowers regardless of season, and to preserve the illusion of a garden untouched by the ravages of pests and weather, the Victorian head gardener succeeded in creating a world apart, a kind of nineteenth-century Arcadia in which the natural world could be gathered in, sorted out and made to behave. It was the supreme artifice of the Victorian garden. The mansion was indeed in Paradise.

ASSEMBLING THE PALETTE

The vivid geometry of the parterre depended on the massing of tens of thousands of tender bedding plants. Each year, these had to be propagated mainly from cuttings, overwintered under glass, and planted out during May and June to provide a blaze of colour when the family returned at the end of July. The quantities involved were enormous. The great Italianate gardens at Shrubland and Trentham Park each consumed 100,000 plants annually, as did the flower garden at Lambton Castle. Thomson at Archerfield used 55,000 a year, and at Drumlanrig, in 1880, the gardeners were raising '300,000 bedding plants of which 30,000 were Pelargoniums.'[3]

Not surprisingly, the whole enterprise imposed an enormous strain on space and labour, even at the largest establishments. Preparations for the following year began in August with the propagation of pelargoniums which formed the basis of any display. Cuttings were taken from a reserve ground if possible, so as not to break into the flower beds, and after rooting in a sheltered spot were overwintered as resources allowed. At Archerfield, where there was plenty of spare room under glass, Thomson liked to strike his finest plants 20 to an 8-inch pot, while the more routine scarlets were packed into boxes.[4] There might be a dozen or more varieties involved, and he usually had at least 750 pots – some 15,000 – plants overwintering on the floor of an orchard house, and almost as many boxes. All the plants were potted up singly in February and grown on in a vinery until the vine leaves started to shade out the light. Finally, they were moved into frames to harden off and by mid-May were 'strong and stocky bristling with bloom and bloombuds', all set for planting out.

At Putteridge Bury, where Fish did not have the space to overwinter any but the most tender, variegated-leaved varieties in a glasshouse, thousands of plants had to be nursed through until January and February in unheated pits and frames. This was an altogether more risky affair, requiring considerable ingenuity to fit in all the plants, and to conquer the cold and damp. Cuttings were taken deliberately small, and the low temperatures discouraged vigorous growth, so saving on space. 'It is all very well to talk of potting cuttings off,' Fish wrote, 'if we did so we would have no place for them all winter. We like them better the smaller they are until January, and then we let a few of them grow larger.'[5] He would take cuttings from these to make up the numbers required, and in the spring, with a little bottom heat, new plants would be made 'in as many days as weeks in the autumn'.

During severe weather, the main problem was to protect the occupants of the frames from the cold, while allowing sufficient ventilation to avoid damp. Any errors in this respect would often 'render abortive all the care of young stock since September.' The frames could be insulated with wooden covers and dry litter, but it was down to the skill of the gardener to judge how much and how often to let in the air. If the weather was very damp, 'a piece of lime might be put inside' to absorb moisture or 'a bottle or two with warm water in, which with air on, would cause a more rapid circulation inside, and make the atmosphere drier.'[6]

Pelargoniums made up the greater part of most displays in the 1860s and 1870s, but there were also thousands of verbena and calceolaria cuttings to be taken as well. Verbenas were propagated with the aim of producing stock plants from which cuttings could be taken the following spring. Verbenas were prone to thrips and mildew, but taking cuttings early, in August, helped avoid infection. 'Nice stubby side shoots were selected' and as an extra precaution against pests the heads were pulled through a dish of weak tobacco and sulphur water. They were then rooted in a cold frame, and by October were strong healthy plants ready for their winter quarters. Thomson liked to move them into earthenware pans 14 inches in diameter. Each of these took 30 plants and he would have at least 100 such pans overwintering alongside the pelargoniums in the orchard house. Followed by a fortnight or so in the warm, moist atmosphere of the vinery in February, these would provide 20,000 spring cuttings, that would later be potted up singly, and be readied for hardening off in May.

Fish's verbenas, on the other hand, had to survive 20 to a 3-inch pot in frames and pits until January or February, when he would move them into larger pots after giving them another dip in laurel or tobacco water. These, after putting on growth in a vinery, would be 'headed across for cuttings ever so often, but we never find room to single pot any.' They did not all always make it. As Fish related sadly in 1863, 'many fine batches of Verbena last year on Christmas-day could hardly be said to see the 1st of February. Thrips and other evils did for them as soon as the sun gained a little strength.'[7]

Verbena and pelargonium cuttings were taken throughout August and September, by which time the calceolarias, which had flowered throughout summer 'with such great profusion', would nearly have achieved sufficient growth to provide cuttings in October. Meanwhile there were other occupants of the flower garden also requiring attention. Dahlias, gladioli, and cannas had to be lifted and stored in frost-free sheds, and specimen fuchsias, dracaenas and other foliage plants potted and brought under cover. Coleus plants also had to be housed to give spring cuttings, and seed from the best lobelia plants collected and sown in a frame.

When it came to propagating the calceolarias, it was, perhaps, fortunate for the hard-pressed gardener that they needed only frost-free frames to survive the winter – although a few hot water pipes were undoubtedly an advantage. The cuttings would be inserted straight into a bed made up of light sandy soil over a firm base of dry leaves to guard against damp, and remain in the frame until the beginning of March when they would be moved on to give them extra space. They were not, however, immune to disaster. At Putteridge Bury, where Fish had upwards of 14 lights tightly packed with calceolarias, he lost the whole of one particular variety to mice in the same year that thrips did for the verbenas.

By March, pressure on space, labour and materials could be acute. The bedding plants vied for time and attention with the kitchen garden and early grapes competed with the forced potatoes and lettuces for space in the frames, and with dahlias and cannas for room on the vinery floor. In 1863, for example, Fish recorded that he was 'smothered up with plants', and wished he could have every pair of hands multiplied threefold. 'Few people know before they try', he sighs wearily, 'what it is to fill large flower gardens in the present fashion.'[8] He had to turn his bedding plants out into makeshift earth pits and, when these were full, into trenches in the old cabbage ground. Here they were planted in sandy soil over a layer of leaf mould, and protected against heavy rain and a late frost with calico cloths.

Keeping thousands upon thousands of pots watered, and successfully hardening off the tender plants, were other tasks which consumed immense amounts of time and effort. Gradually acclimatising the bedding plants to the outside air was a stage requiring meticulous attention to detail if they were not to become 'sickly weaklings that were only half a plant.' Gardeners had to choose their day carefully. It had to be calm, without a hint of frost or chilly easterly wind, and they often reflected that it was necessary to fall victim to the warning twinges of sciatica or 'rheumatics' before the art could be entirely mastered. Having made the decision, the plants all had to be moved in the morning, before the sun had warmed up the houses or frames, and while there was the least difference between the outside and inside temperatures.

Watering was a chore which could be alleviated by a certain ingenuity. At Linton, for example, Robson cut down on both space and effort by a practice he called 'mossing'.[9] At the beginning of April boys were sent out into the woods to collect moss, which was then scalded with boiling water to kill the insect and animal life within it.

Pelargoniums were then 'knocked out' of their pots and wrapped around with a piece of moss containing a handful of soil, to resemble 'a small plant growing in a little mossy bundle the size of a large goose egg, the moss reaching to the lower leaves.' It was grand wet weather work, well-suited to the nimble hands of the garden boys, and a great number of plants could be disposed of in a day. The bundles were then packed in rows in the soil of a gentle hotbed, and covered by a makeshift frame. They grew on splendidly, and only needed a run across the rows with the watering can instead of a stoop to every pot. Furthermore, a thousand 'mossed' plants were a fraction of the weight of the same number in pots to wheel down to the terraced flower garden, and there were no pots to return to the store and wash.

Enamelling the Parterre

Every August, the gardener took a critical look at his flower garden to see how it could be improved or varied the following year. Without the annual introduction of new colour associations or other novelties, Fish observed, 'the eye wearies and one half of the interest and pleasure is lost.' In the New Year, when he could see how his stocks had fared through the worst of the winter and there was still time to increase the numbers of a particular batch if necessary, he would make his final decisions. The designs were then worked out on paper as precisely as those for tapestry work or literal embroidery, and translated into instructions for the planters.

Robson drew his designs straight onto the great oval bed with a stick, while Fish provided his men with numbered plans. Even the simplest pattern was far from straightforward. At Putteridge Bury, an arrangement of 30 beds consisting of two sets of three rows of five squares took over 1,000 plants, and ten different sorts of pelargoniums alone. It was sited immediately below the drawing and dining room windows, and in 1863 each square was planted in two colours to form a centre section and a border. Even fragrance entered his calculations. The purple colour in the beds nearest the house was provided by heliotrope, 'chiefly for the scent near the windows.'[10]

The ground itself had to be thoroughly prepared. At Linton, the winter shrubs were removed and the patterns of crushed bricks, cinders and sand dug in with extra manure. Beds were levelled, or raised if they were to be planted as pyramids. Then came the laborious business of the planting itself. The men were instructed to work from boards as 'no bed will look well with tattered irregular edges', and at Putteridge Bury the soil was so heavy that each plant had to be individually provided with compost. 'As the planter makes a hole and sets the plant in it, a little boy pitches down to him a little soil as he goes on. This compost is formed of two parts of road drift and road scrapings, chiefly for the ground flint they contain; one part of sifted leaf mould, one part of old mushroom dung and one part of burnt clay and charred materials, generally pretty hot, which thus makes the compost when well turned very comfortable as respects temperature and a little lime is added to settle the worms.'[11] Fish also had to stake almost every plant with the twiggy branches of spruce, which added greatly to the labour but 'in such an exposed situation such as this we should have things swept off without them.'

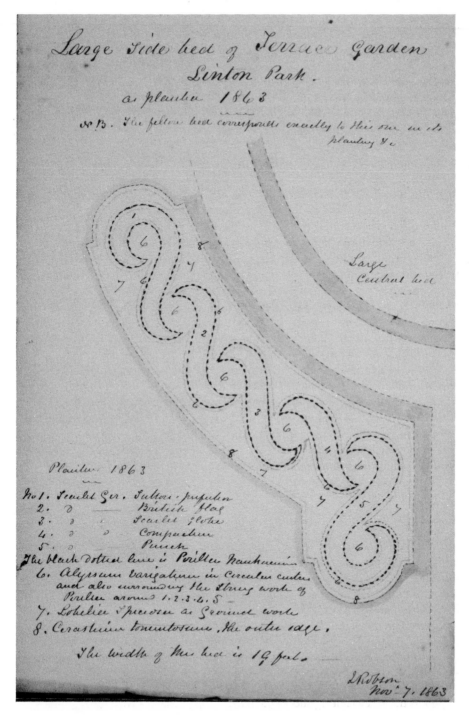

A detail from one of Robson's plans for the Linton flower garden.

By the beginning of July planting was complete and, after hoeing to remove any weeds, the parterres would be mulched to save on both on weeding and the watering can. At Putteridge Bury, the mixture usually consisted of 'a slight layer of leaf mould and old Mushroom dung', which was passed through a 1-inch sieve with the addition of a little soot and lime to keep 'the beautiful birds from scratching it about over the lawn' although 'this they can hardly attempt when the beds are too thick for their bills and shoulders.' Taylor, at Longleat, employed chopped wheat straw which, although a little unsightly, was soon concealed by the verbenas 'that had to cover a foot of ground before July is out.'

Once established, the flower beds continued to need attention. Heights had to be controlled, lines kept distinct and 'no earth, dirty leaves, dirty foliage etc should be seen.' By mid-August, it was necessary to undertake 'a little tying and pegging to keep all in their places.' This task was by no means quickly accomplished. In preparation for expected company, the 30 beds under the windows at Putteridge Bury, 'took two first rate workmen the best part of two days to make the very best of them.'

There would also be the inevitable casualties of rain and drought to repair. Dry weather would see the gardeners 'dispensing water like wine', but, even so, several weeks without rain, as in the summer of 1863, had Fish cutting the wilted feverfew out of the ribbon border, and closing the gaps by drawing the pelargoniums and perilla closer together. Fortunately, he wrote, as 'they are both strong the loss of the Feverfew is not noticed, farther than the white told well between the rose and the purple.'[12]

With care and good weather the appearance of the flower garden could be maintained until October, or even November if the frosts stayed away, although to be on the safe side, any tender specimen plants would be taken inside somewhat earlier. Then everything had to be cleared to make way for the winter display, or planted up with pansies, wallflowers and bulbs for spring. Emptying the beds seemed, if anything, more arduous than filling them. Often the plants proved so thick and strong that 'the men seem much more tired of it than they were of the planting time.'[13]

CRAFTING THE SETTING

The success of the parterre also depended on the display having the perfect foil in the immaculate lawns, paths and edgings which set it off. Often the flower beds were bounded by low box hedges which would be trimmed annually with geometric precision. A line stretched along the middle of the hedge was all that was needed, 'a good workman needing no guide but his eye.' Both the box and the gravel paths, however, could be ruined by weeds or moss, and it took the frequent attentions of a couple of industrious boys to keep the offenders at bay. Terraces had to be brushed every morning, paths swept and lawns rolled so that, as Fish observed, 'it might be as smooth and easy for the feet as a Turkey carpet. Even the pleasure derived from seeing a fine flower bed is much diminished if you must reach it by a walk enough to make a corn scream, or a lawn in hard lumps that the thin slipper of a lady is a poor protection against.'[14]

It was this standard which the gardener tried to achieve throughout the dressed grounds. Indeed, in Thomson's opinion, the very terms 'flower garden' and 'pleasure ground' were synonymous with 'order, high-keep, cleanliness, and neatness'.[15] Weedy, uneven, uncomfortable walks, ragged edgings, patchy and ill-kept grass, and flower beds and plants 'standing in confusion in green' were all to be avoided, as they deprived the dressed grounds of their principal charm.

On such a scale, however, the task was a herculean one. As well as providing an ideal foil for the parterre, well-kept grass made a perfect background for clumps of ornamental shrubs and specimen trees. Nothing was considered to add more to the picturesque effect of the pleasure ground than a spacious, well-kept lawn, especially in winter, when 'the bright green grass, if kept nice is one of the greatest attractions of the demesne.'[16] In consequence, many establishments had a total area under grass in excess of 100 acres. At Blenheim Palace, for example, the 'pleasure grounds cover three hundred acres, 160 of which are under the machine and scythe',[17] while in Drumlanrig's 45 acres of dressed grounds there were great expanses of lawn with 'grass as smooth as velvet' and 40 miles of 'soft silent carriage drives through the woods kept like lawns.'[18] At Mount Edgcumbe in Cornwall, grass bounded by shrubberies formed sheltered enclosures for fine trees, and included a Cedar Lawn displaying eight magnificent cedars of Lebanon.[19]

The time and manpower required to keep such areas mown and properly cared for were prodigious. Keeping just one acre of lawn 'exhibiting the hue of emerald . . . that shade of colour so refreshing to the sight, and on which the eyes love to rest' in first rate condition, required as much work as the same extent of kitchen garden cropped in the usual way, and negotiating intricate parterres or steeply sloping banks added to the labour as the grass here required 'a man in his shirt sleeves at the everlasting task of clipping to keep it short.' Many gardeners were only too ready to agree with Thomson that overambitious owners with understaffed gardens would be far better off with only half the amount.

He had once inspected 'a garden where the attempt was made to keep one hundred or more acres of grass short, and where the horse in the mowing-machine was kept at the trot.' On being asked by the owner if he could suggest anything to improve the place, he replied, 'Let a third of the grass go into hay, and then the remainder could be maintained in a pleasurable condition.'[20]

Work on the lawns began during March and April when dandelions and unsightly plantain were knifed out. Heights and hollows were smoothed away by lifting the turf and raising the soil to the right level. Poor lawns were rejuvenated by a top dressing of fine soil, and a scattering of grass seed. After sweeping and rolling to solidify any ground loosened by frost, they would then be ready for the first mowing.

Keeping the grass cut had become much easier since the invention of the mechanical mowing machine by Edwin Budding in 1830.[21] By the 1860s, these machines had been adopted almost everywhere, doing away with the need to rise before dawn and scythe while the dew was still on ground, in order to achieve a good finish. Machines also reduced the labour and time involved. They varied in size from those which could be pushed by a single man and were useful for cutting small and fiddly areas, to the 24-inch-wide mowers drawn by active, fast-walking, but light-footed ponies.

These could only be used where there was plenty of open space, and not too many trees or clumps of shrubs to negotiate. Even the best machines, however, left 'some bents uncut, which detract from the look of the sward and their removal requires the occasional application of the scythe.' Apart from this, as regular mowing kept the surface smooth and compact, it took only a daily rolling to disperse the dew near the flower garden, so allowing the ladies to walk out, to provide the finishing touch.

Come the autumn, however, the lawns had to be kept clear of fallen leaves. Although 'many of us', observed Fish, 'will become almost poetic about the wondrous beauty of the many colours', it could not be denied that they were also 'suggestive of desolation and melancholy ideas, and we are never quite satisfied until they are removed out of our sight.' As some proprietors insisted on the daily clearing of lawns and paths, keeping even the area around the mansion tidy involved 'no small amount of labour', causing gardeners to look as anxiously at the wind direction as at the thermometer. Fish recalled in the autumn of 1867 that 'only the other day we had as pretty a piece of short green carpet lawn as the eye ever rested on, and the direction of the wind was such that we hoped the appearance would last for a long time without our being at further trouble; but a change of wind during the night covered the whole of this piece of lawn with a livery of varied yellow from the Horse Chestnut, the Elm and the Maple.'[22]

He employed the following strategy to keep the grass pristine on his exposed site. 'Near the mansion we have tried to keep the grass shorter and smoother even than in the height of summer, and on that, if there was more than the slightest breeze of wind, the dry leaves would not remain. . . Then on the pleasure grounds farther from the house and but little seen, we have let the grass grow longer at this season, or we have scythe cut it without cleaning it up for a few days, and in these cases the long grass, or the small ridges when cut, held the leaves where they fell, and prevented them so easily careering over the neighbourhood.'

Battle also had to be waged against daisies, worm casts and any mole that dared to make an appearance. The latter was swiftly dealt with by placing fearsome traps in its runs or calling in the molecatcher. Daisies, weeds and moss could be individually spotted with acid from a dispenser although this tended to leave bare patches. A better treatment for moss was to apply a mixture of one part lime to three parts soil, and since it was only the daisy heads which offended, these could be despatched by a good switching with the daisy knife. Worm casts were 'licked' up by a light wooden roller, which at Putteridge Bury was made out of the rounded bole of a tree, but if the worms were really tiresome around the parterre, an application of lime water soon sent them underground.

The verges, where the grass met the walks and drives, also required attention. Fish recalled that, in his youth, the ideal was 'a good clear earth outline to the sides of walks . . . so that the edges might shine like a pair of well-polished boots.'[23] Now it was the order of the day that 'no raw earth edge will be presented to the eye during the pleasant summer months.' Some were so particular on this point 'that in forming new walks through lawns, the sides of walks are lined with hard bricks set on edgewise . . . 'Ere long the bricks will be concealed by the out-jutting grass, and by this means, if shears are constantly used, they can clip close to the brick and no cutting with the

'Some proprietors are most particular and insist leaves are swept up every day.'

edging irons will be required.'

All walks 'where appearance is an object', in Robson's opinion, required a defining edge. This might be a living boundary of box or a low 'hedge' of ivy, but a whole range of other materials could be used. These included stone, lumps from iron and glass furnaces, slate slabs, pebbles, flints and clinker, and there were numerous manufactured iron and basket work edgings. Stone with a plain round edge was considered far the most superior, and was to be found lining all the grand parterres and gravel walks at Trentham and other extensive Italianate gardens. Pretty designs in artificial stone and earthenware were also available, but some gardeners, like Robson, objected to the latter because of its colour. If driven to using it he considered it 'better to adhere only to simple forms, and avoid all pointed, notched and beaded tops, which are liable to breakage or to become so covered with dirt that all the beauty which they possess is destroyed.'[24] He much preferred edgings made of well-burnt bricks set diagonally. These lined all the walks at Linton right out to the edge of the pleasure ground and as well as being cheap and eminently serviceable, Robson found 'their red glare quickly softens down to the ordinary colour of ground or gravel.'

These miles of walks also took considerable maintenance to keep the surface pristine. The grounds were often at their most enjoyable on a balmy summer's evening after heavy rain, so walks had to be well made, the surface firm and finished with fine gravel. If they became soft through poor drainage, half the guests' pleasure, not to mention the appearance of the garden, was lost. Frequent rolling preserved the hard surface, and ironed out scuffing by the gentlemen's boots, while weeds were usually disposed of by hoeing or hand weeding by the garden boys. A sprinkling of salt on a dry spring day also helped to keep the weeds and moss at bay, but it had to be kept well clear of the box to which it was fatal, and could only be used in the family's absence as many proprietors disliked its dusty appearance. It could also could make the paths slippery.

A smooth, well-rolled walk was easier to keep clear of leaves and, 'in this respect' opined Fish, 'the less the verge is elevated above the walk the better.' Like the lawns, they required regular sweeping in the autumn, although brushing could wonderfully improve their appearance at any time of year. The ideal implement was 'a new birch broom, from which the slender points had been nipped off with a knife' but 'to render [the surface] fresh and level, and leave scarcely a mark of the broom', was something of an art. 'If you begin at the north end of a walk', Fish instructed his apprentices 'you must brush continuously and only to the south, making no back strokes to the north. In this way with a little practice scarcely a mark of the birch will remain.'[25]

Detailed to Perfection

With so much attention devoted to achieving a high, craftsman-like finish, the eye inevitably became attuned to registering the minutest detail of the garden's composition. When Fish visited Trentham Park in 1863, for example, he was careful to draw his reader's attention to the harmonies of the window-boxes and the house. After noting that the terrace in front of the mansion was paved with slate, and the house coloured a deep, creamy stone colour, he launched into a long description of the ground floor aspect.

'Close to the base are semicircles cut out of the slate terrace and these were filled with blue masses of Lobelia speciosa, and we can conceive of no colour more striking in the position close to the walls. Then the whole of the sills of the lower windows of this centre front were filled each with a China box just to fit it. Plants are grown in other boxes just made to slip in, so that the China boxes look as full and overflowing as if the plants had never been anywhere else. These China boxes are kept filled all year round with plants suitable to the season. When we saw them each box was a dense mass of Golden Chain Geranium. What, and so close to such a coloured wall? Yes, it is true, and most beautiful they looked. But that you may take our word for it, we must also tell you that the pretty Wedgwood ware was chiefly white and green . . . and the glass of the windows behind the boxes was of a light mauve colour. We thought at first that the blinds were so coloured, but found out it was the glass. Under such circumstances the Golden Chain was peculiarly at home.'[26]

Most establishments would also give similar thought to the colouring of the glazing bars of the conservatory. The idea was that externally these should complement the house, while internally should appear to merge into the sky. For the exterior, Robson's opinion in 1867 was that 'nothing . . . is better than a good stone colour, several coats being laid on. Effect may, perhaps, to a certain extent be given by painting some of the glazing bars in the fronts or the sides of a chocolate colour; but this is less required than in the windows of a dwelling house. Now and then the ribs or rafters, or a part of them, may be of a distinct colour; a good Spanish brown, is perhaps as good as any, though not better than bronze and all gay colours ought to be avoided. Although . . . a very pale blue and white may be employed for the inside colouring with effect, outwardly plainness is best.'[27]

The appropriate colour for vases, stonework and fencing was also a matter for careful consideration. The choice of paint, asserted Robson, should not depart 'from that harmony of colour which ought to prevail in all places where floral or vegetable beauty is the main attraction . . . however there are many instances in which artificial colouring has been carried too far, and, I think, done in an manner not consistent with propriety.' As an example he cited 'vases, or tazzas, out-of-doors intended to be planted with flowers, painted of a glaring white, which was stained and spoiled by the first waterings the plants received. These vases were of artificial stone, or some composition resembling it and so far as durability was concerned, did not require painting. Cast-iron vases might require a coat of paint; but in all cases where such is wanted, let the finishing colour be some soft grey, or other tint resembling the stone of the district. I would avoid both white and green, which I think ought not to be used for outside work of any description. When it is desired to render iron fencing invisible, green may perhaps be admissible; but then the fence ought to be a long distance from the eye, as objects near at hand cannot be so concealed, and it is useless to attempt doing so. . . . The same rule holds good with other features in the garden, as pillars, stands, walk-edgings when of stone or resembling it, sun-dial stands, and in most cases balustrading and copings. Perhaps if the latter are in contact with new work of a highly-polished character they may be kept free from lichen and dirt, but they will rarely be improved by paint; while I must confess I admire the grey hue which age gives such objects' .

Avoiding paint was also one of the best ways of rendering the more mechanical aspects of the garden inconspicuous. 'Dahlia stakes and similar supports look best when they are of Ash, Chestnut, Hazel, Willow, or other straight-growing wood of the proper size with the bark on, and no more taken off the knots than is necessary. Most other stakes, both large and small, also look better when made of a similar material, rather than of dressed deal painted green or any other hue; but if deal sticks must be used, let them be painted with some colour not too conspicuous. Green, in my opinion, is the worst, and next to that a clear white. Of course, no one would think of painting stakes bright red, or yellow; but green which is very commonly employed is certainly objectionable.' He advised a dull ash grey for stakes, and most iron work such as arches, trellises and fences. This medium lead colour was 'one of the most durable paints employed, certainly much more so than green. All light iron work might be so treated, but elaborate work of a heavier character such as gates, balustrading and pillars, might have what is called a bronze finishing.'

Even the shade of gravel on the terrace was carefully selected to complement the mansion. At Linton, for example, the addition of crushed cockle shells made it as bright and sparkling as the white façade, and cart loads of shells were bought in each year from the Kent coast to surface the walks in the formal flower gardens.

As one moved away from the house, formality gave way first to the shrubberies, then to wooded dells and finally to the surrounding parkland. The nature and degree of finish in each area had to be finely judged. Walks were still well-maintained, however far one penetrated into the wilderness, but trimmed larch poles rather than a stone or iron balustrading might, for example, be deemed more appropriate for a bridge over a distant stream. Plants here did not have to be vigorously constrained as in the dressed ground, but they still needed to be strong, well-grown specimens, thickly-foliaged with no bare trunks or straggly stems exposed. Leaves could be allowed to lie under the trees, but any areas of bare earth near paths would be covered with ferns and ivy.

DECORATIVE AS WELL AS FUNCTIONAL

Although the kitchen garden was hidden behind high walls, it had to be as much a showcase as any of the 'public' areas of the pleasure ground. Its plant and fruit houses were glorious at any time of year, and the trained wall fruit, whether in blossom or laden with fruit, made a wonderful display. The neat rows of vegetables and walks edged with box to keep the soil off the paths had the satisfying orderliness of a parterre, and were just as likely to be visited. This was certainly the case at Sandringham where the perimeter walk in front of the wall fruit was a continuation of the carriage drive from the house. It swept around in a great oval curve, and was a feature so appreciated by the Princess of Wales that the kitchen gardens formed 'a frequent resort when her Royal Highness was taking a carriage outing.'[28]

Trentham Park's kitchen garden was no less inviting, and 'so banked and flanked with shrubberies and its main walks so skirted with flowers, that the idea of a pleasure ground is at first sight thrown over the whole.'[29] The north-south cross walk was the site of a famed ribbon border backed by apple and pear trees trained into alternate bell and pyramid shapes, while the east-west walk, in line with the main entrance, was arched over with pear trees which provided 'a pleasant promenade on a hot summer's day, and the fruit can also be easily seen and examined.'

As everywhere else in the grounds, the whole effect depended on everything being kept immaculate. In the kitchen garden, this tended to follow inevitably from the strict standards required to reduce pests and disease, but it also required a sharp eye and constant diligence on the gardener's part. Boot scrapers were set into each corner of every quarter to keep the mud off the paths, which also had to be kept clear of garden debris. All 'houses and borders and walks near them should always be neat and clean', reminded Fish.[30] Wheel marks and unwashed pots were no more acceptable here than they would be in the flower garden or conservatory, and weeds were not to be tolerated either. 'A few large weeds in a distant quarter will not strike the eye so much as similar weeds near the houses,' he continues, 'whilst such weeds *inside* the houses always convey the idea of slovenliness and idleness.'

It also helped the illusion of perfection to keep some parts of the garden away from close scrutiny. The fruit trees that usually lined the walks served this purpose, and further screening was provided by the borders of flowers. At Archerfield, where the ribbon borders and 18-foot wide flower panels in front of the glasshouses consumed as many bedding plants as the Dirleton flower garden, Thomson's choice of flowers in the cross walks helped to mask both sights and smells of vegetable production. Rows of tall, sweetly scented stocks were planted behind the ribbon borders, while behind these grew dwarf apple trees. These alternated with standard roses, and the spaces in between were filled with mignonette.[31]

Achieving and maintaining a state of decorative perfection was a good deal easier at establishments such as Archerfield and Drumlanrig which were only used by their owners for about three months of the year. These gardens might supply luxury items such as pineapples and orchids to other residences, but they did not have to meet the heavy all-year-round demand for flowers, fruit and vegetables that, for example, Taylor faced at Longleat. Under his circumstances, Taylor considered practicalities had to prevail. He did not see any merit in lining the paths with flowers and fruit trees, a custom that 'starts with the idea that there is something loathsome in growing Cabbages, and that we must screen such crops from the eye of the refined.'[32] Those people, he continues, 'who cannot see any beauty or take any interest in a well kept vegetable garden are to be pitied.'

His scorn was compounded by the fact that to form an effective screen the fruit trees had to be planted too close together to be of any use, and that their roots were often damaged by the vegetable man's spade, as he strove to fit another cauliflower into the end of a row. Taylor preferred to see fruit and vegetables kept separate, so allowing the rows of vegetables to run at right angles up to the main walks with 'every variety . . . carefully labelled, where it can be read from the walk, and all kept in the highest state of cultivation.' With a neat brick edge rather than the slug haven of box, this scheme was, in his opinion, 'more systematic and economical than the usual arrangement, and there are not many proprietors who would fail to interest themselves as much in a crop of Onions averaging three-quarters of a pound in weight as they would in a row of prettily trained but often fruitless Pear trees.'

Under glass, however, there was little conflict between production and display. An October visitor to Longleat was dazzled by a house of winter-flowering carnations, another of 'rosy crimson' pelargoniums and yet another filled with a mass of white begonias. Nearby, there was a stove house glowing orange-scarlet with gesneras, and the great vinery, with its amber muscats and huge, dark-bloomed bunches of Alicante, was alone worth a pilgrimage to Wiltshire.[33] Everything was destined for the mansion but, in the meantime, the scale and out of season splendour made for a display which was as magnificent as it was fruitful.

The distinction between production and display in the glasshouses was blurred still further by the fact that at many places a section of the kitchen ranges might be taken up by anything from a relatively modest conservatory to a major collection of exotic specimens. Owners and guests would thus pass freely, and without a second thought, between houses composed expressly for their delight, and those whose primary purpose was more practical.

At many establishments, for example, the central portion of the range was a display house filled with seasonal blooms, such as chrysanthemums in the autumn and

Eucharis destined for Eaton Hall's floral decorations and bouquets also made a splendid picture in the lean-to.

azaleas in the spring. At Archerfield, this showpiece opened straight on to the vineries on one side and the peach houses on the other. Linton had no central show house, but in the plant houses there were not only orchids destined for the drawing room, but also other less robust, yet exquisite species, such as the hanging basket of a *Stanhopea*, whose flowers lasted only a day and 'might be mistaken for some huge insect or shell fish of peculiar form.'[34]

At the other extreme there was Dangstein, the Sussex home of the Nevill family. In addition to the usual plant and fruit houses, this had an orangery, its tropical fruit collection and a whole series of ranges housing orchids, ferns, and palms. These were open to the public every day except Sunday and during the 1860s the orchid collection was considered to be one of the finest in the country.[35] It was housed, like most collections, according to the requirements of the different species. In the East India house, which was the warmest, were grand specimens of vandas and moth orchids from Burma, Java and the Philippines. A cool house contained odontoglossums and lycastes from the cloud forests of Columbia. These were set off by 'ornamental leaved Begonias ranged on each side of the central pathway, and a covering of Lycopod on the end wall.' The principal house, measuring some 50 feet by 24 feet, presented 'a striking appearance: the Cypripediums, Calanthes, Dendrobes, etc., furnishing an ample supply of bloom even without the Poinsettias, which had been introduced to give loveliness to the whole.' There were several houses devoted to fine foliage plants, and in one there were tropical waterlilies and a Madagascan lace plant, or water yam, growing in tanks. A new fernery had been made for 'a charming collection of Filmy Ferns which for completeness and rarity would vie with any . . . The walls are all encrusted with shells from the East Indies and on the back wall are the letters L.D.N. 1872 in white coral upon red.' Most remarkable of all was the huge palm stove house, filled to overflowing with economically important as well as beautiful tropical plants. Here, the Peruvian wax palm grew alongside cotton plants, tea and coffee trees, sugar cane, as well as mangoes, guavas and bananas.

Few places, however, had collections on this scale and, as at Longleat, most of the kitchen garden's glasshouses would be devoted to producing fruit for the dessert and flowers for the mansion. Even so, before the family left for town after Easter, they might take the chance to admire the forced peaches, grapes and strawberries, while in the cooler houses they could stroll among trees magical with blossom. When they returned in August, not only were the wall fruit and the apple and pear trees lining the paths in fruit, but house after house was laden with grapes, figs, peaches, nectarines and, in many places, pineapples.

Even more spectacular would be the yards of glasshouses devoted to supplying the mansion's flowers. These often took up as much, if not more, space as the fruit. At Dalkeith, which was not even a noted 'plant place', some 500 feet of glasshouses were taken up with growing plants for decoration.[36] One range about 200 feet long began with a house of South African heaths, followed by one 60 feet long of camellias partly shaded by Maréchal Niel and Gloire de Dijon roses, and passion flowers climbing along the rafters. Next there was a warmer orchid house, which also contained stove ferns and an adjacent house filled with foliage plants such as 'Palms, Crotons, Marantas, Anthuriums, Dracaenas, Caladiums and Alocasias, etc., all grown with a view to usefulness during winter and spring for decorative purposes.' There were also many pots of the maidenhair fern, *Adiantum farleyense*, for table decoration. Another range 300 feet long was divided into a cooler greenhouse containing 'Cineraria, Amaryllis, Heliotropes, Primulas, Mignonette, Pelargoniums, etc.' and a warmer house filled with 'nice lots of standard Epiphyllums, Poinsettia pulcherrima, Euphorbia jacquiniaeflora, Begonias, Gesnera etc.', all for decoration.

At Westonbirt, the Gloucestershire home of the Holford family, whose town house later became The Dorchester Hotel in Park Lane, there were by the 1870s nine span roof ranges given over to growing plants for the mansion. One house alone held 1,000 pots of amaryllis, another was filled with double pelargoniums for cutting, another with azaleas, another with perpetual flowering carnations and another with fuchsias. A whole range was given over to an orchid collection, while ferns and foliage plants filled another. The central and largest range was a camellia house, which also formed 'an artery of communication' leading to the flower garden beyond. In consequence, it was 'more ornamental in its construction with ornamental plate glass doors, deluding the eye by the reflections of its contents.'[37]

All this production of flowers under glass would, of course, be in addition to the outside borders and beds which provided baskets of summer roses and armfuls of dahlias, gladioli, pyrethrums and Japanese anemones. Taylor had 1,000 rose bushes at

Longleat and his long, mixed and herbaceous borders provided him with 'the greatest quantity of cut flowers'. Dahlias in all their variety were the most valuable as they lasted well into the autumn, but there were rudbeckias and red hot pokers for bold displays along the corridors and landings. When these beds died back, however, the whole of the floral burden reverted to the glasshouses, whose jewel-like colours glowed with even greater intensity amidst the winter drear of their surroundings.

FLOWERS PERPETUAL

That pot plants and cut flowers had to be cultivated on such a scale was determined by the fact that, like the parterre and the pleasure ground, the interior of the mansion had to present an unfaltering picture of floral perfection. Whatever the time of year or upheavals of the social calendar, the conservatory had to be brilliant with colour, the boudoir and drawing room sweet with perfume, and the dining table suitably majestic.

The parterre and the pleasure ground had of necessity to be governed by the seasons but, inside the mansion, summer could be made perpetual by the displays of plants grown under glass and the forcing of early spring flowers. At Longleat, for example, '30-40 buttonholes were needed daily in the darkest days of winter' and 'fourteen hand-barrow loads of plants in flower (fine foliage and Ferns count for nothing here) all through the dullest months of winter.' Similarly at Norris Green, home of the Liverpool banker, Heywood, 'two hundred plants or more are in daily request for months through the winter for room decoration, . . . the majority being flowering plants.'[38]

The demand for roses was met by pots of hybrid perpetuals, which were brought into the glasshouses in December, or earlier, and in the gentle heat bloomed in the New Year. China roses, too, were forced, and ideal for bouquets, while tea roses furnished 'beautiful flowers of a fair size in January' and, Taylor found, kept 'up a succession of excellent buttonhole blooms for nearly three months afterwards'.[39]

In addition, hundreds of spring bulbs potted up in the autumn and housed in pits and frames were introduced to heat in batches, providing relays of blooms for the mansion and conservatory. At Rangemore, the Bass residence, for example, the gardener recorded forcing '1,600 Roman Hyacinths . . . upwards of 600 Dutch Hyacinths, 1,200 Crocuses' annually.[40] Similarly, shrubs such as deutzia, grown outside in pots in a sheltered spot, were brought under glass to produce showy bushes of flowers in January and February, while pots of lilac in a warm, dark shed yielded chaste, white sprays for the dining table. From beds in the kitchen garden, clumps of lily of the valley, were dug up in the autumn and put on the vinery floor to provide cut flowers throughout the winter, or the crowns were potted up to take into the mansion as they came into bloom. At Scone Palace in Scotland there was an acre devoted to lily of the valley alone,[41] and most places also forced Russian violets in frames. These were for picking throughout the hunting season, when they adorned the ladies' riding habits and their boudoirs.

As in the parterre, there was no place for fading blooms in the mansion and displays had to be renewed at the first sign of fatigue. As many of the forced and hothouse plants were not ideally suited to mansion life, turnover was high and large reserves a necessity. Fragile ferns survived only one evening in the dining room, and a careless housemaid opening the windows on a frosty morning could ruin months of hard work in a trice. 'A vase of Lily of the Valley, produced during November, when delicate and tender is soon spoiled by cold draughts and its time of lasting in good condition considerably reduced,' observed Heywood's gardener.[42]

Mignonette, too, imposed a great strain on resources. The same gardener noted that 'a vase that will hold a pot 9 or 10 inches in diameter, and that has to be filled with a trained standard Mignonette, and nothing else, until Hybrid Roses can take its place, causes a great deal of work. Mignonette in rooms does not last long, at least the fragrance is soon gone, and the plant must be removed and replaced with another. The damage done to the plant by a short stay in the dwelling-house takes a long time to repair.'

Although at kinder seasons a large proportion of the mansion's cut flowers could come from beds outdoors, few hardy plants could compete with the lush qualities and bright colours of tropical flowers. Even in August, glasshouses would still supply pots of gloxinias and anthuriums for the drawing room, and sprays of stephanotis and allamanda for the ladies' hair and boudoirs.

Glass also ensured greater reliability. It allowed the gardener to dictate when his plants would flower and to obtain the finest quality. Tea roses and camellias, for example, could survive outdoors in the south, but under glass they achieved an earlier and longer season and, protected from the elements, were insured against the possibility of frost marring the porcelain perfection of their petals.

As weddings, christenings and balls had to be catered for in addition to all the usual entertainments, glass enabled the gardener to mount a magnificent display whatever the time of year, and by forwarding or holding back stocks of plants as required, the huge demand for extra plants could be met. When the Prince of Wales visited Longleat in 1881, for example, John Wills of Kensington was called in to supply 'large Palms, Tree Ferns, Dracaenas, etc.,' to decorate the grand staircase, the principal corridors and the great hall which served as a ballroom, but everything else in the way of flowers and foliage including 500 carnations and, by implication, as many trusses of pelargoniums and gardenias, as well as hundreds of pots of gesneras and tuberoses had to come from the gardens.[43]

Spring saw the beginning of the many repeating and overlapping cycles of preparation and renewal which were essential if the mansion was not to fall short of the floral ideal. While the planning of the parterre was in full swing, there would also be innumerable plants to repot or propagate for the house and conservatories. The first stage in this process was the mixing of all the different composts. For most purposes, soil from the waiting stacks of turfy loam would be sieved, and then depending on how it was to be used, enriched with old pulverized manure and leaf mould, and lightened with sharp sand, in various proportions. For the orchids, a special mixture of sphagnum moss, fibrous peat and charcoal would be prepared. Thousands of earthenware pots and the 'crocks' to cover the drainage holes, would also have been washed and stacked in order of size. They ranged from 'thumbs' which were only 2½ inches in diameter, and used for the rooted cuttings, to those 12 inches across which would take a full grown chrysanthemum.

Meanwhile, camellias and orange trees were carefully washed and cleaned, and the surface soil renewed and top-dressed with manure. The stove house stephanotis, and other climbers such as the bougainvillea on the back wall of a vinery would be similarly refreshed. Ferns were divided to increase stocks, while hundreds of bulbs, corms and tubers would be brought out from under the benches, shaken out and potted up. These would include the recently introduced gloxinias, achimenes and begonias, as well as the more familiar cyclamen and tuberoses. Bulbs were very accommodating and could be started into growth in batches to extend their flowering season. *Eucharis amazonica*, an essential white flower, could even be induced to flower three times a year and, by retarding some batches and forwarding others, the gardener could have supplies almost all year round. At Drumlanrig Thomson had 60 large pots of eucharis and another expert reported that he succeeded in picking eucharis flowers on 314 of the 365 days of the year.[44]

Other plants such as cockscombs, mignonette, cinerarias and the more ethereal Chinese primulas had to be raised annually from seed sown in the spring, while the azalea collection was increased and replenished by grafting the best varieties on to home grown stocks.

Numerous other decorative species had to be renewed by taking cuttings of soft young growth from stock plants. This produced a generation of new vigorous plants, which generally yielded the best crop of blooms. Gardenias, fuchsias, tea roses, chrysanthemums, pelargoniums, perpetual flowering carnations and heliotrope were all propagated by the hundred in this way, while foliage plants, such as dracaenas, were either mossed to root the tops, or raised from stem cuttings.

Mr Green, for example, who was head gardener at Draycot Manor, the home of Earl Cowley, had a whole series of pits devoted entirely to gardenias and was able to furnish the mansion with cut blooms all year round. In 1873, he achieved a total of 15,396 blooms, of which 3,331 were cut in May for the London house.[45] The chrysanthemums, which with their rich, bright colours were the autumn cut flower and pot plant *par excellence*, would make good flowering plants by September and, by employing a wide range of varieties, and holding some batches back in a cool pit, gardeners could maintain a show until the New Year. Meanwhile pelargoniums would also be prepared for the winter display. Pelargoniums of one kind or another were in flower all year round, but for the prized winter blooms, plants from spring cuttings would be kept disbudded throughout the summer until just before the time came to wheel them into the conservatories or warm houses. The best varieties, such as the esteemed Vesuvius, would then give 15 to 20 trusses per plant and Taylor's stock of the semi-double, rosy crimson Guillon Mangilli were capable of yielding several hundred trusses for a single event.

Perpetual flowering carnations were to become an even more important cut flower. Taylor, who was later credited with laying the foundations of carnation culture, would have several hundred new plants by May which could be moved into the carnation house in the autumn. His stocks would provide him with hundreds upon hundreds of blooms right through the winter to the following Easter.

The care and energy that gardeners put into producing the mansion's pot plants and flowers was matched by their devotion to the preparation and maintenance of the displays themselves. Where cut flowers were concerned, Luckhurst recommended that 'in all large establishments where floral decoration is valued, there should be a "flower room" especially devoted to the work.'[46] He certainly had one in 1881, and at Linton there was a flower room in the kitchen garden complex. Ideally equipped with a sink, a table under the window, and space for all the necessary tools and materials, such a facility allowed the gardener to prepare arrangements and execute the most delicate of construction tasks in cool, clean and peaceful surroundings.

In Luckhurst's flower room, the drawers of the window table contained 'scissors, knives, wire, string, dusters, cotton wool' and a packet of gum arabic which, when dissolved in water, could be dropped into the centre of pelargoniums and azaleas to prevent the petals dropping. A 'bundle of flower sticks' , on to which the flower heads were wired for bouquets, was also to hand. Under the table were boxes of 'white sand, charcoal, and moss'. A small piece of charcoal was added to each vase to keep the water sweet, and sand was often used to hold the flowers in position, while damp moss sustained the flowers in the bouquets. 'A set of water jugs, a very small water pot with a finely perforated rose for moistening sand, a sponge, and a set of brushes for cleaning vases, and a clock' were also essentials, while in a cupboard were large numbers of different-sized blocks to raise bowls above the level of table tops, and stands, vases and bowls of all descriptions.

Flowers would be gathered in the cool of the early morning, the gardener having previously discussed the forthcoming programme of entertainments with his employers, and resolved any special arrangements for the dining table with the butler. Certain flowers such as lily of the valley and hyacinths were best pulled, but most were cut with a sharp knife and put into water as soon as possible. Every effort was made to extend a cut flower's life in the drawing room. The tulip's tendency to hang its head could be overcome by standing the whole length of stem in warm water, and lilies lasted best if cut with short stems. Gathering the flowers young was also important if they were to remain good for any length of time, although 'some kinds of orchids may be left on plants for weeks . . and last almost as long as those cut when just expanded.'[47]

The first call of the day might be for bunches of violets or little pots of primulas for the ladies' breakfast trays, and if the hunting season was under way there would be all the buttonholes to prepare for the guests' riding habits. Meanwhile, the arrangements downstairs would have to be repaired or renewed while the housemaids lit fires and tidied up in preparation for the family's appearance. 'Lord and Ladyship must never hear or see you doing it. There was never a dead flower. It was as if flowers, for them, lived for ever. It was part of the magic in their lives.'[48]

The conservatory also had to be checked and watered before there was any danger of visitors strolling in. Windows had to be opened, canvas screens pulled down if necessary, and condensation carefully avoided if the appearance of the camellias was not to be ruined. Decaying leaves and faded flowers were swiftly removed, and pots brought in from the plant houses if rejuvenation was required. Finally the marble or Minton floor tiles would be swept or washed clean so that not a drop of water or trace of debris should remain.

The lunchtime flowers would then be assembled, if these were required, followed by the buttonholes, bouquets and hair flowers for the evening. These would be sent down two or three hours before dinner, and while the family and guests were preparing themselves, the gardeners went to the dining room to lay out the dinner table decorations. Much of this had to be done after the table had been laid, and required immense care to avoid a range of possible disasters from water on the tablecloth, or in the salt cellars, to the breaking of a piece of crystal.

When the family was in London, the gardener could not usually attend to the floral displays personally. His contribution under these circumstances was to select and prepare plants for their journey to Town with the utmost care. Only flowers which could stand 'the oscillations of the luggage van' would be despatched, and the more delicate blooms reserved for the earlier, cooler months of the family's sojourn, when the stresses of the journey would be less. Plants grown under glass would be hardened off in cooler quarters to 'stiffen up' their flowers and foliage, and prepare them for the rigours of travel, while some, like the pelargoniums, would receive the gum arabic treatment to help keep their petals together.

Packing itself was a highly specialized art. Young spinach leaves were often used to keep the flowers fresh and, in William Iggulden's experience, these were preferable to tissue paper, cotton wool or moss as a packing material. He would line the sides and base of a flower basket with spinach leaves and 'on these are flatly disposed fronds of Ferns, Spiraea leaves and other greenery, and on these are placed a layer of the most robust flowers, next another layer of leaves, lining the sides as before, then follows a layer of more tender flowers in the case of the smaller baskets, or moderately sturdy flowers in the largest baskets and so on till these are filled, the topmost layer invariably consisting of the most fragile flowers.'[49] If the blooms were to reach the ladies in perfect condition it was equally important that 'those who unpack them should never attempt to drag out the under layers before finishing the topmost or much damage may easily result.'

Taylor always sent up immense numbers of roses, and through experience had devised perforated stands to hold and protect them.[50] These would be taken out to the rose bushes early in the morning where, with the dew still on their petals, the half-open flowers would be picked. 'A qualified lad or man selects the roses and places two or three blooms in each hole, but keeping a half inch clear all round the sides.' When filled, the stand would contain between 4 and 6 dozen roses and would be taken to the packing shed. Here it would be checked, faulty blooms replaced, and the stems wedged with a piece of soft wood so that the flowers could not possibly move. The stands were then fitted into carrying boxes with the blooms facing downwards and the stems shortened. Finally, the remaining space was filled with 'long loose flowers, the stalks of the Roses sticking up between them and preventing them rubbing and crushing.' A piece of soft paper was laid over the top, the lid nailed down, and the case declared ready for despatch. In this way between seven and ten boxes carrying 60 dozen roses were sent up for one occasion.

Flowers could be sent up by train, horse van, or even post. Parcel post was not introduced until 1883 but, before this, the daily despatch of choice flowers was possible using small boxes measuring 6 inches by 3 inches. These would be securely tied, and a threepenny stamped addressed parchment label attached 'which receives most of the punching.' Iggulden 'frequently sent six Gardenias, or as many Roses' in this way, and a box in May 1882 contained 'two large Catherine Mermet Roses, two sprays of Stephanotis, and two large blooms of Souvenir de la Malmaison Carnation' which, packed in spinach leaves, invariably reached their destination 'beautifully fresh'.[51] As in everything the gardener did, attention to detail was all.

Men of Influence

he outer reaches of the pleasure ground may have been the limit of the head gardener's domain, but they were not the limit of his influence. Books, journals, horticultural shows and generations of pupils ensured that his opinions and expertise extended far beyond the boundaries of the estate, while his contributions to the raising and testing of new material played a major role in determining the contents of gardens throughout the country. That gardening 'as an art and a science has made great improvement in this country, [was] chiefly though the intelligence and industry of gardeners,' pronounced Robert Fish[1] in the *Journal*, and at a time when there were no horticultural colleges and research institutes and comparatively little relevant academic biology, Victorian head gardeners were indeed the stewards of all past knowledge and a main source of horticultural advance. It was a monopoly which, for the century or so it lasted, gave them unprecedented power over the direction of private and commercial horticulture and a dazzling opportunity to interpret the taste and aspirations of the most powerful groups in society.

HANDING ON THE TRADITION

Every head gardener learned his craft directly from the previous generation of masters and, in turn, passed on his accumulated knowledge to the apprentices and journeymen who came to learn from him. The usual pattern was for a prospective gardener to be taken on in a mansion's gardens as a lad of 12 or 14 years of age. For the first year he would stoke fires, wash pots and, perhaps, help around the glasshouses. This would then be followed by a year in the kitchen garden, and a further twelve months learning the skills of the flower garden.

After three or four years, and if he was able and ambitious, he would qualify as a journeyman and move on to another garden to specialize in a particular skill. After two years or so he would move again, and then perhaps again, the aim being to acquire proficiency in all aspects of horticulture and gain experience of different regional climates and soils. Taylor, for example, began his career at Shrubland in Suffolk, which Donald Beaton, who was one of the acknowledged masters of the flower garden, had made so famous during the 1840s.[2] Later he was employed at

Knowsley near Liverpool, which was renowned for its hardy fruit, and then at Meredith's commercial vinery where he learnt the skills of 'modern grape growing'. Many young gardeners went to work in nurseries or, as Taylor also did after he left Shrubland, at the Horticultural Society's gardens in Chiswick. Others trained at a botanic garden, such as Kew or Edinburgh, and Scottish gardeners, also, made sure they sought some experience in the south. William Ingram, son of the Royal gardener, even went as far afield as France to study.[3]

A successful journeyman would rise through the probationary ranks to qualify for the post of foreman, who took overall charge of one department such as the plant houses, or acted as the head gardener's second-in-command. This entitled him to his own set of tools, and gave him responsibility for the welfare and behaviour of the undergardeners. By the time he reached his late twenties or early thirties he would be in a position to apply for a headship, although this could happen somewhat earlier. David Thomson, for example, became a journeyman at Bothwell Castle when he was 16, then spent two years under the celebrated Robert Marnock at the Royal Botanic Gardens in London and, after a brief spell as foreman to his brother at Wrotham Park in Hertfordshire, took his first post as head gardener at the age of 24.[4]

The main source of posts were advertisements in the journals, and a recommendation from an editor, or one of the top nurserymen, such as Veitch, was undoubtedly a great help in securing one of the better positions. So, too, was to have been at one of the gardens considered a particular centre of excellence. Foremost amongst these were Chatsworth, under Paxton, and Bicton in Devon, where James Barnes was in charge.[5] He was famous for rationalizing pineapple culture, raising the Bicton Pine Strawberry and growing many of the new conifers and shrubs from seed. From his stable came the next head gardener of Chatsworth, Taplin, and Westcott of Raby Castle, Bennett of Rangemore and Snow of Saltram.

Many of the best schools were in Scotland. At the beginning of the century the plant hunter David Douglas and Robert Fish were contemporaries at Scone Palace, the Earl of Mansfield's estate, where Fish's younger brother David also began his career. The Thomson brothers were slips from Bothwell Castle under the renowned plantsman, Andrew Turnbull, while the M'Intosh brothers, and later the Thomsons themselves, made the Duke of Buccleuch's gardens at Dalkeith and Drumlanrig a sure stepping stone to a good placing. Pupils of theirs included Muir of Margam Park, Pettigrew of Cardiff Castle, and Rose of Chatsworth who went on to become Royal gardener in 1868.

Having secured his first post as head gardener, the keen young man – encouraged, no doubt, by the equal ambition of his employer – would then seek to make his mark on the horticultural world or, as Thomas Speed put it more picturesquely, 'to rear a mound of excellent gardening on which I could stand and be seen.'[6] This was the sure route to a more prestigious post at a larger or wealthier establishment. Speed's mound was sufficiently impressive that he went on to become head gardener at Chatsworth, and it was Thomson's transformation of the gardens at Dyrham Park in Barnet, London, that led to his appointment at Archerfield.

Not surprisingly, given the intense competition between garden owners, a certain amount of gentlemanly horticultural headhunting was inevitable. Sometimes, it was only the fortunate foreman to whom visiting guests, impressed by the flower garden or the quality of the dessert, might issue the flattering invitation to pastures new. Sometimes, it was the head gardener himself. In Thomson's case 'there occurred petty annoyances [at Archerfield] which caused him to consider the advisability of transferring his services elsewhere, on hearing of which the Duke of Buccleuch gave him the refusal of the superintendency of Drumlanrig gardens on the retiral of Mr M'Intosh in 1868.'[7]

The training the young gardener received was undoubtedly thorough. In addition to a range of horticultural skills he was required to master reading, writing and arithmetic, the essentials of trigonometry and perspective drawing, aspects of botany and plant physiology, and the management skills to deal with a large staff, tight budgets and difficult employers. Such a schooling was, however, a privilege for which, in the early days at least, he often had to pay dearly. Days were long, wages and living conditions poor, and the apprentices had to share many of the heavy and laborious tasks which were the lot of the lowly garden labourers. It was part of the young men's job, for example, to hand weed the miles of paths, and keep the gravel and acres of grass free from leaves. They had to help hump the hundredweights of coal for the boilers, and the loads of manure and bark for the hotbeds. Looking back on his early days as an apprentice, Thomson recalled 'the kitchen men carrying in all the bark for the pine pits, and they carried in tons of it on their backs up steep stairs, for the ground was deep behind the houses, and I have helped do this in December with stinging frosts, and the sweat dripping off my nose like peas.'[8]

The basic working day for everyone in the garden began at 6 o'clock in the morning and lasted until 6 at night with an hour off for breakfast and another for dinner.[9] In winter, the breaks were reduced in order to squeeze in ten hours of work despite the fewer daylight hours. In addition to this the apprentices also had extra duties. Even the most modern boilers needed stoking late at night to keep up the forcing temperatures, and fires needed tending, ventilators opening and plants watering on Sundays and festivals just as on any other day of the week. Even Christmas day for those on duty 'meant no running to the bothy [their lodgings] save but for meals . There was not, indeed, time for more, but in any case, that was the rule fixed and unalterable.'[10] On this particular occasion, 'At dinner-time (the Christmas dinner, mind) we duty ones went in to find the fire out, for the off duty ones had been ordered off to the railway station to load slack, which, owing to the season, had been delayed in transit . . . With a crust of bread and butter we sought the more congenial clime of the houses or stoke holes. At teatime, fire still out, though the grimy ones had just come in, and we all had to wash and be off for table decoration.'

At busy times of year, the apprentices would have to be thinning grapes at dawn, and potting by candlelight. At some places, evening work was routine. Richard Gilbert of Burghley remembered his early days when 'we used to work every night at something, the gardener declaring he always got the most out of the men after six o'clock, and perhaps twice a year he would make a point by handing us 2s. 6d. each, saying "This will encourage you." ' However we did not think so, still we kept on working.'[11]

Two shillings and sixpence was at that time the equivalent, or more, of an appren-

Dusting crops with insecticidal powder was just one of the unpleasant jobs which fell to the garden apprentices.

tice's entire week's wages. Taylor recalled that while he was an apprentice at Shrubland in the early 1850s he received 2 shillings a week, which was a quarter of the wage that the garden labourers took home to their families. Some head gardeners also extracted a premium for taking on an apprentice, which could amount to £5 or £10 deducted in weekly instalments from his wage, or a lower rate of pay *in lieu*. The practice appeared, however, to be dying out by the 1870s, and some of the most noted gardeners claimed never to have extracted a penny. By this time, too, wages had also improved. Robson, for example, paid the boys at Linton 1s. 4d a day or 8 shillings a week in 1873, and there is no suggestion in his accounts of any deductions.[12]

The young gardeners also received their lodgings. They lived in the bothy, which was a room, or collection of rooms behind the kitchen garden, and in the early part of the century this contributed further to their hardship. Many bothies were remembered as cold, damp miserable hovels, as at Lord Melbourne's residence in Hertfordshire in the 1830s. Situated between and linking two stoke holes, the room looked out 'on a high grassy bank about 10 feet distant, the roof covered with the old-fashioned pantiles, without any ceiling, so that when there came drifting snow it found its way to us as we lay in bed.'[13]

Later in the century conditions, like the wages, had become somewhat better. A visitor to Denbies, the Dorking residence of a wealthy widow, Mrs Cubitt, in 1867, found 'airy dormitories; good, clean, comfortable beds; places for their clothes; a library for them to read in, and means for cooking their food.'[14] At Hamilton Palace, home of the Duke of Hamilton, the bothies were 'princely', in Robson's opinion, with each young man provided with 'a separate sleeping apartment, [and] a dining room, kitchen, scullery and bathroom',[15] while at Lambton Castle there was 'every requisite . . . for promoting health, and provision is also made for sickness.'[16] At Linton, a Mrs Wood was paid 1s. 6d a week in 1873 'for cleaning out the young men's rooms,'[17] and at Drumlanrig the 14 undergardeners enjoyed the full time services of a housemaid, while another woman cooked and cleaned for a second bothy attached to the flower garden, where four more men were housed.[18]

The young gardeners were encouraged to keep themselves to themselves. Attempting to court a housemaid would be certain to blight a young man's prospects, and thoughts of marriage were, in any case, out of the question until he could command a house. Mixing with the stable lads was also frowned upon, as that way led the downhill path to gambling and drink. There was, in any case, little time for such distractions if the apprentice was to apply himself properly to all the demands made upon him.

Underlying a gardener's early training was not only the requirement that he learn the basic horticultural skills, but also, and more fundamentally, that he develop a meticulous and methodical approach to all gardening operations. 'Even the simplest and minutest of these', said Fish, should not be considered 'beneath his careful attention . . . much of the neatness and the comfort of a gentleman's garden depends on the superintendent being practically conversant with the best mode of doing everything, and the quality and quantity of work that ought to be done in certain circumstances . . . We knew an otherwise bright young fellow to whom the sight of a spade was like a nauseous dose of medicine in prospect. For the life of him he could not turn over a 5 foot flower bed without leaving one side some 8 or 9 inches higher than the other, and aye, he would plant it too in that condition.' This misguided lad's performance on the lawns was also to be an example to those similarly inclined. He 'knew as little about a scythe as the man who never saw one.'[19]

Fish also laid great stress on the value of forethought and efficient organization. He believed that the motto written over the door of every tool shed should be 'In doing work avoid making work', and contrasted the man who, once set a task, would take with him all he needed 'hoe, rake, ties, stakes, broom and basket or barrow' to tidy up a flower bed, with the second-rate workman who would muddle along, so that 'ultimately there is the double journey for a broom and a barrow, to the no small wearing of shoe leather.' Indeed, Fish observed, 'want of method, more than want of knowledge, is often the cause of want of success.'

Fish took his role of teacher extremely seriously, to the extent of dispensing detailed advice to young gardeners through the pages of the *Journal*. He exhorts them to carry a notebook with them at all times in which to record even the smallest details, and to keep a diary 'especially of sowing, planting, gathering, [and] changes of temperature produced either naturally or artificially.' Everything that was sent to the mansion or planted in the flower garden was also to be noted, together with when and how much was required, how long it lasted, and so on. On log books such as these, painstakingly compiled over his years as an apprentice and journeyman, the success of a head gardener could depend.

The need to maintain good and careful records, keep accounts, follow the journals, and draw up plans also meant that 'the young gardener should be well up in reading, writing and arithmetic.' As many only had a smattering of the three Rs, this might need 'resolute determination'. In Fish's experience 'some of our ablest, most intelligent gardeners can look back to the time when, as they handled the fire-shovel, they could scarcely spell their way through a simple sentence. What they have done others may do.'

At Putteridge Bury, as at many other places, the apprentices and journeymen were encouraged to read as much as possible as 'it must be the chief means of increased information to the young gardener.' The list of recommended titles ran from Loudon's *Encyclopaedia of Gardening*, Lindley's *Theory of Horticulture* and Johnson's *Science and Practice of Gardening*, through to Hogg's *Fruit Manual* and nurseryman Williams's *Orchid Growers' Manual*. He also had to read the gardening journals which, as at Linton, could be taken for him by his employers, and he might purchase for himself the inexpensive reprints of particularly useful articles. Five postage stamps, for example, would obtain a copy of *Fruit Gardening for the Many*, or *Manures and Muck for the Many* from the *Journal*'s office, while 16 stamps could purchase *Flower Gardening, Greenhouse and Florists' Flowers* or *Garden Plans*.

The question of a lad's writing and spelling also received detailed attention as, in Fish's view, 'writing down what he knows is one of the best agents by which he can plumb the depths or the shallowness of his information, and is often the only agent he can use for making his knowledge influential upon others.' As far as the writer's hand was concerned, Fish considered 'that writing is the best that can be read as easily as print.' On the question of style, he is equally definite. The 'shorter the sentences are, the more pleasant and perspicuous the reading.' Spelling was best helped by reading 'the good authors slowly with an occasional turn-up of the dictionary', and this was also the way to acquire the art of composition. The 'clear expression of ideas, natural sequence of these ideas, and a pleasing impression and clear comprehension by the ear when . . . read aloud', would not be gained by reading popular novels with their 'high sounding rodomontade and abundance of low slang'. Even after a hard day in the garden it had to be 'The Book of Books, the pages of the "Spectator", and the volumes of the "Gardener's Magazine" especially after the great Loudon was united to Mrs Loudon, for seeing how massive strength and vigour may be combined with the terse, simple, old Saxon, with its short words and short sentences.'

Equally important the prescription continued, were the four rules of arithmetic. All too often, Fish had 'met with otherwise bright young lads who could not count above a certain number, and whose calculations, even of simple sums, had to be done by the fingers instead of by the pencil or the pen.'[20] Gardeners needed to be able to cope with fractions, square roots, volume calculations, decimals and geometry if they were to plan gardens and garden structures, and estimate quantities for builders and carpenters. In addition, for anything 'much in the way of land-surveying, an acquaintance with logarithms and trigonometry will be a very great advantage.'

Ambitious young men were also urged to become familiar with the principles of isometric and perspective drawing. 'We have known some men get easily to the top of their profession, because when their employers did not know what they meant . . . they could render it all clear in a few minutes by means of a pencil and pocket notebook.' Fish's colleague, Robson, was particularly renowned for the excellence of his plans, and such skills were fostered by competitions sponsored by horticultural organizations. In 1878, all three of the prizes offered by the Scottish Horticultural Society were won by the young men from Linton.[21]

Young gardeners everywhere were also expected to show a healthy interest in the science of their chosen calling. Botanic studies could be pursued in the surrounding countryside which offered ample scope for the assembly of a personal herbarium during the spring and summer months, and the exotic material in the garden extended their range still further. At Bothwell Castle, for example, in addition to all the tropical flowers in the glasshouses, the young men had a herbaceous border containing '700 different kinds all named and numbered' for them to examine.[22]

Punctiliousness in the use and spelling of Latin names on plant labels was expected, but pronunciation could follow local custom with more, or less, of a nod in the direction of the basic rules laid down by Loudon.[23] A wider knowledge of the classics was considered desirable, but 'not at all likely to be general until employers show their appreciation of such requirements by a suitable remuneration.' As it was more important to most proprietors to have a decent gardener than a learned scholar this was an unlikely prospect. 'There are very many who will excuse a comparative ignorance of botany, who will not even find their ears tingle at the uncouth pronouncing of the name of a plant, who will be slow to find any excuses for rickety plants, half-filled flowerbeds, a want of crisp vegetables, and a deficiency of ripened, perfect, well flavoured fruit.'

Having mastered the basics of systematic botany, it was more profitable for the young men to expend their scientific efforts on plant physiology.[24] They had to observe 'the different structures of plants, tracing the whole movements that take place from the germination of a seed or the striking of a cutting until the time comes when the plant dies from disease, age, or accident; this including the functions of the different parts of the plant, especially roots, leaves and stem; how these are influenced by soils; mechanically and chemically by air, by dryness, and moisture, by heat, and cold, by sunlight and shade and darkness; by diversity of seasons, varieties and peculiarities of climate, not merely as to the highest and lowest temperature, and medium temperatures, but as to how these are conjoined with shade or bright sunshine and altitude as well as latitude of the natural home of a plant.' The industrious student would also be drawn into other related subjects such as the nature of soils, character of manures, hydraulics, meteorology and entomology.

The more fortunate pupils did, however, receive considerable support and encouragement in what must at times have seemed like an unequal struggle. At some places, for example, they would gather together for discussion and the submission of prepared talks under the guidance of the head gardener. Gilbert of Burghley notes that with '5 in rooms' in 1879 'among the pleasant hours I spend are those engaged in evening's chat with them.'[25] At Drumlanrig, the gardeners formed themselves into a Mutual Improvement Association in 1871, and in their tenth anniversary year the range of topics covered was comprehensive to say the least. They considered the 'Eradication of Garden Insects; Protection of Wall-Fruits; Formation of Character; Certain Trades and Professions as Causes of Disease; Cultivation of the Cyclamen; Cultivation of the Azalea; Progress in Australia; The Pansy; Cultivation of the Strawberry; The Conservatory; Temperance; Forcing of the Fig; Government by Party; Does Civilisation necessitate Demoralisation? Food; Potato Disease; Cultivation of the Balsam; Cultivation of the Bouvardia; Movements of Plants; Garden-

Walks; Hardy Plants for Walls; Cultivation of the Raspberry; Pruning of outdoor Fruit-trees; The Camellia; Man's Inhumanity to Man; Hotbeds and their uses' and 'Cultivation of the Orange'. The list concluded with 'Window plants, and their Injuriousness to Health'.[26]

LEARNING TO MANAGE

Important as it was to acquire an intimate knowledge of plants and their predilections, no aspiring head gardener was going to succeed unless he acquired a manager's skills in equal measure. This was a much less precise subject both to learn and to teach, and the example set by a young man's mentor in this respect could set the tone for the whole of his future career. It was a matter to which Taylor, in particular, devoted considerable thought and attention. 'All soldiers', he wrote, 'have not the capacity to become generals, and it is possible that management is to some degree a natural gift, but it is quite certain that much may be gained by cultivation.'[27]

As a large establishment had to fulfil the combined tasks of market garden, commercial orchard, pot plant nursery, florist's shop and pleasure ground, and would employ between 20 and 50 gardening staff to do so, it was not easy to ensure that everything was done efficiently, economically and at the right time. 'Management of oneself and the management of those under our command are mixed together so intimately,' Taylor continues, 'that if we succeed in doing the first the other becomes very much simplified.' But, he observes, 'self-management has another aspect besides that which has to do with the workmen. There is often great and frequent provocation from unsympathetic employers, employers' friends and their children, as well as from servants, ranging from the scullery maid to the agent, with all of whom the gardener must keep on good terms if he would live in peace and have the most made of his produce.'

Managing employers was, perhaps, the most difficult task. Luckhurst advised the young learner that there was 'no necessity for cringing or an excessive display of humility' but rather he should 'quietly study the wishes of his employers without officiousness.'[28] Taylor is also adamant that, however sorely tried the gardener may feel, 'self control in the presence of employers is particularly to be insisted upon.'[29]

The trials, it seems, were many. Fanciful and impulsive employers, who were forever changing their minds, were among the most trying to serve, but equally hard to please were those who expected miracles, such as grapes all year round when they had only half the number of vineries as their neighbours. Ladies who wrenched off camellia blooms, splitting the branches and preventing the development of flowers in the future, made great demands on tact and patience, while similar diplomacy was needed when, as another gardener recounts, they took the tops off the amaryllis bulbs, as well as the blooms, because they 'liked green with the flowers.'[30] Somehow, these ladylike transgressors had to be gently taught that 'plants will not live without leaves, and with such treatment the bulbs would die.'

The gardener also had to be prepared to spend hours repairing the destruction which could be unthinkingly wrought anywhere in his immaculate garden or pleasure ground. The crinoline of the 1860s, recalled one gardener, would sweep through the parterres like 'a besom of destruction', snapping off flower heads, while the same 'armour plated ladies' could pass through the narrow alleys of the conservatory, bringing blooms to the ground by the dozen.[31] Even walks could be ruined by visitors after several days of rain. 'They will come out and perambulate backwards and forwards as if a task were assigned to them to make as many marks as they could with hob-nailed shooting-boots.' Even though there might be stone walks and rougher walks 'they must choose the smooth walk', leaving as many marks as 'if they had been dancing a hornpipe on it.'[32]

Satisfying the big house also involved the gardener in successfully negotiating his relationships with the cook and butler. Here again, the gardener could often find himself in a difficult position. 'Cooks and housekeepers knew no substitutes' yet seemed unaware of the difficulties gardeners sometimes faced in meeting their demands.

The gathering of fruit could also be a contentious issue. At some establishments it was customary to allow the cooks or parlour maids to pick a dish of strawberries whenever they wished, and for children to go strawberry picking as they pleased. For a new head gardener, with the clear remit to send in the best for the table, this was an impossible situation. He had to restrict access to his crop, even if it meant taking the matter up with his employer. No one, said Fish, but 'the gardener should gather fruit or someone with clean hands and a quick eye on whom he can rely.'[33] If the butler was accustomed to arranging the displays for dinner, however, the new gardener was well advised to bide his time until extra help was needed and he could make his superior skills tactfully apparent.

When it came to managing the workforce in the garden, many of the most successful head gardeners published advice. High on their list of essentials was that of discipline. 'Strict government is the kindest' they affirm.[34] No scamping is to be allowed amongst the youngsters, chatterboxes are to be separated and it is recommended that unpunctuality be discouraged by a docking of wages. 'Harsh language', however, 'should never be resorted to' emphasizes Luckhurst.

Fines were often suggested as a means of punishing lapses in method and workmanship but Fish was the advocate of a more enlightened scheme.[35] His approach was to keep the fine small – a penny or twopence at the most – and instead of giving them to the master, have them collected by the best of the men, and spent as the majority wished. He reports how he once introduced such fines for shortcomings such as 'going out with insufficient tools, taking tools to a shed dirty, stepping on a walk with dirty boots, taking a dirty barrow wheel over a walk, or on a walk at all, when it could be avoided.' It was 'astonishing', he asserts, 'how well the system worked, and how keenly every man took hold of a slip in his fellow-workman', and he did not recollect 'a single unpleasantness'.

After discipline, next in importance came the organization of the workforce so that no one should ever be without a job to do. This usually required a head gardener to walk around at dawn or twilight, with his notebook in hand, listing and planning the next day's operations. He is reminded to keep back some dry jobs in the houses so that on days when the weather is bad there will be no shortage of 'washing, cleaning, scrubbing, tying, pruning, top dressing etc. [which] can be done much better on a wet than sunny one – that is with more ease by the workman . . . a little consideration will thus ensure that a wet day in a garden shall be the farthest removed from idleness and its natural consequences. The very change of work and scene promotes activity.'[36] This was not only an efficient use of labour, it also helped to keep the men happy. As Fish observed, the days of sending men out to nail wall fruit in snowy weather or mowing with the rain streaming down their backs belonged, he hoped, to 'the barbarous past . . . when the gardener cared naught for the welfare of his men.'[37]

The essence of good management stemmed also from attention to detail in every department. It was as important to ensure that trenching in the kitchen garden did not turn into mere digging as it was to check several times a day that the vinery was up to temperature. As an undergardener's slip could easily ruin the early grapes, endanger the orchid collection, and everybody's reputation into the bargain, the head gardener was exhorted to have eyes everywhere and keep all but the most experienced on a very tight rein. A new recruit in particular, however proud he might be of serving in 'the celebrated gardens of my Lord Duke' needed to be treated 'as an exotic for which you do not fully know the use nor the requirements.'[38]

Nevertheless, it was inevitable that even in the best run garden there would occasionally be failures. In 1879, for example, a noxious fungus overran the mushroom beds at Longleat,[39] and, another year, blight decimated the tomatoes. The gardener had to learn to cope with such disasters. When Robson was faced with a poor carrot crop at Linton in 1865 he arranged to buy in from a neighbouring garden.[40] When the boiler cracked in the middle of the forcing season, there was nothing for it but to nurse it through with patches and bungs until the warm weather came and it could be replaced.

Finally, there was the question of finance. Managing the garden's budget, calculating the wages, keeping the accounts and paying the bills were all the head gardener's responsibility. At all but the wealthiest establishments, ambition was always ahead of the resources available, and economies of every kind were a matter of both pride and necessity to the gardener. Robson, for example, would often use the foliage of box rather than hot-house flowers for the winter table arrangements, or employ the palm-like leaves of the wild hellebore to dress the base of the March stands. Out in the garden, nails from the fruit walls would be re-used, watering cans mended by the itinerant tin-man, and a 'diamond, putty and glass [kept] to hand.' The better a head gardener managed his resources, the more he was able to achieve in the garden, and the happier both he and his employer would be.

The records that survive for Linton for the years 1864 to 1873 give an indication of the kinds of constraints within which a gardener at a moderately sized establishment worked. Robson's total expenditure on the garden in 1873 came to £680. 13s. 1½d, while the mansion's bills just for 'replastering kitchen, doing roof, carting coals and other stuff to house, brewing, [and] cleaning windows' came to £344. 10s. 4½d.[41] The mansion also seems to have consumed five times as much coal as all Robson's hot-houses put together. It is clear, too, that gardeners would take every opportunity to create a little extra revenue. In 1865, for example, Robson's accounts show he made

£23.7s.6d from the sale of surplus fruit.

The largest expenditure by far was on wages. With these ranging in 1873 from 8 shillings for the garden boy and 14 shillings for a skilled journeyman to 19 shillings for the most senior man, the weekly wage bill was rarely less than £10. The numbers employed fluctuated over the years between a dozen and twenty men, with wives and workers from other estate jobs being drafted in as required. Learning how to judge the amount of labour required was, therefore, one of the first lessons an aspiring head gardener had to master, and the inverse relationship between wages and other forms of expenditure underlined still further the importance of organizing work and the workforce as efficiently as possible.

After the men had been paid, the gardener's budget had to meet all the expenses of maintenance and renewal, while also allowing for the acquisition of novel material. Employers would advance extra finance for major projects such as the building and stocking of Linton's new conservatory, but how to make the most of the funds available was down to the gardener. Plants, for example, could be expensive. For the new conservatory, Lady Holmesdale spent £106.15s.0d. at Veitch's on ferns alone. This is, perhaps, why plants were often sought at auctions. Robson's accounts for 1865 show not only his purchases at the Combermere Abbey sale in Cheshire, but also at other auctions. On one occasion he bought wellingtonia seed for £1.6s.0d, and '7 lots of roses, 84 in all' and on another, acquired over a thousand shrubs. The London auction rooms were another way of assembling the latest novelties. In 1865 Robson also purchased 'new Japanese plants, all newly introduced from that country and consisting of 140 plants', as well as *Lilium auratum* bulbs and some new orchids. In matters such as this, as in all the less tangible aspects of garden management, the example of an astute and experienced mentor was the best training the aspirant could receive.

SPREADING THE WORD

The education of apprentices and undergardeners may have been the most direct way in which head gardeners passed on their philosophy and techniques, but they reached a much wider audience through books, gardening journals, the world of competitive horticulture, and the widespread custom of garden visiting.

Loudon's *Gardener's Magazine*, which he launched in 1826, provided gardeners for the first time with a forum for critical discussion and the free exchange of ideas. Such openness contrasted strongly with the self-conscious mystery which had previously surrounded horticulture. Looking back to his youth in the early years of the century, Robson recalled that 'the age was one of exclusiveness, as there was assumed a sort of secrecy in the art of cultivating certain plants, which it was thought improper to make too generally known. Modes of growing Auriculas, Pinks, Tulips, Ranunculuses, etc, were pretended to be kept as profound secrets by those entrusted with them.' He recounts how well he remembered when 'it was customary for a visitor to a nursery at grafting-time to find when he approached the man performing the operation that the knives all wanted sharpening, and that scissors were not at hand, but had to be sent for, and did not arrive till the stranger had gone.'[42]

As the century progressed, Loudon's example, combined with the advent of cheap paper, the growing interest in gardening, and the flood of new plants and technology on which information and guidance were required, paved the way for many more publications. These ranged from Scotland's *The Gardener*, which was edited first by William Thomson and then his brother David, to Shirley Hibberd's weekly for amateur gardeners *The Gardener's Magazine* and William Robinson's polemical *The Garden*. There was also the monthly proceedings of the Royal Horticultural Society and a number of specialized journals, such as the *Florist and Pomologist*. The most important, however, were the *Gardeners' Chronicle and Agricultural Gazette*, and its chief rival the *Cottage Gardener, Country Gentleman's Companion, and Poultry Chronicle* which was to become the *Journal of Horticulture, Cottage Gardening, and Country Gentleman*. The *Gardeners' Chronicle*, which was the more academic of the two, was founded in 1841 by Paxton and John Lindley, who was Secretary of the Horticultural Society and also became Professor of Botany at London University. He acted as the magazine's editor until his death in 1865, when he was succeeded by the botanist Maxwell Masters.

The *Cottage Gardener* was set up some five years later by George W. Johnston, a garden historian and barrister. The pomologist Robert Hogg became its joint owner and editor in 1860, and it was in 1861, following comments that the contents were more suited to an establishment with a double coach house than a cottage, that its title was changed. It had an 'editorial board' composed of about a dozen advisers, most of whom were head gardeners. In 1863, these included Robson, who looked after all matters relating to the fruit and kitchen garden, David Thomson, whose responsibility was the flower garden, and Robert Fish, who advised on the stove house. Luckhurst and Taylor were also to join this august company.

These periodicals aired every conceivable subject of horticultural interest from the composition of the soil in the vine borders and the aesthetics of floral decoration to gardeners' wages and the threat of foreign imports to the home fruit and vegetable industry. They were remarkable not only for their range of content but also for the breadth of their readership. The *Journal* and the *Chronicle* would be read as eagerly in the mansion as in the bothy, and contrived to meet the needs of the suburban amateur as well as those of the professional market gardener and the head of a vast pleasure ground. Through their densely written pages head gardeners were able not only to enter into a valuable dialogue with each other but also to influence the shape and content of gardens at every social level. They reported in detail on their own work, reviewed that of others, and dispensed advice and judgements to private and commercial men alike – the industry did not have a separate press until the end of the century. Readers were also invited to write in with their problems and queries, and the uncertain to submit their plans and planting schemes for professional scrutiny and advice.

The questions – and answers – they received were wide-ranging and to the point. One issue of the *Journal* finds an adviser suggesting to an employer who complains that his new gardener is only interested in teaching the coachman Latin, to be patient, while Fish pronounces on the tricky question of the exchange of plants between gardeners: he cautions that all plants belong to the proprietor. Readers' planting schemes receive detailed if sometimes lordly attention. In one issue Fish inveighs against a group of beds one hapless correspondent wishes to plant in stripes of red white and purplish-blue verbenas.[43] 'It is just the old story of having a white-bodied phaeton with one wheel red and the other purple,' he observes loftily.

The periodicals also published papers from nurserymen, and from the gardening clergy, who figured prominently among the amateur botanists, entomologists and fungi experts contributing to the journals. In addition, there were reports on the latest plant introductions, accounts of garden visits, book reviews and detailed show reports. Market prices, meteorological reports and gardening calendars were included in every issue. With advertisements for everything from patent insecticides to pruning knives, and many line drawings, they were weighty tomes – in every sense of the word.

Editing and contributing to the journals not only helped gardeners establish their credentials and demonstrate their authority but it was also an important way of advancing and setting standards in a field that had no formal organization. It must also have provided a useful extra income; certainly enough to make it worthwhile putting pen to paper at the end of a long and demanding day. Fish, for example, produced 2-3,000 words every week for his regular *Journal* column 'Doings of the Last Week', while Luckhurst managed to keep the pieces flowing despite undertaking the massive transformation of Oldlands. Donald Beaton, head gardener at Shrubland in the 1840s and early 1850s, wielded his pen so effectively that when an admirer offered to provide him with an experimental garden, he was able to retire and live off his writing.[44]

These forays into print also led several head gardeners to publish books. Taylor's immensely detailed account of growing grapes, which first appeared in the *Journal*, was later published as *Vines of Longleat* and was even translated into French. David Thomson wrote two widely appreciated books, the *Handy Book of the Flower Garden* and *Fruit Culture under Glass*, and John Wright, who succeeded Hogg as editor of the *Journal* in 1897, produced a book on mushrooms and the enduring *Fruit Growers' Guide*. John Perkins and William Low both wrote books on floral decoration, while William Iggulden produced a volume on tomatoes.

Shows and Visits

In addition to their writing and teaching, gardeners also had other showcases for their skills. The first of these was their own garden which was always on display to visitors to the mansion and to other gardeners, and many were also open to the public. Putteridge Bury, for example, received hundreds of visitors in three days in 1862.[45] The peripatetic nature of Society, the competition between those within it, and the aspirations of those below, all combined to ensure that new ideas spread rapidly. A head gardener's introductions and experiments one year could easily be high garden fashion the next.

Gardeners also tried to make a point of seeing their colleagues' work for themselves. This was not just a question of keeping an eye on the latest trends in the flower garden – though this was important – but of keeping up-to-date with the latest developments whether they were botanical, gastronomic, technical or mechanical. As Fish observed, 'if an employer wants the best out of his gardener he needs to send him to a Metropolitan Exhibition every year and to the most celebrated gardens.' Fish himself spent two weeks making a tour of Irish gardens in 1861, while Robson made a series of visits to Cornish gardens in 1874. Reports of such visits figure prominently in the literature as it was impossible for anyone to visit more than a handful of places personally each year, and a fellow professional's experience was the best substitute. Visiting gardens and other places of horticultural interest was also considered a valuable addition to a young gardener's training.

As an example of an ideal trip, Robson suggested an itinerary centred on Liverpool – a large and prosperous city offering the visitor plenty of opportunity to catch up with the various aspects of his rapidly changing profession.[46] 'Let the traveller make arrangements for starting early . . . and take a stroll in the town till 6 o'clock when he might make his way to the Botanic Garden . . . After breakfast, he may start again towards the great centre of attraction – the Exchange, near which is the fruit and vegetable market, but he must not delay long, for he will have to visit Chester, and the princely seat of the Marquis of Westminster.'

This he could approach on foot, walking the three miles from Chester through the meadows to Eaton Hall. Here he would 'see one of the happiest examples of an embroidered garden intermingled with beds for bedding plants, the whole being on a scale benefiting the richly decorated character of the mansion, which exhibits to the fullest extent the varied embellishments of which gothic architecture is susceptible.'

The next day would see the determined visitor off to Meredith's 'extensive Graperies' at Garston, while the following morning after that might be set aside for a trip out to see Lord Derby's estate at Knowsley. He could also consider heading northwards to Wigan and Haigh Hall, the seat of the Earl of Crawford and Balcarras, which excelled in forcing of all kinds.

A similar visit to London might include a trip to Battersea Park to see the tropical bedding and a visit to Veitch's in the King's Road, or alternatively Low's at Clapton to view the orchid collection and the newest tropical introductions. The visitor might also take in a show or exhibition at the Crystal Palace and catch up on the latest in carpet bedding.

Apart from his garden, the gardener had a second arena in which to perform: the horticultural show. Here he could be either an exhibitor or a judge, depending on the circumstances and his expertise. In both roles he was able to influence the criteria growers aimed for, and contribute still further to the maintenance and raising of standards within the profession and in the world of gardening as a whole.

During the 1860s horticultural shows and exhibitions of every kind proliferated. At one end of the scale were the local shows organized by the hundreds of gardening societies which were becoming a feature of village life. At these, the local head gardener would be the judge while his Lordship provided the prizes and the show tent was pitched in the mansion's grounds. Linton, for example, played host each year to the local Cottager's Show, which merited a staff holiday.

Next came the County and City shows, which followed in the wake of the Royal Horticultural Society's example of 1867 when it staged its first provincial show. These gave professional gardeners the chance to test their skills in open competition against peers and colleagues, and allowed nurseryman an important shop window for their latest developments and acquisitions. They also provided everyone from amateurs right through to the professional and commercial men with a chance to see the enormous range of plants in cultivation and assess the value of new varieties and culture techniques.

In London, the frequent Royal Botanic and Horticultural Society Shows, and those held at the Crystal Palace, were important events in the Social calendar. The Royal family, together with all the more fashionable members of Society, would gather in Regent's Park, Kensington, or out at Sydenham to see the magnificent displays. In March, there would be hyacinths to admire; and in April and May azaleas and rhododendrons. Roses in June provided a fitting climax. Apart from being places to be seen, these occasions also allowed estate owners to see all the latest introductions gathered together in one place, and to bask in the immense social gratification of having a specimen from their orchid house or pinery declared so publicly superior.

The most important shows were those honoured with the title 'International'. Many gardeners, for example, remembered the International Fruit and Flower Show, which opened in Edinburgh on 4th September, 1865.[47] The Fruit Committee sat up all night staging the entries so that the judging could commence at 6 o'clock in the morning and be over by 9 a.m. when gardeners were admitted for a shilling preview before the doors opened to the public at 11 a.m. What the crowds then beheld was a quantity and quality of hothouse fruit 'never witnessed before'.

Entries had come in from all over the country. Third prize in the most prestigious of all the competitions, the award for a collection of twenty fruits, was won by Mr Tillery, head gardener to the Duke of Portland, whose Welbeck estate was in Nottinghamshire, while the Duke of Roxburghe's Mr Rose, from Floors Castle in the Border Counties, took fourth place. The coveted first and second places went, respectively, to William and David Thomson, who were pioneers in the art of exhibiting fruit. The winning entry consisted of 'two excellent Smooth-leaved Cayenne Pines, and a handsome Queen, of the exceptional weight of 6½ lbs; splendid bunches of Black Hamburgh, Lady Downe's, Calabrian Raisin, and Muscat Grapes; two well grown Melons, Crawford's Early and Bellegarde Peaches; Elruge Nectarines, Moor Park Apricots, Jefferson and Victoria Plums, Figs, Morello Cherries, Red and White Currants, Kerry Pippin Apples and Jargonelle Pears'. Ten years later the same occasion witnessed the weighing in of 'the world's heaviest bunch of grapes' and the use of the electric telegraph to wire down the momentous news to Fleet Street.

The year 1866 saw the mounting of the ambitious International Horticultural Exhibition and Congress, at the Royal Horticultural Society's Gardens in Kensington.[48] This was intended to be the gardening equivalent of the Great Exhibition of 1851, and the tented and landscaped site covered 3½ acres. True to its title, it included exhibits from Ghent, Brussels and Paris. London nurserymen brought in plants by the horse van-load and Kew sent palm and banana trees. Gardens of note from as far away as Dumfries and Hereford were represented.

The report in the *Journal* is so vivid that even those who did not number among the thousands of visitors who attended must have almost felt they had been there. Entering the marquee on 22nd May 'you were at once met, very wisely, not by an outburst of colour and beauty, but by a screen of Pines, Yews, pyramidal Box etc.' Once past these, everything had been done 'to give effect to the toute ensemble.' Water trickled over rock work where the ferns were displayed, 'there were little valleys of Rhododendrons, which were planted in the soil; while all around on grass mounds and terraces were placed such gorgeous masses of blooms in [the exhibits of] Azaleas, Geraniums, and Roses; such wonderful variety of form and colour in the different classes; that it was impossible to take in all at once, or indeed at all.' There were foliage plants, palms and tree ferns, conifers, forced fruit and vegetables, dinner table decorations, bouquets and garden ornaments and tools.

As long again as the main marquee was the heated orchid tent which adjoined it. In here it was 'difficult not to feel that satiety which comes after such a visual feast as this, as does the same sense to the alderman of St Thomas Backchurch after my Lord Mayor's feast, when callipash and callipee and salmon, and venison, fat capons, etc. have been laid under contribution!'

Growing specimens for competition was time-consuming and essentially a labour of love. Gardeners grumbled that prize money barely covered their travelling expenses, although a couple of 'firsts' at a big show, where the awards could be as much as £10 or £15, must have been something of a bonus. Nevertheless, the personal satisfaction and, even more important perhaps, the prestige associated with winning was considerable. It helped establish the gardener's authority among his peers, and it certainly did his position at the mansion no harm when an employer conducted his guests around the country's finest collection of stove plants, or set the fruits of his prizewinning vinery before them at dessert. National recognition as a leader in the field would also lead to an invitation to be a judge in his own right, and would admit the head gardener to the ranks of the most distinguished figures in the horticultural world. William Thomson of Dalkeith, Tillery of Welbeck and G.T.Miles of Wycombe Abbey, another celebrated grower of hot-house fruits, all became national judges. James Douglas of Loxford Hall became a judge in the flower classes, specializing in carnations and hyacinths.

As well as aiming for fine quality and perfect appearance, all competitive gardeners then – as now – seem to have been fascinated by size. The 1875 Edinburgh competition for the heaviest bunch of grapes did not, for example, pass off without incident.[49] The runner-up disputed the right of the winner to his prize, on the grounds that his 26 lbs 4 oz bunch of the variety Calabrian Raisin was, in fact, two bunches. The decision was, however, upheld.

Monster specimens were also beloved of the vegetable fraternity who vied to produce the largest leek and heaviest onion. Nevertheless, the most prestigious awards were for perfectly matched selections displaying each variety's particular attributes to its best advantage. The greatest prize of the year was the Carter's Challenge Cup for a collection of twenty vegetables. This was worth £50, of which £10 went to the

Kingston-on-Thames Chrysanthemum Show, November 1886. At the far end are the specimen plants 'some 4 or 5 feet in diameter and bearing hundreds of blooms'. Other tables display single blooms and collections of apples and pears.

gardener, and carried a silver trophy for the employer. It was won three times by Gilbert of Burghley, whose exhibit in July 1875 formed an 'exceedingly fine and beautifully arranged' display. In this the 'Peas, Onions, Beans, Turnips, Carrots, Lettuce, Potatoes, Cauliflowers, and Globe Artichokes were splendid.' Likewise, the 'Melons, Cucumbers, Celery, Mushrooms, Asparagus and Parsley [were] very good.'[50]

Size was also a theme in some flower tournaments. A champion bloom, at least in some classes, combined the greatest size with 'the perfect phase of its possible beauty'. Roses were the speciality of the clergy, who also went in for dahlias and gladioli, but the chrysanthemum king of the 1880s was Edwin Molyneux, head gardener to W. H. Myers of Swanmore Park in Hampshire. Myers was an employer who made no secret of his enthusiasm for the competition stakes and had provided Molyneux with 'all requisite means for high culture, and given encouragement that has contributed in no small degree to the remarkable success.'[51]

Competing at this level involved having a stock of at least 72 varieties and 600 plants. The pots of chrysanthemums formed a promenade at the back of Swanmore's vineries and peach houses, and created a forest of blooms in the central display house. Molyneux swept the board from Southampton to Stoke Newington, the London home of the Chrysanthemum Society. In his triumphant season of 1885 he captured seven firsts, one second and one third at the Crystal Palace, five firsts at Winchester and eight first prizes – including for the fourth time, the top award of the 25-guinea Silver Vase – at Kingston.

In achieving perfection of appearance on the show bench, a certain amount of 'dressing' was permitted. Recalcitrant petals would be drawn into place with forceps, and any dust accumulated on the journey brushed off. As the display was set up, each bloom would be named and then hidden until the last possible minute with a sheet of tissue paper as, in Molyneux's experience, opponents were 'often anxious to know what they have to contend against in each class, and if they are weak in certain points they can marshal their forces, so to speak, to their advantage; therefore take all available means to keep them in the dark until it is too late for them to make any alterations in their stands.'[52]

This kind of devotion, and almost paranoid anxiety, was the pattern repeated in gardens and show tents up and down the country. It differed only in detail between fruit men, vegetable fanciers and flower experts, although it is unlikely, perhaps, that they were all as modest and philosophical as Molyneux. Accept the congratulations and greetings unostentatiously, he advises and, if unlucky, return home 'a wiser if sadder man, but with the spirit of emulation stronger within you. Much information can be gained from defeat, and if turned to account it may enable you to out-distance your rival on the next occasion.'

NEW PLANTS AND NEW INDUSTRIES

As well as cultivating, writing about and judging plants, head gardeners also played a fundamental role in determining what was actually grown in both private and commercial gardens. Controlled hybridization, the deliberate cross-pollination of one species or variety by another had flourished since the pioneering work of the fruit and vegetable breeder Thomas Andrew Knight had shown the way at the end of the eighteenth century. Nurserymen, amateur enthusiasts and professional gardeners all contributed to the raising of new varieties, and it was not unusual for the best of a head gardener's hybrids to join the nurserymen's successes and be grown all over the country. The lengthy list of dessert fruits originally raised in private kitchen gardens included the widely grown Foster's seedling grape, the Ecklinville apple, the Bryanston Gage, and Frogmore cherries and strawberries. Among the vegetables, Douglas' Tender and True Cucumber was a notable addition to the nurserymen's lists, as was the Nuneham Park onion and the 'Chou de Burghley' raised by Richard Gilbert.

The work of the Dean of Manchester, the Honourable and Reverend William Herbert, on amaryllis and gladioli, which was published in the 1820s, similarly encouraged the breeding of ornamentals. Flower gardens everywhere owed a debt to the Trentham Rose pelargonium and the Belvoir wallflower, while Peter Grieve's experiments in hybridization at Culford Hall in Suffolk led to the proliferation of many varieties of variegated-leaved pelargoniums, such as the still famous Mrs Pollock. Malmaison carnations, beloved of Edwardians, were largely developed by James Douglas, and Edwin Beckett, who was head gardener to Vicary Gibbs at Aldenham House, Hertfordshire made an enduring contribution to the modern michaelmas daisy.

The orchards, kitchen gardens and pleasure grounds of country estates also acted as independent trial grounds for the flood of foreign introductions and new hybrids which filled page upon euphoric page of the nurserymen's catalogues. At Margam Park in South Wales, for example, Muir had 30 varieties of peas on trial in 1878, and 36 different named tomatoes in 1881.[53] These included one bred by Thomson at Drumlanrig, and the local variety, Crossling's Glamorgan. Sometimes the gardener's brief would extend beyond the immediate needs of the mansion to those of the estate's farms. Douglas in 1878 was 'testing out potatoes for the Loxford Hall Farm',[54] and Robson was concerned with the selection of apples for Kent's fruit farms, many of which were on the Linton estate.

Often gardeners would get together to pool their experiences. One of Robson's 'red letter days' took place in Woodstock, outside Oxford, when he joined a group of horticultural friends who had met together 'not to settle any angry dispute about extraordinarily heavy Grapes, or the merits of a newly-introduced plant, or the début of some variety of Golden Geranium with astounding qualifications, but simply to devote a specific time to the examination of a great number of varieties of Potatoes, and in some degree to test their merits.'[55]

The host on this occasion was Mr Robert Fenn, a retired head gardener, who had spent much of his spare time since the devastating blight and potato famine of 1845 crossing the old English varieties, renowned for their quality, with the more prolific American varieties in the hope of raising strains which were more resistant to disease. Fenn raised dozens of new varieties, one of which, International Kidney, became the mainstay of the Jersey early potato trade, earning the title Jersey Royal.[56]

After an excellent lunch 'at which more than one Potato was presented in that

SUTTON'S
CHOICE SEED POTATOES.

PRIZE MEDAL, PARIS 1878.

PRIZE MEDAL, PARIS 1878.

FIRST PRIZE MEDAL.

FIRST PRIZE MEDAL.

PARIS, 1878.

PARIS, 1878.

Sutton's Collection of Potatoes

As shown at the International Potato Exhibition held at the Crystal Palace, September 24 and 25, 1878; and also at the Paris Universal Exhibition, October 16, 1878, when we were awarded the highest prize medal then given.

ARATOR (the nom de plume of **M. JULES GODEFROY**, one of the first French horticultural authorities of the day), in an article in 'l'Écho Agricole,' November 1878, writes:—

'The most striking feature of this Exhibition was, without any doubt, the stand of Messrs. Sutton & Sons, of Reading.'

SUTTON & SONS, SEEDSMEN TO H.R.H. PRINCE CHRISTIAN.

Kitchen gardens acted as independent trial grounds for the new varieties which filled the seedsmen's catalogues.

condition in which a Potato's merits are best understood', the guests adjourned to the garden where they found 'a large breadth of ground had been planted with seventy or eighty kinds of potatoes.' The new hybrids were interspersed with specimens of well known varieties and as one kind after another was dug up for consideration the assembled company had every opportunity to study and compare. 'Certain kinds came in for a fair meed of praise, and after their history and pedigree had been discussed, marks of commendation in the reporter's notes were placed against them.'

Flowers, shrubs and trees came in for equal scrutiny as gardeners sought to increase both novelty and practicality in the flower garden and pleasure ground. In 1864, for example, David Thomson reviewed the merits of 52 pelargoniums that had passed through his hands at Archerfield. He found some 'worthless here', but others, such as the crimson Stella 'perfectly wonderful'. Two years later Fish surveyed 41 possibilities for a sub-tropical garden, and in the 1870s Luckhurst examined dozens of new rhododendrons for Oldland's shrubberies.[57]

An essential part of the enterprise was the publishing of reports in the gardening literature, which allowed performance in different localities to be compared and enabled gardeners at all levels to benefit from the collective wisdom. So highly regarded was the information that the detailed reports of cropping potential, quality, susceptibility to disease, and so on would often determine whether or not a variety met with commercial success.

At a more 'official' level the Horticultural Society tested varieties in their own trial grounds. Their Fruit and Vegetable Committee was set up in 1858 and a Floral Committee the following year. With a number of leading head gardeners among their members, these bodies met to consider the results of the trials and any other specimens submitted by growers. The receipt of one of their coveted First Class Certificates was an almost certain guarantee of the variety's success in the market-place.

The head gardener's experiences helped to determine not only the contents and appearance of private gardens at all social levels, but also the emphasis and methods of the expanding horticultural industries. Fruit farming, market gardening, the new hothouse culture and floristry all leaned heavily on the head gardener's technical expertise and knowledge of different varieties.

Tea roses, carnations and the tropical eucharis blooms all owed their availability in the florists' shops to the earlier efforts of gardeners to perfect the techniques of growing them under glass. The industry's success in growing cucumbers, strawberries and, especially, grapes depended almost entirely on the skills acquired by generations of head gardeners as they engaged in contest with the fickle British climate, and stretched the possibilities of glasshouse technology to its limits. When the need came to invigorate English orchards in the face of foreign competition and, later the collapse of British agriculture, it was to the head gardeners that farmers and government turned for advice. At the Royal Horticultural Society's National Apple Congress of 1883, when an attempt was made to identify every variety grown in Britain and select the most merit worthy, the expert committee included John Roberts of Gunnersbury Park, Charles Ross of Welford Park, John Woodbridge of Syon Park, Malcolm Dunn of Dalkeith and Richard Gilbert of Burghley. It was largely the gardeners' consensus of opinion that led to the selection of those varieties chosen to form the basis of orchard renewal.

The Fruits of Success

The head gardener's skill, expertise and knowledge all contributed to his status within and beyond the mansion. While few achieved Paxton's *entrée* into the highest levels of Society, becoming the head gardener at an important establishment was for many humble lads the route to almost, and in some cases wholly, middle-class respectability. Robson, for example, combined his role as head gardener with that of estate steward and became a pillar of the local community. He acted as treasurer to the Linton Parochial Church Council and was for many years Chairman of the Maidstone Gardeners' Society. On his retirement in 1876 his neighbours and friends presented him with 'a handsome silver inkstand, and purse containing £126, with a list of 160 subscribers' bearing public testimony to 'his integrity, industry and urbanity'.[58] John Spencer, head gardener and steward to the Marquess of Lansdowne, even became director of a bank.[59]

Apart from the personal and professional kudos a post at this level brought, it was also, by the second half of the century, comparatively well-paid and entitled the family to a house, and some free fuel and foodstuffs. Robson and Taylor, for example, both received £100 a year, while the post of head gardener at Hampton Court in 1873

The head gardener's house at Lambton Castle, Durham.

carried a salary of £130 with apartments in the Palace and there was talk of rates up to £200.[60] Such wages were high enough to allow at least one household servant to be employed, and the accommodation itself seems to have been of a good standard. Robson moved into a brand new, four-bedroomed house in the early 1860s, while Fleming, at Trentham, had been able to design for himself a splendid dwelling in the Elizabethan style.[61]

For many who got this far – and life was far harder for those who did not – ambition was satisfied. It may have seemed at times an 'arduous pursuit, fraught with many difficulties and demanding increasing diligence, foresight and care' but it offered a unique opportunity to influence the appearance of a pleasure ground, and contribute to the development of everything from gastronomy and garden fashion to that of the commercial grape industry. For some the post became a stepping stone to wealth and success in the commercial world, particularly as the industry became more specialized. Benjamin Williams, for example, who had been head gardener to Robert Warner and in charge of his famous orchid collection, went on to establish one of the leading orchid firms. George Mills, head gardener to Lord Rothschild at Gunnersbury Park, Middlesex, left to take up rose growing for market, while William Thomson resigned from Dalkeith to set up the Clovenford Grapery outside Edinburgh and Taylor moved on from Longleat into business outside Bath.

Others carried the skills learned in the mansion and the pleasure ground out into the homes and gardens of the socially ambitious. The entirely new trade of floristry and flower decoration reached its apogee in the hands of John Wills, the former head gardener at Oulton Park in Cheshire. William Barron of Elvaston Castle went on to exploit his skills in transplanting trees, while others traded on their expertise as landscape gardeners. Paxton's undergardener, Kemp, executed his master's designs for Birkenhead Park, near Liverpool and went on to set up his own successful landscaping business, while Gibson, also a Chatsworth gardener, became superintendent of Battersea and then Hyde Park, Kensington.

For all such gardeners, Queen Victoria's reign was a glorious interlude. By the later years of the century the gardener whose authority exceeded his master's had become a humorous stereotype, and many saw in the suit for libel brought by James Barnes of Bicton against his former employer, Baroness Rolle, in 1869, the final confirmation of the gardener's professional independence. The Baroness alleged that Barnes had left the gardens in disorder, but the judgement went against her and Barnes received damages of £200.[62]

But an interlude was all it was to be. By the end of the century it was already clear that the particular set of circumstances which had thrust the head gardener out of the kitchen garden into the blaze of horticultural celebrity was ceasing to hold. Even before the First World War, the *Gardeners' Chronicle* noted that the day of the 'horticultural giants whose knowledge and skill can influence the length and breadth of the land had passed.'[63]

Epilogue

uccess inspires imitation, and monopolies invite challenge. Social rituals adapt to circumstances, and fashion, by definition, moves on. In the final analysis, it was on inevitabilities such as these that the head gardener's empire foundered.

By the end of the nineteenth century, Taste, Society, and the nature of the country house were changing. As these were among the most important factors shaping the gardener's role 60 years earlier, any significant change was bound to affect his position. In addition, the head gardener's monopoly of his craft almost certainly harboured the seeds of its own destruction. The very nature of the head gardener's productions made it certain that the outside – that is to say, the middle-class – world would strive to attain them and, by the end of the century, the sheer diversity of his activities made them vulnerable to the takeover claims of everyone from the commercial men to academic scientists.

The head gardener's prestige during the middle years of the century depended on his success in providing many of the props on which his employer's social credibility depended. What the mansion demanded above all was exclusiveness – a level of quality, quantity and novelty that was the unique and demonstrable privilege of the landed classes. When this started to become difficult to sustain, as was the case by the end of the century, the head gardener's position was inevitably undermined.

The exclusiveness of the gardener's contribution was eroded in a number of different ways. First, there was the shift in the balance of power between landed and business interests which had begun to take place during the 1880s. Back in the 1850s, it had been essential for any merchant or industrialist seeking to breach the stronghold of Society to acquire a country house with an estate of at least 500 acres, and sever all his links with the commercial world. By 1900 this had changed completely. The new rich were setting up in country houses, being given titles and continuing to take the train up to their offices in order to deal in newspapers, ships, tobacco, coal, gold or linoleum.[1] Their establishments were unlikely to have grounds of more than 150 acres,[2] and often considerably less. Numerous ancestral homes stood empty, or were let or put up for sale.[3] Large estates were being broken up, parks and farms sold off,[4] and kitchen gardens turned into market gardens.[5]

The reason for this about turn was both the agricultural depression of the 1880s, and the increasing volume and familiarity of middle-class wealth. Until the influx of cheap corn from America sent returns from British farming plummeting, land seemed if not the quickest and most profitable way of investing one's wealth, then certainly the safest and most prestigious. With the advent of the agricultural depression, this myth was exploded.[6] Unless they were exceedingly wealthy, old families dependent entirely on rents began to find themselves in difficulties. Suddenly, alternative sources of wealth became a great deal more acceptable. As indigent peers scrambled for directorships, new men bidding for a stake in Society found investment in land not only unwise but in the new climate, socially and politically unnecessary.

Meanwhile, the appeal of the country house itself remained as strong as ever. It continued to provide the necessary facilities for the entertainments around which Society revolved, and with its associations of tradition, dignity and peace enshrined a romantic dream of Englishness. For the businessman it offered a retreat from the demands and urban realities of money making, and for the old aristocracy it provided reassurance that, in spite of everything, their values still held. The important change, however, was that acreage ceased to be a crucial divide between aspirant and *arriviste*, or between minor and major aristocracy.

This meant that the incentive to demonstrate at every turn the superiority of the home-grown over produce that money alone could buy was correspondingly reduced. It is also likely that the greater respectability of commerce itself made outside sources of everything from flower decorations to the dessert fruit more acceptable, especially as, by the end of the century, improvements in quality and availability had greatly narrowed the margin between the bought in and home-grown.

Imported pineapples and the market gardener's grapes were now of the first quality. With the expansion of the railways, fruit such as pears and peaches was beginning to reach the markets as quickly and in almost as good a condition as the fruit sent up to the London house from the country estate. Apples were coming in from New York, Boston, Halifax and even from the Antipodes. Commercial flower culture was expanding and everything from palms and dracaenas to tea roses and carnations were becoming available from the new florists' shops. The head gardener had retained the leading edge for several decades, but although he could still compete, it was now increasingly hard for him to win by more than a hair's-breadth. In this situation employers began to reconsider the wisdom of diverting immense resources into maintaining acres of glass and tropical temperatures if items such as winter pineapples and collections of exotic plants had ceased to confer major social advantages.

The prestige of the gardener's role in the glasshouses was under threat from another quarter, too. During Queen Victoria's reign, it was mainly wealthy invalids who, every winter, took their tubercular lungs to Italy, the south of France and later to the Alps and Upper Egypt.[7] Once Edward VII had ascended the throne, life was allowed to become more enjoyable. Trips to Continental watering holes and spas became legitimate pleasures, and it was increasingly the case that once the Christmas festivities were over the smart set deserted the cold, leafless landscapes of the English winter and established themselves in Cannes, Nice and Menton.[8] With either owners, or the guests they wished to impress, out of the country, the need for forcing fruit, flowers and vegetables through the bleakest months of the year was much reduced. Increasingly, employers discovered they could enjoy perpetual summer through travel, rather than through their own – or their gardener's – domestic efforts.

The exclusiveness of the country house dinner table itself had also been eroded as Society grew larger and more fragmented. This, combined with the increased ease and frequency of well-to-do travel because of railways and steamships, was reflected in the rise of the great fashionable hotels in Europe and America. Unlike the private hotels of London in the middle years of the nineteenth century, these were large, sumptuous, and select by virtue of expense rather than membership of a particular social circle. More novel still, they were respectable places for ladies to dine. This changed the social character of their dining rooms still further. The great chef Escoffier noted that one reason for such hotels becoming so much part of fashionable life was that 'they allow of being observed, since they are eminently adapted to the exhibiting of magnificent dresses.'[9]

The central figures in the rise of the international hotel were, like Escoffier, leading names among French professional chefs of the period. The quality and innovation of the cooking which emerged from their kitchens effectively wrested the gastronomic initiative from the country house. It also introduced French-style *cuisine* to a much wider social circle, encouraging its adoption in households considerably removed from those of the traditional élite. Hotels such as the Ritz, the Carlton and the Savoy in London did not, of course, render the private house-party and ceremonial dinner redundant, but the cachet of superlative, trend-setting cookery had gone. This affected the gardener's position in several ways. He could continue to provide the mansion with quality produce but, in a sense, the currency had been devalued. It was also clear that the standard and variety of fruit and vegetables available to these hotel kitchens was adequate to sustain any culinary aria. Many employers, particularly those who had to make economies, or who had never grown luxury produce, saw less and less reason for not buying in at least those items which were particularly difficult or expensive to grow. In addition, following the lead of the hotel dining rooms the chef's contribution to the dessert was increasingly emphasized at the expense of fresh fruit, and Escoffier even observed that 'nowadays the name is commonly used to describe the sweet course.'

The head gardener's role was also diminishing outside the kitchen garden. The change in his position at the beginning of the nineteenth century had depended both on his power to transform the appearance of the garden, and the escalating demand for his services as new houses were built and old ones refurbished. The boom in country house building reached its peak in the early 1870s and then, with the agricultural slump of 1879-94, came to an abrupt end.[10] With the majority of new gardens by now established, the emphasis of the gardener's role inevitably began to shift away from that of creative genius towards that of guardian of the status quo.

What was more, of the houses that *were* subsequently built, the majority belonged to new men,[11] and in these circles there was an undercurrent of hostility towards the head gardener's power and professional standing. Dismayed by the outcome of the Barnes *v* Rolle court case and impelled, it would seem, to bolster their own social position, certain middle-class correspondents in the gardening press fired the opening shots in a campaign against 'the modern gardener, a tyrannical and prosaic creature'.[12] 'Have you no proper spirit left, that you submit to be dictated to by a servant?', cried John Latouche, while in similar vein Henry Arthur Bright complained that at flower shows, 'The owner of the garden is nobody, and the gardener is almost everything. The prize in almost every case is regarded as the alleged property of the gardener, who has, nevertheless, won the prize by his master's plant, reared at his master's expense, and at the cost of time which has made him too frequently neglect much more important matters.'

Not only did social insecurity make certain new proprietors baulk at the idea of giving the creative upper hand to a professional whose qualifications might overshadow their own, but the style of house – and by extension, garden – building that was becoming fashionable rendered many of the head gardener's skills superfluous. Grandeur and ostentation were 'out'.[13] What new owners most admired in old country houses was the mellowness of age, the sanctity of tradition and continuity, and in the face of increasing industrialization, a sense of rootedness in the landscape. Reflecting the 'deep vein of rural nostalgia',[14] which is everywhere apparent in the art and sensibility of the later nineteenth and early twentieth centuries, architects of the 'arts and craft' generation set out to recreate in their houses a 'quaint', 'homely' pre-industrial simplicity.[15] For their models, they looked to medieval country churches and barns, sixteenth- and seventeenth-century farmhouses, and the red brick early Georgian houses of country towns.

Whether Tudor or neo-Georgian in allusion, new houses in this mould required gardens to match. Architects such as Reginald Blomfield argued forcefully for the superiority of the architect over the gardener, and in place of the bright, modern artifice of high Victorian bedding, introduced their own versions of Tudor and Stuart enclosures and seventeenth-century English formal gardens. The emphasis was primarily on the architectural features of the garden, the aim one of formal simplicity and restraint. The planting was to be similarly 'old-fashioned', with reference to Francis Bacon, the plant-lore of Shakespeare, Tudor herbals, and the dubious antiquity of cottage gardens.[16]

Gardens such as these demanded little of the gardener but obedience to a pre-ordained plan. Many, like those of Lutyens, came equipped with planting schemes by Miss Gertrude Jekyll, often in later years drawn up for clients without ever visiting the site.[17] The 1880s also saw the appearance of the gardening lady – and her husband if she had one – who liked to direct personally, as well as supplement, the labour of the gardening staff.[18] Such employers had no use for a manager or an artist, either outside the house or within. Flower arrangements and dinner table decorations in such households became once again the ladies' province with, perhaps, one of the prestigious firms of floral decorators being called in for special occasions.

Even the conservatory began to disappear. Belief in the virtues of living and working outdoors led to a passion for open windows, bedroom balconies and sunny loggias. Aside from any economic considerations, conservatories began to seem not only too exotic and artificial, but as placing too much of a barrier between indoors and out. After 1900 conservatories were growing rare and were hardly built at all after 1920.[19]

One by one, it seemed, the head gardener's kingdoms were falling. On the commercial front, not only had the glasshouse and market gardening industries began to equal the gardener at his own game, but the fruit farmers were beginning to challenge the head gardeners' expertise. In the face of increasing foreign competition and the build up of disease in the new plantations, there was perhaps an element of the commercial men seeking a scapegoat. The favoured root stocks and varieties did not always live up to expectations and there is a sense, too, in which the expanding industry's centre of gravity was inevitably moving away from the methods and criteria of the domestic circuit. In 1912 the first government-aided institute to advise on fruit growing was set up at Long Ashton, Bristol, to be followed by the John Innes Institute at Merton, south London and the East Malling Research Station in Kent.

What commerce did not take away on the one hand, science began to annexe on the other. The old empirical methods were felt to need re-examination in the light of the emerging disciplines of plant pathology and soil science, while the birth of genetics brought fresh insight to plant breeding. Commercial horticulture and the scientists joined forces, and by the 1920s research institutes began to take over as the trial grounds and sources of new material.

Even the head gardener's role as a sage and teacher was undermined. The new partnership of science and commerce, together with the changing needs of industry and the increasing fragmentation of the gardener's role made this, once again, inevitable. The traditional system of apprenticeship remained in place until the beginning of the last war, but as early as 1893 the Royal Horticultural Society introduced its General Examination in Horticulture and this was incorporated into the National Diploma in Horticulture which was launched in 1913. Independent horticultural colleges were set up. Swanley College in Kent opened in 1889, followed in 1898 by Studley College, Worcestershire. London University's Wye College, also in Kent, introduced the first degree course in 1916.[20]

In practice, the disintegration of the head gardener's empire took place in a slow and piecemeal fashion. For many gardeners, particularly those at large establishments cushioned from economic recession by high and broadly based incomes, life continued much as before until the First World War and even beyond. Others saw the writing on the wall and turned it to their advantage, setting up their own horticultural business or throwing in their lot with the commercial men. In any event, it was not so much the personal status of individuals that was lost, as a gradual ebbing away of the responsibility and prestige the post of head gardener itself implied.

Yet, for all its brevity, the period which saw head gardeners become the glittering stars in the horticultural firmament, remains the dominant influence today. The Parks departments' floral clocks, the garden centres' brilliant bedding plants, and our enduring love of pot plants are constant reminders of the Victorian head gardener's achievements. We continue to rely on fruit and vegetable varieties that he tested and popularized, and which went on to form the basis of the modern industry.

He did, indeed, create Paradise out of a common field, and gardeners continue to make their own Edens in his image.

Appendix

Estates and their Owners

Archerfield

Archerfield, East Lothian, was one of several residences owned by Lady Mary Nisbet Hamilton (also known as Mrs Hamilton Nisbet Ferguson). Her first husband was Lord Elgin. Following her second marriage to R.C. Ferguson M.P., she divided her time between London, Bloxholm Hall in Lincolnshire, and the family estates of Biel and Archerfield in East Lothian. After her husband's death, Archerfield became her favourite residence. David Thomson was head gardener there from 1858 to 1868, and Archerfield's flower gardens and hothouse fruit became renowned during this period.

Belvoir Castle

Belvoir Castle in Leicestershire is the seat of the Dukes of Rutland, who are descended from Thomas Manners, one of King Henry VIII's courtiers. The Castle had been substantially rebuilt at the beginning of the nineteenth century and together with Chatsworth and Trentham completed the trio of great ducal seats in the Midlands. The family also owned the Haddon Hall estate in Derbyshire and lands in adjacent counties. The sixth Duke succeeded to the title in 1857 and died in 1888. The family spent half the year, including the winter, at Belvoir, whose land was acclaimed foxhunting country. The remainder of the time, apart from the two months in London for the Season, was passed at Haddon.

To meet the social demands imposed by the sporting calendar, Belvoir's head gardener from 1853, William Ingram, had a 15-acre kitchen garden, and was among the first to explore the possibilities of spring gardening, a tradition continued by his successor, W. H. Divers, who was appointed in 1894.

Bicton

Bicton, near Exeter, Devon, was the residence of Lord and Lady Rolle, who were enthusiastic collectors of trees and plants. Planting began early in the century under the direction of the nearby Veitch Nursery and the head gardener Glendenning, and continued between 1839 and 1869 under his successor James Barnes. There were extensive glasshouses and Bicton was particularly famous for its pineapples and monkey puzzle avenue.

Burghley House

Burghley House, Cambridgeshire, is a Renaissance palace built by Queen Elizabeth's minister, William Cecil, Lord Burghley, whose son became the 1st Earl of Exeter.

The nineteenth-century Marquess owned estates in Northamptonshire, Rutland and Lincolnshire. The gardens and the celebrated 16-acre kitchen garden were managed between 1868 and 1895 by Richard Gilbert.

CLIVEDEN see TRENTHAM

CYFARTHFA CASTLE
Cyfarthfa Castle, Merthyr Tydfil, was the residence of the Crawshay family, the South Wales iron masters. During the middle years of the nineteenth century, the Cyfarthfa works and those of the rival Dowlais plant belonging to the Guest family were the largest in the world. Cyfarthfa Castle was completed in 1825 and was the residence of R. T. Crawshay from 1846 to 1879. The gardens were famed for pineapples, grapes and the cultivation of all crops under glass.

DALKEITH AND DRUMLANRIG
Dalkeith Palace outside Edinburgh, and Drumlanrig Castle in Drumfriesshire were the chief Scottish residences of the Dukes of Buccleuch and 'two of the finest gardening establishments in the country'. Dalkeith Palace had been the seat of the Dukes of Buccleuch since 1642. Drumlanrig Castle, which was completed in 1689 and was orginally the residence of the Marquess of Queensbury, passed to the Duke of Buccleuch in 1777. During the nineteenth century the Buccleuch family became the wealthiest in the British peerage. They owned estates in seven Scottish and five English counties, as well as Montague House in London and a residence in Richmond. The 5th Duke of Buccleuch and 6th Duke of Queensbury (1806-84) was ADC to Queen Victoria. He was also President of the Royal Horticultural Society from 1862 to 1880, and the family employed a number of leading head gardeners.

At Dalkeith, Charles M'Intosh, who had previously been with the King of the Belgians at Claremont, became head gardener in 1838, and was succeeded in 1855 by William Thomson, who remained until 1871.

At Drumlanrig, where restoration of the house began in 1827 and development of the gardens in the 1840s, James M'Intosh, brother of Charles, was head gardener until 1868, when David Thomson, brother of William, was appointed. He stayed until 1897.

DANGSTEIN
The Dangstein estate, which lay in north-west Sussex near Petersfield, was bought by Lord and Lady Nevill in 1851. Both were connected with the Walpole family and had inherited considerable fortunes. Lord Nevill enlarged the estate, while Lady Dorothy entertained people eminent in politics, literature and science, and pursued her passion for growing exotic plants. She was aided by head gardener James Vair (1825-87), who had a special talent for growing difficult plants. The large and valuable collection was used by Darwin for his studies and plants were exchanged with Kew. After Lord Nevill's death the house and plants were sold in 1879. (See Trotter, W. R., 'The Glasshouses at Dangstein and their contents'. *Garden History*, 1988, vol. 16 pp. 71-89.)

DROPMORE

Dropmore, Buckinghamshire, was the home of Lord and Lady Grenville. Lord Grenville was Prime Minister Pitt's Foreign Secretary, and his wife was Pitt's cousin. Dropmore was famous for its pinetum and also reputed to have seen the origin of the bedding system. Philip Frost was head gardener from 1833 and remained active until his death in 1887.

DRUMLANRIG see DALKEITH

LAMBTON CASTLE

Lambton Castle, in County Durham belongs to the Lambton family who were elevated to the peerage at the beginning of the nineteenth century. The first Earl (*d.* 1840) was a leading member of the government and architect of the Great Reform Bill of 1832. The vast coal seams on the Lambton estate were extensively developed from the beginning of the nineteenth century, when the huge and fortress-like Lambton Castle was built. The 2nd Earl (1828-79) succeeded to the title in 1840. Large flower gardens were laid out and Lambton was also renowned for the extent of the glasshouses, where exotic fruit was cultivated by head gardener James Hunter during the 1870s and 1880s.

LAMORRAN

Lamorran, near Truro in Cornwall, was the residence of the Honourable and Reverend J. T. Boscawen (1820-89), the rector of Lamorran from 1849. He was a descendant of the diarist John Evelyn, and 'a man of science', a horticulturalist and hybridist. For many years he was an active member of the Bath and West of England Society for the Promotion of Agriculture and for a time was a member of the Council of the Royal Horticultural Society. The gardens, which were made by Boscawen, were famed for their range of plants, and he raised a number of hybrid rhododendrons, camellias and orchids.

LINTON

Linton Park, near Maidstone, Kent, was the home of the Cornwallis family, whose ancestors included distinguished soldiers and a Governor-General of India. The present house was erected by Robert Mann, who purchased Linton in 1724, and the estate was largely built up during the eighteenth century. It became the property of the related Cornwallis family in 1820 and of the 5th Earl in 1824. In 1851 it passed to his daughter, the Lady Julia. She married Viscount Homesdale, M.P., the son of Earl Amherst of Montreal, Kent, in 1862. The head gardener was John Robson from c. 1849 until 1876, and during this period extensive alterations and extensions to the grounds were undertaken. Linton was famed for its flower gardens, conifers, shrubs and trees.

LONGLEAT

Longleat in Wiltshire is the residence of the Marquess of Bath, a descendant of Sir John Thynne, who began building the house in the sixteenth century. Estates in Somerset and Wiltshire came into the family at this time. During the nineteenth century it was considered 'one of the most magnificent mansions in the country', set in the midst of a park of 4,500 acres. Early in the century the house was considerably altered to achieve greater domestic convenience and a formal flower garden was laid out near the house. In 1860 the 4th Marquess (d. 1896) embarked on large scale redecoration and there followed a period of intense social activity. Head gardener William Taylor was employed from 1869 to 1883 to help cater for these heavy commitments.

MARGAM PARK
Margam Park, outside Neath in South Wales, was the residence of C. R. Mansell Talbot, M.P., who was called the 'father of the House of Commons', being a Member for 60 years. He was the wealthiest landowner in Glamorgan and created Port Talbot as an outlet for the mineral wealth of the district. Mansell Talbot was descended from the Welsh Norman family of Mansell, and by marriage in the seventeenth century, with the Talbots of Lacock Abbey, Wiltshire. The Victorian mansion, which was known locally as Margam Castle, was erected by him between 1830 and 1840. It was filled with fine works of art and sculpture and in the grounds a terraced Italianate garden was created and many trees and shrubs planted. Within the extensive park lay the ruined Cistercian Margam Abbey and the celebrated eighteenth-century Orangery. James Muir was head gardener from the early 1870s until the end of the century.

MARSTON HOUSE
Marston House, Marston Bigott, Somerset, had been the seat of the Earls of Cork and Orrery since the seventeenth century. The famous 1st Earl was Richard Boyle, who arrived in Ireland almost penniless in 1588, became one of the richest men in the British Isles and bought the estate of Marston. The Boyle family included many distinguished patrons of literature, science and art, including the 4th Earl of Burlington and Cork. The 10th Earl (1829-1904) succeeded to the title in 1856 and was a keen horseman, continuing to ride to hounds at the age of 73. During this period the house was improved and enlarged, and became the scene of great social activity during the winter months. William Iggulden became head gardener in 1881.

NORRIS GREEN
Norris Green, West Derby, outside Liverpool, was the home of J. P. Heywood, the chief banker of Liverpool. The family resided at their Shropshire seat in summer and the gardens at Norris Green were accordingly laid out to be at their best in the autumn and winter, with many shrubs and trees and a large conservatory. The kitchen gardens boasted some of the 'finest glass houses in the North of England'. Their head gardener from the early 1880s until 1890 was William Bardney.

NUNEHAM PARK
Nuneham Park, outside Oxford, was the seat of the Harcourt family who were major Oxfordshire and Berkshire landowners, and figured prominently in political life. The house was built for the 1st Earl in 1757. During the 1860s it was the home of the Reverend William Vernon Harcourt, who was 'an active man of science'. His head gardener Stewart was said to manage one of the best kitchen gardens in the country.

OLDLANDS

Oldlands Hall, built in 1870, was the home of Alexander Nesbitt, F.S.A. (1817-86). He came from an ancient Scottish family, which had long been established in Ireland, with a family seat at Lismore, County Cavan. He was 'distinguished in many branches of archeology'. The grounds and woodlands were developed by his head gardener Edward Luckhurst, who was appointed in 1870. Mrs Nesbitt appears to have left Oldlands in the 1890s.

PETWORTH

Petworth House in Sussex was the seat of Lord Leconfield, heir to Lord Egremont, and the vast estates of the Wyndham family, which were located in Sussex, Northern England and Ireland. The present palatial house was built at the end of the seventeenth century. Lord Leconfield lived in 'princely fashion' and was well served by his head gardener Thomas Jones (1826-1912), who probably came to Petworth in the early 1860s and left in 1872 to became the Royal head gardener at Frogmore, Windsor.

PUTTERIDGE BURY

Putteridge Bury, near Luton in Bedfordshire, was built in 1812 by John Sowerby. The family also owned property in Yorkshire and Cumberland. Extensive development of the grounds was undertaken by his second son, Colonel George Sowerby, during the period from 1841 to 1868, under the direction of the head gardener, Robert Fish.

RANGEMORE HALL

Rangemore Hall, outside Burton-on-Trent, Staffordshire, was the residence of M. T. Bass, M.P. (1799-1884), the brewery magnate, who also owned property in Scotland. The family business was founded in 1777, but it was from 1851 onwards that its trade and fame expanded. Bass was a great local benefactor and lived in grand style. Under head gardener Bennett, Rangemore became famed for its glasshouses and especially the cultivation of fruit and the forcing of all crops under glass.

SANDRINGHAM

The Sandringham estate in Norfolk was bought for the Prince of Wales in 1861 and the new house completed in 1871. In prime hunting and shooting country, it was said to be his favourite residence. The large kitchen garden was created by his head gardener William Carmichael.

SHRUBLAND PARK

Shrubland Park in Suffolk was the home of Lord and Lady William Middleton. The estate, which had been purchased by his father in 1804, came into William's possession in 1829 and improvements commenced the following year. It was here that the head gardener, Donald Beaton, developed the bedding system and his exploration of colour harmonies. Lord and Lady Middleton had lived for a time in Italy and they employed Charles Barry to make the house into 'a perfect Italian villa'. In the gardens Barry made an immense Italianate staircase and a series of terraces. Further formal flower gardens were made and Shrubland was famed for the extent and beauty of its gardens.

Trentham and Cliveden

These were both estates of the Dukes of Sutherland, the Leveson Gower family. During the nineteenth century they were one of the largest landowners in Britain, owning the vast Sutherland estate in Scotland and coal-rich lands in the Midlands. The 2nd Duke (1786-1861) and his Duchess, Harriet (d. 1868) lived on a grand scale. The Duchess was Mistress of the Robes to Queen Victoria and their main residence was the palatial Stafford House in London, now Lancaster House. Here, in 1848, Chopin played before the Queen at one of their musical soirées. Stafford House was designed by Barry who was also employed to refurbish Dunrobin Castle in Sutherland, and rebuild Lilleshall Hall in Shropshire, Trentham Park in Staffordshire and Cliveden Manor in Berkshire. Barry also laid out terraced Italianate gardens at Trentham. The Duchess Harriet, who was known as the 'Queen of Gardening' , enjoyed the services of two renowned head gardeners, George Fleming at Trentham and John Fleming at Cliveden.

Westonbirt

The Westonbirt estate in Gloucestershire was owned by R.S. Holford (1808-92). The Holfords were descended from Sir Richard Holford, Master of Chancery in 1693, who acquired the estate by marriage. The present mansion is the third on the site and was completed in the 1871. Dorchester House, Park Lane – now the Dorchester Hotel – was the family's London residence. The family were keen collectors of plants, especially of orchids and trees, and Westonbirt's Arboretum is now in effect the British national arboretum, run by the Forestry Commission.

References

PERIODICALS

Cottage Gardener, 1848-60, abbreviated as Cott-Gard and continued as Journal of Horticulture, 1861-1915

The Garden, 1871-1927, abbreviated as Garden

The Gardener, 1867-82, abbreviated as Gardener

Gardeners' Chronicle, 1841-, abbreviated as GC

The Gardener's Magazine, 1865-1916, abbreviated as Gardener's Magazine

Journal of Horticulture, Cottage Garden and Country Gentleman, continuation of Cottage Gardener, 1861-1915; abbreviated as JHort

Journal of the Royal Horticultural Society of London, 1866- ; abbreviated as JRHS

The Illustrated London News, 1843-

Chapter One: A Paradise out of a Common Field

1. Steegman, J., Victorian Taste (1950, reprint 1987), p.4
2. Elliott, B., Victorian Gardens (1986), pp.16-18
3. Girouard, M., Life in the English Country House (Penguin 1980), p.268
4. Elliott, op. cit., p.14
5. Stroud, D., Humphry Repton (1962), p.11
6. Williamson, T. and Bellamy, L., Property and Landscape (rev. ed. 1987), p.130
7. Stuart, D. C., Georgian Gardens (1979), p.43
8. Williamson and Bellamy, op. cit., p.136
9. Girouard, op. cit., p.242; Williamson and Bellamy, op. cit., p.151
10. Repton, H., An Inquiry into the Changes of Taste in Landscape Gardening (1806), London, quoted in Williamson and Bellamy, op. cit., p.151
11. Walpole's History of Modern Taste in Gardening, (1784), quoted in Stuart, op. cit., p.77
12. Stuart, op. cit., p.76
13. Elliott, op. cit, p.23
14. Stroud, op. cit., p.83
15. Stuart, op. cit., pp.26-32
16. Ibid., pp.48-50
17. Ibid., pp.55-64, 80-90
18. Steegman, op. cit., p.19
19. Carter, G., Goode, P. and Laurie, K., Humphry Repton Landscape Gardener 1752-1818 (1982), Catalogue of Victoria and Albert Museum and Sainsbury Centre for the Visual Arts Exhibition, p.5
20. Turner, T., English Garden and Design: History and Styles since 1650 (1986), p.131; Boniface, P, ed., In Search of English Gardens, The Travels of John Claudius Loudon and his Wife Jane (1987), p.11
21. Stuart, op. cit., p.61
22. Thornton, P., Authentic Decor, The Domestic Interior 1620-1920 (1984), p.216
23. Elliott, op. cit., p.33
24. 'Trentham Hall', GC, (1848) p.687, 703. See also Elliott, op. cit., pp.75-7, 90-2
25. Ibid., pp.121-123
26. Ibid., p.32
27. Gorer, R., The Growth of Gardens (1978), p.60, p.43. For introductions of garden plants, see also Coats, A. M., Flowers and their Histories (1956); Coats, A. M., Garden Shrubs and their Histories (1963); Fisher, J., The Origins of Garden Plants (1982)
28. Gorer, op. cit., pp.52-3
29. Scourse, N., The Victorians and their Flowers (1983), p.3
30. Festing, S., Country Life, June 19, 1986, p.1772
31. Scourse, op. cit., pp.3-5
32. Fisher, op. cit., p.169
33. Gorer, op. cit., p.90-98
34. Ibid., p.163
35. Scourse, op. cit., p.15
36. Wills and Segar catalogue, (1897); RHS Lindley Library. For growth of interest in orchids, see also Curtis, C. H., Orchids (1950), p.7-15; Fisher, op. cit.; White, T., The Plant Hunters (1970)
37. Scourse, op. cit., p.10
38. Thompson, F. M. L., English Landed Society in the Nineteenth Century (1980), pp.25-7
39. Ibid., p.2
40. Girouard, M., The Victorian Country House (1985), p.5
41. Thompson, op. cit., p.44
42. Girouard, M., Life in the English Country

House op.cit., p.270

43. Thompson *op. cit.*, p.2
44. Girouard, *op.cit.* (1980), p.270
45. Girouard, M., *The Victorian Country House op.cit.*, p.7
46. *Ibid.*, p.6
47. Sproule, A., *The Social Calendar* (1978), p.27
48. Girouard, M. *Life in the English Country House op.cit.*, p.268; Davidoff, L., *The Best Circles: Society, Etiquette and the Season* (1973), pp.15-17
49. Girouard, *ibid.* pp.214-18
50. Robinson, J. M., *The English Country Estate* (1988), pp.113-129
51. Sproule, *op. cit.*, p.29
52. Davidoff, *op. cit.*, p.26; and Lady Tweedsmuir, *The Lilac and the Rose* (1952), quoted in Davidoff, p.26
53. Franklin, J., *The Gentleman's Country House and its Plan 1835-1914* (1981), p.41

Chapter Two: Geometry and Geraniums

1. Franklin, J., *The Gentleman's Country House and its Plan 1835-1914*, (1981), p.43
2. Robson, J., 'The Massing System and its Origin', *CottGard*, (1860), XXIV, p.312
3. Elliott, B., *Victorian Gardens* (1986), p.88
4. Elliott, *op. cit.*, pp.89-90.
5. Robson, J., 'The Rise and Progress of the Bedding Geranium', *JHort* (1871), XXI, pp.481-3
6. Gorer, R., *The Growth of Gardens* (1978), pp.146-7
7. Thomson, D., *Handy Book of the Flower Garden* (1868), p.18
8. Elliott, *op. cit.*, pp.138-9
9. Robson, J., 'Flower Gardening on a New Principle', *CottGard* (1859), XXI, pp.396-7. For descriptions of flower gardens see: Fish, R., 'Linton Park', *CottGard* (1859), XXIII, pp.143-4, 160; *JHort* (1861), II, pp.185-188; *JHort* (1863), V, p.169
10. Fish, R., 'Linton Park', *CottGard* (1859), XXIII, p.160
11. Robson, J., 'Putteridge Bury and its Flower Gardening', *CottGard* (1860), XXV, pp.59-60, 74, 102, 212-214; 'Putteridge Bury', *JHort* (1864), VI, pp.113-115, 176-7 (note *Brugmansia* now *Datura*)
12. Robson, *op. cit.*, *CottGard* (1860), XXV, p.102.
13. *Ibid.*
14. 'Putteridge Bury Gardens', *Luton News*, reprinted *JHort* (1862), III, pp.491-2, 512-3
15. Robson, J. 'Archerfield' *JHort* (1865), IX, pp.447-8; see also 'Archerfield and Dirleton

Gardens', GC (1860), p.795
16. Bristow, I., 'Prismatic Principles, 19th-century colour theory', *Country Life* (1987), pp.146-7. Contemporary works: Field, G., *Chromatics* (1817); Hay, D. R., *Laws of Harmonious Colouring adapted to Interior Decorations* (1844); Chevreul, M-E., *The Principles of Harmony and Contrast of Colour* (1854); Jones, O. *Grammar of Ornament* (1856, reprint 1988)
17. Axton, W. F., 'Victorian Landscape Painting: A Change in Outlook' in *Nature and the Victorian Imagination*, ed. Knoepflmacher, U.C. and Tennyson, G. B. (1977), pp.281-308
18. Discussion during the 1830s and 1840s took place at, for example, the West London Gardeners' Association, of which John Caie and Robert Fish were founder members. For Maidstone see *JHort* (1864), VI, pp.395-7
19. Thomson, D., *Handy Book of the Flower Garden* (1868) pp.276-285
20. Interpretation based upon Thomson, *ibid.*; diagram and planting details, *JHort* (1865), IX, p.447; Thomson, *ibid.* and *JHort* (1864), VI, pp.172-4
21. Shirley Hibberd (1864), quoted Elliott, *op. cit.*, p.148.
22. 'Garibaldi among the Gardeners', *JHort* (1864), VI, p.347
23. Pearson, J. R., 'Planting Flower Gardens', *JHort* (1863), IV, p.308; *JHort* (1868), XV, p.477. See also Divers, W. H., *Spring Flowers at Belvoir Castle* (1909)
24. Robson, J., 'Summer Flower Gardening and Winter Decoration at Linton Park', *CottGard* (1861), II, pp.227-9
25. Robson, J., 'The Claims of Winter Ornamental Gardening', *JHort* (1868) XV, pp.477-8, 499-501; 'Winter Bedding Plants', *JHort* (1869), XVII, pp.431-2, 475-76
26. Elliott, *op. cit.*, pp.148-9
27. Thomson, D., *JHort* (1863), V, p.162
28. Luckhurst, E. 'What is Repose?' *JHort* (1874), XXVI, p.397
29. *JHort* (1865), IX, p.417
30. Luckhurst, E., 'Flower Garden Arrangements', *JHort* (1871), XX, p.42
31. Gorer, R., *The Growth of Gardens* (1978), p.171
32. Fish, R., 'Planting our Subtropical and other Handsome-Foliaged Plants', *JHort* (1866), X, pp.375-77
33. Robson, J., 'Battersea Park', *JHort* (1864), VII, pp.214-5; see also *JHort* (1865), IX, p.124; *JHort* (1878), XXXV, p.184
34. Fish, *op. cit. JHort* (1866), X, p.375

35. Elliott, *op. cit.*, p.155; GC (1868), p.487; 'Bedding-out at Cliveden', *JHort* (1868), XV, pp.284-5

36. Luckhurst, E., 'The Flower Garden', *JHort* (1875), XXVIII, p.450

37. *JHort* (1878), XXXV, p.329

38. 'Cleveland House', Clapham, *JHort*, (1875), XXIX, pp.205-8, 226-8; *JHort* (1877), XXXIII, pp.182-3, 308, (note *Dracaena indivisa* syn. *Cordyline indivisa*)

39. 'Belvoir Castle', *JHort* (1876) XXX, pp.404-5, Fig.110

40. Luckhurst. E., 'The Crystal Palace Gardens', *JHort* (1875), XXIX, p.316

41. Elliott, *op. cit.*, p.157

42. *Ibid.*, p.160

43. *JHort*, (1863), V, pp.265-6

44. *JHort* (1865), IX, pp.293-4; see also Thomson, D., *Handy Book of the Flower Garden*

45. Elliott, *op. cit.*, p.162

46. Sutherland, W., 'On the Formation and Planting of Homes for Herbaceous Plants', *Gardener* (1878), pp.21-4, 75-79, 147-52; Sutherland, W., *Handbook of Hardy Herbaceous and Alpine Flowers* (1871)

47. Taylor, W., 'Hardy Perennials', *JHort* (1879), XXXVII, p.264

48. Taylor, W., 'Hardy Perennials', *JHort* (1878) XXXV, pp.121-2

49. Thomson, D., 'The Flower Garden', *JHort* (1864), VI, pp.109-110. For survey of plant introductions, see Coats, A. M., *Flowers and their Histories* (1956)

50. Thompson, R., *Gardener's Assistant* (new ed. Moore, T., 1878), pp.688-90; survey of popular plants, pp.690-718

51. Luckhurst, E., 'The Perennial Border', *JHort* (1876), XXXI, p.440

52. Taylor, *op. cit.*, *JHort* (1879), XXXVII, p.264

53. Taylor, W., 'Gems of the Herbaceous Border', *JHort* (1875), XXIX, pp.149-50; 'Hardy Perennials in Mid-October', *JHort* (1878), XXXV, p.307; 'Hardy Perennials', *JHort* (1879), XXXVII, p.264; 'A Peep at the Perennials', p.302

54. 'Munstead, Godalming', *Garden* (1882), XXII, p.191.

Chapter Three: The Mansion in Bloom

1. Steegman, J., *Victorian Taste* (1950, reprint 1987), p.31

2. Girouard, M., *Life in the English Country House* (1980), p.214

3. Woods, M. and Warren, A., *Glass Houses* (1988), p.51

4. Taylor, W., 'Flowering Plants for Halls and Corridors', *JHort* (1875), XXVIII, pp.385-6

5. *JHort* (1875), XXIX, p.220

6. Wills, J., 'Plants for House Decoration', *JRHS* (1892), XIV, pp.84-88; *JHort* (1874), XXVI, p.365

7. Bear, W. E., *Fruit and Flower Farming in England* reprinted from *Journal of Royal Agricultural Society of England* (1898, 1899); Shaw, C. W., *London Market Gardeners* (1879). For range of pot plants and flowers popular in the period, see Burbidge, F. W., *Domestic Floriculture* (1874)

8. Taylor, *op. cit.*, *JHort* (1875), XXVIII, pp.385-6

9. Wills, *op. cit.*, *JRHS* (1892), XIV, pp.84-88

10. Taylor, W., 'Fine Foliage Plants for Indoor Decoration', *JHort* (1875), XXVIII, pp.443-4

11. *Ibid.*

12. Taylor, *op. cit.*, *JHort* (1875), XXVIII, p.385

13. *Ibid.*

14. Taylor, *Ibid.* and 'December Flowers', *JHort* (1880), I(NS), pp.544-5.

15. Thomson, D., *Gardener* (1878), 'Cool Orchids', pp.1-5; 54-6; 182-4; 'Cypripediums', *Gardener* (1878), pp.343-46. For orchids used in floral decoration see Burbidge, *op. cit.*; Nicolson, G., *The Illustrated Dictionary of Gardening* (1885-8); Curtis, C. H., *Orchids* (1950), (note *Cypripedium* orchids now *Paphiopedilum*)

16. Bardney, W., 'Flowering Plants for Room Decoration', *Gardener* (1881), pp.52-55

17. 'Longleat', *JHort* (1881), III(NS), p. 399, 538

18. Luckhurst, E., 'The Arrangement of Cut Flowers', *JHort* (1881), III(NS), pp.270-1

19. Brotherston, R., 'About Cut Flowers', *JHort* (1880), I(NS), pp.505-6

20. Bardney, W., 'Allamandas for Autumn and Winter', *Gardener* (1881), pp.492-95

21. *Gardener* (1880), p.492

22. Taylor, W., 'Roses for Non-Exhibitors', *JHort* (1875), XXVIII, p.307. The merits of rose varieties was an important subject in all the gardening journals. For popular varieties of the period see Paul, W., *The Rose Garden*, (1848, reprint 1978); Hibberd, S., *Amateur's Rose Book* (1894); Rivers, T., *The Rose – Amateur's Guide* (1867)

23. 'Calanthes at Drumlanrig', *JHort* (1875), XXVIII, p.213

24. Thomson, D., 'Notes from the North', *JHort* (1883), VII(NS), p.435

25. Jeaffreson, J.C., *Book about the Table* (1875), vol. I, p.154.

26. Davidoff, L., *The Best Circles: Society, Etiquette and the Season* (1973) p.48
27. Robson, J., 'Dinner Table Decoration – No 1', *JHort* (1871), XX, pp.103-5, (note *Aralia veitchii* now *Dizygotheca veitchii*,or *D. elegantissima*)
28. *Ibid.*
29. Robson, J., 'Dinner-Table Decoration – No. 3', *JHort* (1871), XX, p.200; 'Linton Labour Book, 1873', Kent County Archives U24A12
30. Robson, J., 'Dinner Table Decorations – No. 2', *JHort* (1871), XX, p.181
31. Robson, J., 'Devices for Dinner Table Decoration', *JHort* (1862) III, p.347; *op. cit.*, *JHort* (1871), XX, p.104
(note Christmas cactus, *Epiphyllum truncatus*, now *Zygocactus truncatas*,but correctly *Schlumbergerax buckleyi*
32. Perkins, J., *Floral Designs for the Table* (1877), p.26, 16, 19
33. Robson, *op. cit.*, *JHort* (1871), XX, p.105
34. Low, W., *Table Decoration* (1887), p.47
35. Luckhurst, E., 'The Arrangement of Cut Flowers', *JHort* (1881), III(NS), pp.237-8
36. *Ibid.*, p.237
37. *JHort* (1881), II(NS), p.314
38. Iggulden, W., 'Dinner Table Decoration', *JHort* (1881), III(NS), pp.555-6
39. Webber, R., *Early Horticulturalists* (1968), p.154. For hand flowers etc. see Burbidge, *op. cit.*, Thompson, R., *Gardener's Assistant* (new ed. Moore, T. 1878), pp.918-24
40. *Illustrated London News* (1863), p.311
41. Lichten, F., *Decorative Art of Victoria's Era* (1950), pp.158-9
42. Robson, J., 'Hand Bouquets', *JHort* (1871), XX, p.215
43. 'Princess Louise's Bouquet', *JHort* (1871), XX, p.232
44. 'Flowers and their Fitness', *JHort* (1867), XII, p.294
45. Thomson, *op cit.*, *Gardener* (1878), pp.54-6, (note *Odontoglossum Alexandrae* syn. *Odontoglossum crispum*)
46. Luckhurst, E., 'A Half Hour among the Tea Roses', *JHort* (1875), XXIX, pp.1-2; Taylor, W., 'Tea Roses', *JHort* (1878), XXXIV, p.387
47. Brotherston, R. P., *The Book of Cut Flowers* (1906), p.100

Chapter Four: Gardens under Glass

1. Franklin, J., *The Gentleman's Country House and its plan, 1835-1914* (1981), p.63; see also Boniface, P., *The Garden Room* (1982)
2. Woods, M. and Warren, A., *Glass Houses*

(1988), p.56
3. *Ibid.*, p.39, 46
4. *Ibid.*, p.51
5. *Ibid.*, p.98, Franklin, *op. cit.*, p.63
6. Elliott, B., *Victorian Gardens* (1986), pp.28-9
7. Woods & Warren, *op. cit.*, p.90, pp.121-4
8. Lemmon, K., *The Covered Garden* (1962), p.140
9. From Knight, C., *Encyclopaedia of London* (1851), quoted in *The Marriage of Iron and Glass*, Ironbridge Gorge Museum Trust (1980), p.2
10. Franklin *op. cit.*, pp.63-4
11. 'Linton Garden Book 1865', Kent County Archives U24A8
12. Loudon, J. C., quoted in Elliott, *op. cit.*, p.28
13. Fish, R., 'Trentham', *JHort* (1863), V, pp.413-5; see also 'Trentham Hall', GC (1848), p.719; 'Trentham Hall' in Brooke, E. A., *The Gardens of England* (1857)
14. 'Harlaxton Manor', *JHort* (1875), XXVIII, p.259
15. Fish, *op. cit.*, *JHort* (1863), V, pp.392-3; O.S Map, *c.* 1880
16. 'Dangstein', *JHort* (1872), XXIII, pp.515-8; *JHort* (1873), XXIV, p.33
17. Fish, *op. cit.*, *JHort* (1863), V, p.393
18. 'Linton Labour Book 1865', Kent County Archives U24A8; 'A Day at Linton Park', *JHort* (1866), X, pp.208-9
19. Robson, J., 'Dutch Flower Garden at Linton Park', *JHort* (1861), I, p.101
20. Franklin, *op. cit.*, p.63
21. Muir, J., Gardener (1881), p.514. Successions of pot plants based upon weekly calendar of gardening instruction in *Gardener*, and 'Doings of the Last Week' in *JHort* written by Fish and after his death in 1873, by John Douglas, head gardener at Loxford Hall, Essex (note *Dracaena australis* syn. *Cordyline australis*; *Habrothamnus elegans* syn. *Cestrum elegans*).

Chapter Five: Pleasures of the Table

1. Dallas, E. S., *Kettner's Book of the Table* (1877 reprinted 1968), pp.173-76; see also Kirwan, A. V., *Host and Guest*, (1864)
2. Addison in *The Tatler*, no. 148, March 21, 1709, quoted in Mennell, S., *All Manners of Food* (1985), p.126; see also Mennell, *op. cit.*, pp.125-7
3. Haywood, A., *The Art of Dining* (1883 ed.), pp.30-31
4. Mennell, *op. cit.*, p.151
5. quoted in Mennell, *op. cit.*, p.132
6. Willan, A., *Great Cooks and their Recipes*

(1977), p.134; Montagne, P., *Larousse Gastronomique* (1961 ed.)

7. Mennell *op. cit.*, p.279

8. Walker, T., 'Art of Dining', *The Original* (1835, ed.1874), vol. II, pp.178-185; Mennell, *op. cit.*, p.279

9. Mennell, *op. cit.*, p.267

10. Dining *à la Russe*, see Tabitha Tickletooth, *The Dinner Question* (1860); Kirwan, A.V., *Host and Guest* (1864). Development of china and cutlery, see Somers Cocks, A., *The Art of Dining, Masterpieces of Cutlery and the Art of Eating*, Victoria and Albert Museum (1979)

11. Taylor, W. ,'Mushroom Growing', *JHort* (1875), XXIX, p.459; 'Mushroom Growing', *JHort* (1880), XXXVIII, p.37

12. *JHort* (1870), XX, p.242

13. 'Sandringham', GC (1861), p.735

14. 'Winter Protection for Celery', *JHort* (1867),XII, p.27

15. Fish, R., 'Doings of the Last Week', *JHort* (1863), IV, p.121

16. Fish, R., 'Doings of the Last Week', *JHort* (1863) V, pp.217-8

17. Dallas, *op. cit.*, pp.475-77. Prejudices still persist among elderly people; see also, Mennell, S., 'Indigestion in the 19th century, aspects of English taste and anxiety' in Jaine, T., ed. *Oxford Symposium on Food and Cookery, 1987: Taste* (1988), pp.153-60

18. Taylor, W., 'Celeriac or Turnip-Rooted Celery', *JHort* (1874), XXVI, p.144

19. Dallas, *op. cit.*, p.43

20. *Ibid.*, p.46

21. 'Asparagus', *JHort* (1881), II(NS), p.415

22. Luckhurst, E., 'Asparagus Culture under Difficulties', *JHort* (1883), VI(NS), pp.338-9

23. *JHort* (1881), II(NS), p.415

24. Fish, R. 'Doings of the Last Week', *JHort* (1863), V, p.218

25. Taylor, W., 'Things out of Season', *JHort* (1874), XXVII, pp.249-50

26. D'Ombrain, H., 'Potatoes', *JHort* (1866), XI, pp.462-3

27. Thomson, D. 'Potatoes and their Culture', *JHort* (1867), XII, p.21

28. 'Longleat', *JHort* (1881), III(NS) p.379

29. Longleat Archives

30. 'Late Peas', *JHort* (1875), XXVIII, p.486

31. Taylor, W., 'A Selection of Vegetables for Early Sowing', *JHort* (1875), XXVIII, p.156

32. Taylor, W., 'The Seed Order', *JHort* (1881), II(NS), pp.23-24

33. Taylor, W., 'Flavour of Vegetables', *JHort* (1876), XXX, p.320

34. *Ibid.*

35. Taylor, W., 'The Seed Order', *JHort* (1881), II(NS), p.66

36. Luckhurst, E., 'Early Snowball Cauliflower', *JHort*, (1875), XXIX, p.113

37. 'Veitch's Autumn Giant Cauliflower', *JHort* (1875), XXVIII, p.348

38. Luckhurst, E. 'The Leamington Broccoli', *JHort* (1875), XXVIII, p.310

39. 'Small or Large Brussels Sprouts?' *JHort* (1863) V, p.509

40. 'Longleat', *JHort* (1881), III(NS), p.379.

41. Taylor, W., 'The Seed Order', *JHort* (1881), II(NS), p.66

42. Francatelli, C. E., *The Modern Cook*, (1846) p.30

43. 'Nuneham Park', *JHort* (1867), XIII, p.351

44. Luckhurst, E., 'Queen Onion', *JHort* (1875), XXVIII, p.404

45. 'Turnips all Year Round', *JHort* (1884), VIII(NS), p.258

46. Dallas, *op. cit.*, p.465

47. Fish, R., 'Doings of the Last Week', *JHort* (1866), XI, p.50

48. Taylor, W., 'Winter Cucumbers', *JHort* (1874), XXVII, p.463

49. *Ibid.*

50. D'Ombrain, H., 'Lettuces', *JHort* (1873), XXV, pp.266-7; see also Dallas, *op. cit.*, pp.391-401; Hayward, A. *op. cit.*, p.117

51. Fish, R., 'Doings of the Last Week', *JHort* (1873), XXIV, p.287

52. D'Ombrain, *op. cit.*, *JHort* (1873), XXV, p.267

53. Luckhurst, E. 'Standstead Park Cabbage Lettuce', *JHort* (1875), XXVIII, pp.311-12

54. Taylor, W., 'Notes on Vegetables', *JHort* (1878), XXXV, p.401

55. Keane, W., 'Work for the Week', *JHort* (1867), XIII, p.200

56. Muir, J., 'Chicory', *JHort* (1880), XXXVIII, pp.321-2

57. Fish, R., 'The Herbary', *JHort* (1873), XXIV, p.276-7; 'Doings of the Last Week', *JHort* (1873), XXIV, p.287; see also Dallas, *op. cit.*, pp.400-1

58. Robson, J., 'Endive Culture', *JHort* (1862), III, pp.191-2

59. Iggulden,W., 'Tomato Culture', *JHort* (1880), I(NS), pp.179-80; see also Stuart, D. C., *The Kitchen Garden* (1984), p.245

60. Iggulden, *op. cit.*, *JHort* (1880), I(NS), pp.179-80

61. Taylor, W., 'Things out of Season', *JHort* (1874), XXVII, pp.249-50; *JHort* (1875), XXVIII, p.138

62. Record, T., 'A Few Sorts of Tomatoes', *JHort* (1873), XXV, p.328

63. Fish, R., 'The Herbary', *JHort* (1873), XXIV, pp.276-5

64. Dallas, *op. cit.*, pp.328-9

65. Fish, *op. cit.*, *JHort* (1873), XXIV, p.276

66. 'Thoresby', *JHort* (1876), XXX, p.451

67. 'Bicton', *JHort* (1871) XX, p.222

68. 'Lord Leconfield's Petworth House, Sussex', *JHort* (1863), V, p.186

69. Hayward, *op. cit.*, p.118

70. Fish, R., 'Doings of the Last Week', *JHort* (1865), IX, p.56

71. Loudon, J., *An Encyclopaedia of Gardening* (1824), p.689. For range of cooking properties of culinary varieties of apples see Morgan, J., 'A cooker for all seasons', *JRHS, The Garden* (1980), vol. 105, pp.435-439; Morgan J., 'Culinary Apple Varieties and their Uses' in *Cooking Apples* (1982), ed. Hatton, E. & Miles, C., Ampleforth Abbey, Yorkshire

72. Francatelli, *op. cit.*, p.429

73. Luckhurst, E., 'Raspberry Culture', *JHort* (1875), XXVIII, p.200

Chapter Six: The Dessert Triumphant

1. For the history and nature of the dessert see: Bunyard, E. A., *The Anatomy of Dessert* (1929); Bunyard, E. A. and Bunyard, L., *The Epicure's Companion* (1937); Ketcham Wheaton, B., *Savouring the Past* (1983). For varieties of dessert fruits grown during the nineteenth century, see Hogg, R., *The Fruit Manual* (1884); Bunyard, G. and Thomas, O., *The Fruit Garden*, (1904), Bunyard, E., *A Handbook of Hardy Fruits*, vol. I, (1920); vol. II, (1925)

2. At the Duke of Chandos' garden at Canons, Edgware, Middlesex, pineapples were grown in 1719 – see Stuart, D., *The Kitchen Garden* (1984), p.190. Pineapples were also grown in the early eighteenth century by Thomas Knowlton, gardener to the Earl of Burlington and the Dukes of Devonshire – see Henrey, B., *No Ordinary Gardener, Thomas Knowlton 1691-1781* (1986). In 1781, a bunch grown at the Duke of Portland's garden at Welbeck in Nottinghamshire weighed 19 lb 8 oz – see Stuart, *op. cit.*, p.250. His collection included more than 100 varieties (*JHort* [1875], XXVIII, p.123). The Duke of Portland's gardener, William Speechley, wrote *A Treatise on the Culture of the Pineapple* (1779) and *A Treatise on the Culture of the Vine* (1790)

3. Faujas Saint-Fond, B., *Travels in England, Scotland and the Hebrides* (1799), vol. 1, pp.251-58, quoted in Horn, P., *Life and Labour in Rural England 1760-1850* (1987),

p.32

4. Robson, J., 'The Pineapple', *JHort* (1872), XXII, p.455

5. Bear, W., *Flower and Fruit Farming in England*, reprinted from *Journal of the Royal Agricultural Society* (1898, 1899)

6. Tabitha Tickletooth, *The Dinner Question* (1860), p.9

7. Thomson, D., 'Grape Judging', *JHort* (1867), XII, p.250; Hogg, R. 'Judging Fruits', GC (1870), p1056-7

8. Low, W., *Table Decoration* (1887), p.22; see also Kirwan, A. V., *Host and Guest* (1864)

9. 'Christmas Dessert', JHort (1878), XXXIV, p.482

10. Taylor, W., 'Keeping Grapes', *JHort* (1879), XXVI, p.360

11. Perkins, J., 'Ornamental Leaves for Garnishing the Dessert', *JHort*, (1863), IV, p.337

12. Perkins, J. 'An Ornamental Fruit for the Dessert', *JHort* (1866), XI, p.255

13. Collins, J. L., *The Pineapple*, (1960), p.10; Kirwan, A. V., *Host and Guest* (1864)

14. Woods, A. and Warren, A., *Glass Houses* (1988), pp.60-2.

15. Robson, J., *op. cit.*, *JHort* (1872), XXII, p.455

16. Robson, J. 'The Pineapple', *JHort* (1866), X, pp.340-1

17. 'Half an Hour at Cyfarthfa Castle', *JHort* (1875), XXIX, p.288

18. Robson, J., 'The Pineapple and its Culture', *JHort* (1877), XXXII, pp.51-2

19. Thomson, D., *The Culture of the Pineapple* (1866); 'Drumlanrig', *JHort* (1880), XXXVIII, p.270

20. Thomson, D., *The Culture of the Pineapple* (1866), pp.8-11; Hogg describes 25 pineapple varieties in cultivation

21. Collins, *op. cit.*, p.71

22. Thomson, *op. cit.*, p.9

23. 'The Château De Ferrières', *JHort* (1884), IX(NS), p.351

24. 'Sandringham', GC (1866), p.735; according to Hogg the largest recorded weight was 14 lbs 12 oz

25. Thomson, D. 'Notes from the North', *JHort* (1883), VII(NS), p.435

26. Barron, A. F., *Vines and Vine Culture* (1887), p.6

27. Thomson, W., 'Vines and Vine Borders', *JHort* (1867), XII, p.206

28. For Victorian dessert grapes see Hogg, R., *The Fruit Manual*, (1884); Barron, *op. cit.*; Thomson, D., *Fruit Culture under Glass* (1872)

29. Thomson, D., 'Grape Judging', *JHort*

(1867), XIII, p.250; Taylor, W., 'Vines at Longleat', *JHort* (1882), IV(NS), p.252

30. Barron, *op. cit.*, p.167

31. Thomson, D., 'Notes on Grapes', *JHort* (1879), XXXVI, pp.21-2

32. Taylor, W., 'Keeping Grapes', *JHort* (1880), I(NS), p.365

33. 'The Large Vinery at Longleat', *JHort* (1874), XXVII, p.125

34. For melon varieties see: Nicholson, G. ed. *The Illustrated Dictionary of Gardening*, vol. 2, (1886); Bunyard, E. A., *The Anatomy of Dessert* (1929)

35. Taylor, W., 'Melon-Growing and Judging', *JHort* (1874), XXVI, p.47

36. *Ibid.*; 'Cutting Melons', *JHort* (1874), XXVI, p.63; Nicholson, *op. cit.*

37. 'Sandringham', GC (1866), p.735

38. For origins and history of the strawberry see : Darrow, G. M., *The Strawberry* (1966); Hyams, E. *Strawberry Cultivation*, (1953); Stuart, D., *The Kitchen Garden* (1984), p.235-38.

39. Radclyffe, W. F., 'Selection of Strawberries and their Culture', *JHort* (1865), IX, pp.41-2

40. Taylor, W., 'Strawberry Forcing', *JHort* (1875), XXVIII, pp.135-6, 'Strawberries for Forcing', *JHort* (1879), XXXVI, p.393; 'Strawberries', *JHort* (1880), I(NS), p.22. For flavours and merits of strawberry varieties see also Hogg, *op. cit.*; Laxton Brothers, *The Strawberry Manual* (c. 1899, not dated)

41. Radclyffe, *op. cit.*, *JHort* (1865), IX, p.41; Laxton Brothers, *ibid.*, p.26

42. Austen, J., *Emma* (1816, Penguin Classic, 1985 ed.), p.354

43. 'New Strawberries', *JHort* (1864), VII, p.11

44. Taylor, *op. cit.*, *JHort* (1875), XXVIII, p.135

45. Fish, R., 'Doings of the Last Week', *JHort* (1867), XII, p.380

46. Thomson, D., *Fruit Culture under Glass* (1872), p.138

47. Taylor, W., 'Peach Forcing', *JHort* (1874), XXVI, p.217

48. Thomson, *op. cit.*, p.147. For merits and flavours of peaches and nectarines see Hogg, *op. cit.*; Bunyard, E. A., *The Anatomy of Dessert*; Bunyard, E. A., *A Handbook of Hardy Fruits*, vol. II

49. Luckhurst, E., *JHort* (1875), XXIX, p.164

50. Ruskin, quoted in Bunyard, *The Anatomy of Dessert*, p.35.

51. Robson, J., 'Apricot Management', *JHort* (1863), IV, pp.163-4; Gilbert, R. 'The Apricot Crop', *JHort* (1874), XXVI, p.309. For varieties in cultivation see: Hogg, *op. cit.*;

Bunyard, *op. cit.*

52. For popular fig varieties and their flavours, see Thomson, *op. cit.*; Hogg, *op. cit.*; Bunyard, *The Anatomy of Dessert*, *op. cit.*

53. 'Petworth House', GC (1878), ii, p.524. The fig trees at Petworth were described as 'the Green Italian Fig' and as the Nerii Fig, both of which seem to be synonyms for White or Green Ischia

54. 'A Good Fig', *JHort* (1874), XXVI, p.161

55. Fish, R. 'Doings of the Last Week', *JHort* (1866), XI, p.71

56. 'Dangstein', *JHort* (1864), VI, p.10

57. 'The Culture of the Mangosteen for the Dessert', *JHort* (1865), IX, p.357

58. Wright, J., 'Dalkeith', *JHort* (1875), XXVIII, p.204

59. Robson, J., 'Lambton Castle', *JHort* (1873), XXV, p.314; 'Musa Cavendishii', *JHort* (1863), V, p.399

60. Robson, *op. cit.*, *JHort* (1873), XXV, p.314; Drumlanrig: see *JHort* (1874), XXVII, p.348

61. 'Passiflora Edulis', *JHort* (1875), XXVIII, p.258; Bunyard, and Thomas, *op. cit.*, p.213

62. Stuart, *op. cit.*, p174-6

63. 'Oranges', *JHort* (1878), XXXV, p.490

64. Rivers, T. 'Dessert Orange Culture', *JHort* (1869) XVI, pp. 59-60

65. Luckhurst, E., 'Pears and their Culture', *JHort* (1876), XXX, pp.71-2

66. 'The Gardens of Nuneham Park', *JHort* (1866), XI, p.255; Luckhurst, E. 'Pears', *JHort* (1880), I(NS), pp.521-2

67. Pear varieties and flavours see: Hogg, *op. cit.*; Bunyard, *op. cit.*

68. Morgan, J. 'A historic centenary', *JRHS, The Garden* (1983), vol.108, pp.383-388

69. Loudon, J.C., *Garden Encyclopaedia* (1824) p.689

70. For diversity and flavours of apples see Morgan, J., 'Vintage apples', *JRHS, The Garden* (1982), vol. 107, pp.308-313; Morgan, J. 'The Dimensions of Flavour of the Apple', in Jaine, T., ed. *Taste, Proceedings of the Oxford Symposium on Food and Cookery 1987* (1988), p.162-64; Morgan, J. 'In Praise of Older Apples', BBC Radio 3, October 12, 1983, produced, Richards, A.; Hogg, *op. cit.*; Bunyard, *op. cit.*

71. Estates from all over Britain supplied apples for the 1883 Congress. Many of their collections contained over a hundred varieties, see Morgan, *op. cit.*, *JRHS, The Garden* (1983), vol.108, pp.383-388

72. Plum varieties see Hogg, *op. cit.*, Bunyard, *op. cit.*

73. Cherry varieties see Hogg, *ibid.*; Bunyard,

ibid.

74. Gooseberry varieties see Hogg, *ibid*; Bunyard, *ibid*

75. Robson, J., 'The Filbert and Cob Nuts', *JHort.* (1864), VII, p.485

Chapter Seven: Producing the Plenty

1. For kitchen garden layout, see Thompson, R., *Gardener's Assistant* 1878, (new ed. Moore, T., 1878)

2. 'Nuneham Park', *JHort* (1867), XIII, pp.314-5, 351-2

3. 'Nuneham Park', *ibid.*, and OS Map *c.* 1880; 'Burghley House', *JHort* (1872), XXII, pp.13-14

4. 'Drumlanrig', *JHort* (1877), XXXIII, pp.195-8

5. 'Trentham', *JHort* (1863), V, pp.354-6

6. 'Longleat', *JHort* (1881), III(NS), p.379

7. Fish, R., 'Doings of the Last Week', *JHort* (1867), XIII, p.12

8. 'Liquid Manures', *JHort* (1865), IX, pp.2-4; Muir, J. 'Manure Water', *Gardener* (1881), pp.450-3

9. Fish, R., 'Rubbish Heaps', *JHort* (1866), XI, p.273;

10. Linton: Kent County Archives U24F25 gives indoor staff of 20 for 1841, which was approximately the number employed at the end of the century; Longleat: Thynne, D. W L. (Marchioness of Bath), *Before the Sunset Fades* (1951)

11. Taylor, W. 'Strawberry Forcing', *JHort* (1875), XXVIII, p.135

12. Elliott, B., *Victorian Gardens* (1986), p.18

13. 'Drumlanrig', *JHort* (1877), XXXIII, p.197

14. 'Longleat', *JHort* (1873), XXV, p.10; Longleat Archives – Estate map 1887

15. 'Linton Park Labour Book, 1864', Kent County Archives U24A7; 'Rangemore Hall, The Seat of M. T. Bass, Esq., MP', *JHort* (1876), XXX, p.55

16. 'Drumlanrig', *JHort* (1877), XXXIII, p.197; 'Blenheim House, the Seat of the Duke of Marlborough', *JHort* (1874), XXVI, p.277

17. Robson, J. 'The Cold Pit, and its uses in Winter', *JHort* (1867), XIII, pp.1-2; OS map *c.* 1880

18. Thomson, D., *Fruit under Glass* (1873), pp.42-45

19. 'Drumlanrig', *JHort* (1877), XXXIII, p.197

20. 'Gardening at Cyfarthfa Castle, Merthyr Tydvil', *JHort* (1878), XXXV, pp.411-12

21. Thomson, *op. cit.*, pp.35-45

22. see Thomson, *op. cit.*; Thompson, R., *op.cit.*, see 'Fruit Forcing'

23. Taylor, W., 'Catching Sunbeams', *JHort*

24. Fish, R. 'Doings of the Last Week', *JHort* (1863), IV, p.282, 299

25. 'Petworth House', GC (1878) ii, p.523; 'Windsor Castle', *JHort* (1877), XXXIII, p.215; 'Ingram Strawberry House', Thompson, *op. cit.*, p.596

26. 'Dalkeith', *JHort* (1875), XXVIII, p.203

27. 'The Large Vinery at Longleat', *JHort*, (1874), XXVII, p.125

28. 'Longleat', *JHort* (1881), III(NS), p.399; 'Royal Visit to Longleat', *JHort* (1881), III(NS), p.538

29. 'The Gardens of Nuneham Park', *JHort* (1866), XI, p.256

30. 'Christmas Vegetables', *JHort* (1878), XXXIV, p.484

31. Thompson, *op. cit.*, pp.535-6

32. 'Rangemore Hall', *JHort* (1876), XXX, p.55

33. 'Jottings on Last Year's Gardening', *JHort* (1875), XXVIII, p.166

34. Taylor, W., 'Mushroom Growing', *JHort* (1875), XXIX, p.459; 'Mushroom Growing', *JHort* (1880), XXXVIII, p.37

35. Hinds, W., 'On Vegetable Forcing', *Gardener* (1878), p.60

36. 'Longleat', *JHort* (1881), III(NS), p.380

37. Fish, R. 'Doings of the Last Week', *JHort* (1867), XII, p.183

38. 'Oldlands Hall', *JHort* (1875), XXIX, p.247; D'Ombrain, 'Lord Leconfield's, Petworth House', *JHort* (1863), V, p.186; OS map, *c.* 1880

39. 'Oldlands Hall', *JHort* (1875), XXIX, p.247

40. 'Barham Court', *JHort* (1877), XXXII, p. 50

41. Rivers, T., *The Miniature Fruit Garden* (12th ed., 1891)

42. Fish, F., 'Doings of the Last Week', *JHort* (1863), IV, pp.156-7

43. Rivers, T., *The Orchard – House*, (14th ed., 1870), p.2

44. 'Drumlanrig', *JHort* (1877), XXXIII, p.196; *JHort* (1880), XXXVIII, p.271; *JHort* (1883), VI(NS), p.158

45. Taylor, W., 'The Seed Order', *JHort* (1881), II(NS), pp.23-4

46. Taylor, W., 'Kitchen Garden Arrangement', *JHort* (1877), XXXII, p.360

47. 'Rangemore Hall', *JHort* (1876), XXX, p.75

48. Iggulden, W., *Gardener* (1881), p.56

49. Taylor, W., 'Kitchen Garden Cropping' *JHort* (1878), XXXIV, p.141

50. Iggulden, W., 'How to make the most of wall borders in kitchen gardens', *Gardener* (1881), p.205

51. 'Mulching', *JHort* (1874), XXVI, p.472

52. Fish, R. 'Doings of the Last Week', *JHort*

(1863), IV, p.175

53. Fish, R. 'Doings of the Last Week', *JHort* (1863), IV, p.156

54. 'Knowsley Hall', GC (1865), p.199

55. Iggulden, W., 'Packing Cut Flowers', *JHort* (1882), IV(NS), pp.397-8

56. 'Bloxholm Hall', *JHort* (1876), XXX, p.352

57. Luckhurst, E., 'Packing Fruit and Cut Flowers', *JHort* (1875), XXIX, p.289

58. Taylor, W., 'Packing–No. 1', *JHort* (1877), XXXIII, p.30; 'Packing–No. 3', *op. cit.*, p.129

Chapter Eight: The Mansion in a Landscape

1. Elliott, B., *Victorian Gardens* (1986), pp.102-5; 'Biddulph Grange, the Residence of James Bateman, Esq.', GC (1862), pp.478-80, 527-8, 575-6, 670-2, 719-20

2. 'Trentham Hall', GC (1848), p.703; OS map, *c.*1880

3. Luckhurst, E., 'Lamorran', *JHort* (1877), XXXIII, pp.177-180; 'Lamorran', GC (1881), i, p.751-2

4. Loudon, J. C., 'Remarks on the improvements proposed to be made at Linton Place in Kent, the seat of the Right Honourable the Earl Mann Cornwallis', (1825); manuscript held Maidstone Museums and Art Gallery, Maidstone, Kent

5. 'Mr Alderman Masters', GC (1874), ii, p.437

6. See: Robson, J., 'Flower gardening on a new principal', *CottGard* (1859), XXI, pp.396-7; Fish, R. 'Linton Park', *CottGard* (1859), XXIII, pp.143-145, 160-163; 'Linton Park', *CottGard* (1861), II, pp.185-8; 218-220; 238-40; 'Linton Labour Books', 1864, 1865, 1868, 1869, 1871, 1873, Kent County Archives, U24 A7-12; OS map, *c.*1880

7. Fish, *op. cit.*, *CottGard* (1859), XXIII, pp.144-5; Robson, J., 'The Yucca', *JHort* (1873), XXIV, pp.164-5

8. Thomson, D., *Handy Book of the Flower Garden* (1868), pp.193-7

9. Elliott, *op. cit.*, p.190

10. For development of modern roses see: Thomas, G. S., *Shrub Roses of Today* (1962), Thomas, G. S., *Climbing Roses Old and New* (1965); Beales, P., *Classic Roses* (1985)

11. Discussion on the merits of the new varieties was a continuing topic in the journals; see also Hibberd, S., *The Amateur's Rose Book* (revised ed. Gordon, G., 1894)

12. Luckhurst, E., 'A Rose Garden', *JHort* (1878), XXXV, p.430

13. 'Rose Garden at Mentmore', *JHort* (1879), XXXVI, pp.81-2

14. 'Linton Park', *JHort* (1861), I, p.239; 'Fes-

toons of Climbing Roses', *JHort* (1867), XII, p.110

15. 'Nuneham Park', *JHort* (1867), XIII, p.404

16. Douglas, J. 'Hardwick House', *JHort* (1875), XXVIII, pp.54-7

17. viz. 2nd Duchess of Portland had an American Garden at Bulstrode, see Festing, S. *Country Life*, June 19, 1986, p.1772; Repton made American Gardens for Duke of Bedford at Woburn in 1804, and one at Ashridge in 1813 – see Carter, G., Goode, P., Laurie, K., *Humphry Repton, Landscape Gardener 1752-1818* (1982),Catalogue of Victoria and Albert Museum and Sainsbury Centre for the Visual Arts Exhibition, p.60

18. Gorer, R., *Growth of Gardens* (1978), pp.139-41; for rhododendrons of the 19th century see Millais, J.G., *Rhododendrons: and the Various Hybrids* (1917)

19. 'Linton Labour Book 1865', U24A8, Kent County Archives; Robson, J., 'Garden Reminiscences of the Past Fifty Years', *JHort* (1876), XXXI, p.553

20. Luckhurst, E., 'Hardy Rhododendrons', *JHort* (1873), XXIV, p.93; see also Thompson, R., *Gardener's Assistant* (revised ed., Moore, T., 1878), pp.668-75

21. Luckhurst, E., 'Ornamental Planting – No. 6', *JHort* (1873), XXV pp.98-9

22. 'The Dell, Egham', *JHort* (1886), XII(NS), p.513

23. see this chapter p.165

24. For lily introductions see Singe, P., *Lilies* (1980)

25. D'Ombrain, 'Lilium Auratum and its Culture', *JHort* (1867), XII, p.257

26. 'Duneevan', *JHort* (1875), XXIX, pp.294-97; *JHort* (1885), X(NS), p.483

27. Luckhurst, E. 'Ornamental Planting – No. 2', *JHort* (1873), XXIV, pp.433-5

28. Luckhurst, E. 'Ornamental Planting – No. 3', *JHort* (1873), XXIV, p.464

29. For coverage of conifers and history of their introduction see James Veitch & Sons, *A Manual of Coniferae* (1881); 'Report of the Conifer Conference', JRHS (1892), XIV; Mitchell, A. and Wilkinson, J., *The Trees of Britain and Northern Europe* (1982); Johnson, H., *The International Book of Trees* (1973)

30. 'Dropmore', *JHort* (1884), IX(NS), pp.169-2; Herrin, C. 'Conifers at Dropmore', JRHS (1892), XIV, pp.61-6

31. 'Dropmore', *JHort* (1864), VI, pp.456-7

32. *Catalogue of Taxacea and Coniferae planted in the Pinetum at Linton Park in 1844*; (entries bring records up to 1877), RHS Lindley Library Archives; see also Robson, J., 'Coni-

fers at Linton Park', *JHort* (1872), XXIII, pp.247-248; 287-288

33. Luckhurst, E., 'Ornamental Planting – No. 2', *JHort* (1873), XXIV, pp.433-5

34. Luckhurst, *op. cit.*, *JHort* (1873), XXIV, p.433

35. Veitch and Sons, *op. cit.*, pp.320-1

36. Luckhurst, E., 'Ornamental Planting – No. 8, Avenues', *JHort* (1873), XXV, p.187

37. Coats, A. M., *Garden Shrubs and their Histories* (1963), p.115; see also Gorer, *op. cit.*

38. Luckhurst, E., 'Ornamental Planting – No. 6', *JHort* (1873), XXV, p.98

39. Gorer, *op. cit.*, p.75

40. Luckhurst, E., 'Ornamental Planting– No. 10', *JHort* (1873), XXV, pp.347-8

41. 'Oldlands Hall', *JHort* (1875), XXIX, p.246; OS map, 1874

42. Luckhurst, E., 'Ornamental Planting – No. 1', *JHort* (1873), XXIV, p.19

43. *Ibid.*

44. Luckhurst, E., 'Shrub Grouping', *JHort* (1884), IX(NS), pp.498-9

45. Luckhurst, *op. cit.*, *JHort* (1873), XXV, pp.19-20; *JHort* (1873), XXIV, p.433

46. Luckhurst, *op. cit.*, *JHort* (1884), IX(NS), pp.498

47. Luckhurst, E., 'Ornamental Planting – No. 4', *JHort* (1873), XXIV, pp.499-500

48. Elliott, *op. cit.*, pp.93-4

49. Robson, J., 'The Snowdrop and its uses for naked places', *JHort* (1874), XXVI, pp.179-189, 'Eranthis hyemalis, or Winter Aconite', *JHort* (1874), XXVI, pp.198-9

50. Robson, J., 'Flowers of Hardy Trees and Shrubs, No. 1', *JHort* (1875), XXIX, p.92; 'Flowers of Hardy Trees and Shrubs, No. 2' *JHort* (1875), XXIX, pp.163-4

51. Taylor, W., 'Semi-natural Gardening', *JHort* (1875), XXVIII, pp.485-6; see also *JHort* (1911), LXII, p.497; Robinson, W., *The Wild Garden* (reprint 1894 ed., 1983), p.177, 193, 253

Chapter Nine: The Perfect Whole

1. Axton, W. F., 'Victorian Landscape Painting: A change in outloook', in *Nature and the Victorian Imagination*, (1977), ed. Knoepflmacher, U. C. and Tennyson, G. B., p.299

2. Christopher Falconer, quoted in Blythe, R., *Akenfield*, (1969, reprint, 1988), p.118

3. 'Archerfield'. *J Hort* (1865), IX, pp.447-8; 'Drumlanrig', *JHort* (1880), XXXVIII, p.271

4. Thomson, D., 'Autumn Propagation of Bedding Plants', *JHort* (1863), V, pp.81-2; 'The Flower Garden', *JHort* (1864), VI, pp.109-110

5. Fish, R., 'Doings of the Last Week', *JHort* (1863), V, p.257

6. Fish, R., 'Doings of the Last Week', *JHort* (1863), IV, p.13

7. Fish, R. 'Doings of the Last Week', *JHort* (1863), V, p.154; *JHort* (1863), IV, p.13

8. Fish, R., 'Doings of the Last Week', *JHort* (1863), IV, p.249

9. Robson, J., 'Bedding Geraniums, and an easy Way to Promote their Growth', *JHort* (1875) XXVIII, pp.313-4; 'Linton Labour Book, 1865', Kent County Archives U24A8

10. Fish, R., 'Doings of the Last Week', *JHort* (1863), IV, pp.383-4

11. *Ibid.*, p.384

12. Fish, R., 'Doings of the Last Week', *JHort* (1863), V, p.196

13. Fish, R., 'Doings of the Last Week', *JHort.* (1863),V, p.418

14. Fish, R., 'Doings of the Last Week' *JHort* (1863), V, p.94

15. Thomson, D., 'Order', *Gardener* (1878), pp.391-3

16. Fish, R. 'Doings of the Last Week', *JHort* (1866), XI, p.468

17. 'Blenheim House', *JHort* (1874), XXVI, p.275,

18. 'Drumlanrig', *JHort* (1880), XXXVIII, p.270

19. Luckhurst, E., 'Mount Edgcumbe', *JHort* (1877), XXXIII, p.419

20. Thomson, *op. cit.*, *Gardener* (1878), p.393

21. Elliott, B., *Victorian Gardens* (1986), p.16

22. Fish, R., 'Doings of the Last Week', *JHort* (1867), XIII, pp.336-7

23. Fish, R., 'Doings of the Last Week', *JHort* (1866), XI, p.225

24. Robson, J., 'Edgings for walks in places where there is no vegetation', *JHort* (1867), XIII, pp.257-8

25. Fish, *op. cit.*, *JHort* (1866), XI, p468

26. Fish, R., 'Trentham', *JHort* (1863), V, p.413

27. Robson, J., 'Painting and Colouring Garden Structures', *JHort* (1867), XIII, pp.172-3

28. 'Sandringham', GC (1866), p.735

29. Fish, R., 'Trentham', *JHort* (1863), V, pp.354-5

30. Fish, R., 'Doings of the Last Week', *JHort* (1867), XIII, p.201

31. Robson, J., 'Archerfield', *JHort* (1865), IX, p.426

32. Taylor, W., 'Kitchen Garden Arrangement', *JHort* (1877), XXXII, p.360

33. 'Longleat', *JHort* (1881), III(NS), p.398

34. Robson, J., 'Stanhopea tigrina and oculata', *JHort* (1867), XIII, pp.115-6

35. 'Dangstein', JHort (1872), XXIII, p.517-8; JHort (1873), XXIV, pp.33-4

36. 'Dalkeith', JHort (1875), XXVIII, pp.181-3

37. 'Westonbirt', JHort (1873), XXV, pp.82-83

38. Taylor, W., 'Catching sunbeams', JHort (1875), XXVIII, p.91; Bardney, W., 'Flowering plants for room decoration', Gardener (1881), pp.52-5

39. Taylor, W., 'Tea Roses – No. 3', JHort (1880), XXXVIII, p.448; see also Thompson, R., Gardener's Assistant, 'The Forcing Calendar'

40. 'Rangemore', JHort (1876), XXX, p.75

41. 'Scone Palace', JHort (1885), X(NS), p.90

42. Bardney, op. cit., Gardener (1881), pp.52-5

43. 'Royal Visit to Longleat' JHort (1881), III(NS), p.538

44. 'Drumlanrig', JHort (1880), XXXVIII, p.271

45. 'Draycot', JHort (1873), XXV, p.491

46. Luckhurst, E. 'The Arrangement of Cut Flowers', JHort (1881), III(NS), pp. 270-1

47. Brotherston, R. 'The Book of Cut Flowers', (1906), pp.43-54

48. Blythe, op. cit., p.119

49. Iggulden, W., 'Packing Cut Flowers', JHort (1882), IV(NS), pp.397-8

50. Taylor, W., 'Packing – No. 2' JHort (1877), XXXIII, p.89

51. Iggulden, op. cit., JHort (1882), IV(NS), p.388

Chapter 10: Men of Influence

1. Fish, R., 'A Few Words to Young Gardeners on Education and Attention', JHort (1863), IV, p.27. The (Royal) Horticultural Society maintained experimental gardens at Chiswick, and introduced a formal training scheme and examinations in the 1836, but only a few gardeners trained here. The Society's General Examination in Horticulture was introduced in 1893.

Rothamstead Experimental Station was established in 1843 by Sir John Bennet Lawes, but was primarlily concerned with agriculture and field crops. The first experimental fruit farm was set up at the Duke of Bedford's Woburn estate in 1894. Government-funded horticultural research commenced in 1912 with the founding of the Long Ashton Research Station, Bristol. See Fletcher, H. R., The Story of the Royal Horticultural Society (1969)

2. 'Mr William Taylor', JHort (1910), LXI(NS), pp.436-7

3. 'William Ingram', GC (1875), i, p.336

4. 'Mr David Thomson, V.M.H.', JHort (1908), LVII(NS), pp.294-8

5. 'James Barnes', GC (1874), i, pp.655-6

6. 'Thomas Speed', GC (1874), ii, p.783

7. JHort (1908), LVII, p.295

8. Thomson, D., JHort (1879), XXXVI, p.3

9. Fish, R. 'Gardeners' Hours and Holidays', JHort (1862), III, pp.209-11

10. 'Memories and Morals of Bothydom', JHort (1896), XXXIII (NS), p.270

11. Gilbert, R. 'Extra Work and Wages in Gardens' JHort (1879), XXXVI, p.380; JHort (1910), LXI(NS), pp.436-7

12. 'Linton Labour Book, 1873', Kent County Archives U24A12

13. see 'Daniel Judd', GC (1875), i, p.785

14. 'The Denbies, Dorking, The Seat of Mrs Cubitt', JHort (1867) XII, p.143

15. Robson, J., ' Hamilton Palace', JHort (1865), IX, p.315

16. Robson, J., 'Lambton Castle', JHort (1878), XXXV, p.87

17. 'Linton Labour Book 1873', Kent County Archives U24A12

18. 'Drumlanrig', JHort (1880), XXXVIII, p.271

19. Fish, F., 'Knowledge Desirable for Gardeners', JHort (1863), V, pp.63-66

20. Fish, op. cit., JHort (1863), V, pp.105-108

21. GC (1878), i, p.732

22. 'Bothwell Castle', JHort (1879), XXXVII, p.482

23. Fish, op. cit., JHort (1863), V, p.64

24. Fish, op. cit., JHort (1863), V, p.107

25. Gilbert, op. cit., JHort (1879), XXXVI, p.380

26. Gardener (1881), p.225

27. Taylor, W., 'Management: Hints to Learners Only', JHort (1879), XXXVI, p.301

28. Luckhurst, E., 'Gardeners and Gardening', JHort (1871), XX, pp.21-22

29. Taylor, op. cit., JHort (1879), XXXVI, p.301

30. JHort (1883), VI(NS), p.530

31. JHort (1867), XII, p.321

32. Fish, R., 'Doings of the Last Week', JHort (1863), V, p.196

33. Fish, R., 'Who Should Gather the Garden Produce?', JHort (1865), IX, p.504.

34. Luckhurst, op. cit., JHort (1871), XX, pp.21-2

35. Fish, R., 'Doings of the Last Week', JHort (1867), XIII, p.407

36. Fish, R., 'Doings of the Last Week', JHort (1867), XIII, p.84

37. Fish, R., 'Doings of the Last Week' JHort (1863), V, p.317

38. Taylor, W., 'Management-2' *JHort* (1879), XXXVI, p.338
39. Taylor, W., 'Difficulties Overcome', *JHort* (1879), XXXVI, p.75, 93
40. 'Linton Labour Book, 1865', Kent County Archives U24A8
41. 'Linton Labour Books', 1864, 1865, 1868, 1869, 1871, 1873, Kent County Archives U24A7-12
42. Robson, J., 'Gardening Reminiscences of the Past Fifty Years', *JHort* (1876), XXXI, pp.551-3
43. Fish, R., 'Telling Beds or Flower Gardens', *JHort* (1863), V, p.294
44. Elliott, B., *Victorian Gardens*, (1986), p.13
45. *JHort* (1862), III, p. 513
46. Robson, J., 'Visiting Some Distant Gardens and How to See Them', *JHort* (1864), VII, pp.129-130
47. 'The Edinburgh International Fruit and Flower Show', *JHort* (1865), IX, pp.210-1; GC (1865), p.841, 844-5
48. 'International Horticultural Exhibition and Botanic Congress', *JHort* (1866), X, pp.390-7; GC (1866), pp. 481-2
49. 'Grapes at the Edinburgh Show', *JHort* (1875), XXIX, p.270
50. 'Royal Horticultural Society', *JHort* (1875), XXIX, p.27
51. Molyneux, E., *Chrysanthemums and their Culture* (1888), p.vii; 'Swanmore Park', *JHort* (1884), IX (NS) pp.439-40
52. Molyneux, *op. cit.*, p.97, 106
53 *JHort* (1878), XXXV, p.130; *JHort* (1881), III(NS), p.261
54. GC (1878), ii, p.601
55. Robson, J., 'Mr. Fenn and his Potatoes', *JHort* (1874), XXVII pp.248-9
56. Salaman, R. N., *History and Social Influence of the Potato* (1949, reprint 1985), p.167
57. Thomson, D., 'The Flower Garden', *JHort* (1864), VI, pp.172-4; Fish, R. 'Planting out Sub-Tropical and Other Handsome Foliage Plants', *JHort* (1866), X, pp.375-7; Luckhurst, E. 'Hardy Rhododendrons', *JHort* (1873), XXIV pp.93-4
58. *JHort* (1886), XII (NS), p.91
59. GC (1881), i, p.89
60. Longleat Archives; 'Linton Labour Books', *op. cit.*
61. *JHort* (1861), II, pp.258-9; 'Trentham', *JHort* (1863), V, p.354
62. Elliott, *op. cit.*, p.214; GC (1869), p.1305
63. GC (1909), ii, p.296

Epilogue

1. Girouard, M., *Life in the English Country House* (1980), p. 301
2. Franklin, J., *The Gentleman's Country House and its Plan, 1835-1914* (1981), p.38
3. Girouard, *op. cit.*, p. 300
4. Franklin, *op. cit.*, p. 38
5. Elliott, B., *Victorian Gardens*, (1986), p.15
6. Girouard, *op. cit.*, pp.300-2
7. Pemble, J. 'Death in San Remo'; 'Resurrection in the Alps', BBC, Radio 3, 1984; produced, Richards, A.
8. Buckland, B. *The Golden Summer*, (1989), pp.11-12
9. Escoffier, G. A., *A Guide to Modern Cookery* (1903), p.xi, quoted in Mennell, S., *All Manners of Food* (1985), p.158
10. Girouard, M., *The Victorian Country House* (1985), p.9
11. Girouard, M., *Life in the English Country House, op. cit.*, p.304
12. Elliott, B., *op. cit.*, (1986), pp.214-15
13. Girouard, *op. cit.*, p.306
14. Bradbury, M., *The Social Context of Modern English Literature* (1971), p.46, quoted in Weiner, M. J., *English Culture and the Decline of the Industrial Spirit, 1850-1980* (1985), p.50
15. Girouard, M., *Sweetness and Light, The 'Queen Anne' Movement, 1860-1900* (1977), p.5
16. For full discussion see: Elliott, *op. cit.*, chap 9, 'In search of a vernacular'
17. Elliott, *op. cit.*, p.237
18. Girouard, M., *Life in the English Country House op. cit.*, p.314
19. *Ibid.*, p.314
20. Fletcher, H. R., *The Story of the Royal Horticultural Society* (1969), pp.215-7, 284-94, 310-12

Bibliography

For list of periodicals consulted, see page 234.

ALLEN, D. E., *The Victorian Fern Craze*, 1969, Hutchinson, London

AXTON, W. F., in *Nature and the Victorian Imagination*, ed. Knoepflmacher, U. C. and Tennyson, G. B., 1977, University of California Press, California

BARRON, A. F., *Vines and Vine Culture*, 1887, Journal of Horticulture Office, London

BEALES, P., *Classic Roses*, 1985, Collins Harvill, London

BEAR, W. E., *Fruit and Flower Farming in England*, reprinted from *Journal of Royal Agricultural Society of England* for 1898 and 1899

Beeton's All About Gardening, reprint 1987, Bracken Books, London

Beeton's Dictionary of Everyday Cookery, 1865 reprint 1984, Bracken Books, London

BLYTHE, R., *Akenfield*, 1969, 1988, Penguin, London

BONIFACE, P., *The Garden Room*, 1982, HMSO, London

BONIFACE, P., ed. *In search of English Gardens: The travels of John Cladius Loudon and his Wife Jane*, 1987, Lennard Publishing, Herts

BRIGGS, A., *Victorian People*, 1954, Odhams, London; reprint 1987, Penguin, London

BRIGGS, A., *Victorian Things*, 1988, Batsford, London

BROOKE, E. A., *The Gardens of England*, 1857

BROTHERSTON, R. P., *The Book of Cut Flowers*, 1906, T. N. Foulis, Edinburgh & London

BUCKLAND, B., *The Golden Summer*, 1989, Pavilion Books in association with Michael Joseph, London

BUNYARD, E., *A Handbook of Hardy Fruits*, vol. I, 1920; vol. II, 1925, John Murray, London

BUNYARD, E. A., *The Anatomy of Dessert*, 1929, Dulau & Company, London

BUNYARD, E. A. and BUNYARD, L., *The Epicure's Companion*, 1937, J. M. Dent & Sons, London

BUNYARD, G. and THOMAS, O., *The Fruit Garden*, 1904, Country Life, London

BURBIDGE, F. W., *Domestic Floriculture*, 1874, William Blackwood & Sons, Edinburgh & London

CAMPBELL, S., *Cottesbrooke, An English Kitchen Garden*, 1987, Century Hutchinson, London

CARTER, G., GOODE, P. and LAURIE, K., *Humphry Repton Landscape Gardener 1752-1818*, 1982, Catalogue of Victoria and Albert Museum and Sainsbury Centre for the Visual Arts Exhibition

CARTER, T., *The Victorian Garden*, 1984, Bell & Hyman Ltd., London

CHEVREUL, M-E., *The Principles of Harmony and Contrast of Colour*, 1854

Cassell's Dictionary of Cookery, Cassell Petter & Galpin, London, Paris, New York

CLAYTON-PAYNE, A., *Victorian Flower Gardens*, 1988, Weidenfeld & Nicolson, London

COATS, A. M., *Flowers and their Histories*, 1956, Hulton Press, London

COATS, A. M., *Garden Shrubs and their Histories*, 1963, Vista Books, London

COATS, P., *Flowers in History*, 1970, Weidenfeld & Nicholson, London

COLLINS, J. L., *The Pineapple*, 1960, Leonard Hill [Books] Ltd., London, Interscience Publishers, New York

CURTIS, C. H., *Orchids*, 1950, Putnam & Co. Ltd., London

DALLAS, E. S., *Kettner's Book of the Table*, 1877, reprint 1968, Centaur Press, London

DAVIDOFF, L., *The Best Circles: Society, Eti-*

quette and the Season, 1973, Croom Helm, London

DESMOND, R., *Dictionary of British and Irish Botanists and Horticulturalists*, 1977, Taylor Francis, London

DESMOND, R., *Bibliography of British Gardens*, 1984, St Paul's Bibliographies, Winchester, Hants

DIVERS, W., *Spring Flowers at Belvoir Castle*, 1909, Longman Green and Co., London

Dumas on Food, translated by A. and J. Davidson, 1978, The Folio Society, and Michael Joseph

ELLIOTT, B., *Victorian Gardens*, 1986, Batsford, London

ESCOFFIER, G. A., *The Complete Guide to the Art of Modern Cookery*, 4th ed. 1921, trans Cracknell, H. L. and Kaufmann, R.J., 1979, Book Club Associates, by Arrangement with William Heinemann, London

EVANS, H., *Our Old Nobility*, 1909, Morning Leader Office, London

FIELD, G., *Chromatics*, 1817

FISHER, J., *The Origins of Garden Plants*, 1982, Constable & Co. Ltd., London

FLETCHER, H. R., *The Story of the Royal Horticultural Society 1804-1968*, 1969, Oxford University Press for the Royal Horticultural Society

FORD, C. and HARRISON, B., *A Hundred Years Ago, Britain in the 1880s in Words and Photographs*, 1983

FRANCATELLI, C. E., *The Modern Cook*, 1846, Richard Bentley, London

FRANKLIN, J., *The Gentleman's Country House and its Plan 1835-1914*, 1981, Routledge & Kegan Paul Ltd., London

GIROUARD, M., *Sweetness and Light, The 'Queen Anne' Movement, 1860-1900*, 1977, Oxford University Press

GIROUARD, M., *Life in the English Country House*, 1978, Yale University Press, New Haven and London, reprint 1980, Penguin, London

GIROUARD, M., *The Victorian Country House*, 1985, Yale University Press, New Haven and London

GORER, R., *The Growth of Gardens*, 1978, Faber & Faber, London

GORER, R., *The Development of Garden Flowers*, 1970, Eyre & Spottiswoode, London

GRIEVE, P., *Ornamental Foliaged Pelargoniums*, 1869, reprint 1977, The British Pelargonium & Geranium Society

HARTCUP, A., *Below Stairs in Country Houses*, 1980, Sidgwick & Jackson, London

HATTON, E. and MILES, C., *Cooking Apples*, 1982, Ampleforth Abbey, Yorkshire

HAY, D. R., *Laws of Harmonious Colouring adapted to Interior Decorations*, 1828, 1844, W.S. Orr & Co., London; Fraser & Co., Edinburgh

HAYWOOD, A., *The Art of Dining, or Gastronomy and Gastromes*, 1853, new ed. 1883, John Murray, London

HENREY, Blanche, *No Ordinary Gardener, Thomas Knowlton 1691-1781*, 1986, British Museum (Natural History), London

HIBBERD, S., *Amateur's Rose Book*, revised ed. Gordon, G., 1894, W. H. and L. Collingridge, London

HIBBERD, S., *Rustic Adornments for Homes of Taste*, 1856, reprint 1987, Century in association with the National Trust, London

HOBHOUSE, P. and WOOD C., *Painted Gardens*, 1988, Pavilion Books in association with Michael Joseph, London

HOGG, R., *The Fruit Manual*, 5th ed. 1884, Journal of Horticulture Office, London

HORN, P., *The Rise and Fall of the Victorian Servant*, 1975, reprint 1989, Alan Sutton

HORN, P., *Life and Labour in Rural England 1760-1850*, 1987, Macmillan Educational Ltd., Basingstoke, Hants and London

HYAMS, E., *Strawberry Cultivation*, 1953, Faber & Faber

JAINE, T., ed. *Oxford Symposium on Food and Cookery, 1987: Taste*, 1988, Prospect Books, London

JEAFFRESON, J. C., *A Book about the Table*, Books I, II, 1875, Hurst and Blackett, London

JOHNSON, G. W., *Kitchen Garden*, 1836, Orr and Smith, London

JOHNSON, G. W., *Johnson's Garden Dictionary*, new ed. 1894, Wright, C. H. and Dewar, D., George Bell and Sons, London.

JOHNSON, H., *The International Book of Trees*, 1973, Mitchell Beazley, London

JONES, O., *The Grammar of Ornament*, 1856, reprint 1988, Omega Books, London

KEMP, E., *How to Lay out a Garden*, 3rd ed. 1864, Bradbury & Evans, London

KETCHAM WHEATON, B., *Savouring the Past*, 1983, Chatto and Windus, London

KIRWAN, A. V., *Host and Guest*, 1864

LAXTON BROTHERS, *The Strawberry Manual*, c.1899 (undated), Hulatt & Richardson, Bedford, Beds

LEMMON, K., *The Covered Garden*, 1962, Museum Press, London

LICHTEN, F., *Decorative Art of Victoria's Era*, 1950

LINDLEY, J., *The Theory and Practice of Horticulture*, 1855, Longman, Brown, Green, and Longmans, London

LOUDON, J., *An Encyclopaedia of Gardening*, 1824, Longman, Rees, Orme, Brown and Green, London

Low, W., *Table Decoration*, 1887, Chapman Hall, London

MALING, Miss, *Flowers for Ornament and Decoration*, 1862, Smith, Elder and Co., London

MARCH, T., *Fruit and Flower Decoration*, 1862

MATYJASZKIEWICZ, K., *James Tissot*, 1984, Phaidon Press and Barbican Art Gallery

MENNELL, S., *All Manners of Food*, 1985, Basil Blackwell Ltd., Oxford

MEREDITH, J., *The Grape Vine*, 1876, George Philip & Son, London

MILLAIS, J. G., *Rhododendrons and the Various Hybrids*, 1917, 2nd series 1924, Longmans Green and Co., London

MINGAY, G., *English Landed Society in the Eighteenth Century*, 1963, Routlege & Kegan Paul, London

MITCHELL, A. and WILKINSON, J., *The Trees of Britain and Northern Europe*, 1982, Collins, London

MOLYNEUX, E., *Chrysanthemums and their Culture*, 1888, Journal of Horticulture Office, London

MONTAGNE, P., *Larousse Gastronomique*, 1961 ed., Paul Hamlyn, London

MONTGOMERY-MASSINGBERD, H., *Great British Families*, 1988, Webb and Bower, Exeter, Devon, in association with Michael Joseph, London

MORRIS, F. O., *A Series of Picturesque Views of Seats of the Noblemen and Gentlemen of Great Britain and Ireland*, 1866-80, vols. 1-6, William Mackenzie, London, Edinburgh and Dublin

NICHOLSON, G., *The Illustrated Dictionary of Gardening*, 1884-1886, vols I-IV, L.

Upcott Gill, London

PAUL, W., *The Rose Garden*, 1848, reprint 1978, Heyden, London, Philadelphia, Rheine

PAUL, W., *Roses in Pots etc*, 1844, 9th ed., 1890, Simpkin,Marshall, Hamilton, Kent, & Co., London

PERKINS, J., *Floral Designs for the Table*, 1877, Wyman & Sons, London

ROBINSON, J. M., *The English Country Estate*, 1988, Century Hutchinson Ltd., London

ROBINSON, W., *Hardy Flowers*, 1871, Macmillan, London

ROBINSON, W., *Alpine Flowers for English Gardens*, 1870, John Murray, London

ROBINSON, W., *The Wild Garden*, 1870, reprint 1983, Century Publishing, London

ROBINSON, W., *The English Flower Garden*, 1883, John Murray, London

RIVERS, T., *The Rose – Amateur's Guide*, 1867, Longmans, Green and Co., London

RIVERS, T., *The Orchard House 1859*, 14th ed. 1870, Longmans, Green, and Co., London

RIVERS, T., *The Miniature Fruit Garden*, 1854, 12th ed. 1891, Longmans, Green and Co., London

SALAMAN, R. N., *History and Social Influence of the Potato*, 1949, reprint 1985, Cambridge University Press, Cambridge

SCOURSE, N., *The Victorians and their Flowers*, 1983, Croom Helm, Beckenham, Kent

SHAW, C. W., *London Market Gardeners*, 1879, London

SOMORS COCKS, A., *The Art of Dining, Masterpieces of Cutlery and the Art of Eating*, 1979, Victoria and Albert Museum and Michael Joseph, London

SOYER, A. *The Gastronomic Regenerator*, 1846, Simpkin Marshall, London

SPEECHLEY, W., *A Treatise on the Culture of the Pineapple*, 1779

SPEECHLEY, W., *A Treatise on the Culture of the Vine*, 1790

SPROULE, A., *The Social Calendar*, 1978, Blandford Press, Poole, Dorset

ST. CLAIR, LADY HARRIETT, *Dainty Dishes*, 1866, Edmonston and Douglas, Edinburgh

STEEGMAN, J., *Victorian Taste*, 1950, reprint 1987, Century in association with the National Trust, London

STRONG, R., *The Renaissance Garden in England*, 1979, Thames and Hudson, London

STROUD, D., *Humphry Repton*, 1962, Faber, London

STUART, D., *Dear Duchess, Millicent Duchess of Sutherland, 1867-1955*, 1982, Victor Gollancz Ltd., London

STUART, D. C., *Georgian Gardens*, 1979, Robert Hale, London

STUART, D. C., *The Kitchen Garden*, 1984, Robert Hale, London

STUART, D. C., *The Garden Triumphant*, 1989, Viking, London

SUTHERLAND, W., *Handbook of Hardy Herbaceous and Alpine Flowers*, 1871, William Blackwood & Sons, Edinburgh & London

TABITHA TICKLETOOTH, *The Dinner Question*, 1860

THOMAS, G. S., *The Old Shrub Roses*, 1957, reprint 1986, J. M. Dent & Sons, London

THOMAS, G. S., *Shrub Roses of Today*, 1962, reprint 1985, J. M. Dent & Sons, London

THOMAS, G. S., *Climbing Roses Old and New*, 1965, new ed. 1983, J. M. Dent & Sons, London

THOMAS, G. S., *Perennial Garden Plants*, 1986, J. M. Dent & Sons, London

THOMPSON, F. M. L., *English Landed Society in the Nineteenth Century*, 1980, Routledge & Kegan Paul, London

THOMPSON, R., *Gardener's Assistant*, revised ed. Moore, T., 1878, Blackie & Sons, London

THOMSON, D., *The Culture of the Pineapple*, 1866, William Blackwood & Sons, Edinburgh & London

THOMSON, D., *Handy Book of the Flower Garden*, 1868, new ed. 1887, William Blackwood and Sons, Edinburgh and London

THOMSON, D., *Fruit Culture under Glass*, 1872, William Blackwood and Sons, Edinburgh and London

THOMSON, W., *The Grape Vine*, 1862, William Blackwood and Sons, Edinburgh and London

THORNTON, P., *Authentic Decor, The Domestic Interior 1620-1920*, 1984, George Weidenfeld & Nicolson, Ltd., London

THYNNE, D. W. L. (Marchioness of Bath), *Before the Sunset Fades*, 1951, Longleat Estate

TRIGGS, H. I., *Formal Gardens in England and Scotland*, 1902, reprint 1988, Antique Collector's Club, Woodbridge, Suffolk

TURNER, T., *English Garden and Design: History and Styles since 1650*, 1986, Antique Collector's Club, Woodbridge, Suffolk

VEITCH AND SONS, *A Manual of Coniferae*, 1881, James Veitch & Sons, London

VILMOURIN-ANDRIEUX, *The Vegetable Garden*, English translation 1885 with added notes relating to Britain; reprint 1976, John Murray, London

WALKER, T., *The Original*, 1835, vol. I, vol II., ed. 1874, Grant & Co, London

WATERSON, M., *The Country House Remembered*, 1985, Routledge & Kegan Paul, London

WEBBER, R., *The Early Horticulturalists*, 1968, David and Charles, Newton Abbot, Devon

WEINER, M. J., *English Culture and the Decline of the Industrial Spirit, 1850-1980*, 1985, Penguin, London

WHITE, T., *The Plant Hunters*, 1970, William Heinemann Ltd., London

WILLAN, A., *Great Cooks and their Recipes*, 1977, Elm Tree Books, London

WILLIAMS, B., *The Orchid Grower's Manual*, 4th ed. 1871, Victoria and Paradise Nurseries, London

WILLIAMS, B., *Stove and Greenhouse Flowering Plants*, 1883, Victoria and Paradise Nurseries, London

WILLIAMSON, T. and BELLAMY, L., *Property and Landscape*, 1987 ed., George Philip, London

WOOD, C., *Victorian Panorama, Paintings of Victorian Life*, 1976, Faber & Faber, London

WOODS, M. and WARREN, A., *Glass Houses*, 1988, Aurum Press, London

WOODS, S., *The Forcing Garden*, 1881, Crosby Lockwood and Co., London

WRIGHT, H., *The Fruit Grower's Guide*, vols I and II, revised ed. 1924, Virtue & Co. Ltd., London

WRIGHT, J. and WRIGHT, H., *The Vegetable Grower's Guide*, vols I and II, 1908, Virtue & Co. Ltd., London

WYNDAM, J. E. R., *Lord Egremont, Wyndam and Children First*, 1968, 1969, Macmillian, London

YOUNG, G. W., *Victorian England, Portrait of an Age*, 1977, ed. G. Kitson Clarke

Imperial/Metric Conversion Chart

1 inch		= 25.4 millimetres
1 foot		= 0.3048 metre
1 yard		= 0.9144 metre
1 mile		= 1.609 kilometres
1 acre	= 4,840 sq. yd.	= 0.405 hectare
1 pint	= 20 fluid oz.	= 0.568 litre
	= 34.68 cu. in	
1 quart	= 2 pints	= 1.136 litres
1 gallon	= 4 quarts	= 4.546 litres
1 peck	= 2 gallons	= 9.092 litres
1 ounce		= 28.35 grams
1 pound		= 0.4536 kilogram
1 hundredweight		= 50.8 kilograms
1 ton		= 1.016 tonnes

Temperature conversions

(approximate equivalents)

32°F	=	0°C	59°F	=	15°C
41°F	=	5°C	68°F	=	20°C
50°F	=	10°C	77°F	=	25°C
			86°F	=	30°C

Index